Praise for Pa

It's the first and only book that covers Disney cruises in detail. And what splendid detail! Jennifer and Dave tell you everything you need and want to know, from embarkation to debarkation. Even if you don't currently have a Disney cruise planned, this is great armchair reading. It certainly took me back to happy thoughts of my last Disney cruise and made me want to plan the next one!

— Mary Waring
MouseSavers.com

I love everything! The excursion ratings, the hints that you can only get from people that have been before, what to do on your first day aboard, and the web site to get free updates since the book was released!

— Kris C. in New Jersey

PassPorter makes organizing my trip so easy and fun.

— Colleen Anastasi in Pennsylvania

WOW ... PassPorter is so comprehensive!!

— Andrea Lampert in Massachusetts

PassPorter is concise! It gives me all of the information in one spot that would have taken hours of searching through web sites and board postings. I love all the great tips and ideas for trip planning.

— Curtis S. in Indiana

PassPorter has a vast amount of information and spells it out in simple terms. All the hints and tips are awesome! It is very easy to read and use by our children, too.

— Pete F. in Michigan

I love your honesty. If you don't like something, you just say so. I also like the down-to-earth nature of the book. It's as if a friend wrote the book.

— Lisa Amico in New York

What's New in This Edition

Major Enhancements:

✓ **More than 30 brand new pages** filled with valuable information, advice, details, reviews, ratings, and photos.

✓ **More photos** than our previous edition—many of which include your authors in the picture, too!

✓ **Coverage of new ports**, including the South Caribbean (Barbados and St. Kitts), and Mexico (Costa Maya)

✓ **Sneak peek at new itineraries and possibly new ships**—our thoughts and speculations on the future of the Disney cruises.

✓ **Coverage of the recent changes** aboard the Disney Magic, including the expanded spa, the new Ocean Quest kids area, outdoor "Dive-In" movies, and more!

✓ **Updated details** on shore excursions for all ports.

✓ **More information** on the new passport regulations, including how and when to get yours.

✓ **More details** on access the Internet, including wireless access.

✓ **Expanded information** on the Vista Spa and its updated offerings, including the new Spa Villas on the Disney Magic.

✓ **Enhanced details** on activities for kids, including a new section about toddlers. We also expanded the pages on Oceaneer Club and Lab.

✓ **Updated planning timetable** to help you stay on track of important dates and indicate completed tasks.

Fun Features and Information:

✓ Thousands of small tweaks to further improve our guide.

✓ Current rates, prices, menus, and shore excursions.

✓ Expanded index to make it easier to find things.

✓ More new reader tips, magical memories, and stories.

✓ New peer reviewers to ensure accuracy and thoroughness.

...and much, much more! Visit us at http://www.passporter.com/dcl for a complete list of what's new and changed in this edition!

Disney Magic/Wonder Deck Plans

Tip: Once you know your stateroom number, note it on this page and highlight the section of the ship where it is located in the profile map to the left.

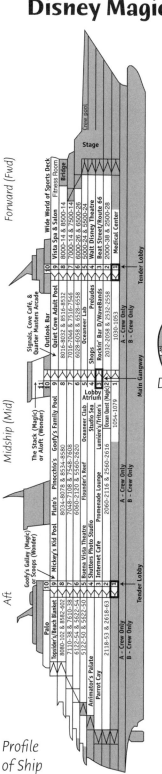

Our stateroom number: ____________________

Profile of Ship

Forward (Fwd) · Midship (Mid) · Aft

Deck	Forward (Fwd)	Midship (Mid)	Aft
11		The Stack (Magic) or Aloft (Wonder)	
10	Wide World of Sports Deck; Fitness Room; Bridge	Outlook Bar	Palo
9	Vista Spa & Salon	Quiet Cove Adult Pool; Goofy's Family Pool; Pinocchio's; Pluto's	Mickey's Kid Pool; Topsider's/Beach Blanket
8	8000-14 & 8500-14	8016-8032 & 8516-8532; 8034-8078 & 8534-8580	8080-102 & 8582-602
7	7000-14 & 7500-14	7016-7046 & 7516-7546; 7048-7108 & 7548-7608	7110-38 & 7610-38
6	6000-26 & 6500-26	6028-6058 & 6528-6558; 6060-2120 & 5560-2620	6122-54 & 5622-54
5	5000-24 & 5500-24	Oceaneer Lab; Oceaneer Club; Flounder's Reef	Buena Vista Theatre; 5122-50 & 5622-50; Animator's Palate
4	Walt Disney Theatre	Shops; Preludes; Lobby Atrium; Studio Sea	Shutters Photo Studio
3	Beat Street/Route 66	Rockin' Bar D/WaveBands; Lumière's/Triton's; Promenade Lounge	Internet Cafe; Parrot Cay
2	2000-38 & 2500-28	2032-2058 & 2532-2558; Ocean Quest (Magic); 2060-2116 & 2560-2616	2118-53 & 2618-63
1	Medical Center; Tender Lobby	1030-1053; 1054-1079; Main Gangway	Tender Lobby
A	A - Crew Only	A - Crew Only	A - Crew Only
B	B - Crew Only	B - Crew Only	B - Crew Only

Other profile labels: Stage; Crew pool; Signals, Cove Café, & Quarter Masters Arcade; Goofy's Galley (Magic) or Scoops (Wonder)

Deck 11: The Stack

Deck 10 (Port / Starboard): Wide World of Sports Deck; Outlook Bar; Palo

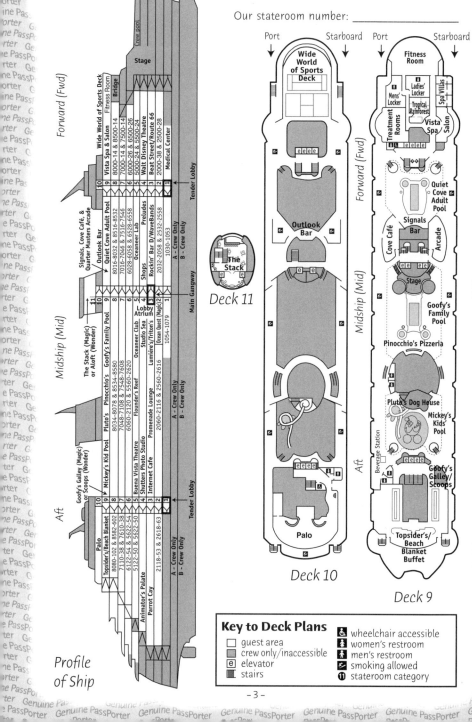

Deck 9 (Port / Starboard; Forward (Fwd), Midship (Mid), Aft): Fitness Room; Ladies' Locker; Mens' Locker; Spa Villas; Tropical Rainforest; Treatment Rooms; Vista Spa; Salon; Quiet Cove Adult Pool; Signals Bar; Cove Café; Arcade; Stage; Goofy's Family Pool; Pinocchio's Pizzeria; Pluto's Dog House; Mickey's Kids' Pool; Beverage Station; Goofy's Galley/Scoops; Topsider's/Beach Blanket Buffet

Key to Deck Plans

- guest area
- crew only/inaccessible
- e elevator
- stairs
- wheelchair accessible
- women's restroom
- men's restroom
- smoking allowed
- stateroom category

Decks 8, 7, 6, and 5

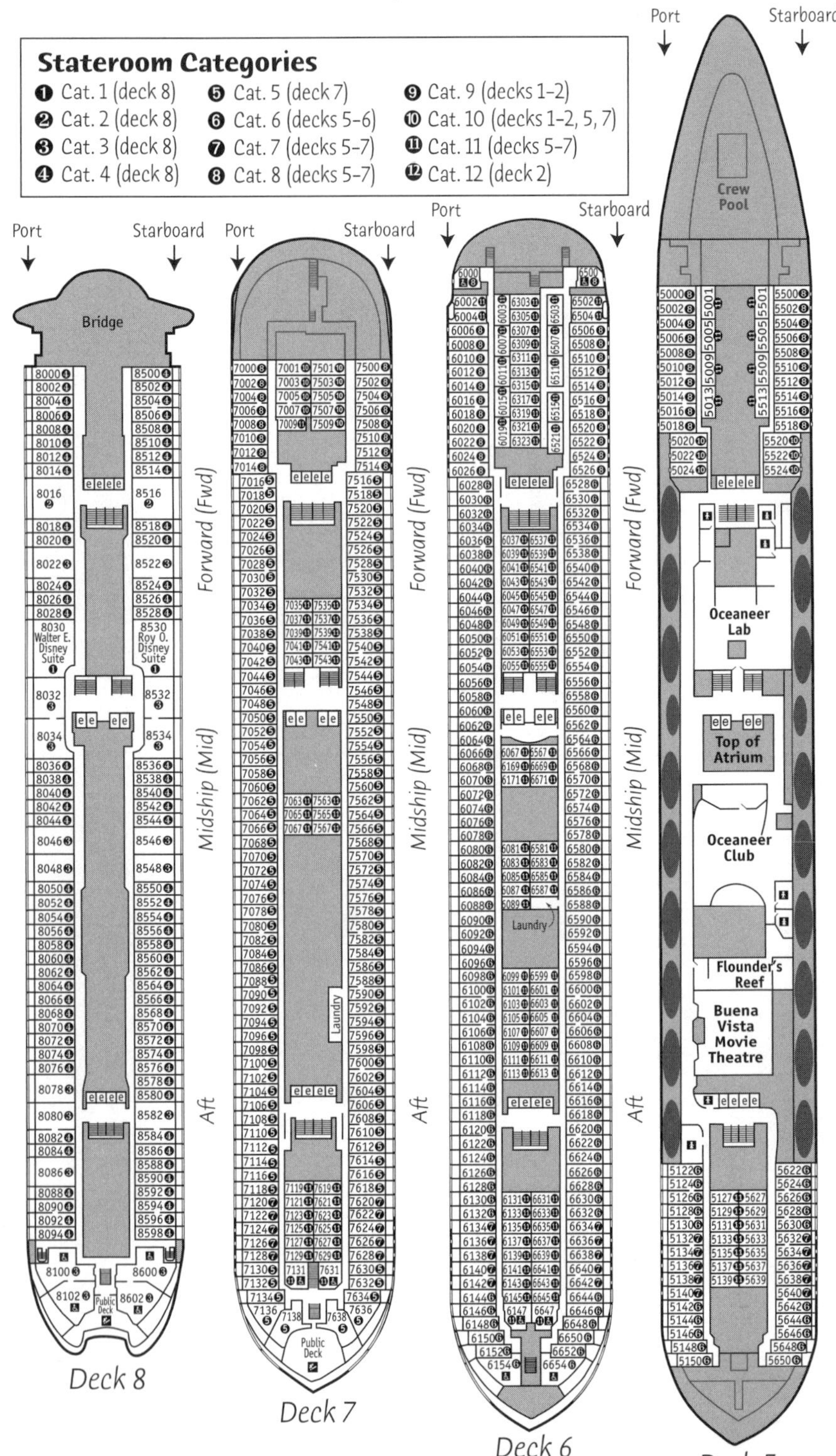

Decks 4, 3, 2, and 1

Get These Deck Plans Online!
Owners of this guide have free access to more detailed, color versions of all our deck plans—you can even zoom in closer! Access requires an Internet connection for downloading the files. Visit http://www.passporter.com/dcl/deckplans.htm

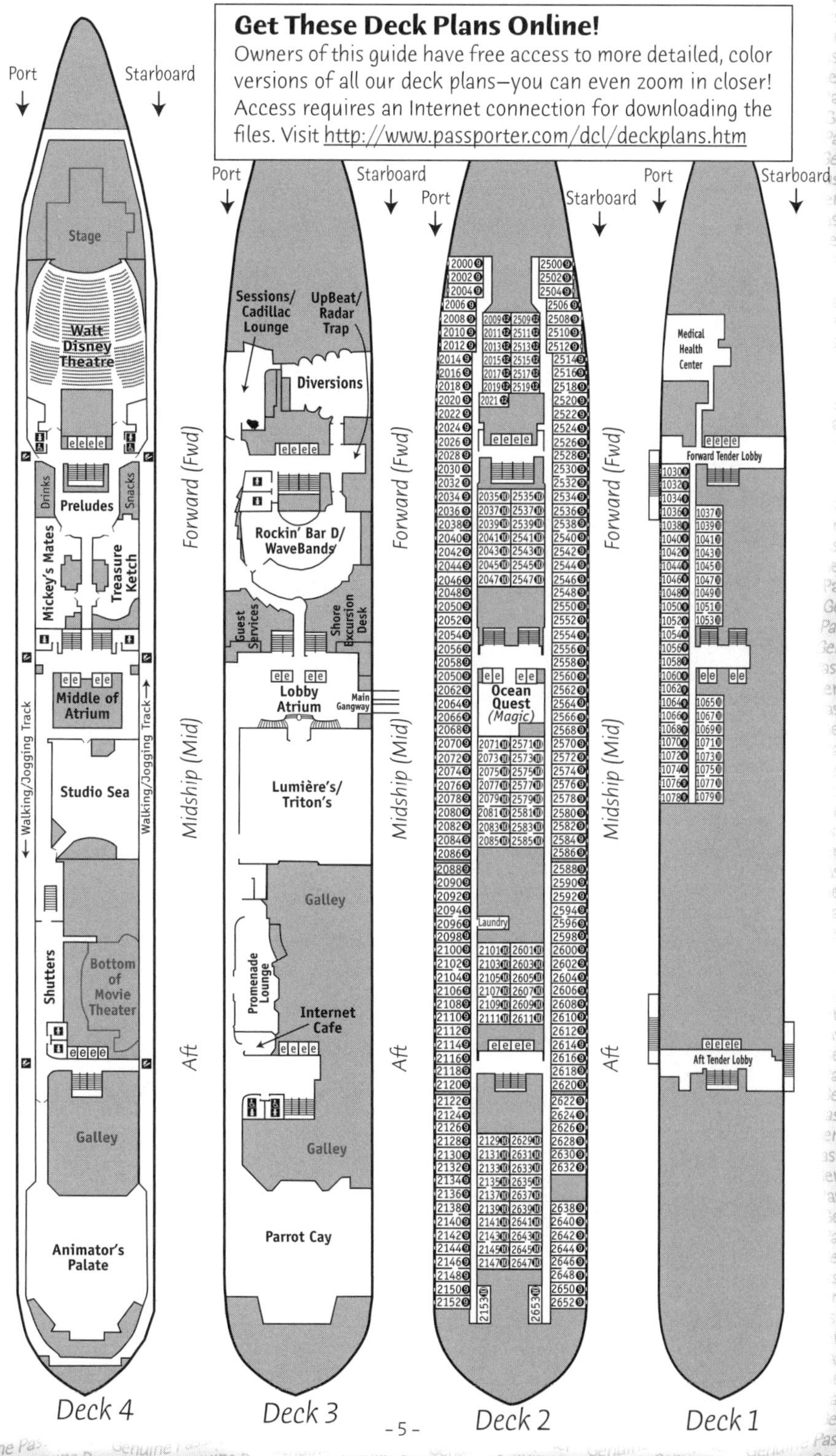

Port ↓ Starboard ↓

Forward (Fwd) — Midship (Mid) — Aft

Deck 4
Stage
Walt Disney Theatre
Drinks
Preludes
Snacks
Mickey's Mates
Treasure Ketch
Middle of Atrium
Studio Sea
← Walking/Jogging Track
Walking/Jogging Track →
Shutters
Bottom of Movie Theater
Galley
Animator's Palate

Deck 3
Sessions/ Cadillac Lounge
UpBeat/ Radar Trap
Diversions
Rockin' Bar D/ WaveBands
Guest Services
Shore Excursion Desk
Lobby Atrium
Main Gangway
Lumière's/ Triton's
Galley
Promenade Lounge
Internet Cafe
Galley
Parrot Cay

Deck 2
2000 2002 2004 2006 2008 2010 2012 2014 2016 2018 2020 2022 2024 2026 2028 2030 2032 2034 2036 2038 2040 2042 2044 2046 2048 2050 2052 2054 2056 2058 2060 2062 2064 2066 2068 2070 2072 2074 2076 2078 2080 2082 2084 2086 2088 2090 2092 2094 2096 2098 2100 2102 2104 2106 2108 2110 2112 2114 2116 2118 2120 2122 2124 2126 2128 2130 2132 2134 2136 2138 2140 2142 2144 2146 2148 2150 2152
2009 2011 2013 2015 2017 2019 2021
2509 2511 2513 2515 2517 2519
2035 2037 2039 2041 2043 2045 2047
2535 2537 2539 2541 2543 2545 2547
Ocean Quest (Magic)
2071 2073 2075 2077 2079 2081 2083 2085
2571 2573 2575 2577 2579 2581 2583 2585
Laundry
2101 2103 2105 2107 2109 2111
2601 2603 2605 2607 2609 2611
2129 2131 2133 2135 2137 2139 2141 2143 2145 2147
2629 2631 2633 2635 2637 2639 2641 2643 2645 2647
2153 2653
2500 2502 2504 2506 2508 2510 2512 2514 2516 2518 2520 2522 2524 2526 2528 2530 2532 2534 2536 2538 2540 2542 2544 2546 2548 2550 2552 2554 2556 2558 2560 2562 2564 2566 2568 2570 2572 2574 2576 2578 2580 2582 2584 2586 2588 2590 2592 2594 2596 2598 2600 2602 2604 2606 2608 2610 2612 2614 2616 2618 2620 2622 2624 2626 2628 2630 2632 2638 2640 2642 2644 2646 2648 2650 2652

Deck 1
Medical Health Center
Forward Tender Lobby
1030 1032 1034 1036 1038 1040 1042 1044 1046 1048 1050 1052 1054 1056 1058 1060 1062 1064 1066 1068 1070 1072 1074 1076 1078
1037 1039 1041 1043 1045 1047 1049 1051 1053
1065 1067 1069 1071 1073 1075 1077 1079
Aft Tender Lobby

Deck 4 Deck 3 Deck 2 Deck 1

What's Your Heading?

(M) = Disney Magic; (W) = Disney Wonder

Location	Deck	Page
Adult pool	9 Fwd	3
Adult cafe	9 Mid	3
Adult district	3 Fwd	5
Adult restaurant	10 Aft	3
Aerobics studio	9 Fwd	3
Aloft (W)	11 Mid	3
Animator's Palate	4 Aft	5
Assembly stations	4	5
Atrium (Lobby)	3-5 Mid	5,4
Arcade	9 Mid	3
Bars	3,4,9,10,11	5,4,3
Beach Blanket Buffet (W)	9 Aft	3
Beat Street (M)	3 Fwd	5
Beverage station	9 Aft	3
Bridge overlook	9 Fwd	3
Buena Vista Theatre	5 Aft	4
Buffet restaurant	9 Aft	3
Cadillac Lounge (W)	3 Fwd	5
Casual dining	9	3
Children's clubs	5 Mid	4
Children's pool	9 Aft	
Computer cafe	3 Aft	5
Conference rooms	2 Mid	5
Cove Café	9 Mid	3
Dance club	3 Fwd	5
Deck parties	9 Mid	3
Diversions	3 Fwd	5
Duty-free shops	3 Fwd, 4 Mid	5
Family nightclub	4 Mid	5
Family pool	9 Mid	3
Fantasia Reading Rm. (M)	2 Mid	5
Fast food	9	3
Fitness center	9 Fwd	3
Flounder's Reef	5 Mid	4
Fruit station	9 Aft	3
Goofy's Family Pool	9 Mid	3
Goofy's Galley (M)	9 Aft	3
Guest Services	3 Mid	5
Hair salon	9 Fwd	3
Hot tubs	9	3
Internet Cafe	3 Aft	5
Kids pool	9 Aft	3
Kids clubs	5 Mid	4
Laundry rooms	2,6,7 Mid	5,4
Liquor shop	3 Fwd	5
Lobby (Atrium)	3 Mid	5
Lounges	3,4,9,10,11	5,3
Lumière's (M)	3 Mid	5
Medical Center	1 Fwd	5
Mickey's kids' pool	9 Aft	3
Mickey's Mates	4 Mid	5
Movie theater	5 Aft	4
Nightclubs	3 Fwd	5
Nursery	5 Mid	4
Ocean Quest (M)	2 Mid	5
Oceaneer Club & Lab	5 Mid	4
Outlook Bar	10 Mid	3
Palo	10 Aft	3
Parrot Cay	3 Aft	5
Photo studio	4 Aft	5
Piano lounge	3 Fwd	5
Ping-Pong tables	9	3
Pinocchio's Pizzeria	9 Mid	3
Pluto's Dog House	9 Aft	3
Pools	9	3
Preludes Bar	4 Fwd	5
Promenade Lounge	3 Aft	5
Pub (Diversions)	3 Fwd	5
Quarter Masters arcade	9 Mid	3
Quiet Cove adult pool	9 Fwd	3
Restrooms	3,4,5,9,10	5,4,3
Rockin' Bar D (M)	3 Fwd	5
Route 66 (W)	3 Fwd	5
Salon	9 Fwd	3
Scoops (W)	9 Aft	3
Sessions lounge (M)	3 Fwd	5
Shore excursion desk	3 Mid	5
Shuffleboard	4	5
Shutters photo studio	4 Aft	5
Shops	4 Mid	5
Sickbay	1 Fwd	5
Signals	9 Mid	3
Snack bars	9	3
Spa (Vista Spa)	9 Fwd	3
Sports deck	10 Fwd	3
The Stack (M)	11 Mid	3
Teen club	11 Mid	3
Tender lobbies	1 Fwd & Aft	5
Theater (movies)	5 Aft	4
Theater (stage shows)	4 Fwd	5
Topsider's Buffet (M)	9 Aft	3
Treasure Ketch	4 Mid	5
Triton's (W)	3 Mid	5
UpBeat duty free (W)	3 Mid	5
Vista Spa & Salon	9 Fwd	3
Walt Disney Theatre	4 Fwd	5
Waterslide	9 Aft	3
Whirlpools	9	3
WaveBands (W)	3 Fwd	5
Wide World of Sports Deck	10 Fwd	1

Fwd, Mid, or Aft? These common abbreviations are for the Forward (front), Midship (middle), and Aft (rear) of the ship. Refer to the labels on our deck plans.

PassPorter's® Field Guide to the Disney Cruise Line®

Fourth Edition

The take-along travel guide and planner

Jennifer Marx
and
Dave Marx

PassPorter Travel Press

An imprint of MediaMarx, Inc.
P.O. Box 3880, Ann Arbor, Michigan 48106
877-WAYFARER
http://www.passporter.com

PassPorter's® Field Guide to the Disney Cruise Line® and Its Ports of Call–Fourth Edition
by Jennifer Marx and Dave Marx

P.O. Box 3880, Ann Arbor, Michigan 48106
877-WAYFARER or 877-929-3273 (toll-free)
Visit us on the World Wide Web at http://www.passporter.com

Special Sales: PassPorter Travel Press publications are available at special discounts for bulk purchases for sales premiums or promotions. Special editions, including personalized covers and excerpts of existing guides, can be created in large quantities. For information, write to Special Sales, P.O. Box 3880, Ann Arbor, Michigan, 48106.

Distributed by Publishers Group West

ISBN-10: 1-58771-030-7
ISBN-13: 978-1-58771-030-8

10 9 8 7 6 5 4 3 2 1

Printed in the United States of America

About the Authors

Name: Jennifer Marx
Date of birth: 10/09/68
Residence: Ann Arbor, MI
Signature: Jennifer Marx

Jennifer Marx grew up in Michigan, where you can stand anywhere within the state and be less than six miles from a lake, river, or stream. Her shipboard experiences include two weeks aboard a sailboat as a crew member and nine months working aboard the sternwheeler "Michigan" on Lake Biwa, Japan. Her first Disney Cruise Line adventure was for three nights in October 1999. A four-night cruise followed in May 2001. She had the good fortune to be aboard the Panama Canal crossing (eastbound) in August 2005. Her most recent cruise was aboard the Disney Wonder on the four-night MouseFest cruise in December 2005. Jennifer is the author of more than 20 books, including the guide that started it all: *PassPorter Walt Disney World Resort*. Jennifer makes her home in the university town of Ann Arbor, Michigan, where she lives with her husband Dave and their son, Alexander.

Dave Marx may be considered a Renaissance Man, a jack-of-all-trades, or a dilettante, depending on how you look at things. He took a 20-year hiatus between his early journalism training and the start of his full-time writing career. Beyond co-authoring more than twenty books with Jennifer, he's been a radio writer/producer; recording engineer; motion picture music editor; broadcast engineer supervisor; whitewater safety and rescue instructor; developer of online publishing courses; and newsletter editor and promotions chief for an online forum. He discovered the Walt Disney World Resort in March 1997 and first cruised in October 1999. He's since cruised ten more times, including his award cruise for being a Million-Point Winner at "Who Wants To Be a Millionaire—Play It!" at Walt Disney World. Dave lives in Ann Arbor, Michigan.

Name: Dave Marx
Date of birth: 04/07/55
Residence: Ann Arbor, MI
Signature: Dave Marx

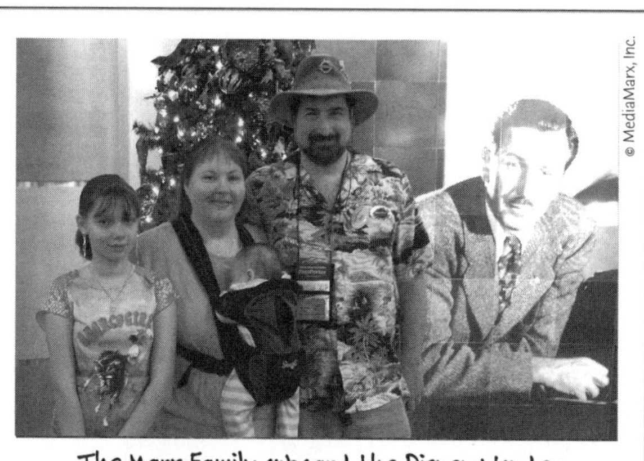

© MediaMarx, Inc.

The Marx Family onboard the Disney Wonder

PassPorter Team

What's behind our smiling faces on the previous page? An incredible team of people who help us make PassPorter the best it can be!

Our Expert Peer Reviewers—We recruited a group of very knowledgeable Disney and travel experts. Each painstakingly checked our guide to ensure our accuracy, readability, and thoroughness. Thank you from the bottom of our hearts!

LauraBelle Hime is a PassPorter message board guide and enjoys 4–5 Disney trips a year. Disney cruising is her newest passion and she finds each cruise to be a unique experience whether she travels solo, with family, or with friends.

Susan Kulick took her first Disney Cruise in 2002 with her husband Steve. She loved cruising so much she took another in January 2005, and has a third booked for April 2007. Sue is a PassPorter guide and a DVC member.

Barb Lesniak and her husband, Tony, will exceed 50 Disney cruises by the end of 2006. Their web site at http://www.castawayclub.com started as a hobby but quickly became one of the most popular unofficial sources for Disney cruise information. In 2004, Barb became a travel agent to parlay her love of cruising into a business of helping others make the most of their trips.

Bruce Metcalf works at a major Central Florida theme park, so cruising is his preferred form of vacation. He enjoys "messing about in boats" of all sizes, which is fortunate, as he's working on a book-length treatment of "The Disney Navy."

Cheryl Pendry is a PassPorter message board guide and a Disney Vacation Club member. She and her husband Mark are regular Disney visitors and are planning their next Disney cruise, despite the fact that they live in England.

Marnie Urmaza and her family have taken many trips to Walt Disney World and have another trip, including their first Disney cruise, in the near future. Marnie also enjoys being a PassPorter Message Board guide.

Deb Wills is a veteran of twelve cruises, mostly Disney, and countless trips to Walt Disney World. She is recognized as a Disney expert in the national press and the Disney planning field. She is the co-author of "PassPorter's Walt Disney World For Your Special Needs" and founder of AllEarsNet.com® and the All Ears® weekly newsletter.

Sandy Zilka is a proofreader for a Big Four accounting firm. She's taken more than 20 Disney trips, including a four-night Disney cruise. She loves to travel and share her experiences as a PassPorter message board guide.

Printer: Malloy Lithography in Ann Arbor, Michigan
Visibility Specialists: Kate and Doug Bandos, KSB Promotions
Online Promotions and Newsletter Editor: Sara Varney
Office Managers and Research Assistants: Nicole Larner, Chad Larner
Proofreader: Sandy Zilka
Sorcerers' Apprentices: Kim Larner, Carolyn Tody, and Tom Anderson
Special thank yous to Christie Erwin, Ernie Sabella, Phil Adelman, Jeff Howell, Fred Marx, Paul McGill, and the crews of the Disney Magic and the Disney Wonder.

Acknowledgments

Oceans of thanks to our readers, who've contributed loads of tips and stories since the debut of the first PassPorter in 1999. A special thanks to those who allowed us to include their contributions in this field guide:

Mary Waring, Kris C., Colleen Anastasi, Andrea Lampert, Curtis S., Pete F., and Lisa Amico (page 1); Amy Bedore and Kimberly King (page 30); Gina Walck, Dave Huiner, and Jill Koenigs (page 74); Angie J., Jeanne Sacks, and Joan Welch (page 98); Dawn Dobson and Stacy G. (page 122); Penny DeGeer, Amanda Poole, and Margo Verikas (page 154); Kris Romero and Jennifer Litera (page 256); and Melissa Hatcher, Brenda S., and Mary Jane Ross (page 274). May you each receive a new memory for every reader your words touch.

PassPorter would not be where it is today without the support of the Internet community. Our thanks to the friendly folks below and to all those we didn't have room to include!

- AllEarsNet.com (http://www.allearsnet.com). Thanks, Deb!
- CruiseCritic.com (http://cruisecritic.com). Thanks, Laura!
- CruiseDirections.com (http://www.cruisedirections.com). Thanks, Gordon!
- Dave's DCL Tribute (http://www.dcltribute.com). Thanks, Dave!
- Hidden Mickeys of Disney (http://www.hiddenmickeys.org). Thanks, Tom!
- Intercot (http://www.intercot.com). Thank you, John!
- LaughingPlace.com (http://www.laughingplace.com). Thanks, Doobie and Rebekah!
- Magical Disney Cruise Guide (http://www.allearsnet.com/cruise/cruise.shtml).
- MEI-Travel (http://www.mei-travel.com). Thanks, Beci!
- MouseEarVacations.com (http://www.mouseearvacations.com). Thanks, Jami!
- The Mouse For Less (http://www.themouseforless.com). Thanks, Binnie!
- MousePlanet (http://www.mouseplanet.com). Thanks, Mike!
- MouseSavers.com (http://www.mousesavers.com). Thanks, Mary!
- The Platinum Castaway Club (http://www.castawayclub.com). Thanks, Barb & Tony!
- Planning Strategy Calculator (http://pscalculator.net). Thanks, Scott!
- Spencer Family's Disney Page (http://home.hiwaay.net/~jlspence). Thanks, Jeff!
- Unofficial Disney Information Station (http://www.wdwinfo.com). Thanks, Pete!

A special thank you to the Guides (moderators) of our own message boards: Maureen Austin, Kelley Baker, Kelly Charles, Michelle Clark, Dianne Cook, Joanne and Tim Ernest, Kristin Grey, Debbie Hendrickson, LauraBelle Hime, Christina Holland-Radvon, Robin Krening-Capra, Susan Kulick, Marcie LaCava, Denise Lang, Tara McCusker, Bill Myers, Michelle Nash, Allison Palmer-Gleicher, Cheryl Pendry, Tina Peterson, Susan Rannestad, Jennifer Sanborn, Ann Smith, Donna Sonmor, Nate Stokes, Suzanne Torrey, Marnie Urmaza, Sara Varney, Margo Verikas, Dave Walsh, Suzi Waters, Brant Wigginton, and Debbie Wright and the 11,000+ readers in our amazing community at http://www.passporterboards.com.

A heartfelt thank you to our family and friends for their patience while we were away on research trips or cloistered at our computers, and for their support of our dream: Allison Cerel Marx; Alexander Marx; Carolyn Tody; Tom Anderson; Fred and Adele Marx; Megan and Natalie Larner; Dan, Jeannie, Kayleigh, Melanie, and Nina Marx; Gale Cerel; Jeanne and David Beroza; Robert and Sharon Larner, Gordon Watson; and Marta Metcalf.

Last but not least, we thank Walter Elias Disney for his dream.

Contents

Jennifer poses by a porthole

List of Maps, Worksheets, and Charts

© MediaMarx, Inc.

Dave anticipates a fine meal at Palo

© Disney

Goofin" around at the Mickey Pool

Contents
(continued)

Bon Voyage!

You're about to embark on a marvelous voyage aboard one of the most beautiful and celebrated cruise lines in the world. You couldn't have made a better choice—the Disney Cruise Line will surprise and delight you with its stunning architecture, legendary service, and fun-for-the-whole-family activities. Boy, we wish we could go with you!

Our original travel guide, *PassPorter Walt Disney World*, contains the basic information for the Disney Cruise Line. Even so, our readers sent in many requests to add more details on the cruises. Our answer is this field guide, which is chock-a-block with information on virtually every aspect of cruising with Disney. We designed it to stand alone or work with our Disney World guidebook and/or the PassPorter travel planning system. Everything you need to know to plan and enjoy a magical cruise is within these pages!

You're holding the fourth edition of the first guidebook dedicated to the Disney Cruise Line! As always, we include in-depth coverage of scheduled "special itinerary" ports along with Disney's regular stops. Changes and updates aboard the Disney Cruise Line since our last edition are highlighted in gray, too! The Disney Cruise Line is constantly evolving, which makes this travel guide a perpetual work in progress. Please tell us what you like and where we've missed the boat so we can improve our next edition!

This field guide is the embodiment of not just our knowledge and experience, but that of our fellow cruisers and PassPorter readers as well. In essence, this is a cruise guide by cruisers, for cruisers. We share what we like and don't like, and you may find some differing opinions just within the pages of this guide. Reader opinion plays a big part of our shore excursion reviews in chapter 6. And our expert reviewers shared their own opinions and experiences to enrich our information.

Use this field guide for planning before you embark, and then keep it handy onboard during your voyage. We hope you find this field guide a useful companion on your adventure!

Jennifer and Dave

We'd love to hear from you!
Visit us on the Internet
(http://www.passporter.com)
or drop us a postcard from
Castaway Cay!

P.S. This edition was last revised in February 2006. To check for new revisions or view our latest online update list, visit us on the Internet at this address: http://www.passporter.com/dcl

Preparing to Cast Off

Cruising doesn't just refer to the time you're onboard—it's a state of mind. To help you get into the spirit of the adventure that awaits, try out our favorite ways to build excitement for a Disney cruise. You may discover they help you "cruise" through the planning process without a hitch!

Check Out the Literature

A trip to your local travel agent will reward you with the free Disney Cruise Line Vacations booklet—it's in full color and crammed with photos. You can also request one at 888-325-2500 or at http://www.disneycruise.com. The Disney web site is also a great source for photos, excursions, etc.

Watch the Video or DVD

Request your free Disney Cruise Line video or DVD by calling 888-325-2500 or on the web at http://www.disneycruise.com. It arrives in about 3-4 weeks. Both the video and DVD offer a fun peek at the ship and ports.

Network With Other Cruisers

Fans of Disney cruises are scattered far and wide—chances are you know someone who has been on a Disney cruise. If not, come join us on the Internet, where many Disney cruisers congregate to share tips. See page 28 for links to popular gathering places, including PassPorter.com.

Tune In to TV

Watch the Travel Channel and the Discovery Channel for specials about cruises and the Caribbean. Or have fun with reruns of "The Love Boat."

FROM CASTAWAY CAY

Being on Castaway Cay and hearing all this great music reminds us that there's nothing like steel drums to conjure up visions of cruising through the Caribbean. Find some Caribbean-style music and play it as you plan. We guarantee it'll get you in the mood. If you have access to iTunes, try the Reggae/Island radio stations. If you're on AOL, try the Surf or Reggae channel at AOL keyword: Radio.

Your field guide authors,
Jennifer and Dave

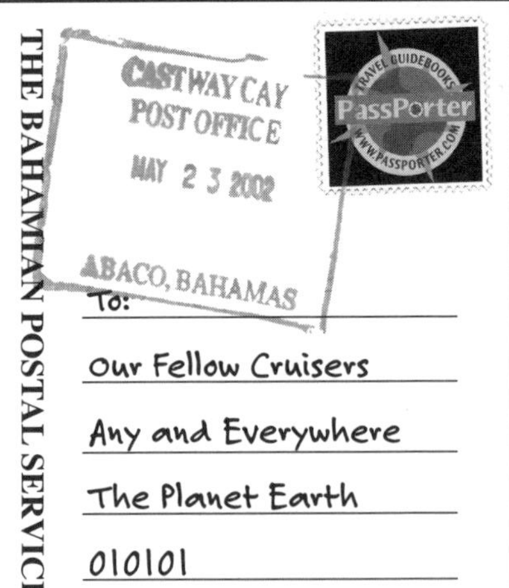

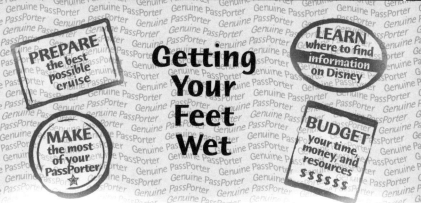

Getting Your Feet Wet

So, you've decided to take a Disney cruise! The Disney cruise attracts many first-time cruisers. If you're among them, welcome to the world of cruising! If you're a cruise veteran, welcome back!

Now that you've decided to cruise, you're likely to have one of two reactions. You may feel overwhelmed by the complexity that looms ahead. Or you may be lulled into a sense of complacency, sure that all the details will be taken care of. We understand—before our early cruises, we wavered between these two reactions ourselves. It wasn't until we learned more about the Disney cruise that we received a welcome splash of cold water. Thanks to a boatload of knowledge and the experience of other cruisers, we were able to dispel that feeling of drifting into uncharted waters.

We figure you don't want a splash of cold water in your face, so instead we offer this chapter as a friendly introduction to the world of cruising with Disney. We filled the chapter with highlights and histories, as well as facts and figures. You can read the chapter straight through or jump to the sections that interest you. We've included articles on the Disney Cruise Line, cruising in general, hints for first-time cruisers, comparisons with other cruise lines and Walt Disney World, fleet facts, the differences between the two ships, budgeting, money-saving ideas, and the best places to find more information. We wrap up the chapter with tips and memories.

Before you delve deeper, we want to share a secret. Yes, it's true that you could plunk down your money and just show up. But you wouldn't be getting your money's worth—not by a long shot. Planning is the secret to any successful vacation. Not only do you learn the tips and tricks, but you get to start your cruise early through anticipation. By the end of this guide, you'll know more than the vast majority of your shipmates. You'll know the way to get those coveted reservations. You'll know the way to pack and what to bring. You'll even know your way around the ship before you board it. In short, you'll be cruising your way ... straight out of those uncharted waters and into the true "magic" and "wonder" of a cruise.

The Disney Cruise Line

The Disney Cruise Line is more than just another cruise. Disney designed its ships to be **innovative**, offering unique facilities and programs, each with Disney's hallmark, first-class service.

The **history** of the Disney Cruise Line began in November 1985, when Premier Cruise Lines become the official cruise line of Walt Disney World Resort. Premier's "Big Red Boat" offered Disney characters and packages that included stays at the Walt Disney World Resort. When the ten-year contract with Premier was up, Disney set off on its own with an ambitious goal: To become the best cruise line in the world. Disney commissioned the Fincanteri Shipyard (in Venice, Italy) to build a 350-million-dollar liner reminiscent of the grand, trans-Atlantic liners of the early 20th century. A private island was developed into the delightful Castaway Cay, a stop on each cruise itinerary. On July 30, 1998, the Disney Magic set sail on her maiden voyage. The magnificent new ship boasted a classic, streamlined silhouette, twin funnels, and well-appointed interiors. The Disney Magic sailed from her dedicated, art deco-inspired cruise terminal in Port Canaveral, FL on three- and four-night cruises to the Bahamas. The Disney Wonder set sail on August 15, 1999. Seven-night itineraries to the Eastern Caribbean on the Disney Magic were added in 2000, leaving the shorter cruises to the Wonder. In 2002, seven-night Western Caribbean cruises were added. In summer 2005 the Disney Magic visited the West Coast to celebrate Disneyland's anniversary. Both ships have received upgrades over the years, enhancing their comforts. What lies ahead? See page 29 for a discussion of the future, including scuttlebutt and our own personal theories.

The **Disney Magic** and the **Disney Wonder** are almost identical vessels, with only a few minor differences (see page 23). The ships' hulls are painted dark blue-black, white, yellow, and red (Mickey's colors) with elegant gold scrollwork that cleverly reveals the silhouettes of classic Disney characters. As you board, you are greeted by friendly crew members in the three-story lobby atrium, distinguished by a sweeping staircase and a bronze statue (Mickey on the Magic, Ariel on the Wonder). Warm woods, polished metal railings, and nautical touches embrace passengers in elegance. Subtle Disney touches are abundant, from character silhouettes along the staircase to valuable Disney prints and artwork on the walls. Every area of the ship is decorated and themed. Both ships are a delight to the senses.

©Disney

The Disney Magic and the Disney Wonder

Why Cruise?

Cruising is something very special. Imagine yourself on a big—really big—beautiful ship. A low hum of excitement fills the air. The ship's whistle sounds smartly (Where have you heard that tune before?) and the ship begins to glide out of her berth. The ship is yours—deck upon deck of dining rooms, lounges, theaters, and staterooms.

People cruise with Disney for many reasons. Some love everything Disney, some want to be pampered, others enjoy the onboard activities, and still others want to visit foreign ports. Some families love the together-time they can have onboard, while other families appreciate the many activities for different ages. Adults love the peace of the adults-only pool, the gourmet tastes at Palo, and the evening fun at Beat Street/Route 66. Teens love having their own hangout and meeting fellow teens. Kids love the Oceaneer Club/Lab and the pools. What about us? Our first Disney cruise was to experience Disney's "next new thing." What brought us back again and again? Pure relaxation! A vacation to Disney World is wonderful, but very intense. On the cruise, we take a deep breath and slow down. We disembark refreshed and renewed, ready to tackle anything.

Dave enjoys a tropical drink during a deck party

Cruising Myths

Here are some oft-quoted reasons why some people don't cruise—each is a common myth that we're happy to dispel. *Myth #1: It's too expensive.* Actually, cruising costs the same as a land-based vacation—a Disney Cruise is equivalent to a comparable stay at the Walt Disney World Resort. *Myth #2: I'll be bored.* If anything, there's too much to do! You'll find it hard to choose between activities, and you'll probably disembark with a list of things you wish you'd had time to do. *Myth #3: I'll get seasick.* Most people don't, but there's a chance you could be one of the unlucky few. But if you follow our tips on page 267, you should be just fine. *Myth #4: Cruises are too formal.* Hey, this is a Disney cruise! Yes, the cruise is luxurious, but you won't feel out of place. Casual clothing is the norm onboard (most of the time). *Myth #5: The Disney Cruise is for kids (or people with kids).* Kids love the Disney Cruise, but so do adults (we cruised many times sans kids). There are plenty of adult activities and areas. *Myth #6: I'll feel claustrophobic or unsteady on my feet.* Disney ships' staterooms are 25% larger than most other lines, and the ships have stabilizers to minimize rolling.

First-Time Cruisers

Are you going on your first cruise and wondering what to expect?

You're not alone—many of your fellow cruisers will also be on their first cruise. We remember our first cruise well—we had only "The Love Boat" reruns and stories from friends and family to rely upon. We fretted over getting seasick, which wasn't a problem at all. We worried there wouldn't be enough to do, but in fact there was too much—a cruise is quite overwhelming (especially for first timers) and we wished we had more time. We were even concerned we'd feel like "poor relations" mingling with wealthier cruisers, but we fit right in.

Life aboard a Disney cruise ship is unlike most land-based vacations, unless perhaps you live the lifestyle of the rich and famous. Even if you're staying in budget lodgings, you'll receive the same level of luxurious, personal service as the deluxe guests. Your stateroom attendant will keep your room ship-shape (cleaning twice a day), see to your special needs, and turn down the bed every night (perhaps even with a cute animal made from towels). You'll form a personal relationship with your dining room team, who'll attend you at every shipboard dinner (apart from Palo).

And you'll eat! **Nearly all food and soft drinks onboard are included** in your Disney cruise—meals, snacks, room service, more snacks—so order anything you want, even if it's "seconds" or two different entrées.

The **ship hums with activity**, from sunup to the wee hours. Parties, live shows, children's programs, recreational activities, first-run movies, seminars, and guest lectures ... nearly everything is included in the price of your cruise, as is the right to do "none of the above."

Some say that modern cruise ships are "floating hotels," but "traveling resort" is a better description. Each day brings new vistas and often a new port. No matter how distracted you may be by onboard activities, the subtle vibration and motion of the ship whispers that your **luxurious little world** is going somewhere. Unlike long road trips or jet flights, your life doesn't go into an uncomfortable state of suspended animation while en route to your destination. Getting there can be far more than half the fun!

Our **advice to first-time cruisers** is two-fold: learn as much as you can about cruising, and then leave your expectations at home. Keep an open mind and be willing to try new things. You can rest assured that Disney has taken the needs of first-time cruisers into mind and considered your needs even before you realize you have them.

What's Included in a Disney Cruise?

Shipboard Accommodations: Up to 25% larger rooms than other ships—from 184 sq. ft. to 304 sq. ft. for non-suite staterooms.

Shipboard Meals: Three full-service dining room meals daily (breakfast, lunch, and dinner). Alternatives for breakfast, lunch, and dinner, such as buffets, quick-service, and room service, are also included. Let's not forget the snacks (ice cream, fruit, hot dogs, pizza), afternoon cookies, evening hors d'oeurves, and at least one late night dessert buffet. The seven-night cruises serve-up even more late-night munchies. Soft drinks (Coke, Diet Coke, Sprite, and ginger ale), milk, coffee, tea (hot and iced), cocoa, lemonade, fruit punch, water, and ice are always free at meals and at the Beverage Station (deck 9). Lunch (with soda) at Castaway Cay is also included.

Shipboard Entertainment and Activities: Disney offers a wide variety of entertainment, including a different live stage show each evening, first-run movies, deck parties, live bands, dancing, nightclubs, karaoke, trivia games, bingo, Disney character meet and greets, seminars, tours, art auctions, and social gatherings.

Sports and Recreation: There are three pools, four whirlpool tubs, fitness center, aerobics studio (and some classes), walking/jogging track, Ping-Pong, shuffleboard, basketball, and the Wide World of Sports deck.

Kids Activities: Participation in kids programs is included for ages 3-17, with activities and areas for varying age groups. Kids' shore excursions (other than Castaway Cay programming) are not included, however.

Ports of Call: Stops at all ports on the itinerary are included, as is transportation to the shore by tender (small boat), if necessary. Port charges are included in the price quote, unlike some other cruises.

What Isn't Included?

Your airfare may or may not be included in your cruise package—check when making your reservation. This goes for insurance and ground transfers from the airport to the ship (and back) as well. Accommodations, meals, and park passes for any time you spend at Walt Disney World are not included, unless you book a land/sea package that specifically includes these. Other extras: alcoholic beverages, specialty beverages (i.e., smoothies), soft drinks (at a bar or from room service), Internet Cafe, bingo games, spa and beauty treatments, Palo meals ($5–10/adult), childcare for kids under 3, arcade games, onboard or off-ship shopping, photos, formalwear rental, shore excursions, meals off-ship (except Castaway Cay), medical treatment, laundry services (including the self-service washers and dryers, though you can use the iron and ironing board freely), parking at the cruise terminal, and gratuities.

How Do They Measure Up?

Compared to **other cruise ships**, the Disney Magic and the Disney Wonder are among the most spacious ships afloat. Staterooms are 25% larger on average than those found on other ships. Other unique aspects of the Disney Cruise Line include split bathrooms (in stateroom categories 10 and up), rotational dining (different dining rooms, same servers), half a deck designed just for kids (with programs for specific age groups), areas reserved just for adults (pool, restaurant, Cove Café, spa, beach on Castaway Cay, and an entertainment district that's reserved just for adults after 9:00 pm), a visit to Castaway Cay (Disney's private island), Disney's famous characters, and that Disney magic!

Experienced cruisers may miss having a casino or a library aboard. The sentiment seems to be that the Disney Cruise Line offers the best family cruise afloat, but that it lacks enough activities for adults without children. We disagree (especially after several "drydock" upgrades)—we've sailed without kids and never lack adult activities. The generous adults-only areas deliver welcome isolation and surpass other "family" cruise lines. Some cruisers have also reported that the Disney Cruise Line is too, well, "Disney." Let's face it: if you don't like Disney, you may not like this cruise either. But these aren't theme parks. The quality service and elegant surroundings could easily outweigh any negative associations you have with Mickey Mouse.

Safety and **cleanliness** is a big deal on cruise ships, and all international ships are inspected by the U.S. Centers for Disease Control (CDC) on a regular basis. The Disney Magic and Disney Wonder were most recently inspected in November 2005 and July 2005. Both passed their inspections, receiving 96 and 99 out of 100 points, respectively. To view the latest inspection results, visit: http://www.cdc.gov/nceh/vsp/default.htm.

If you've been to the Walt Disney World Resort and wonder how a Disney cruise compares to a **resort vacation**, it is really quite different. The cruise feels more laid-back yet formal at the same time. The excitement of dashing from attraction to attraction is gone, and you may feel like you're missing "something" that you can't identify. On the upside, everything is within walking distance, the food is "free," and rain isn't the same party-pooper it is at the theme parks. You'll take things a bit slower on the cruise (although there's still plenty to do), all the while feeling pampered by the gorgeous setting and excellent service. The Walt Disney World Resort and the Disney cruise do share many perks, however: single key-card access for rooms and purchases, Disney character greetings, and that "red carpet" guest service. Don't expect to find "Walt Disney World on water." You'll discover the Disney Cruise Line has its own unique charm.

Fleet Facts

Home Port: Port Canaveral, Florida, USA
Country of Registry: The Bahamas
Radio Call Signs: C6PT7-Magic and C6QM8-Wonder
Captains: Captain Tom Forberg, Captain Henry Andersson, Captain John Barwis, Captain Gus Verhulst, and Captain Thord Haugen
Crews: 950 crew members, multinational
Guests: 2400 (1750 at double occupancy)—maximum is near 3000
Space ratio: 48.3 (the ratio of passengers to space, namely 4830 cubic feet per passenger; a ratio this high means a roomy, uncrowded ship.)
Tonnage: 83,000 (measured by volume, not weight—for an explanation, see http://www.m-i-link.com/dictionary/default.asp?s=s&q=tonnage)
Length: 964 ft./294 m. (longer than the *Titanic* at 882 ft./268 m.)
Beam: 106 ft./32.25 m. (the width of the ships at their widest)
Draft: 25.3 ft./7.7 m. (the depth below the waterline when full)
Speed: 21.5 knots, or 25 mph/40 kph (max. is 24 knots/28 mph/44 kph)
Systems: Five 16-cylinder diesel engines, two 19-megawatt GE propulsion motors, three bow thrusters, two stern thrusters, and 1 pair fin stabilizers
Passenger Decks: 11 (see front of book for our detailed deck plans)
Lifeboats: 20, with each seating 150 passengers (plus 50 life rafts)
Staterooms: 877 (252 inside, 625 outside)—see chap. 3
Theatres: 2 (975 seats and 268 seats)
Restaurants: 4 (138 seats in Palo, 442 seats in the others)—see chap. 4
Buffets and Snack Bars: 4 (294 seats inside, 332 seats outside)
Lounges: 5 (or 8 if you count the three nightclubs)
Shops: 5 **Pools**: 4 (one is for crew) **Hot Tubs**: 4 **Spa**: 1

Differences Between the Magic and the Wonder

Feature	Disney Magic	Disney Wonder
Year built	1998	1999
Itineraries	7-night cruises	3- and 4-night cruises
Decor:	Art Deco	Art Nouveau
Bow decoration:	Sorcerer Mickey	Steamboat Willie (Mickey)
Stern adornment:	Boatswain Goofy	Donald and Huey
Atrium statue:	Helmsman Mickey	Ariel, The Little Mermaid
Grand dining room:	Lumière's	Triton's
Casual dining room:	Topsider's Buffet	Beach Blanket Buffet
Adults-only district:	Beat Street + Cove Café	Route 66 + Cove Café
Dance club:	Rockin' Bar D	WaveBands
Jazz piano bar:	Sessions	Cadillac Lounge
Teen club:	The Stack & Ocean Quest	Aloft
Navigator's Verandah:	Round porthole	Larger oblong porthole

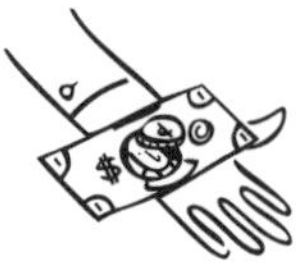

Can I Afford It?

Cruises were once reserved for wealthy globetrotters. These days, cruises are **more affordable**, but not always "inexpensive." DCL's popularity and "demand-based" pricing keep pushing rates up. Still, a seven-night Disney cruise can be comparable in price to a seven-night land vacation at Walt Disney World. To determine what you can afford, make a budget (see below). Budgeting not only keeps you from spending too much, it encourages you to seek out ways to save money. With a little research, you can often get **more for less**. To get an idea of what an actual cruise costs, check out our December 2005 cruise expenses at the bottom of the page.

A **cruise package** may include ground transportation, airfare, insurance, lodging at Walt Disney World, theme park admission, and other extras. This may seem convenient, but planning each aspect of your cruise yourself saves you more money. Learn about cruise packages on pages 42–43.

Your **cruise expenses** fall into six categories: planning, transportation, lodging, cruise passage, port activities, and extras. How you budget for each depends upon the total amount you have available to spend and your priorities. Planning, transportation, lodging, and cruise passage are the easiest to factor ahead of time as costs are fixed. The final two—port activities and extras—are harder to control, but we provide sample costs throughout this field guide to help you estimate.

Begin your budget with the **worksheet** on the next page (use pencil at the start). Enter the minimum you prefer to spend and the most you can afford in the topmost row. Set as many of these ranges as possible before you delve into the other chapters of this book. Your excitement may grow as you read more, but it is doubtful your bank account will.

As you uncover costs and ways to save money, return to your worksheet and **update it**. Your budget is a work in progress—try to be flexible within your minimums and maximums. As plans crystallize, write the amount you expect (and can afford) in the Goals column. If you are using PassPockets (see the Deluxe Edition on page 301), **transfer the amounts** from the Goals column to the back of each PassPocket when you are satisfied with your budget.

Our Dec. 2005 Expenses
(2 adults, 1 infant)

Round-trip airfare: $411
Rental mini-van: $150
4-night cruise (cat. 6): $2215
Port activities: $60
Souvenirs: $159
Beverages/Palo: $60
Phone/Internet: $100
Childcare: $30
Gratuities: $138

TOTAL: $3323

Budget Worksheet

As you work through this field guide, use this worksheet to identify your resources, record estimated costs, and create a budget. We provide prices and estimates throughout the book.

	Minimum		Maximum		Goals	
Total Projected Expenses	$		$		$	
Planning:						
Phone calls/faxes:						
Guides/magazines:						
Transportation: *(to/from)*						
Travel/airline tickets:						
Rental car:						
Fuel/maintenance:						
Ground transfer/shuttle:						
Town car/taxi:						
Wheelchair/ECV:						
Parking:						
Lodging: *(Pre-/Post-Cruise)*						
Resort/hotel/motel:						
Meals/extras:						
Cruise Passage:						
Cruise:						
Protection plan/insurance:						
Port Activities:	Per Port	Total	Per Port	Total	Per Port	Total
Excursions:						
Meals:						
Attractions:						
Rentals:						
Transportation/taxis:						
Extras:						
Souvenirs/photos:						
Beverages:						
Resortwear/accessories:						
Palo/formal wear:						
Spa treatments:						
Childcare (nursery):						
Phone/Internet/stamps:						
Gratuities/duties:						
Other:						
Total Budgeted Expenses	$		$		$	

Money-Saving Ideas and Programs

The Disney Cruise Line enjoys great popularity, so discounts can be scarce. Here are the ways we've found to save money on your cruise:

Reserve Early to Get Early Booking Savings
Reserve early enough and you could save approximately $100–$890 per stateroom (7-night cruises) or $30–$650 per stateroom (3- and 4-night cruises). Staterooms at this discount are limited, however. To get the best early booking savings, reserve your cruise as soon as dates are announced (generally up to 18 months in advance).

Go à la Carte
Disney emphasizes the 7-night Land and Sea package combining 3 or 4 nights at the Walt Disney World Resort with a cruise. This is appealing to many vacationers, but it is pricier than making your own arrangements as you can usually find better deals on hotel rooms at Walt Disney World.

Find Promotions and Discounts
As with most cruise lines, Disney uses demand-based pricing. Unlike most cruise lines, this means prices almost always rise as a cruise date approaches. The last-minute specials common with other lines are rare at Disney. With Disney Cruise Line, the earlier you reserve, the better your rate. That said, deals and specials are available, if you're alert. Check about 75 days before you want to cruise (this is the final payment deadline for current reservations). Visit http://www.disneycruise.com to learn more. Also visit MouseSavers.com (http://www.mousesavers.com), which summarizes available discounts, and http://www.themouseforless.com.

Use a Travel Agent
Larger travel agents, such as MouseEarVacations.com, are able to pre-book blocks of staterooms, locking in discounts for you to snag later on. Check with agents before booking on your own (see page 46 for a list). Travel agents are very good at finding the best prices, too! Mouse Fan Travel (http://www.mousefantravel.com) and MouseEarVacations.com (http://www.mouseearvacations.com) have saved us considerable money on our cruises, and other agencies can do the same.

Watch for Onboard Credits
Wouldn't it be nice to have an extra $25 or $100 sitting in your onboard account? Keep an eye out for onboard credit specials. At the time of writing, guests who book online get a $25 credit. Onboard credits may also be available when you book onboard (see next page) and through special deals offered by travel agents. Credits for repeat cruisers have generally been replaced by in-stateroom gifts.

Move to Florida

We're not serious about moving, but if you're already a Florida resident you may get discounts up to 50% off select cruises (limited staterooms). Call Disney at 888-325-2500 to inquire about Florida resident discounts, or check http://www.mousesavers.com. Proof of residency is required.

Book Your Next Cruise Onboard

On your next Disney cruise, check the *Personal Navigator* or the Cruise Sales Desk on Deck 4 for onboard specials. Not only can booking onboard offer great prices ($100 less than land-based prices recently), but sometimes onboard credits, too. Two catches: the best rates are often for cruises sailing the same time next year, and you must reserve before you disembark. If you see a deal, grab it - you can change or cancel your reservation later if necessary; just call Disney at 888-325-2500. Tip: You can transfer your booking to your travel agent when you return home.

Stay Off-Site Before Your Cruise

If you're like us and prefer to arrive at least a day ahead of your cruise, look for an inexpensive hotel or motel. In-airport hotels can be pricey—to save money, see page 59. See pages 58–59 and 64–66 for lodging. It can sometimes be less expensive to fly in a day early, so always investigate.

Compare Local Transportation Costs

Depending on your party size, it can be less expensive to rent a car to drive from the airport to the port and back again. On the other hand, transportation companies such as Quicksilver Tours & Transportation may offer price plus convenience. Explore your options on pages 60–62

Special Tips for Special People

- ✔ **Infants and kids** 12 and under are less expensive than adults, but only if there are two adults along as well (the first two stateroom guests always pay full adult fare). The third and fourth adults in a stateroom also cruise at a lower price. See page 44.
- ✔ **AAA and Costco** members can get rates and make reservations through these companies and often get excellent deals. AAA members: Ask about your local AAA chapter's "Disney Month" for extra savings and goodies, and be sure to inquire about any extras (such as an onboard credit) with your AAA Disney package.
- ✔ **Disney Vacation Club** members and **Annual Passholders** may be eligible for exclusive cruises at good rates. Check with those programs or the Disney Cruise Line for details.
- ✔ **Canadian residents** may get special rates on select cruises. Contact the Disney Cruise Line or a travel agent.
- ✔ **Military personnel** may be eligible for some last-minute rates, similar to those offered to Florida residents. Call the Disney Cruise Line or a travel agent for more details.
- ✔ **Repeat cruisers** are automatically members of the Castaway Club. You'll receive a gift (one per stateroom) when you cruise again, and enjoy special features at the Castawsay Club web page. For details and rates, call Disney Cruise Line, or visit http://www.disneycruise.com and click Castaway Club.

Porthole to More Cruising Information

While this field guide could serve as your single source, we recommend you gather as much information as possible. Each of the sources described below offers its own unique porthole into the world of Disney cruising.

Official Disney Information—Definitely get the free booklet and video/DVD we mention on page 16, and visit the web site (http://www.disneycruise.com). Any other brochures you can get from your travel agent will be helpful, too. Disney also sends cruise documentation (more about this on page 48) which contains some basic information.

Books—Disney published an official guidebook, "Birnbaum's Disney Cruise Line," starting in 2004, but we were disappointed to find little detail beyond what's available at the Disney Cruise Line's web site—the shore excursion reviews are insightful, however. And while virtually all Walt Disney World Resort guidebooks mention the Disney Cruise Line, most only give it a few pages. The two with the most information are "Walt Disney World with Kids" by Kim Wright Wiley (Fodor's) and "The Unofficial Guide to Walt Disney World" by Bob Sehlinger (Wiley). Both have about 10 pages on the topic. Two other PassPorter books contain information on Disney Cruise Line: "PassPorter's Walt Disney World For Your Special Needs" and "PassPorter's Treasure Hunts" have sections on Disney Cruise Line.

Magical Disney Cruise Guide—This excellent, free online guide offers a detailed overview of Disney cruising, including reviews. http://www.allearsnet.com/cruise/cruise.htm.

Web Sites—Some of the best sources of information are the official and unofficial sites for the Disney Cruise Line. Here are our picks:

Disney Cruise Line Official Site—http://www.disneycruise.com
PassPorter.com (that's us!)—http://www.passporter.com/dcl
PassPorterBoards.com (advice from fellow cruisers)—http://www.passporterboards.com
Magical Disney Cruise Guide—http://www.allearsnet.com/cruise/cruise.shtml
Platinum Castaway Club—http://www.castawayclub.com
Dave's Disney Cruise Line Tribute—http://www.dcltribute.com
DIS—http://www.wdwinfo.com (click "Disney Cruise Line")
and http://www.disboards.com (DCL discussion forum)
Disney Echo—http://disneyecho.emuck.com
All Ears Net—http://www.allearsnet.com/cruise/cruise.htm
MagicTrips—http://www.magictrips.com/cruise
ThemeParks.com—http://www.themeparks.com/cruise/index.htm
Kolb Family—http://www.kolbfamily.com/2000cruise/disney_cruise.htm
Disney World Online Guide—http://www.wdisneyw.co.uk/cruise.html
Pettits' Page—http://www.richpettit.com/vacations/ourvacations.htm
epinions.com—http://www.epinions.com (search on the ship names)

These are excellent sites on general cruising:
CruiseCritic—http://www.cruisecritic.com
About.com—http://cruises.about.com
CruiseMates—http://cruisemates.com
AvidCruiser—http://avidcruiser.com
Cruise2.com—http://www.cruise2.com

The Future of the Disney Cruise Line

What's next for Disney Cruise Line? Here are some facts and theories.

Disney Cruise Line fans have long been hoping for **additional ships and broader horizons**. Years ago, Disney execs reported that new ships had been designed and that shipyards had bid on the job. But nothing is being built. The high Dollar/Euro exchange rate has been blamed for several years, with execs saying the diversified media company can get a better return on its investment elsewhere. Perhaps, but the Euro may never drop. Disney Parks and Resorts (which runs Disney Cruise Line) has always been slow to expand hotel capacity, preferring the higher rates that come from scarcity to the heavy discounting that accompanies a room surplus. Heavily-booked Disney Cruise Line is both a cash cow and a first-rate ambassador for Disney quality, generally rating right near the top of the cruise industry and even topping Disney's land-based resorts. Does Parks and Resorts so fear diluting this brand that it will forever put off expansion? Maybe. However, New Disney CEO Bob Iger recently took his first Disney Cruise Line cruise and said, "I'm a believer." With no new theme parks under construction for the first time in many years, maybe it's finally Disney Cruise Line's turn to grow.

And what of the **new ship(s)**? Industry-leading Carnival Corp. (12 cruise lines/79 ships) has 200,000-ton behemoths in the pipeline, compared to Disney's 83,000-ton Magic and Wonder. Still, figure Disney's new ship(s) will be under 100,000 tons, to avoid the risk of over-supply (if nothing else). "Efficiencies of scale" don't always rule the roost.

The Disney Wonder goes into drydock for its two-week, biannual makeover in October 2006. It's expected to get the **same upgrades** the Magic received in 2005: Conference rooms on deck 2 will become Ocean Quest, an additional kid's lounge including a simulated ship's bridge. The Vista Spa more than doubles in size by expanding above the (real) ship's bridge. A 24 x 14-foot electronic video screen will overlook the Goofy Pool area on deck 9 for "Dive In" movies and enhanced live entertainment, and the nearby Scoops ice cream bar will become Pluto's Galley, with expanded snack bar offerings.

As we go to press, it seems all but certain that the Disney Magic will spend the summer of 2007 sailing the **Western Mediterranean**, its first return to Europe since its launch. Expect an official announcement in March or April 2006. Based on the most recent "insider" rumors, here's what to expect: The Disney Magic "repositions" from Port Canaveral to a temporary home port of Barcelona, Spain on May 12 through 26, a 14-night, 4,000-mile voyage with five or six port-of-call stops at spots like Castaway Cay, the Canary Islands, Gibralter, Portugal, and Spain. Alternating 11- and 10-night Mediterranean itineraries commence from Barcelona May 26. Ten-night itineraries often stop in the French ports of Marseille and Villefranche (Nice/Monte Carlo). After that, a mix of Italian and Spanish ports – Livorno (Florence/Pisa), Civitavecchia (Rome), Naples, Sicily, and the Spanish islands of Mallorca and/or Ibiza. Perhaps the 11-night might visit North Africa and Iberian ports like Cadiz (Seville), Gibraltar, and Valencia. There's no time to visit Greece on a Barcelona-based round trip unless there are fewer Italian and Spanish stops, or the Magic sails one-way to Athens on one itinerary and returns to Barcelona on the next. Finally, the Magic should depart Barcelona for Florida on August 18, arriving home September 1. Sign us up!

When **news finally breaks** on new ships and these new itineraries, we'll post all the detail you need at our site (http://www.passporter.com/dcl).

Cruise Reviews You Can Use

Cruiser reviews and reports are one of the absolute best ways to evaluate and get acquainted with the Disney Cruise Line before you embark. With that in mind, we've collected several tips and memories from our own experiences and those of our readers. Enjoy!

- If you have access to the **Internet**, make it a point to get online and explore the web sites listed throughout this field guide. In particular, we recommend you visit MousePlanet's Trip Reports web site, which offers a nice collection of Disney Cruise Line trip reports. The site is located at http://www.mouseplanet.com/dtp/trip.rpt.

- One of the first "guides" to Disney Cruise Line was a free online publication by Mickey Morgan, the "Magical Disney Cruise Guide." You can still find this informative online guide at AllEarsNet. Read it at http://www.allearsnet.com/cruise/cruise.htm.

Magical Memories

- *"This is the first cruise my mom and I have ever been on and it was only fitting it be on the Disney Magic! Being unsure of what a cruise was all about I did a lot of research online and any time I found a tip or found something that caught my eye I would print it out. I started collecting these tips and reviews and wanted a way to save them and have access to them so I got a three-ring binder and protector sheets. I was able to organize the tips into a logical order and now I can make sure I have them with me along with my PassPorter. I also will include some paper to take notes to work on my trip report. Some extra protector sheets to put any photos I might buy while on board will keep them safe from liquids and other things that might stain or damage them. On the front of the binder, I decorated it with a cute design, my name, and my stateroom number so that if I happen to lose it onboard, it will hopefully find its way back to me."*

  ...as told by Disney cruiser Amy Bedore

- *"Our cruise was created out of the incredible marketing that Disney has in place. I went on a cruise (another line) last spring. My son (age 6 now) was left behind with family for the whole week. As a single mom, this was my first ever getaway on my own and badly needed! Before I left, I told him that 'someday' we'd go on a cruise together. Within a few days of my return, my son received a brochure from Disney Cruise Line in the mail. It was even addressed to him. He ran up the drive way shouting... 'Look, Mommy, Mickey Mouse invited me on his boat!' Needless to say, I was online and booking our spring break 2006 cruise within moments. Darn that Disney Marketing department!"*

  ...as told by Disney cruiser Kimberly King

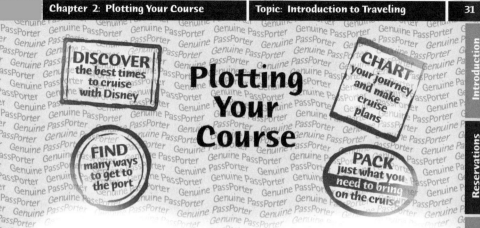

DISCOVER
the best times
to cruise
with Disney

Plotting Your Course

CHART your journey and make cruise plans

FIND many ways to get to the port

PACK just what you need to bring on the cruise

By now, we're certain you're hooked on the idea of a Disney cruise vacation. The time has come, the Walrus said, to turn those Disney dreams into a voyage filled with "wonder" and "magic."

Every journey starts with the first step, and this vacation is no exception. That step, of course, is planning. Planning is the keel upon which the rest of your cruise is built. This chapter is filled with the principal planning steps you'll need to take, plus a cargo of savvy advice and a chartroom filled with maps, charts, and worksheets to help keep you on course.

Some of you may be embarking on a cruise and/or leaving the United States for the very first time. While you will be visiting cozy, nearby ports, you'll encounter some subtle and not-so-subtle differences between cruise preparations and land journeys. Start your planning as far ahead as possible. Not only can you save some money, but you may need that head start to obtain the proper identity documents.

So just how do you plot the course that takes you from your front door to the gangway of your Disney cruise ship? In this chapter we'll chart the many steps in the journey, from selecting your cruise itinerary and sail dates to steering your way around tropical storms. You'll be able to pick your way through the turbulent waters of cruise rates and packages and safely reserve your snug stateroom.

Your ship's captain will ably plot your course on the high seas, but you'll need your own map and compass to get to port. We cover the many highways and byways that form your journey-before-the-journey, including fair lodgings at the port itself.

Finally, it's Embarkation Day! We make sure you aren't waylaid enroute to the cruise terminal, that your important identity papers are all in order, and that your trunks and sea bags are packed!

Introduction | Reservations | Staterooms | Dining | Activities | Ports of Call | Magic | Index

Choosing Your Itinerary

The Disney Cruise Line currently offers **several different itineraries**: one 3-night cruise, one 4-night cruise, two 7-night land/sea combinations, three 7-night cruises, two special 10-night cruises, and one special 11-night cruise. Your choice of itineraries may be solely based on price or length, particularly if you combine your cruise with a stay at Walt Disney World Resort (see page 42). If you can't decide which itinerary works best for you, read our descriptions and comments below for insight:

3-Night Itinerary:
Thursday: Set sail
Friday: Nassau
Saturday: Castaway Cay
Sunday: Return to port

3-Night Cruise Itinerary: The shortest and least expensive cruise, with three nights at sea aboard the Disney Wonder and two ports of call: Nassau and Castaway Cay. Actual time spent afloat: about 68 hours (almost three days). This cruise whizzes by, and you may feel like it's over before it's barely begun. On the flip side, this is a great cruise on which to get your feet wet if you're new to cruising. If you plan to stay at the Walt Disney World Resort before your cruise, the 3-night cruise works best for this as it falls at the end of the week. Also, this cruise departs on Thursdays, which also happens to be the day that most space shuttles depart from Cape Canaveral (see pages 162–163 for more details on shuttle launches).

4-Night Itinerary:
Sunday: Set sail
Monday: Nassau
Tuesday: Castaway Cay
Wednesday: At sea
Thursday: Return to port

4-Night Cruise Itinerary: More sailing time with four nights at sea on the Disney Wonder. Like the 3-night, the 4-night stops at Nassau and Castaway Cay. The extra day is spent at sea–there used to be an alternate itinerary that stopped in Freeport instead of a day at sea, but this ceased in 2004. Actual time spent afloat: about 92 hours (almost four days). If cruising is your focus, you'll be happier with a 4-night cruise than a 3-night–the extra night is more relaxing and it gives you a greater chance of dining at Palo without missing one of the other three restaurants. A benefit: If the Captain has to bypass Castaway Cay due to weather, he has the option to try again the next day. Note: It's possible that the Freeport stop could return in the future.

How Many Days to Cruise?

Should you do three days at Walt Disney World and four days at sea, or vice versa? We don't think you can possibly see everything at Walt Disney World in three or even four days, so take three nights at Walt Disney World, get a taste of it for a future return trip, and spend most of your time at sea. You can always book extra days at Disney after your cruise when you're rested.

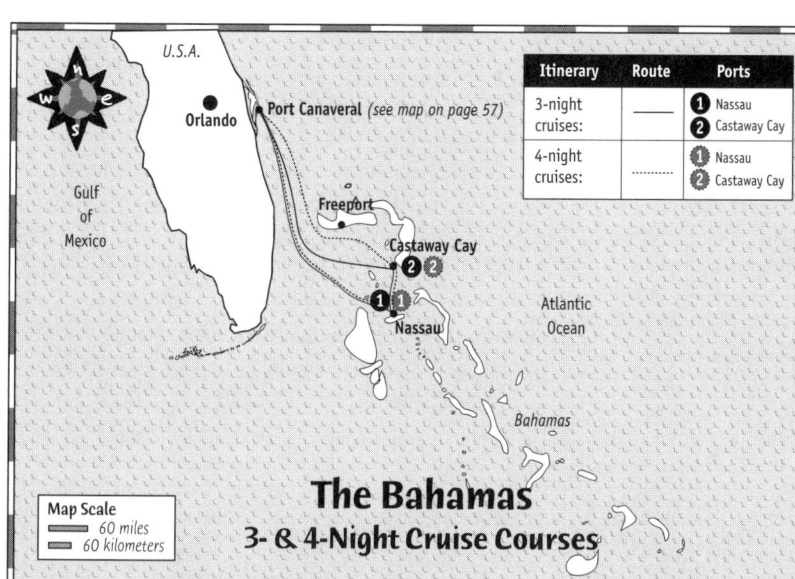

The 7-night land/sea combination itineraries are really just Walt Disney World resort vacations combined with the 3-night and 4-night cruises.

4 Nights on Land/3 Nights at Sea Itinerary: Of the two land/sea itineraries, this is the one we recommend. If you're a fan of Walt Disney World, you may find anything less than four days at Walt Disney World is just too short. With four major parks, you need at least a day to visit each. The cruise portion of this itinerary is identical to the 3-night cruise. The cruise is short, yes, but after four days at Walt Disney World, that may feel just right. Another advantage to this itinerary is how neatly it falls within the space of one week—you leave on Sunday and return on Sunday. If you're new to Walt Disney World and cruising, we think you'll like this itinerary best—it gives you a reasonable amount of time in the parks and a taste of the cruise. Of course, you can book a 3-night cruise-only and arrange your accommodations on your own. See page 42 for details.

3 Nights on Land/4 Nights at Sea Itinerary: We think three days at Walt Disney World is too short. And this itinerary does start and stop on Thursday, which makes for a lopsided week. There are some advantages, however. First, you get four nights on the cruise, which also means four days of meals. If you'd spent that extra day at Walt Disney World, you'd have to feed yourselves for that day, so you get more bang for your buck. And the 4-night cruise has some added perks that you don't get on the 3-night cruise, such as an at-sea day, a variety show, and the Pirates of the Caribbean menu (the theme night itself is the same). (See the chart on page 38 for a comparison.) If your focus is on cruising and you want to save some money on your vacation, then this may be the itinerary for you!

Choosing Your Itinerary *(continued)*

7-Night Caribbean Cruise Itineraries: Almost an entire week onboard the Disney Magic with two regular itineraries (Eastern Caribbean and Western Caribbean) and two special itineraries to the Western Caribbean.

Disney Cruise Line's original 7-night itinerary, the **Eastern Caribbean cruise**, has three ports of call (St. Maarten, St. Thomas, and Castaway Cay) and three days at sea. The **Western Caribbean cruise** offers four ports of call (typically Key West, Grand Cayman, Cozumel, and Castaway Cay) plus two days at sea. Two special Western Caribbean itineraries are available, both featuring two stops at Castaway Cay (no stop in Key West). The first of these itineraries also substitutes Costa Maya, Mexico for Grand Cayman. It stops at Castaway Cay, Costa Maya, Cozumel, and Castaway Cay plus two days at sea. The Costa Maya itinerary departs on May 27, June 24, July 22, August 19, September 16, October 14, November 11, and December 9, 2006. The November 18, 2006 Western Itinerary visits Castaway Cay, Grand Cayman, Cozumel, and Castaway Cay plus two days at sea. It's likely that entirely different special itineraries will be offered in 2007 (see page 29); check with Disney and at our PassPorter.com web site. Actual time spent afloat: 164 hours (almost seven days). The 7-night cruise is a great choice for experienced cruisers or those who really want to relax. Cruisers on 7-night itineraries also enjoy formal and semi-formal evenings, theme nights, and a wider variety of onboard activities. Night for night, the 7-nights are no more costly than shorter cruises. Land/sea packages for these cruises are typically only offered to international guests.

7-Nt. E. Caribbean:
Saturday: Set sail
Sunday: At sea
Monday: At sea
Tuesday: St. Maarten
Wednesday: St. Thomas
Thursday: At sea
Friday: Castaway Cay
Saturday: Return to port

7-Nt. W. Caribbean #1:
Saturday: Set sail
Sunday: Key West
Monday: At sea
Tuesday: Grand Cayman
Wednesday: Cozumel
Thursday: At sea
Friday: Castaway Cay
Saturday: Return to port

7-Nt. W. Caribbean #2:
Saturday: Set sail
Sunday: Castaway Cay
Monday: At sea
Tuesday: Costa Maya
Wednesday: Cozumel
Thursday: At sea
Friday: Castaway Cay
Saturday: Return to port

7-Nt. W. Caribbean #3:
Saturday: Set sail
Sunday: Castaway Cay
Monday: At sea
Tuesday: Grand Cayman
Wednesday: Cozumel
Thursday: At sea
Friday: Castaway Cay
Saturday: Return to port

Note that Cozumel was severely damaged by Hurricane Wilma in 2005. Visits to Cozumel by the Disney Magic resumed in February 2006, but as of this writing, Disney Cruise Line may still temporarily substitute another port for Cozumel if the guest experience is unsatisfactory. Check with Disney Cruise Line for any updates.

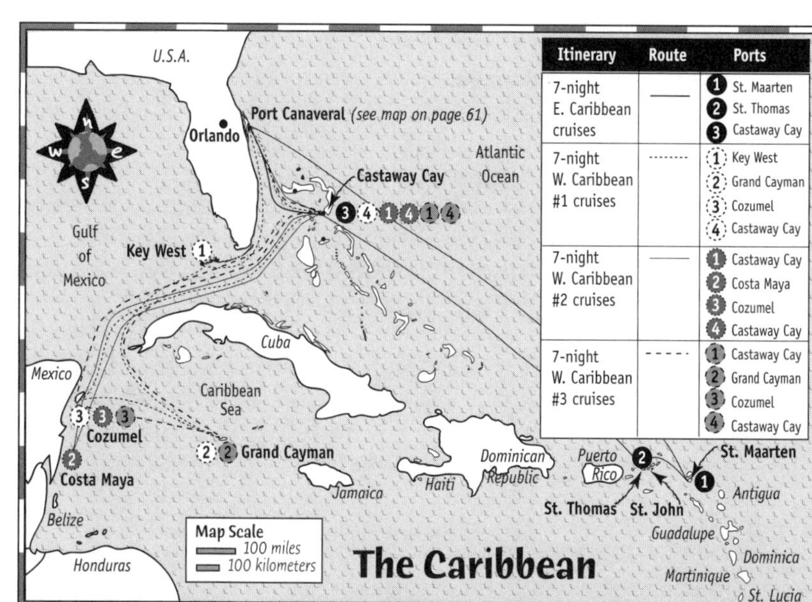

10-Nt. S. Caribbean:
Thursday: Set sail
Friday: At sea
Saturday: At sea
Sunday: St. Thomas
Monday: St. Lucia
Tuesday: Barbados
Wednesday: Antigua
Thursday: At sea
Friday: At sea
Saturday: Castaway Cay
Sunday: Return to port

10-Night Southern Caribbean Cruise Itinerary: In 2006 the Disney Wonder departs on its first-ever itineraries longer than 4 nights. This one-time-only itinerary departs September 7, 2006 and visits St. Thomas/St. John, St. Lucia, Barbados (their first-ever visit), Antigua, and Castaway Cay, with four days at sea. If you've always wanted a longer Disney cruise, this is your chance. Actual time spent afloat: 236 hours (almost ten days).

11-Night Southern Caribbean: Like the 10-night Southern Caribbean itinerary, this is a one-time-only opportunity on the Disney Wonder. Departing September 17, 2006, this sailing visits St. Thomas, St. Lucia, Barbados, Antigua, St. Kitts (their first-ever visit), and Castaway Cay. Actual time spent afloat: 260 hours (almost 11 days).

11-Nt. S. Caribbean:
Sunday: Set sail
Monday: At sea
Tuesday: At sea
Wednesday: St. Thomas
Thursday: St. Lucia
Friday: Barbados
Saturday: Antigua
Sunday: St. Kitts
Monday: At sea
Tuesday: At sea
Wednesday: Castaway Cay
Thursday: Return to port

10-Night Special Holiday Caribbean Itinerary: 2006 features one special holiday cruise to the Eastern Caribbean. Departing December 16, 2006, the Disney Magic will make stops in Key West, St. Maarten, St. Lucia, Antigua, St. Thomas/St. John and Castaway Cay. Christmas Eve will be spent at sea, and Christmas Day will be spent at Castaway Cay.

Choosing Your Itinerary *(continued)*

10-Nt. Holiday:
Saturday: Sail from Port Canaveral
Sunday: Key West
Monday: At sea
Tuesday: At sea
Wednesday: St. Maarten
Thursday: St. Lucia
Friday: Antigua
Saturday: At sea
Sunday: St. Thomas/St. John
Monday: Castaway Cay
Tuesday: Return to Port Canaveral

Future Itineraries: While we don't have a crystal ball, we are reasonably confident that the Disney Cruise Line has some Mediterranean itineraries in store for 2007 (see page 29). Our next edition will detail these, as well as any other new itineraries. Let's get a head start now with a map of the popular Mediterranean ports (see next page), along with some thoughts.

If Disney offers Mediterranean-based cruises, it will likely offer a couple of "repositioning" itineraries between Port Canaveral and Barcelona, Spain across the Atlantic Ocean, crossing eastbound in early May 2007 and returning to the U.S. in late August 2007. What happens once the Disney Magic arrives in Europe is unclear. The best indication is that there will be eight cruises alternating between 10 days and 11 days in length, visiting Spanish, French, Italian, and perhaps Greek and/or North African ports (see page 29 and the map on the next page). That can all change, of course, so don't hold us to it! Disney is characteristically tight-lipped about this possibility, except to confirm that the Mediterranean is being seriously considered.

What about other destinations? Some rumors have floated about Alaskan cruises, which are also a possibility for 2007, though much less likely. We are expecting an announcement about the 2007 special itineraries in early spring 2006—visit http://www.passporter.com/dcl to get the latest news.

2005's special West Coast itinerary and Panama Canal crossings were immensely successful, but are not likely to be repeated in the near term. We think it may take adding a third Disney cruise ship to the fleet before it happens again.

The Disney Wonder will be going into drydock for required maintenence and several upgrades in October 2006. There will be no 3- or 4-night sailings between October 1 and October 14. When the ship returns to service, we expect it to have a greatly enlarged spa; a giant, outdoor video screen overlooking the Goofy Pool; and a new area for the kid's program on deck 2 that caters to the 10–14 age group, among other changes (the same upgrades that were made to the Magic in October 2005).

....➤

The Mediterranean Magical Mystery Tour (with our apologies to the Beatles). If we're right about 2007's Mediterranean itineraries, we thought you might want to see a map. Not every port shown would be included. While current indications are for 10- and 11-night itineraries that begin and end in the same port, there are many other options.

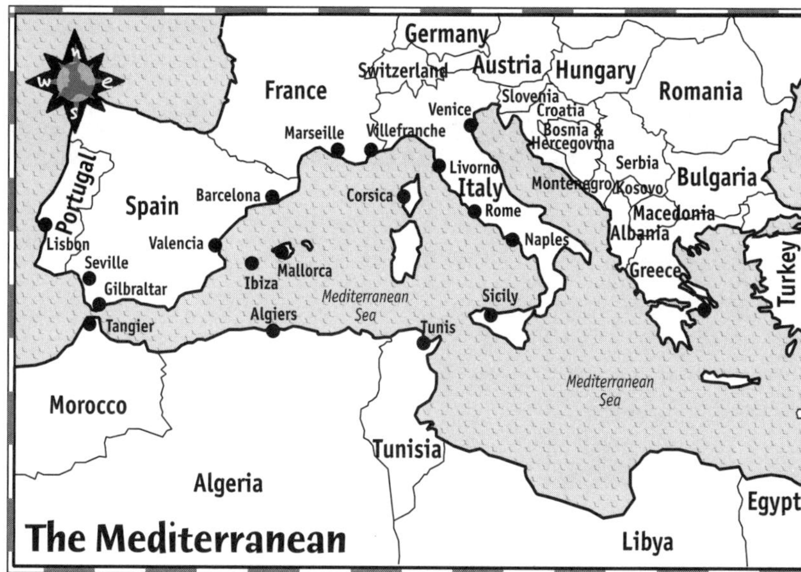

Rather than outline them all, see if you can connect the dots yourselves! One thing is certain about Mediterranean cruises—your port visits can be much more hectic and exhausting than visits to quiet, Caribbean islands. For example, you'll probably have just one day in Rome, and it's a one-hour tour bus ride into town from the port. Six hours in the Eternal City? That's like 15 minutes at Walt Disney World! Just relax and let your tour guide do her thing. Don't expect many days at sea on these cruises either.

Do Itineraries Ever Change?

Yes, as you can see by the mention of the special 2006 cruises, itineraries can and do change. For the most part, these itineraries are announced before reservations are accepted for those sailing dates. Occasionally, though, changes occur after you've made a booking. If so, Disney Cruise Line will contact you about your options. Occasionally itineraries are modified immediately before or during your cruise, but it is rare. Most last-minute itinerary changes are due to bad weather, and usually other ports are substituted. Castaway Cay is most often bypassed due to weather (as it is the most frequently visited), but even that is an uncommon occurrence (it seems to happen most in January and February). If you have plans at a port that cannot be modified (e.g., a wedding), you shouldn't count on a cruise to get you there—you're best off flying in and leaving the cruise for another time.

Itinerary Comparison Chart

Wondering about the specific differences between the various cruise itineraries? Below is a chart of the **differences only** between the regular itineraries (not the special itineraries). As you read through the book, you can assume that any feature mentioned applies to all cruise itineraries unless we specifically state otherwise.

Feature	3-Night	4-Night	7-Night E. Caribbean	7-Night W. Caribbean
Ports of call	2	2	3	4
Sea days	0	1	3	2
Embarkation day	Thursday	Sunday	Saturday	Saturday
Debarkation day	Sunday	Thursday	Saturday	Saturday
Hours afloat	68	92	164	164
Special dinner menus	1	1	4	4
Character breakfast			✔	✔
Champagne brunch			✔	✔
High tea			✔	✔
Tea with Wendy			✔	✔
Dessert buffets	1	1	2	2
Semi-formal nights			1	1
Formal nights			1	1
Stage shows	3	3	4	4
Variety shows	0	1	2	2
Adult seminars		✔	✔	✔

As you might imagine, the 7-night cruise offers more activities than the 3- or 4-night cruises—there are more days to fill, after all! Activities differ from cruise to cruise, but here's a list of some of the extra activities that have been offered on the 7-night cruises in the past:

- ✔ Intro to Internet session
- ✔ Dance lessons
- ✔ Family & Adult Talent Show
- ✔ Team Trivia
- ✔ Family Mini Olympics
- ✔ Mr. Toad's Wild Race
- ✔ Mickey 200 Race
- ✔ Ping-Pong tournament
- ✔ NHL Skills Challenge
- ✔ Mixology demonstrations
- ✔ Ice carving demonstrations
- ✔ Artist-led workshops

See chapter 5, "Playing and Relaxing Onboard," starting on page 123 for many more details on the various activities aboard.

Selecting Your Sail Dates

Once you've selected an itinerary, it's time to choose a sail date. The Disney Cruise Line operates year-round, so you have many choices. Deciding when to go is based on many factors: your schedules, your plans, price, itinerary availability, and weather. Let's go over each of these in detail:

Your Schedules—It's better to book as far ahead as possible, so check now with your employer/school for available vacation dates.

Your Plans—Do you want to go to Walt Disney World? If so, do you want to go before and/or after your cruise? If you do plan a visit to a Disney resort, you'll want to select a sail date that works in tandem with your resort plans—see the "To Go To A Disney Resort or Not?" topic on page 42 for tips. Are you hoping to visit relatives or spend some time at Kennedy Space Center in Cape Canaveral? If so, you will want to go when you can add extra time before and/or after your cruise.

Price—The Disney Cruise Line has rate trends that correspond to demand (check out our rate trends chart on page 45). In general, cruising is more affordable in January and September through early December (excluding Thanksgiving). Spring, summer, and major holidays are the most expensive times to cruise. See pages 44–45 for more pricing details.

Itinerary Availability—The various cruise itineraries depart and return on particular days of the week (see chart below), which may be important to your vacation schedule. Additionally, the 7-night cruise usually alternates between the Eastern Caribbean and Western Caribbean every other week. For specific dates of future cruises, visit http://www.disneycruise.com, or check your Disney Cruise Line booklet.

Cruise	Depart	Return
3-Night	Thurs.	Sun.
4-Night	Sun.	Thurs.
7-Night	Sat.	Sat.

When do we like to sail? We're fond of May—great weather, great rates!

Are Any Dates Unavailable?

Typically, yes. Ships do fill up near certain dates—such as Christmas and New Year's Eve. And some dates may be reserved for members of a certain group only. There may even be private charters for a company or the Disney Vacation Club. Also, the ships go into drydock for maintenance once every couple of years. For example, the Disney Wonder will be in drydock in October 2006. A quick call to the Disney Cruise Line can tell you if your preferred dates are available.

Caribbean and Bahamian Weather

The Caribbean and the Bahamas generally enjoy **delightful weather** year-round. Even so, it can get cool in the winter and a little warm in the summer. The summer also brings more rain than usual. See our weather chart below for details. The most important weather condition to consider is hurricane season, which runs from late May through November (see tropical storm levels in the chart below). The worst months for hurricane activity are August and September. Cruising during hurricane season means you're more likely to have a port change or two and have a rocky ride on rough seas. Even so, cruising during hurricane conditions isn't very dangerous, as modern storm forecasting gives the cruise lines plenty of time to modify itineraries to dodge the storms.

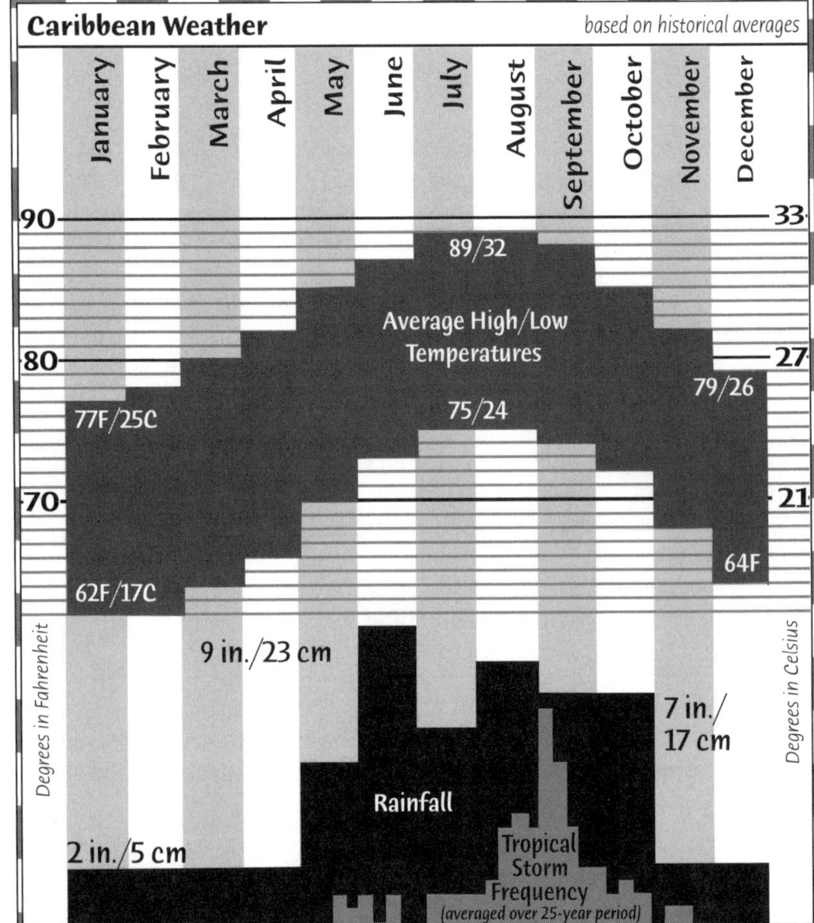

Hurricanes

Following historic Atlantic hurricane seasons in 2004 and 2005, we can't blame you for thinking long and hard on whether a major storm will affect your vacation. However, we were at sea for three and a half weeks during the 2005 season, and the **impact was far less than you might expect**. A storm near Baja, California forced the Disney Magic to bypass Cabo San Lucas and took us to the alternate port of Manzanillo, but the rest of our two-week Panama Canal journey was smooth sailing (although farther north, Hurricane Katrina was doing its worst). On a Western Caribbean cruise in June, our ship changed the order of its port visits and dashed to dodge a storm near Cuba. Other cruisers didn't do as well. Port Canaveral closed for several days, with embarkation/debarkation delayed and relocated to Fort Lauderdale (Disney bused cruisers there and back). Another time, the Disney Magic and Wonder huddled together in Galveston, Texas, dodging a storm. Most important is that the passengers and ships were kept safe. Modern mariners have plenty of warning about storms and are quite adept at keeping their passengers safe. We all hope for risk-free journeys, but it helps to prepare yourself mentally for the chance that all may not go as planned. When compared to the dangers of bygone eras, we're way far ahead of the game. One thing we wouldn't do is dissuade you from taking a hurricane-season cruise. After unexpectedly cold, icy, soggy, or scorching vacations on land, there's something to be said for a trip where you can lift anchor and head for fair weather. We'd rather be "stuck" on a cruise ship with all its facilities than be holed up in a motel room playing endless hands of cards, even if the deck heaves occasionally.

Unfortunately, we have **more stormy weather in our future**. Atlantic hurricanes follow roughly 25-year cycles of above- and below-average activity, and we're not quite halfway through an up cycle. Alas, the current El Niña in the Pacific bodes ill for the Atlantic storm season in 2006.The National Weather Service releases its annual storm outlook in May, with an update in August (see http://www.nhc.noaa.gov). We hope everyone on land and sea enjoys a respite from the recent extremes, but a return to relatively fair weather seems unlikely.

There's not much you can do to **prepare for a stormy voyage**. Bring seasickness medication if you're susceptible, but Meclizine is often distributed on board during rough seas (see page 267). Vacation insurance may add peace of mind, but insurance is typically more useful for your journey to and from the cruise ship than for the voyage itself. Disney Cruise Line has to put passenger safety first, and the company is not obligated to "make good" weather-related changes, but they have an admirable record of delivering passenger satisfaction, even in such difficult cases.

To Go To A Disney Resort or Not?

Perhaps you're tempted by the Caribbean land/sea vacation package, or you just can't resist the urge to visit Walt Disney World. Whatever your reason for visiting Walt Disney World Resort, you're not alone—the majority of your fellow cruisers will also visit the parks on their trip. If you're just not quite sure yet, let's weigh the pros and cons:

Reasons to Visit the Mouse House:

- ✔ You love Disney and can't be nearby without a visit.
- ✔ You've never been, and this is a great opportunity.
- ✔ You're not sure you'll feel the "Disney magic" if you skip the parks.
- ✔ You have the time and money.

Reasons to Just Cruise:

- ✔ You want a laid-back, really relaxing vacation.
- ✔ You've been there, done that, and don't need to go back yet.
- ✔ You don't have the time or money.

If you do **decide to go** to Walt Disney World, you'll need to choose between a land/sea vacation package and arranging it yourself. We always make our own arrangements—we save money and enjoy greater flexibility. The Walt Disney World land/sea package offers a limited choice of Disney resort hotels, based on your choice of stateroom (though you can pay to upgrade to a different resort). Would you like to stretch your dollars at a value resort but book a comfortable verandah stateroom? Not on the land/sea! You also can't grab hotel-only discounts that are often available. We prefer a minimum of a four-night cruise and at least a four-night stay at Walt Disney World. That's not in the package, either, though you can add it. You finally, however, get the full value out of the Magic Your Way Premium tickets that come with the packages—you no longer pay for the day you embark on your cruise. And you can't beat the land/sea for convenience—you'll be ushered everywhere with a minimum of fuss. No matter what, we refer you to our PassPorter Walt Disney World guidebook for loads of details, tips, strategies, maps, and plans. PassPorter's Walt Disney World for Your Special Needs guidebook adds invaluable information for travelers with all sorts of special requirements. You can pick up our guidebooks at most bookstores, online at http://www.passporter.com, and at 877-929-3273.

Should you visit Disney parks **before or after** you cruise? The Disney land/sea vacation package places the Walt Disney World leg before the cruise leg by default, though you can request it be switched. If you're new to Walt Disney World, visit the parks first—Walt Disney World is an intense vacation experience, and the cruise will be a relaxing break. Walt Disney World fans may prefer visiting the parks after the cruise, as "dessert."

Cruise Add-Ons

If you decide to let Disney make the arrangements for your visit to Walt Disney World, there are a number of packages and add-ons designed to help you get the most out of it. Below are the basic packages offered at press time. Please call the Disney Cruise Line for specific packages and prices. Prices quoted below are good through 12/31/2006.

Romantic Escape at Sea—Guests on a 3-, 4-, or 7-night cruise can add a collection of "romantic" services and items to their cruise. This package includes a romantic gift amenity (this may be a gift basket with photo album or frame, sparkling wine, and chocolates, but some cruisers report getting two spa robes instead of the sparkling wine), romance turndown service (one night), champagne breakfast in bed (one morning), priority seating and $10 per person fee at Palo (one evening), a bottle of wine at Palo, and a Tropical Rainforest pass for two at the Vista Spa for the length of the cruise. Some cruisers also report receiving a free 8 x 10 photo with their package. Another unadvertised perk of this package is the ability to book your reservations (such as Palo and Vista Spa) up to 105 days in advance (assuming you've paid for your cruise in full). The massage previously included in this package is no longer included. The ability to make reservations early may be the best piece of this package considering the popularity of Palo. Cruisers report mixed feelings about this package—some love the extra goodies and feel they are "worth the price," while others enjoy the services but think the gifts are "less than stellar" and of "mediocre quality". Price is $339 per couple (ages 21 and older only). Confirm all amenities before booking. This package must be booked prior to 30 days before sailing. (Booking Code: ESC)

Family Reunion—Guests on a 3-, 4-, or 7-night cruise or 7-night land/sea package can add a personalized Disney Cruise Line family reunion shirt (one per person), a leather photo portfolio with a complimentary photo (one per stateroom), and a commemorative family reunion certificate (one per person). Families booking 8 or more staterooms can also choose one of the following: an hour-long reception with open bar and snacks, a Bon Voyage Memory Box (one per stateroom), or a bottle of wine (one per stateroom). Costs $39 per person for the first and second guests in the room, $19 per person for extra guests in the same room. Package must be purchased for all guests (regardless of age) in the party. (Booking Code: FAMILY)

Two other "packages" are the **Wedding at Sea** starting at $3,878 per couple and the **Vow Renewal** starting at $,1978 per couple. Both are available on 3-, 4-, and 7-night cruises. See page 266 for more information.

Walt Disney World Packages

If you book your stay at Walt Disney World separately from your cruise, you can take advantage of a number of other packages. The Magic Your Way packages start with the basics (accommodations plus Magic Your Way base tickets) and add on dining plans, recreation plans, and premium Magic Your Way tickets. Magic Your Way packages start at about $330/person. To learn more about the available packages for Walt Disney World vacations, call the Walt Disney Travel Company at 800-828-0228, ask your travel agent, or visit http://www.waltdisneyworld.com.

Cruise Rates

While we can't give you exact prices, we can give you rate ranges for various itineraries and stateroom categories. The rates below are based on our own research of 2006 rates—we feel these are realistic numbers, but we can virtually guarantee that you'll get different rates when you do your own research. Use these as **guidelines only**. Actual rates are based on demand and fluctuate during the year. To get actual rate quotes, call the Disney Cruise Line, visit http://www.disneycruise.com, or talk to your travel agent. Note that the rates below are for **two adult fares** with early booking savings, but do not include air, insurance, or ground transfers.

Typical Cruise Rate Ranges (for two adults in one stateroom)

Category	3-Night Cruise	4-Night Cruise	7-Night Cruise	7-Night Land/Sea
	Low to High	*Low to High*	*Low to High*	*Low to High*
1	$4598-5998	$5398-7998	$8998-10,798	$7798-10,798
2	$3998-5398	$4598-5998	$8298-10,398	$7198-10,398
3	$2478-4798	$2998-5198	$6198-9398	$5598-9398
4	$1998-4198	$2198-4598	$3798-7398	$3638-7398
5	$1758-3598	$1958-3798	$2998-6398	$3038-6398
6	$1658-3398	$1858-3598	$2898-6198	$2838-6198
7	$1458-3198	$1618-3398	$2598-5998	$2638-5998
8	$1358-2998	$1418-3198	$2398-5198	$2438-5198
9	$1258-2798	$1318-2998	$2198-4798	$2238-4798
10	$1058-2398	$1118-2598	$1898-4398	$2038-4398
11	$958-2198	$1058-2398	$1798-4198	$1938-4198
12	$858-1998	$998-2198	$1698-3998	$1878-3998
3rd & 4th Guest: Kids Under 3	$149	$149	$169	$169
3rd & 4th Guest: Kids 3-12	$229-1099	$329-1199	$399-2199	$399-2199
3rd & 4th Guest: Ages 13 & up	$279-1099	$379-1199	$599-2199	$599-2199

- ✔ Each stateroom booked must include at least one adult, and no more than 3-5 total guests may occupy a stateroom, depending upon occupancy limits. If your party size is greater than five, you'll need to book a suite (categories 1-2) or more than one stateroom.
- ✔ Staterooms with just one adult and one child are charged the price of two adults.
- ✔ Guests cruising alone (one adult in a room) are charged roughly 80% of the above rates.
- ✔ Guests booking a land/sea package can choose to stay at the Grand Floridian Resort with categories 1-3; a deluxe resort (Beach Club, Polynesian, Animal Kingdom Lodge, Swan, or Dolphin) with categories 4-7; or a moderate resort (Port Orleans-French Quarter, Port Orleans-Riverside, or Caribbean Beach) with categories 8-12. No other resorts are options.
- ✔ Note: Women who are past their 24th week of pregnancy and infants under 12 weeks cannot sail with the Disney Cruise Line.

Confused by all those rate ranges? We feel the same way. Before we went to press, **we researched every regular 2006 cruise** and its rates (at early booking discounts). We then graphed the minimum rates (for two adults in a category 12 stateroom) into the chart below. This chart gives you a very useful overview of the general trends for specific times in 2006 (and 2007 will likely be very similar). Rates for higher categories follow the same basic trends as category 12, so you can use this chart to pinpoint seasons for the best rates. Keep in mind, however, that these rates can change at any time. Don't take the numbers in this chart at face value—concentrate on the trends instead. Also note that this chart does not take into account seasonal discounts which may be offered, thereby reducing the rates for a specific period. You may want to compare this to the chart on page 40 to pick the best compromise between great cruise rates and great weather (we're partial to May ourselves).

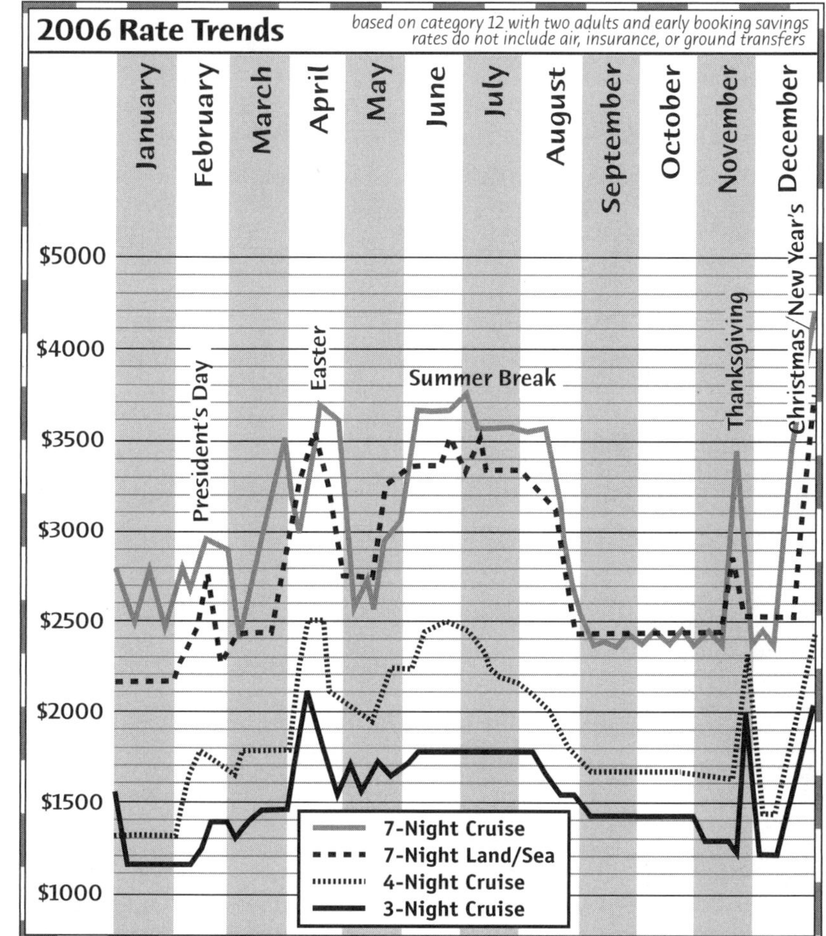

Reserving Your Cruise

Once you know when, how, and where you want to cruise, it's time to **make reservations**. You can call the Disney Cruise Line directly, book online at DisneyCruise.com, or use a travel agent (see sidebar at bottom). There are pros and cons to all. Dealing directly with Disney may give you more control over stateroom selection, while travel agents may get better deals. Disney Vacation Club (DVC) members who want to cruise on points (see sidebar on page 48) should contact DVC directly.

Before you make your reservations, **use the worksheet** on page 49 to jot down your preferred sailing dates along with alternates. Even a small change in your travel dates can open the door to a great deal. Be familiar with all stateroom categories (see chapter 3) in your price range, too.

Reservations can be made by calling **888-325-2500**, 8:00 am to 10:00 pm ET (weekdays) and 9:00 am to 8:00 pm (weekends). From outside the U.S., call +1-407-566-6921. Representatives offer assistance in English, Spanish, Japanese, French, Portuguese, and German. Castaway Club members have a special phone number (see page 273). You can also reserve at http://www.disneycruise.com and at cruise-related sites—see below.

Call Disney Cruise Reservations as far in advance as possible. Ask for any **special deals or packages** for your dates—Disney generally doesn't volunteer this information. If you have a Walt Disney World Annual Pass or Disney Visa, or are a Disney Vacation Club member or Florida resident, ask about those discounts. If your dates aren't available, check alternates.

Make any **special requests**, such as a handicap-accessible room or the need for special meals, at the time of reservation. If you have a particular stateroom or deck in mind (see chapter 3), make sure to tell the reservations agent at the time of booking.

Shopping Around

You can also make reservations through various travel reservation sites or travel agents specializing in Disney Cruise reservations (in alphabetical order):

Travel Reservation Sites

http://www.cruise.com
http://www.cruise411.com
http://www.cruise-locator.com
http://www.expedia.com
http://www.orbitz.com
http://www.travelocity.com
http://www.vacationstogo.com

Travel Agents

http://www.aaa.com
http://www.costco.com
http://www.cruisedirections.com/disney
http://www.dreamscruise.com
http://www.mei-travel.com
http://www.mouseearvacations.com
http://www.themagicforless.com

Get Your Passports and/or Birth Certificates Together Now

Your cruise takes you to foreign ports, so you must have proper ID. Passports will be mandatory for all travelers arriving in the U.S. from the Caribbean on or after 12/31/2006. Until then photo IDs along with certified birth certificates with raised seals work for U.S. citizens, too. You also need passports/birth certificates for kids. It can take months to obtain these if you haven't already, so get started now! See pages 50–51.

You will be asked if you want the **Vacation Protection Plan**, and the cruise line agents automatically include it in their quote. This insurance plan covers trip cancellations, travel delays, emergency medical/dental, emergency medical transportation/assistance, and baggage delay, loss, theft, or damage. The plan price is based on the length of your cruise vacation—$49 (3 nights), $59 (4 nights), and $99 (7 and 10 nights) per person for the first and second individuals in your stateroom (additional guests are $39, $49, and $59, respectively). If your flight could be affected by weather, seriously consider insurance. Note that your airfare and your air travel-related delays will not be covered unless you're also using the Disney Air Program. Also note that the Protection Plan does not cover some preexisting medical conditions. If you don't want this insurance, ask to have it removed from your quote.

Save on **vacation insurance** by booking it yourself—visit http://www.insuremytrip.com or call your insurance agent. But don't delay—most companies will waive preexisting medical conditions only if you buy insurance within 7-14 days after making your trip deposit. Trip interruption/cancellation coverage is great for circumstances beyond your control, but it doesn't help if you simply change your mind. If the cruise is only part of your vacation, make sure your policy covers the entire trip. Policies vary, so shop carefully. You may already have life, medical, theft, and car rental protection in your regular policies (be sure you're covered overseas). Credit cards, AAA, and/or other memberships may also include useful coverage. Airlines already cover lost baggage—make sure your policy exceeds their limits. Seniors and travelers with preexisting conditions should seriously consider insurance—the costs of evacuation, overseas medical care, and travel/lodging for a companion while you're under treatment are very high.

You may also be asked if you want **airfare**. In general, we've found it is less expensive to book our own airfare, but you may prefer to leave the flight details up to Disney. The biggest drawback to using the Disney Air Program is that they decide which flight you'll take, and you may arrive later than you prefer or have tight flight transfers. If you do use Disney Air, ground transfers are automatically included in your package (see below).

Ground transfers are automatic for those using the Disney Air Program and an option for those arranging their own flights. Disney Cruise Line ground transfers are available to/from the airport to the cruise terminal. Price is $59/guest. The ground transfers include pickup at the airport, round-trip ground transportation, and baggage handling. For cruisers arriving at Orlando International Airport, your bags go directly from the plane to your resort/ship (provided you affix the Disney-supplied labels prior to checking your bags with your airline and you're flying in on the day of your cruise). One-way transfers to or from the airport are also available for $30/guest. See page 62. If you're also going to or from Walt Disney World Resort and staying at a Disney resort hotel, those transfers will be included free of charge as part of Disney's Magical Express program (see below).

Disney's Magical Express

Since May 5, 2005, Disney has offered free bus transportation between Orlando International Airport (MCO) and Disney resort hotels. Modeled after Disney Cruise Line's ground transportation program, guests arriving at MCO can bypass baggage claim and head right to the bus loading area—as long as they've affixed special luggage tags back home, their luggage will be gathered right off the plane and delivered to their resort room. Provided their airline participates in the program (check with Disney), guests headed back to the airport can do their airline check-in (including baggage) right at their hotel before boarding their bus. Reservations must be made at least 10 days in advance. If you're staying at a Disney resort hotel before or after your cruise, inquire with Disney reservations at 407-WDW-MAGIC. If you're on a Disney Cruise Line land/sea package, Disney's Magical Express is already built in—ask your reservation agent for details. Disney may start charging for this service in 2007.

Reserving Your Cruise *(continued)*

A **deposit** of $200/guest (3-/4-night) or $250/guest (7-/11-night) is required to confirm your reservation. Reservations are held for seven days without confirmation, and then they are deleted if no deposit is received. Pay your deposit by 8:00 pm ET on the seventh day—you can do it over the phone with Visa, MasterCard, Discover, JCB, Diner's Club, American Express, or The Disney Credit Card. Record deposits on the worksheet on page 49.

Once your cruise is confirmed, Disney mails a **confirmation** of your reservation. Payment is due in full 90 days (stateroom categories 1–3) or 75 days (stateroom categories 4–12) prior to sailing. Starting with cruises departing on or after December 28, 2006, you must provide passport numbers 75 days prior to departure (see pages 50–51). If you need to cancel, reservations can be cancelled for full credit up to 90 days (categories 1–3) or up to 75 days (categories 4–12) prior to your vacation. If you cancel 45–89 days (categories 1–3) or 45–74 days (categories 4–12) prior to your cruise/package, you lose your deposit. (Beginning in 2007, the deposit is nonrefundable for reservations in stateroom categories 1–3.) If you cancel 8–44 days prior, you lose 50% of the cruise fare. There is no refund if you cancel seven days or less prior to your cruise/package. There is a $35/person fee for document reissue and name/air changes within 30 days of your vacation. There is a $50/person fee if you change your sail dates 0–59 days prior to your cruise, and you may need to pay that $35/person fee on top of it if your documents must be reissued. Insurance may help with these penalties.

Your **cruise documents** are mailed to you within 28 days of sailing, though most cruisers get them about two weeks prior to their cruise. Read everything in your cruise document package and fill out the embarkation form, immigration form, cruise contract, and payment authorization before you leave home. Luggage tags are included in each cruise booklet and should be placed on your bags before you arrive (see page 70 for details). Other items in your cruise document package include a guide to the document package, shore excursion booklet and advance reservation form, onboard gift brochure, Disney's Vacation Plan (insurance) brochure/policy, and the Passport to Disney Magic/Wonder booklet (a brief guide to the cruise). Your cruise documents are required to board, and you should have them with you (or in your carry-on) on the day of depature. Don't make the mistake of putting them in a suitcase that gets checked through.

Once your cruise is reserved, you may be eager to **meet other families** sailing with you on the same cruise. You can do this in advance of your cruise by posting your own sail dates on Disney Cruise Line message boards such as our own PassPorter Message Boards (http://www.passporterboards.com) or at DIS (http://www.disboards.com). You can use these resources to plan get-togethers, find companions for your table in the dining rooms, or find playmates for your kids. You'd be surprised at how many of your fellow cruisers are online and eager to make friends!

Disney Vacation Club Members
Members of Disney's innovative time-share program, the Disney Vacation Club (DVC), have the option to use their points for cruises. Contact Disney Vacation Club directly at 800-800-9100 or visit http://www.disneyvacationclub.com to get point charts and details on reserving cruises. Note that you can use a combination of points and cash (or credit) for a cruise. Reservations with points can be made up to 11 months in advance. We've heard mixed reports from guests who use DVC points to cruise—some feel it works out well for them, while others feel the cruise requires too many points. Disney Vacation Club members booking cruises without points may also be entitled to an onboard credit—inquire when making reservations.

Cruise Reservation Worksheet

Use this worksheet to jot down preferences, scribble information during phone calls, and keep all your discoveries together. Don't worry about being neat—just be thorough! Circle the cruise you finally select to avoid any confusion.

Cruise length: *3 nts. 4 nts. 7 nts. 7 nts. land/sea 10 nts. 11 nts.*

Departure date: ____________ Alternate: ____________

Return date: ____________ Alternate: ____________

We prefer to stay in category: ________ Alternates: ________

Discounts: *Disney Visa Disney Vacation Club Castaway Club AAA Seasonal Florida Resident Canadian Resident Other:* ______

Dates	Itinerary	Category	Rates	Insurance	Total

Reservation number: ____________

Confirm reservation by this date: ____________

Deposit due by: ____________ Deposit paid on: ____________

Balance due by: ____________ Balance paid on: ____________

Do we need to order passports/birth certificates? ____________

➤

Have Your Passports Ready

Starting December 31, 2006 (yes, later this year), everyone entering the United States by sea or air from the Western Hemisphere (including the Caribbean and Bahamas) **must have a valid passport**. This goes for U.S. citizens as well as international visitors, so put that driver's license back in your wallet and leave those birth certificates in your safe deposit box.

Formerly, U.S. citizens could use a variety of government-issued photo IDs plus a birth certificate to re-enter the country. The Intelligence Reform and Terrorism Prevention Act of 2004 changes all that. The **law requires a passport** or other "accepted, secure document" for all entry into the U.S. from the Western Hemisphere as of January 1, 2008. Before you get your hopes up, "accepted, secure document" refers to certain special ID cards issued to workers who cross the border on a frequent basis. Driver's licenses and Green Cards do not qualify.

While the law doesn't go into effect until 2008, the U.S. Departments of Homeland Security and State want an **earlier phase-in of these requirements**, to smooth the transition. Originally, passports for Caribbean/Bahamas cruisers were going to be required as of December 31, 2005, but the agencies bowed to public objections. The current proposed regulations may change again before they are finalized. Check at http://travel.state.gov and/or the Disney Cruise Line web site for updates.

If your cruise returns to the U.S. **on or after December 31, 2006** (any Disney ship departing Port Canaveral on or after December 28, 2006) you will need a valid passport for each member of your party, even infants. This requirement may be especially challenging for newborns (who may cruise as early as 12 weeks), as there's barely time to get the birth certificate, apply for and receive a passport in that 12 weeks.

Disney Cruise Line has an extra requirement—**all guests will be required to supply their passport numbers to Disney Cruise Line at least 75 days prior to their departure.** If you have applied for passports but fear you may not receive them in time, discuss the situation with a Disney Cruise Line representative prior to the 75 day deadline.

Passport applications are accepted at **more than 7,000 locations** in the U.S., including many post offices, county clerks, and city halls. For a full listing, including hours of operation, visit http://travel.state.gov or call the National Passport Information Center (NPIC) phone number at 877-487-2778. The same site also provides application forms for download and full information on the application process.

It typically takes **6–8 weeks to receive a passport** after you file the application, so we suggest that you apply for your passport(s) no later than 135 days (four months) prior to sailing (or pay extra for expediting your application)! If you're cruising sooner than four months from now and have no passport yet, you'll want to expedite your passport application—see the top of the next page for details on getting a rush passport.

New applications for everyone including infants must be made in person, but passport renewals can be made by mail provided the current passport is undamaged, your name hasn't changed (or you can legally document the change), the passport is no more than 15 years old, and you were 16 years or older when it was issued.

Are you in a rush? **Expedited passport applications** can be processed for an additional fee. If you apply through a regular passport "acceptance facility," you can get your passport within two weeks. Expedited service adds $60 to the cost of each application, plus overnight shipping fees. If you are traveling within two weeks, you can get urgent passport applications processed even faster at 15 Passport Agencies in the U.S., by appointment only. If you cannot get to one of those Agencies, services such as U.S. Birth Certificate.net (http://www.usbirthcertificate.net) can do it for you, provided you first visit a local passport acceptance facility to handle the preliminaries.

Important: You will need a **birth certificate or other birth/naturalization record** before you can apply for your passport, so you may need even more time! While there are services (such as U.S. Birth Certificates.net) that can obtain a domestic birth certificate in as little as 2–3 days, if you were born outside the U.S., the process may take weeks or even months.

Yes, you're only planning this one vacation, so the extra cost of obtaining passports seems burdensome. Look on the bright side—an adult passport is good for 10 years, and in that time you'll **probably need it again**, if only to visit the Canadian side of Niagara Falls, play the slots in Windsor, Ontario, attend the 2010 Winter Olympics in Vancouver, or spend the afternoon in Tijuana. And who knows? You may get hooked on cruising!

Budget **$97 for a "standard" adult passport application**, $82 for each child under 16. Expedited (two-week) processing brings the budget up to $157/adult, $142/child, plus next-day shipping costs. Passport renewals are $67. Duplicate/replacement birth certificate fees vary by state, but cost at least $15. Naturally, the help of a passport/birth certificate service adds even more to the price—typically an extra $100/passport, $50/birth certificate.

Make sure you **don't get caught without your papers**. Use this timeline to calculate your due dates, and use the following worksheet to get all your ducks in a row.

Passport Timeline

My Cruise Date:	
Subtract 75 days from cruise date:	Passport # to Disney Cruise Line due:
Subtract 90 days from cruise date:	Passport application (expedited) due:
Subtract 135 days from cruise date:	Passport application (regular) due:
Need birth certificates, too? Subtract 15 days from the passport application due date (for those born in the U.S.), 120 days (for those born outside the U.S.):	

Passport Worksheet

Name	Passport Number	Completed Application	Proof of Citizenship	Proof of Identity	Passport Photos (2)	Fees

Getting to Florida

By Car, Van, Truck, or Motorcycle

Most vacationers still arrive in Florida in their own vehicle. It's hard to beat the **slowly rising sense of excitement** as you draw closer or the freedom of having your own wheels once you arrive (helpful when you're combining your cruise with a land vacation). Driving may also eliminate any concerns you or family members may have with air travel. And driving can be less expensive than air travel, especially with large families. On the downside, you may spend long hours or even days on the road, which cuts deeply into your vacation time. And you'll need to park your car while you're cruising, which is pricey (see pages 63 and 67).

If you opt to drive, carefully **map your course** ahead of time. You can do this with a AAA TripTik—a strip map that guides you to your destination. You must be a AAA member (see page 27) to get a TripTik, but you can easily join for $70/year. If you're driving I-75, we recommend "Along Interstate-75" (Mile Oak Publishing, http://www.i75online.com) by Dave Hunter. I-95 drivers will benefit from the "Drive I-95" guide by Stan and Sandra Posner (Travelsmart, http://www.drivei95.com) or a visit to http://www.usastar.com/i95/homepage.htm. For navigating the Sunshine State, look for Dave Hunter's "Along Florida's Freeways" guidebook. Or try a trip-routing service such as AutoPilot at http://www.freetrip.com.

If you live more than 500 miles away, **spread out your drive** over more than one day, allotting one day for every 500 miles. If your journey spans more than a day, decide in advance where to stop each night and make reservations. If possible, arrive a day ahead of your cruise departure day for a more relaxing start to the cruise (see pages 64–66 for lodging in Cape Canaveral). Compare the price of driving versus flying, too.

By Train

The train is a uniquely relaxing way to travel to Central Florida. **Amtrak** serves the Orlando area daily with both **passenger trains** and an Auto Train, which carries your family and your car. The **Auto Train** runs between suburban Washington, D.C. and suburban Orlando (Sanford, FL). Prices vary depending upon the season, the direction, and how far in advance you make your reservation. The Auto Train is also available one-way, and in many seasons, one direction is less expensive than the other. Late arrivals are the norm, so allow extra time. Keep in mind that you may need to take a taxi or town car from the train station, or you can rent a car from the nearby Hertz office. For Amtrak's rates, schedules, reservations, and more information, call 800-USA-RAIL or visit them at http://www.amtrak.com.

By Bus

Greyhound serves Cocoa, Orlando, and Kissimmee. Buses take longer to reach a destination than cars driving the same route. Fares are lowest if you live within ten hours of Central Florida. For fares and tickets, call Greyhound at 800-231-2222 or visit them at http://www.greyhound.com.

By Airplane

Air travel is the fastest way for many vacationers, but we recommend you fly in at least a day before in the event there are any flight delays. You have two choices: use the Disney Air Program and let them include your airfare in your package—inquire about pricing when you book your cruise—or book your own flight. It'll be less expensive and more flexible if you book your own flight—Disney Air Program arrival and departure times aren't always optimal. To find an **affordable flight**, be flexible on the day and time of departure and return—fares can differ greatly depending on when you fly and how long you stay. Second, take advantage of the many "fare sales" available—to learn about sales, visit airlines' web sites or travel sites such as Travelocity (http://www.travelocity.com), Expedia (http://www.expedia.com), or Orbitz (http://www.orbitz.com). Third, try alternate airports and airlines (including low-fare airlines like Song and jetBlue). Fourth, be persistent. Ask for their lowest fare and work from there. When you find a good deal, put it on hold immediately (if possible), note your reservation on page 53, and cancel later if necessary. Consider researching fares on your **airline's web site**—you can experiment with different flights and may get a deal for booking online. Priceline.com (http://www.priceline.com) is an option—you can name your own price. But only use it if you are flying out a day or more ahead and/or returning a day or more later. To arrange **ground transportation**, see pages 60 and 67.

Our Top 10 Tips, Reminders, and Warnings

1. Call your airline/airport for any new or changed requirements, and check the status of your flight before departing for the airport.
2. Pack (or pick up) a meal for the flight.
3. Leave potentially dangerous items at home—they aren't allowed on the plane or the ship. This includes pocket knives, hand tools, and many kinds of sporting gear. If you must bring needles or syringes, also bring a note from your doctor. Nail clippers, tweezers, and eyeglass repair kits can be packed in your carry-on. Call the Disney Cruise Line to confirm any questionable objects.
4. Carry undeveloped film in your carry-on as the checked luggage screening devices may damage undeveloped film. Film at 800 speed and up should be hand-checked.
5. Limit your carry-ons to one bag and one personal item (purse, briefcase, etc.) and assume they will be searched.
6. Plan to arrive at the airport two hours prior to departure.
7. A boarding pass will be required for you to pass through security.
8. Before passing through security, put all metal items in the provided tray.
9. E-Ticket holders should bring a confirmation and/or boarding pass.
10. Be patient with long lines and polite with travel personnel.

Getting Around the Orlando International Airport

Most cruise-bound passengers will arrive in the Orlando International Airport, a large, sprawling hub and one of the better airports we've flown into. Your plane docks at one of the **satellite terminals** (see map below). Follow the signs to the automated **shuttle** to the main terminal—there you'll find **baggage claim** and ground transportation. Once you reach the main terminal follow signs down to baggage claim (Level 2). If you're using Disney ground transportation (and previously affixed Disney luggage tags), head directly to the Disney's Magical Express check-in desk on "A" side, Level 1. Shuttles, town cars, taxis, and rental cars are also found on Level 1 (take the elevators opposite the baggage carousels). Each transportation company has its own ticket booth, so keep your eyes open. If you get lost, look for signs that can get you back on track.

As your authors used to live in entirely different parts of the country, we became quite good at **meeting up at the airport**. It's best to meet your party at their baggage claim area as you won't be allowed past security without a valid boarding pass. The trick here is knowing which airline and baggage claim area. Use the map and airline list below, or call the airport directly at 407-825-2001. Be careful when differentiating between the side A and side B baggage claim. Also note that gates 1–29 and 100–129 use side A, while gates 30–99 use side B. Check the arrival/departure boards in the main terminal for flight status, too!

Another meeting option is an **airport restaurant**, especially for long waits. Call 407-825-2001 or visit http://www.orlandoairports.net for details on the airport's eateries. Travelers can be paged at 407-825-2000.

American Airlines, America West, ATA, Continental, SunWorld, Thomas Cook, and TWA use gates 1–29; Air Canada, ANA, Northwest, United, and U.S. Air use 30–59; Delta, British Airways, Midwest, Song, Sun Country, and Virgin use gates 60–99; and AirTran, jetBlue, Southwest, and Spirit use gates 100–129.

Getting Around the Orlando Sanford Airport

Travelers flying to Orlando **from Europe or via group charter** may arrive at the smaller Orlando Sanford International Airport (FSB), located about 18 miles northeast of Orlando and 67 miles from Port Canaveral. Airlines with scheduled service into Sanford include Allegiant Air, Iceland Air, Pan Am Clipper Connection, and Vacation Express, as well as nine international charter services with flights from the United Kingdom and Ireland (Air Atlanta Europe, aviajet, Excel Airways, First Choice Air, Monarch, MyTravel, Thomas Cook, Thomsonfly, and Travel City Direct).

Alamo/National, Avis, Dollar, Enterprise, Hertz, and Thrifty all operate **in-terminal car rental desks**. Mears Transportation and several shuttle services provide bus/van service from Sanford to Orlando-area attractions and Port Canaveral.

International passengers arrive and depart from Terminal A, while domestic travelers use Terminal B. A Welcome Center is located across the street from Terminal A and is home to ground transportation services.

Dining options here include Chadwick's Pub and a basic food court.

For more details on the Orlando Sanford International Airport, phone 407-322-7771 or visit http://www.orlandosanfordairport.com. If you plan to rent a car at the airport and drive to Port Canaveral, use a map routing service such as MapQuest.com before you leave home to get directions (the airport is located at 1 Red Cleveland Blvd., Sanford, FL 32773).

Travel Worksheet

Use this worksheet to jot down preferences, scribble information during phone calls, and keep all your discoveries together. Don't worry about being neat—just be thorough! Circle the names and numbers once you decide to go with them to avoid confusion.

Arrival date: ________________ Alternate: ________________________

Return date: ________________ Alternate: ________________________

We plan to travel by: ❑ Car/Van ❑ Airplane ❑ Train ❑ Bus ❑ Tour

❑ Other: ____

For Drivers:

Miles to get to Port Canaveral: ______ ÷ 500 = ____ days on the road

We need to stay at a motel on: ____________________________

Tune-up scheduled for: ________________________________

Rental car info: ____________________________________

____

For Riders:

Train/Bus phone numbers: ______________________________

Ride preferences: ____________________________________

Ride availabilities: ___________________________________

Reserved ride times and numbers: _______________________

Routes: ____

For Tour-Takers:

Tour company phone numbers: __________________________

Tour preferences: ____________________________________

Tour availabilities: ___________________________________

Reserved tour times and numbers: _______________________

Routes: ____

For Fliers:

Airline phone numbers: ____

Flight preferences: ____

Flight availabilities: ____

Reserved flight times and numbers: ______________________________

For Ground Transportation:

Town car/shuttle/rental car phone numbers: ______________________

Town car/shuttle/rental car reservations: ________________________

Package ground transportation details: ___________________________

Additional Notes:

Reminder: Don't forget to confirm holds or cancel reservations (whenever possible) within the allotted time frame.

Lodging Near Orlando Intl. Airport

If you fly into Orlando a day ahead of time but arrive too late in the day to make the trek to Port Canaveral, consider bunking near the airport the night before. We describe several hotels near the airport below—even one hotel that's actually in the airport itself! Here are the details:

Hyatt Regency Orlando $219+ 0 mi/0 km from airport

You can't beat the convenience of staying right in the airport at this Hyatt, but you will pay for the privilege. This six-story hotel is built right into the main terminal at the Orlando International Airport, offering 446 sound-proof, luxurious rooms at a whopping 400 sq. ft. each. While we haven't had the opportunity to stay here, a walk around the hotel spaces gives the impression of a very upscale business hotel. Standard room amenities include two double beds, oversized work desk with dataport, armchairs, cable TV, balcony (terminal-side rooms only), coffeemaker, hair dryer, iron and ironing board, daily newspaper, voice mail, and wireless Internet access available upon request—there are no in-room safes. Hotel amenities include room service, arcade, beauty salon, heated outdoor pool, sundeck with a view of the runway, fitness room, and access to the shopping mall in the airport. The Hyatt has two restaurants: Hemispheres serves breakfast buffets and elegant dinners on the top two floors of the hotel; McCoy's Bar and Grill is a casual eatery serving American food for lunch and dinner. The Lobby South lounge offers drinks and appetizers in front of its big screen TV. Check-in time: 4:00 pm; check-out time: 12:00 pm. The hotel was built in 1992 and renovated in 2000. Visit http://orlandoairport.hyatt.com or call 407-825-1234. Address: 9300 Airport Boulevard, Orlando, FL 32827. Note that when you purchase air travel through Disney Cruise Line and they fly you in the night before your cruise, this appears to be the hotel that Disney puts you up at most frequently (but no guarantees, of course!).

Orlando Airport Marriott $269+ 2.5 mi/4 km from airport

A standard room

© MediaMarx, Inc.

We enjoyed a night at this Marriott before a Disney cruise in May 2003 and found it both convenient and affordable (we got a great rate here via Priceline.com—see sidebar on next page). The Marriott is a mere 5 minutes from the Orlando Airport via a complimentary shuttle (available by using a courtesy phone in the terminal). The 484 rooms at this 10-story business hotel offer two double beds, work desk with dataport, 27 in. cable TV, two-line speakerphone, coffeemaker, hair dryer, iron and ironing board, daily newspaper, voice mail, and high-speed Internet access—there are no in-room safes or balconies. Hotel amenities include room service, arcade, indoor/outdoor heated pool, hot tub, sauna, fitness center, tennis courts, and basketball court. A full-service restaurant, Murphy's Chop House, is open daily for dinner. For more casual meals, Paradise Cafe has American foods for breakfast, lunch, and dinner. A pool bar, The Landing, serves drinks and sandwiches seasonally. Kick's Lounge offers appetizers and drinks in the evening. The hotel was built in 1983 and renovated in 1998. Check-in time: 3:00 pm; check-out time: 12:00 pm. Visit http://marriott.com/property/propertypage/MCOAP or call 407-851-9000 or 800-380-6751. Address: 7499 Augusta National Drive, Orlando, FL 32833. See our detailed review of this hotel, complete with photos, at http://www.passporter.com/articles/orlandoairportmarriott.htm. We would stay here again without hesitation.

Sheraton Suites — $195+ — 2.5 mi/4 km from airport

This all-suite, three-story hotel offers 150 suites at affordable rates. Suite amenities include a separate living room with sofa bed, work desk, two-line phones with dataports, TV, armchair, and kitchenette area with refrigerator, coffeemaker, and microwave, private bedroom with French doors, two pillowtop double beds (or one king bed), another TV, marble bathroom with hair dryer, iron and ironing board, voice mail, and high-speed Internet access—there are no in-room safes, but there are balconies in some rooms. Hotel amenities include room service, a heated indoor/outdoor pool, sundeck, hot tub, and fitness room. The on-site restaurant, Mahagony Grille, offers a breakfast buffet plus lunch and dinner. Several restaurants—Chili's, Tony Roma's, and Bennigan's—are within walking distance. A 24-hour shuttle is available between the airport and hotel—use the courtesy phone in the terminal to request it. Check-in time: 3:00 pm; check-out time: 12:00 pm. Visit http://www.sheratonairport.com or call 407-240-5555 or 800-325-3535. Address: 7550 Augusta National Drive, Orlando, FL 32833.

La Quinta Inn & Suites — $94+ — 3 mi/5 km from airport

This five-story, 148-room motel offers clean rooms, free continental breakfasts, and free high-speed Internet access in all rooms. Room amenities include two double beds (or one king bed), 25 in. cable TV, dataport phone, coffeemaker, hair dryer, iron and ironing board, voice mail, free local calls, and newspaper delivery—there are no balconies or in-room safes. There are also five suites with a separate living room, sofa bed, microwave, and refrigerator. Motel amenities include an outdoor heated swimming pool, hot tub, sundeck, and fitness center. No on-site restaurant, but a TGI Friday's is adjacent and Tony Roma's, Denny's, Bennigan's, and Chili's are within walking distance. This motel was built in 1998. A free airport shuttle is available from 5:00 am–11:00 pm daily. Check-in time: 3:00 pm; check-out time: 12:00 pm. Visit http://www.laquinta.com or call 407-240-5000. Address: 7160 N. Frontage Rd., Orlando, FL 32812

AmeriSuites Airport NW — $83+ — 3 mi/5 km from airport

Enjoy a 480 sq. ft. suite in this seven-story hotel. Each suite has a living room with a cable TV, two-line phone with dataport, desk, and sofa bed, kitchenette with wet bar, coffemaker, refrigerator, and microwave, and a bedroom with two double beds (or one king bed), hair dryer, iron and ironing board, and voice mail. Note that the living and sleeping areas are separated by half walls. Hotel amenities include an outdoor heated splash pool and fitness center. Complimentary continental breakfast each morning. TGI Friday's, Tony Roma's, Denny's, Bennigan's, and Chili's are within walking distance. A free shuttle is available within a 5-mile radius of the hotel. Check-in time: 3:00 pm; check-out time: 11:00 am. Visit http://www.amerisuites.com or call 407-816-7800. Address: 5435 Forbes Place, Orlando, FL 32812

Priceline.com

We've had great success with Priceline.com (http://www.priceline.com), where you can bid on hotel rates in particular areas. In May 2003, we got the Marriott Orlando Airport (see previous page) through Priceline.com for about $35. If you do decide to try Priceline.com, read the directions thoroughly, and keep in mind that once your bid is accepted, you can't cancel. We recommend you visit BiddingForTravel.com (http://www.biddingfortravel.com) for Priceline.com advice and tips. Note that as of March 2005, each of the hotels we describe in the Lodging Near Orlando Intl. Airport section is a potential hotel available via Priceline.com. Not sure about Priceline.com? Another place to try for hotel deals is Hotwire.com at http://www.hotwire.com.

Want to stay near or at Walt Disney World before or after your cruise? For Disney resorts and hotels nearby, we recommend you pick up a copy of PassPorter Walt Disney World Resort (see page 301)—it goes into great detail on Walt Disney World lodging.

Getting to Port Canaveral

Port Canaveral, Florida is Disney's home port. Situated in the city of Cape Canaveral, it's easily accessible from anywhere in Central Florida.

From the Orlando International Airport
Port Canaveral is about one hour (45 mi./72 km.) east of the airport. You have five options: transfer, shuttle, town car/limo, taxi, or rental car.

Disney Cruise Line Ground Transfer—If you're sailing the day you arrive at the airport and you've booked ground transfers, a Disney Cruise Line representative meets you at the airport and directs you to a motorcoach. Check your cruise documents for transfer details. If you're not on a package, you can purchase these transfers for $59/person—inquire at 800-395-9374, extension 1. For more details on motorcoaches, see page 62.

Shuttle—You can take a shuttle, which you share with other passengers bound for Port Canaveral, in two ways. You can use the Transfer Coupon (in your cruise documents) at the designated counter on the first floor of the airport, and the charges will appear on your shipboard account. Or, if you prefer, you can arrange your own transportation through Mears (800-759-5219). Cost is about $30 per person, round-trip.

Town Car/Limo—A luxurious alternative is a town car or limo, through a company like Quicksilver (888-468-6939) or Tiffany Town Car (888-838-2161). The driver meets you in baggage claim, helps you with your luggage, and drives you to the port. Cost is around $210 for a round-trip town car to and from the port.

Taxi—At approximately $90 one-way for up to nine people, it's not the best value. You can get taxis at the airport on level 1.

Rental Car—This option works well if you'll be spending time elsewhere before you cruise and need the wheels, it can also be less expensive than the other options, but you must spend time for pickup/dropoff. All the major car rental companies are located at the airport, but we prefer Budget (800-527-7000), Hertz (800-654-3131), or Avis (800-831-2847) because they are convenient, affordable, and offer a complimentary shuttle to the cruise terminal. Note that while National/Alamo has an office in Port Canaveral, it does not offer a complimentary shuttle. All four rental car companies have offices near the cruise terminal for drop-off/pick-up.

Driving directions from the Orlando airport: Follow airport signs to the "North Exit" and take the Bee Line Expressway (528) east 43 mi. (69 km.) to Cape Canaveral. You'll need $1.25 in small bills/coins for tolls.

Introduction Reservations Staterooms Dining Activities Ports of Call Magic Index

Getting to Port Canaveral

(continued)

From Orlando and Walt Disney World—You have four options: shuttle, town car/limo, rental car, and your own car. Mears offers shuttles and Quicksilver and Tiffany offer town cars/limos/vans to Port Canaveral (see previous page). If you're driving, take I-4 to exit 72 and then take the Bee Line Expressway (528) east 53 miles (85 km.) to Cape Canaveral. Allow at least one hour and $2.75 for tolls. See directions below to the terminal.

From I-75—Take I-75 south to Florida's Turnpike. Take the turnpike south to exit 254 and take the Bee Line Expressway (528) east 50 miles (80 km.) to Cape Canaveral. Expect $6.00 in tolls. See directions below to terminal.

From I-95—Take I-95 to exit 205 East and take the Bee Line Expressway (528) east 12 miles (19 km.) to Cape Canaveral.

From Cape Canaveral to the Disney Cruise Line Terminal—As you drive east on the Bee Line Expressway (528), you'll cross two bridges (see if you can spot your ship when you're atop these bridges). After the second bridge, take the Route 401 exit to the "A" cruise terminals and follow the signs to the Disney Cruise Line Terminal (detailed on page 67).

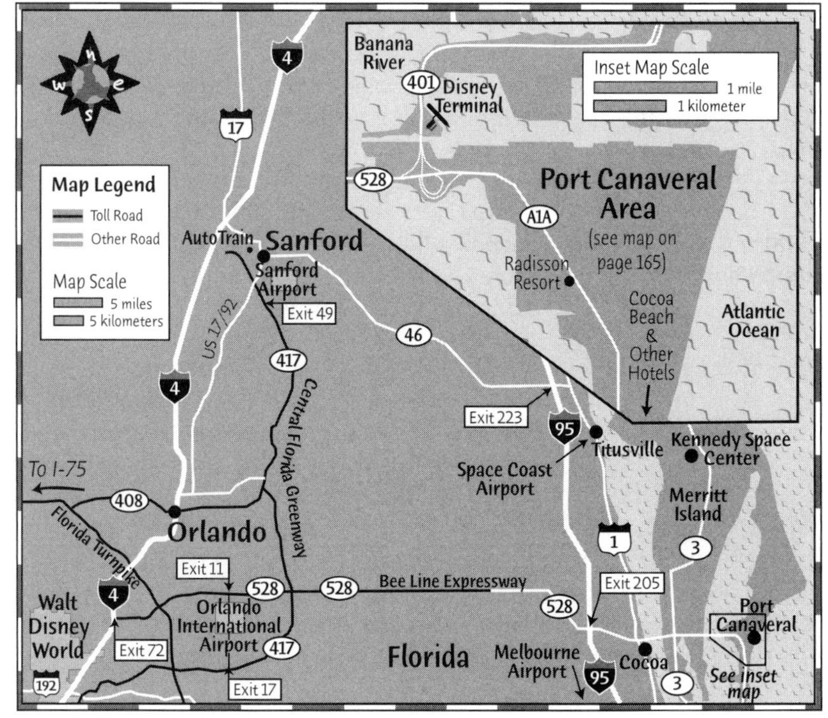

Disney Cruise Line Motorcoach (Ground Transfers)

Passengers on a Disney land/sea vacation package and those who've booked ground transfers separately (see page 47) may get to ride in a comfy Disney Cruise Line motorcoach. These handicap-accessible **deluxe buses** are painted to look like classic motorcoaches. On board, the cushy seats recline and there's even a restroom in the back. On the way to Port Canaveral, you're treated to a delightful video that heightens your anticipation. On the way back, you may watch a Disney movie on the overhead monitors.

© Disney

Disney Cruise Line Motorcoach

There are some **downsides** to the ground transfers. There's no guarantee you'll get a Disney Cruise Line motorcoach just because you purchased the transfers. When we used the transfers, we rode in the motorcoach on the way to Port Canaveral, but on the way back to the Walt Disney World Resort, we were squeezed into a drab shuttle van instead. This is more likely to happen if you're going to the Walt Disney World Resort after your cruise. Another downside is that you usually need to wait to board the bus. This could mean you miss the opportunity to get reservations for Palo and the spa or feel rushed when you arrive at the airport. And check-in goes slower, since you're in the midst of a large group of people who've arrived with you. You'll need to decide which is more important: convenience (take the bus) or speed (use another method). If you opt for the transfer, sit as near to the front as you can to be among the first off.

Boarding at the airport: Passengers with ground transfers who arrive between 9:00 am and 1:30 pm will be met in the terminal by a Disney representative and told where to board the motorcoach. Your luggage (if properly tagged) is intercepted and transported to the ship.

Boarding at Walt Disney World Resort: If you're staying at one of the Disney hotels affiliated with the Disney Cruise Line (Grand Floridian, Beach Club, Polynesian, Disney's Animal Kingdom Lodge, Swan, Dolphin, Port Orleans, and Caribbean Beach), you'll be instructed to set your luggage by the door for pick-up on the morning of your cruise. Around 10:00 am to 11:00 am, you meet in a central location in the resort and then proceed to the motorcoach, which generally leaves between 11:00 am and 11:45 am. You may have the option to depart from Disney's Animal Kingdom theme park the morning of your cruise, giving you an extra half-day in the park—inquire at the cruise desk at your resort (generally open from 8:00 am to noon daily).

Ground Transportation Worksheet

Use this worksheet to research, record, and plan your transportation to and from Port Canaveral.

Method	Price	Details	Reservation #
Disney Cruise Line Transfers: *800-395-9374*			
Shuttle: *Mears: 800-759-5219*			
Town Car/Limo/Van: *Quicksilver Tours 888-468-6939* *Tiffany Town Car: 888-838-2161*			
Rental Car: *Avis: 800-230-4898* *Budget: 800-404-8033* *Hertz: 800-654-3131*	*(don't forget tolls)*		

Scheduling Pick-Up and Departure Times

Allow 90 minutes to get to Port Canaveral from either Orlando Airport or Walt Disney World. Thus, if you hope to board the ship as soon as possible, a pick-up/departure time of 9:30 am or 10:00 am is good. If necessary, you could depart as late as 1:00 pm or 1:30 pm to reach Port Canaveral by 3:00 pm at the latest. For your return trip, the earliest you can expect to disembark the ship is 7:45 am to 8:30 am (and yes, you can still do the sit-down breakfast). It takes about 15 to 20 minutes to collect your bags and go through customs. Thus your pick-up/departure time could be set between 8:00 am and 9:15 am. We do not recommend you book a flight with a departure time before 11:30 am. A 1:00 pm or later flight would give you more breathing room.

Lodging Near Port Canaveral

You may want to take advantage of the visit to the "Space Coast" to squeeze in a trip to Kennedy Space Center or a day at the beach. Or perhaps you want to arrive in advance to avoid stress on the morning of your cruise. While there are many motels and hotels in the area, we've stayed at four (Radisson, Quality Suites, Ron Jon, and Motel 6), all of which we recommend. We also detail two other hotels. To see the location of each, check the map on page 165.

Radisson Resort at the Port $139+ 2.7 mi/4.3 km to port

This 284-room luxury resort is the closest lodging to the Disney Cruise Line terminal (until the Marriott Residence Inn opens next door) and is quite popular with cruisers. While it is not an oceanfront hotel, it does feature a themed pool (see photo below), wading pool, hot tub, tennis, fitness center, room service, and 1- and 2-bedroom suites in addition to its standard, Caribbean-themed rooms (see photo at left). All rooms have ceiling fans, TVs, coffeemakers, hair dryers, voice mail, and dataports. Suites add another TV and phone line, whirlpool tub, microwave, refrigerator, and walk-in showers. An on-site restaurant, Flamingos, is open from 6:30 am to 10:00 pm daily and serves American food, with Caribbean/Floridian cuisine on Saturday nights and a champagne brunch on Sundays. Check-in time: 3:00 pm; check-out time: 12:00 pm.

© MediaMarx, Inc.

Our standard, king bed room at the Radisson

One notable feature is the complimentary shuttle between the hotel and the port (you can make your shuttle reservation up to two weeks in advance—don't wait until you check-in to reserve it or you may get a late pick-up or none at all). Avis has moved; the closest car rental office is now Budget. Special cruise prices allow you to park in their lot while you cruise. Great promotional rates are often available on the Internet for less than $100, but pay attention to the cancellation details as you may have to pay a $25 fee to cancel. Visit http://www.radisson.com/capecanaveralfl or call 321-784-0000.

Address: 8701 Astronaut Boulevard, Cape Canaveral, FL 32920

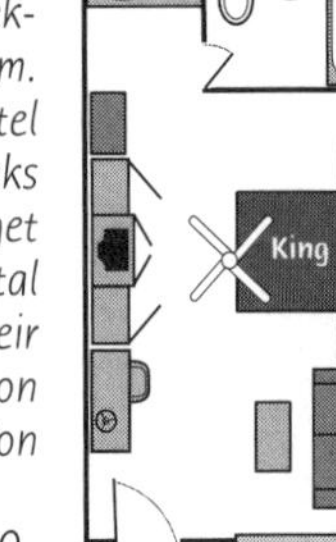

Typical floor plan

© MediaMarx, Inc.

The beautiful, themed pool, complete with a waterfall and perching lioness and eagle

Quality Suites $89+ 6.1 mi/9.8 km to port

Quality Suites

© MediaMarx, Inc.

This small, all-suite hotel offers 48 spacious rooms and reasonable rates. The two-room suites offer a living room with a queen sofa bed, TV, phone, kitchenette with sink, microwave, refrigerator, and coffeepot, and in the bedroom a king bed (no double beds available), another TV, phone, and a desk. All rooms have hair dryers, irons, and dataports. A free continental breakfast is offered on the second floor. There's no on-site restaurant, but a Taco Bell and Waffle House are next door. This hotel has no swimming pool; it does have a large whirlpool, and the ocean is 300 feet away. Ron Jon Surf Shop is one block away. Free shuttle to the port—make a reservation at the desk the day before. Cruise parking packages are available, but you'll need to drive to and park at the Radisson. Check-in time: 3:00 pm; check-out time: 12:00 pm. For details, visit http://www.qualitysuitescocoabeach-portcanaveral.com or call 321-783-6868. 3655 N. Atlantic, Cocoa Beach, FL 32931

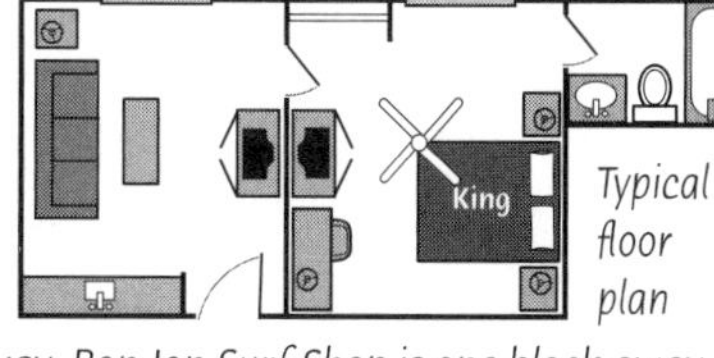

Typical floor plan

Suite living room

© MediaMarx, Inc.

Motel 6 Cocoa Beach $63+ 6.1 mi/9.8 km to port

The Motel 6 in Cocoa Beach has the lowest published rates in the area. The clean motel features an outdoor swimming pool, cable TV, and a laundry room. While there is no restaurant on-site, a Waffle House is within walking distance. This motel is also close to tourist attractions such as Ron Jon Surf Shop, and it's only one block from the beach. No shuttle is available to the port; expect to pay about $11 to $15 for a taxi. Check-in time: 2:00 pm; check-out time: 12:00 pm. Visit http://www.motel6.com or call 321-783-3103. Address: 3701 N. Atlantic Avenue, Cocoa Beach, FL 32931

© MediaMarx, Inc.

Motel 6 room

Resort on Cocoa Beach $130+ 7.2 mi/11.6 km to port

Resort on Cocoa Beach

© MediaMarx, Inc.

A gorgeous, 8-story beach resort within reasonable distance of the port. The 147-suite resort features two-bedroom "condominums" which sleep six with one king bed, two queen beds, and a sleeper sofa. Features include balconies, two bathrooms, full kitchens, two phone lines, two TVs, VCR, whirlpool tub, and washer/dryer. Resort amenities include beach access, outdoor pool with kid's water play area, sauna, hot tub, fitness center, playground, tennis and basketball courts, a 50-seat movie theater, and a drop-in childcare center. This is a true resort! An on-site restaurant, Mug's, is an ocean grill and sushi bar (open 11:00 am to 10:00 pm daily). No shuttle is available to the port; expect to pay about $11 to $15 for a taxi. Check-in time: 4:00 pm; check-out time: 10:00 am. Visit http://www.vrivacations.com/resorts/rcb/index.html or call 866-469-8222. Address: 1600 N. Atlantic Avenue, Cocoa Beach, FL 32931

Lodging Near Port Canaveral *(continued)*

Holiday Inn Express $152+ 4.7 mi/7.5 km to port

© MediaMarx, Inc.
Holiday Inn Express

This hotel opened in late 2000, offering 60 guest rooms in a variety of family-friendly configurations. Beyond the standard queen bed and king bed rooms, Holiday Inn Express offers KidSuites with a separate room for the kids, Family Suites (for older kids or two couples traveling together), Romantic Suites with whirlpool tubs, and Executive Suites with workspace. All rooms have a microwave, refrigerator, coffeemaker, free high-speed Internet access, hair dryer, iron and ironing board, and free newspaper delivery. A free continental breakfast is provided each morning. Amentities include an outdoor pool, whirlpool, and a fitness center ($3 fee), plus it is just two blocks from the beach. There is no on-site restaurant, but Durango Steakhouse and Perkins are nearby. You can take Art's Shuttle (http://www.artsshuttle.com, 800-567-5099) for $3/person to the cruise terminal. Check-in time: 3:00 pm; check-out: 11:00 am. For details ,visit http://www.hiexpress.com/es-cocoabeach or call 321-868-2525 (local) or 800-465-4329 (toll-free). Address: 5575 N. Atlantic, Cocoa Beach, FL 32931

Ron Jon Cape Caribe Resort $110+ 3.2 mi/5.2 km to port

January 2004 saw the opening of this timeshare resort, which is the closest oceanfront resort to Orlando (as well as to the port). You don't need to own a timeshare to stay here, however—anyone can rent one of the villas. We loved our one-bedroom villa here in December 2004—we found it bright, cheery, very spacious, clean, and full of amenities. Accommodations come in the form of studios (up to 4 people), one-bedroom (6 people), two-bedroom (8–10 people), and three-bedroom villas (12 people). All villas have a sitting or living room, refrigerator, microwave, and coffeemaker. The one-, two-, and three-bedroom villas add a patio/balcony and full kitchen. Two- and three-bedroom villas also have a whirlpool tub (our one-bedroom villa had only a shower, no tub at all).

© MediaMarx, Inc.
Ron Jon bedroom

Resort amenities include a "water park" with large heated pool, 248-ft. water slide, lazy river, and beach, plus an on-site restaurant, fitness center, children's play center, movie theater, miniature golf, and organized activities. This resort is 600 yards (about 3 blocks) from the beach, but it does provide a shuttle to the beach. Guests receive a discount at Ron Jon Surf Shop in Cocoa Beach. You can arrange for a shuttle to the cruise terminal through the concierge for an additional fee, or expect to pay about $9 to $12 for a taxi. Check-in time: 4:00 pm; check-out time: 10:00 am. Visit http://www.ronjonresort.com or call 888-933-3030 or 321-799-4900. Address: 1000 Shorewood Drive, Cape Canaveral, FL 32920

© MediaMarx, Inc.
Ron Jon living room and kitchen

Tip: For more information and good rates on area lodging, visit http://www.travelocity.com. Excellent details on lodging can be found at http://www.dcltribute.com/lodging.

The Disney Cruise Line Terminal

Not content to use an existing, plain-Jane terminal for its cruise line, Disney had a **beautiful terminal** built in Port Canaveral to its exact specifications for $27 million. The Disney Cruise Line Terminal (terminal #8) is easily recognized by its 90-foot glass tower and art deco design. The terminal opens between 10:00 am and 10:30 am on cruise days for embarking passengers.

The cruise terminal

If you're driving to the terminal, a gated, fenced lot with 965 parking spaces is available across from the terminal for $10 per 24-hour period (vehicles over 20 ft. long pay $20/day). You'll need to **pay for parking up front** with cash, U.S. traveler's checks, Visa, or MasterCard. The Canaveral Port Authority operates the parking and we know of no discounts. If you do not drop your luggage off curbside (see below), you can take it to one of the white tents in the parking lot. You may find it less expensive to rent a car, drive, return the car to a rental office in Port Canaveral, and catch a shuttle to the terminal than to park at the terminal. Warning: Ants are plentiful around here and may be attracted to food or crumbs in your car.

Security at the terminal is excellent. Have photo IDs for everyone in the car handy when you drive up. Guests and their luggage may be dropped off at the terminal curbside or the parking lot. A porter **collects all luggage** (tip $1 to $2/bag) except your carry-ons before you enter the terminal—luggage is scanned and delivered to your stateroom later, so be sure to attach those luggage tags. Security scans your carry-ons before you enter the terminal. Inside the terminal doors are escalators and an elevator that take you upstairs for check-in and embarkation. In the terminal, look down at the gorgeous, 13,000 sq. ft. terrazzo tile Bahamas map.

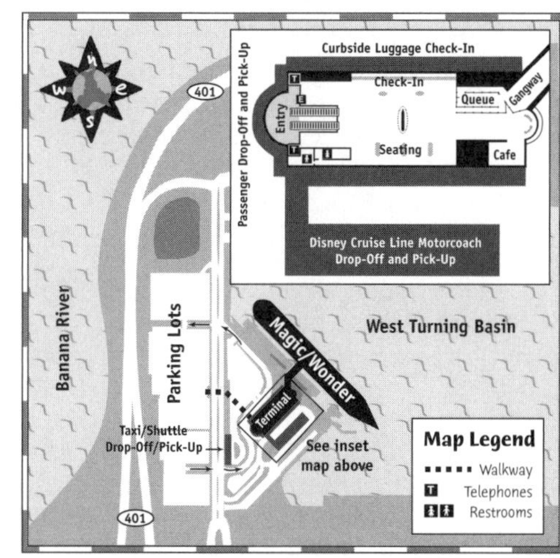

Plan to arrive before 1:00 pm. Ships are scheduled to leave at 5:00 pm, but they have left as early as 4:00 pm when weather dictated.

Address: 9150 Christopher Columbus Drive, Port Canaveral, FL 32920

Telephone: 321-868-1400

Check-In and Embarkation

If you're on a Disney land/sea vacation package, your check-in was completed when you checked in to your Walt Disney World resort hotel. Have your **Key to the World card and photo identification** out and proceed down the gangway (discussed on the next page).

If you've booked a cruise-only or made your hotel arrangements on your own, don't worry—the check-in/embarkation procedure is remarkably smooth, especially if you **fill out the cruise forms before arrival**. Check your Travel Booklet (which comes in your cruise document package—more on this on page 48) for the various forms to be completed in advance.

When you arrive, a cast member may first check to ensure your cruise documents are together. You then proceed to the **check-in counters** (28 in total) which are lined up along the left-hand side. Check-in generally begins around 10:45 am or 11:00 am. If you are a member of the Castaway Club (see page 273) or staying in a suite, you may be directed to special counters.

Have your cruise travel booklets, photo IDs, birth certificates, naturalization certificates, and/or passports handy. If you've misplaced your immigration forms, you can get extra copies in the terminal. Be sure to bring **original or official documents**; no copies will be accepted.

Check-in takes about 10 minutes (you may spend more time in line). Once your forms are filed, you'll each get a **Key to the World card**, which is your ID/charging card and room key for the duration of the cruise (see below). Keep this card with you at all times.

© Disney

A Key to the World card

Your Key to the World Card and Money

It's your stateroom key, ship boarding pass, and shipboard charge card—no wonder Disney calls it your Key to the World. Everyone will have his or her own card—be sure to sign them as soon as you get them, and keep them safe. Disney ships are a cash-free society—everything you buy onboard and at Castaway Cay (except stamps) must be charged to that card. Stash your wallet in your room safe, grab your Key to the World Card, and travel ultra-light. At check-in you'll need to make a deposit of at least $500 towards your on-board spending using credit card (any of those listed on page 48 work), traveler's checks, cash, and/or Disney Dollars. You can even put a different credit card on each person's room key (great for friends traveling together). Disney charges your credit card whenever your shipboard account reaches its limit. If you deposited cash or cash-equivalent, you'll be called down to the Guest Services desk (Purser) to replenish the account. Cruising with kids? You can give them full charging privileges, deny them any charge privileges, or place a limited amount of cash on their account. Whatever you decide, you can make changes later at the Guest Services desk on deck 3 midship.

Non-U.S. citizens (including alien residents of the U.S.) have special check-in counters—look for the signs as you approach the counters. You will need to present your passport with any necessary visas at check-in to ensure that you can reenter the U.S. upon the ship's return. (Canadian citizens must also present a passport, according to Canada's Passport Office at http://www.ppt.gc.ca.) If you live in a country that participates in the U.S. Visa Waiver Program (see http://travel.state.gov) and plan to be in the U.S. for 90 days or less, you don't need a visa, but you do need to present proof of return transport, proof of financial solvency, and a signed visa waiver arrival/departure form (I-94W form) that you get from your airline. For more information on visas, check with the U.S. consulate or embassy in your country (see http://usembassy.state.gov). Note that non-U.S. citizens must surrender their passports at check-in; they will be returned upon disembarkation—see page 272. For this reason, you should bring extra forms of photo identification, which you will use when you leave and reenter the ship in your ports of call.

Embarkation usually begins between noon and 1:00 pm. Typically a line forms in front of the 16 ft. (5 m.) high Mickey-shaped embarkation portal (see photo). Only one member of your party needs to stand in line to hold your place. While you're waiting to embark, you can relax on cushy sofas, watch Disney cartoons, and read the papers Disney gave you (usually a *Personal Navigator* or summary sheet). Around 11:00 am, Captain Mickey, Donald, or other characters may appear for photos and autographs. You may also be able to sign up your kids for Oceaneer Club/Lab—look for a sign-up desk near the far end of the terminal. Be sure to visit the museum-quality, 20-foot-long model of the Disney Magic in the middle of the terminal. You'll also find a small store (where the former R.E. Fresh's cafe was located) with convenience items and stateroom gifts. Look for more than 50 images of Mickey (both obvious and hidden) in and around the terminal! See the terminal map on page 67 to get your bearings before you arrive.

Inside the Disney Cruise Line Terminal

When it's **your turn to board**, you'll present your Key to the World card, which is swiped through a card reader and handed back to you. Just before you reach the ship, photographers will arrange your party for the first of many ships' photo opportunities. Flash! That's it! You've made it! Proceed on up the gangway to the magic and wonder that await you.

Packing for Your Cruise

Some folks hear "cruise" and start packing enough clothes for an around-the-world tour. If you tend to overpack, a cruise is the best place to do it. Guests on land/sea vacations or ground transfers may only need to handle their luggage at the very start and end of their trip. But if you're combining your cruise with a stay in Florida without Disney's help, you'll appreciate having **less luggage**. The Disney Cruise Line limits each guest to two suitcases and one carry-on. Need help packing light? Visit http://www.travelite.org.

When you arrive at the terminal, luggage is collected and you won't see it again until later that day, when it's delivered to your stateroom (usually between 2:00 pm and 6:00 pm). Pack a **separate carry-on** (no larger than 22" x 14"/56 x 36 cm) with your ID, cruise documents, prescriptions, and a swimsuit. Keep this bag light as you may be carrying it around for a few hours. You'll also need this carry-on for your last night, when you place the rest of your luggage outside your stateroom by 11:00 pm for collection.

A word about your **personal documentation**: The Disney Cruise Line requires that all U.S. citizens have one of the following proofs of citizenship: valid U.S. passport, certified birth certificate (with a raised seal or multiple colors), or a certified naturalization certificate with photo ID. Don't have your birth certificate? Try http://www.usbirthcertificate.net. Guests 17 and older should have photo identification, such as a driver's license or government photo ID. We also recommend you bring a backup photo ID for emergencies. Note: Starting 12/31/2006, all U.S. citizens must have a passport to travel to/from the Caribbean (see pages 50–51).

When your cruise documentation arrives, you'll find two **luggage tags** for each individual, with your ship, name, stateroom, and departure date. Read your cruise documentation to find out if you should tag your luggage before or after you arrive at the terminal. In general, if you're not on a land/sea package or haven't booked Disney's ground transfer, don't tag your luggage until you arrive at the terminal. You wouldn't want your bags collected prematurely. Don't forget to ID every piece of luggage with your own tags, too (use http://www.passporter.com/wdw/luggagelog.htm).

Deciding what **clothing** to pack depends a bit on what time of year you're cruising and your itinerary. Cruises in the cooler months require a few more jackets and sweaters, while you'll want to be ready with raingear in the summer. Pack dress clothing for dinner (see page 101) regardless of your itinerary. Guests on the 7-night itineraries will want to add more dress clothing for the formal and semi-formal evenings (see page 262). Everyone may want to consider pirate or tropical garb for the Pirates of the Caribbean evening. Guests on shorter cruises can get by with just one nice outfit.

➢

Packing Tips

Our **packing list** on the next two pages is complete, but for an exhaustive list, visit: http://www.geocities.com/Calgon1/Ultimate_Packing_List.html.

The air-conditioned public rooms on the ships can be **chilly**, as are the winds up on deck. Bring sweaters or jackets.

Pack comfortable **shoes** with non-slip rubber soles for walking around on deck and on shore. You'll also appreciate sandals and water shoes.

While room service is free, delivery is not immediate. If you need snacks on hand, bring packaged **snacks** like crackers or granola bars. You could also bring your own bottled water (it's pricey onboard), but the drinking water tastes fine to most. Note that Disney prohibits personal coolers onboard unless they are for medications, baby foods, or dietary needs. Ice buckets are provided in the staterooms, as are small refrigerators.

The health-conscious may want to consider a well-stocked **medicine kit**, as trips to the onboard infirmary cost you. Beyond the usual items, consider anti-nausea aids (see page 267), antidiarrheal aids, sunblock, sunburn gel, and "Safe Sea," a sunblock that helps protect against the stinging of most jellyfish, sea lice, coral, and sea anemone (see http://www.nidaria.com).

Two-way radios can be handy for keeping in touch onboard—use the ones with extra subchannels. The radios won't work everywhere due to all the metal in the ship—they only seem to work up to a few decks away.

You can bring your own **stroller** or just borrow one free of charge at Guest Services onboard and/or at Castaway Cay (first come, first served). Wheelchairs can also be borrowed free of charge.

Unlike many other cruises, you can bring your own **alcohol** onboard to save money on drinks. Beer and wine are the best items to bring; you can usually buy hard liquor for great prices on the islands. Note that you won't be able to bring opened bottles home with you at the end of the cruise.

Worried about **lost or delayed luggage**? Don't pack all your items in one bag. Instead, split items between bags. Couples can pack half their things in their suitcases and half in their partner's suitcases to be safe.

Knives, pocket tools, and other **potential weapons** are prohibited onboard. All luggage is inspected prior to boarding, and confiscated items will be held until you return to port. This can seriously delay the arrival of your luggage to your room.

Packing List

Packing for a cruise is fun when you feel confident you're packing the right things. Over the years, we've compiled a packing list for a great Disney cruise vacation. Just note the quantity you plan to bring and check them off as you pack. Consider packing items in **bold** in your carry-on.

The Essentials

- ☐ Casual, nice clothing for daytime and late-night wear
  ___ *Shorts* ___ *Long pants* ___ *Shirts* ___ *Skirts/dresses*
  ___ *Underwear (lots!)* ___ *Socks* ___ *Pajamas* ___ *Robes*
- ☐ Jacket and/or sweater (light ones for the warmer months)
  ___ ***Jackets*** ___ *Sweatshirts* ___ *Sweaters* ___ *Vests*
- ☐ Formal and semi-formal clothing for special evenings
  ___ *Suits and ties* ___ *Dresses* ___ *Jewelry* ___ *Tropical dress*
- ☐ Comfortable, well-broken-in shoes, sandals, and dress shoes
  ___ *Walking shoes* ___ *Sandals* ___ *Dress shoes* ___ ________
- ☐ Swim wear and gear (regular towels are provided)
  ___ ***Suits/trunks*** ___ ***Cover-ups*** ___ *Water shoes* ___ *Goggles*
- ☐ Sun protection (the Caribbean sun can be brutal)
  ___ ***Sunblock*** ___ ***Lip balm*** ___ ***Sunburn relief*** ___ ***Sunglasses***
  ___ ***Hats w/brims*** ___ ***Caps*** ___ ***Visors*** ___ ________
- ☐ Rain gear (for your port excursions)
  ___ *Raincoat* ___ *Poncho* ___ *Umbrella* ___ ________
- ☐ Comfortable bags with padded straps to carry items in port
  ___ *Backpacks* ___ *Waist packs* ___ *Shoulder bags* ___ ***Camera bag***
- ☐ Toiletries (in a bag or bathroom kit to keep them organized)
  ___ ***Brush/comb*** ___ ***Toothbrush*** ___ ***Toothpaste*** ___ *Dental floss*
  ___ *Favorite soap, shampoo, & conditioner* ___ *Deodorant* ___ *Baby wipes*
  ___ ***Anti-nausea aids** and **pain relievers*** ___ ***Band aids*** ___ ***First aid kit***
  ___ ***Prescriptions** (in original containers)* ___ *Vitamins* ___ ***Fem. hygiene***
  ___ ***Makeup*** ___ *Hairspray* ___ *Cotton swabs* ___ *Curling iron*
  ___ *Razors* ___ *Shaving cream* ___ *Nail clippers* ___ ***Spare glasses***
  ___ *Lens solution* ___ *Safety pins* ___ *Bug repellent* ___ *Insect sting kit*
  ___ *Mending kit* ___ *Small scissors* ___ ***Ear plugs*** ___ ________
- ☐ Camera/camcorder and more film than you think you need
  ___ ***Cameras*** ___ ***Camcorder*** ___ ***Film/batteries*** ___ ***Memory cards***
- ☐ Money in various forms and various places
  ___ ***Charge cards*** ___ ***Traveler's checks*** ___ ***Bank cards*** ___ ***Cash***
- ☐ Personal identification, passes, and membership cards
  ___ ***Documents*** ___ ***Birth certificate*** ___ ***Driver's license*** ___ ***Passports***
  ___ ***AAA card*** ___ ***Travel perks cards*** ___ ***Discount cards*** ___ *Air miles card*
  ___ ***Other IDs*** ___ ***Insurance cards*** ___ ***Calling cards*** ___ *SCUBA cert.*

Tip: Label everything with your name, phone, and stateroom to help reunite you with your stuff if lost. Every bag should have this info on a tag as well as on a slip of paper inside it. Use our Luggage Tag Maker at http://www.passporter.com/wdw/luggagelog.htm.

→

For Your Carry-On

- ❑ **PassPorter**, **cruise documentation**, **ground/air confirmations**, **multiple photo IDs (driver's license, passport)**, **birth certificates**, and a **pen/pencil**! Remember not to pack any sharp or potentially dangerous items in your carry-on.
- ❑ **Camera** and/or **camcorder**, along with **film/memory/tapes** and **batteries**
- ❑ Any **prescription medicines**, **important toiletries**, **sunblock**, **sunglasses**, **hats**
- ❑ **Change of clothes**, including **swimwear** and **dress clothes** for dinner
- ❑ **Snacks**, **water bottle**, **juice boxes**, **gum**, **books**, **toys**, **games**
- ❑ **PassHolder Pouch** for passports, IDs, cash, etc. (see page 299)

For Families

- ❑ **Snacks** and **juice boxes**
- ❑ **Books**, **toys**, and **games**
- ❑ Familiar items from home
- ❑ Stroller and accessories
- ❑ **Autograph books** and **fat pens**

For Couples

- ❑ **Champagne** for your send-off
- ❑ Wine and favorite adult beverages
- ❑ Portable CD player, speakers, and CDs
- ❑ Good beach novels
- ❑ Massage oil

For Connected Travelers

- ❑ **Handheld/Palm organizer**
- ❑ Laptop, cables, extension cord
- ❑ Chargers
- ❑ GPS system or compass
- ❑ Security cable with lock
- ❑ **Cell phones** and/or **two-way radios**

For Heat-Sensitive Travelers

- ❑ **Personal fan/water misters**
- ❑ **Water bottles**
- ❑ Loose, breezy clothing
- ❑ **Hats** with wide brims
- ❑ **Elastics** to keep long hair off neck
- ❑ **Sweatbands**

Everyone Should Consider

- ❑ **Penlight** or flashlight (for reading/writing in dark places)
- ❑ Battery-operated alarm with illuminated face and nightlight (or just open the closet)
- ❑ Earplugs, sound machine, or white-noise generator (for noisy staterooms)
- ❑ **Water bottles** and personal **fans/water misters**
- ❑ Plastic storage bags that seal (large and small) and plastic cutlery for snacks
- ❑ Address book, envelopes, and stamps (with numeric denominations)
- ❑ Laundry detergent/tablets, bleach, dryer sheets, stain stick, and wrinkle remover
- ❑ **Binoculars** and a **soft-sided, insulated tote** for going ashore
- ❑ Currency exchange calculator or card (if you'll be doing a lot of shopping)
- ❑ Collapsible bag or suitcase inside another suitcase to hold souvenirs on your return
- ❑ **Small bills and coins** for tipping and quarters for laundry
- ❑ Photo mailers or large envelope with cardboard inserts (for safeguarding photos)
- ❑ **Highlighters** (multiple colors for each person to mark activities in your *Personal Navigator*)
- ❑ Closet organizer (the kind used to hold shoes) to store small items and avoid clutter
- ❑ **Sticky notes** (to leave your fellow cabinmates messages)
- ❑ Plenty of **batteries** (and don't forget the charger if you're using rechargeables)
- ❑ An electrical power strip if you'll need extra outlets for lots of chargers
- ❑ Something to carry your small items, such as a **PassHolder Pouch** or evening bag

Your Personal Packing List

- ❑ ______________________
- ❑ ______________________
- ❑ ______________________
- ❑ ______________________
- ❑ ______________________
- ❑ ______________________

Adventuring!

Here are our tried-and-true cruise traveling tips:

- In light of our security-conscious culture, we recommend you bring **more than one photo ID** in the event you lose one. Membership cards (such as Sam's Club) with your photo work fine as a backup. Leave your backup ID in your in-room safe.

- Any travel delay can sink your plans, so don't let the ship sail without you. Plan to **fly (or drive) in the day/night before** you sail to have a stress-free, early start on your vacation. There are many hotels near Orlando International Airport, and good deals can be had by shopping http://www.priceline.com or the hotel web sites in the weeks before you cruise. In the morning, you can take the hotel's shuttle back to the airport and catch Disney's ground transfer to the terminal. Or give yourself a full day in Port Canaveral—many hotels offer free shuttles to the cruise terminal.

- "Use **Space Bags** when you pack for your cruise to save room in your suitcase. If you get the kind that are 'dual valve,' meaning you can use a vacuum at home to remove the air and then just 'roll' out the air when you bring your dirty clothes home at the end of the cruise, it will give you more room for souvenirs. They were also good for packing things that may leak or are still damp, like swimsuits and water shoes from Castaway Cay on the last full day of the cruise.' *– contributed by Disney vacationer Gina Walck*

- "If you're driving, look for the **Ron Jon Surf Shop billboards** along the Florida highways—they count down the mileage remaining to their store, which isn't far from the terminal." *– contributed by Dave Huiner*

Magical Memory

"I am an it's-never-too-early-to-start-planning type of person, especially when it comes to Disney trips. In January of 2005, I booked a Disney cruise for January 2006 for my family and my parents and paid our deposit. One month later, I discovered that I was pregnant and I immediately turned to the PassPorter boards to ask how old an infant had to be before sailing. Upon verifying that it was 12 weeks, I did some quick calculations and learned that our baby would just squeak by if he/she came on the due date. One of my first statements to my doctor was 'this baby cannot be late!' At 15 weeks of age, Madeline Elizabeth sailed away on the Disney Wonder and slept like a dream every night."

...as told by Disney cruiser Jill Koenigs

UNLOCK
the door to
room basics,
information,
and tips

Staying in Style in a Stateroom

VIEW each stateroom's layout

EXPLORE your stateroom in detail with info and maps

Style is, indeed, the operative word for Disney Cruise Line staterooms. Every stateroom, regardless of its price, category, or location onboard, is resplendent in warm, natural woods, luxurious fabrics, imported tile, nautical touches, and dramatic lighting. Robert Tillberg, esteemed naval architect, worked with Disney to design the stateroom interiors with more storage space and the innovative split bathrooms available in categories 10 and up. Unlike many other ships, 73% of the staterooms have an ocean view, while 44% of all rooms have private verandahs. Better yet, staterooms on Disney ships have the "luxury of space"—they are substantially larger (up to 25%) than those on many other ships. Many cruise industry insiders consider Disney Cruise Line staterooms to be among the best afloat. You'll actually enjoy being in your stateroom!

Every stateroom has a generous queen-size bed that can be converted to two twin beds, ample closet space, shower/tub combination (or roll-in showers in the handicap-accessible rooms), hair dryer, desk/vanity, phone with voice mail, safe, color TV with remote, small cooler, individual climate controls, and room service. Most staterooms also have a sitting area with a desk/dressing table and a sofa that converts into a twin bed, and many also have a pull-down single berth. A curtain separates the sleeping area from the sitting area. Staterooms sleep 2–7 guests, though most sleep 3–4. Staterooms are located on decks 1–2 and 5–8, all of which are above the waterline. Crew quarters are on decks A and B, which are off-limits to guests.

Choosing your stateroom is one of the first things you'll do after you decide to cruise, so we put this chapter before dining and playing. We recommend you read this chapter in conjunction with chapter 2 before you make your cruise reservations. This will ensure you make the best possible choice in staterooms. Different stateroom categories offer different amenities, and there are some special rooms and decks that have an added benefit or two. The ship will be your home away from home for several days. Stateroom changes and upgrades are rarely available once you board, as the ships often sail completely full.

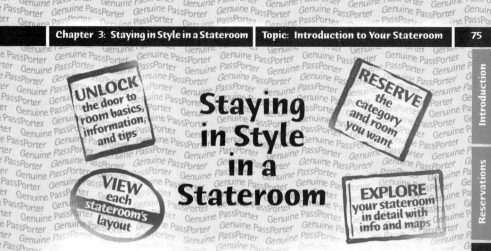

Selecting Your Stateroom

The Disney Cruise Line offers 12 different categories of staterooms on both the Disney Magic and the Disney Wonder. You'll need to specify a category when you make your cruise line reservation, so it is important to know as much as possible about each category in advance.

The most obvious difference between categories is **price**. Category 1 is the priciest, while category 12 is the least expensive. Price may be your only determining factor, and if so, we encourage you to check the current cruise category rates at http://www.disneycruise.com or in your Disney Cruise Line booklet. You can find typical rates on page 44.

Beyond price, we can combine the stateroom **categories** into four groups: outside stateroom suites with verandahs (1–3), outside staterooms with verandahs (4–7), outside staterooms with portholes (8–9), and inside staterooms (10-12). We devote one overview page to each of these four groups, plus one page of delightful detail for each category.

The Disney Cruise Line may offer different "categories," but old-fashioned "classes" are a relic of the past. If you choose a category 12 stateroom, you won't be made to feel like you're in a lower class than any other passenger. You will have **access to all facilities** on your ship and dine in the same style, regardless of your category. We booked our first cruise in a category 12 and never once felt funny about it. (We were later upgraded to category 9, which we loved. For more on upgrades, see page 95.) Guests on a land/sea package stay at different hotels based on their category, however (see chart on the next page). If you want to stay in a nicer hotel, you may be able to upgrade for an additional charge—inquire when reserving.

Another deciding factor may simply be **availability**. This is particularly true of the higher and lower category staterooms, which are in shorter supply. You can find out what categories are available before you make a decision by calling Disney at 888-325-2500. To learn how to check specific stateroom availability, see page 82. Note that you may be booked into a "guaranteed category" rather than a specific stateroom. This tends to happen when all of the staterooms in a certain category are booked. A guaranteed category means you're guaranteed a room in that category *or higher*. Guaranteed category guests do occasionally get upgraded.

Each class of stateroom offers its own **charms and drawbacks**. Check our chart of stateroom pros and cons on the next page for an overview of the staterooms, and then turn the page for a more in-depth look.

➤

Staterooms Side-by-Side

Charms and Delights	Issues and Drawbacks
Outside Stateroom Suites With Verandahs (categories 1–3)	
Huge staterooms, two with room for up to 7 people. Total separation of sleeping and sitting areas. VCRs, CD players, walk-in closets, wet bars, and some whirlpool tubs. Extra-long verandahs. Concierge, 105-day advance reservations, and expanded room service. Guests with land/sea packages stay at the Grand Floridian Resort & Spa.	Very expensive and deals are almost never offered on the suites (although per-guest cost is good if you fill it to capacity). Very popular and are often booked far in advance. There are only 22 suites (all on deck 8). Most cat. 3 staterooms have the pull-down bed in the master bedroom. Can be noisy when crew is cleaning deck 9 above.
Outside Staterooms With Verandahs (categories 4–7)	
Verandahs! It's like having a private deck to watch waves or gaze at passing islands. And the wall-to-wall glass adds light and a sense of extra space. Located on decks 5–8, close to all activities. One category (4) sleeps 4–5; the others sleep 3–4. Staterooms are 268–304 sq. ft. Guests with land/sea packages stay at Disney's deluxe resorts, such as the Beach Club.	Still on the pricey side, and may be out of range for many vacationers. Sitting and sleeping areas are in the same room. Category 5–7 layouts and interior square areas are identical to categories 8–9. Verandahs on deck 5 are slightly more shallow than on decks 6–8. Wind and/or bad weather can make the verandah unusable. Category 7 sleeps only 3.
Outside Staterooms With Portholes (categories 8–9)	
Portholes! Some natural sunlight and the ability to see where you are (i.e., already docked in port!) are real blessings. These staterooms are also more affordable. Some rooms sleep up to 4 guests. Category 8 and 9 staterooms feature split bathrooms (unlike category 11 and 12 staterooms). Provides the same access to the ship as higher categories. Portholes on decks 2 and up are picture window-sized.	No verandahs. Category 9 rooms are on decks 1 and 2, which aren't as accessible as the higher decks. And while category 8 staterooms are on decks 5–7, they aren't in the most desirable of spots, being all located forward in the ship. Sitting and sleeping areas are in the same room, and rooms are smaller at 214 sq. ft. Guests with land/sea packages stay at Disney's moderate resorts, along with category 10–12 guests.
Inside Staterooms (categories 10–12)	
The least expensive staterooms available. Some rooms sleep up to 4. Category 10 has the same square footage as categories 8–9. Some category 10–11 staterooms are on decks 5–7. Six staterooms in category 10 actually have an obstructed porthole (bonus!). Same access to the ship as higher categories. Guests with land/sea packages stay at Disney's moderate resorts, such as Port Orleans or Caribbean Beach Resort.	No windows, making your stateroom seem small, slightly claustrophobic, and dark. Smaller room size (184 sq. ft.) for categories 11–12. Category 12 rooms sleep no more than 3 guests. All staterooms in category 12 are on deck 2, and there are only 13 staterooms in this category (making them hard to get). Categories 11 and 12 don't have split bathrooms (see explanation on page 88).

Outside Stateroom Suites

(categories 1, 2, and 3)

The most luxurious of the ship's staterooms, these suites (all located on deck 8) offer virtually every convenience. All feature extra-large verandahs, VCRs, DVD and CD players, dining areas, wet bars, walk-in closets, robes and slippers, marble bathrooms, plus concierge and expanded room service.

AMENITIES

Suite guests may get **perks** like priority boarding, a separate waiting area in the terminal, a special planning meeting once you're aboard, a private party with the Captain, personalized stationary, and some special surprise gifts. You may be able to request water and soda delivery for your room. All suites come with **concierge service**. You can make reservations for Palo, childcare, Vista Spa, and shore excursions in advance of non-suite guests, and they'll help with other special requests. You can borrow from a library of CDs, DVDs, and games (board and electronic)—check the concierge book in your stateroom for a list.The crew often adds goodies, such as a fruit basket or cookies. Suite guests also get **expanded room service**, meaning you can order a full breakfast in the mornings (same menu as Lumiere's/Triton's breakfast menu—see page 104) and a full dinner from the restaurants during dinner hours—menus are available from concierge, or check our menus in chapter 4. Suite guests can also book massages in their staterooms or on their verandahs.

TIPS & NOTES

The suites are **extremely popular**; if you do not book one far in advance, expect to be put on a waiting list.

Guests with land/sea packages have **first pick of suites**; any suites available 30 days before sailing can be booked by all. No restrictions are placed on the 7-night cruise suites.

Suite guests have online **priority booking service** for shore excursions, spa treatments, Palo reservations, children's programming, and babysitting up to 105 days in advance (see page 125). If you have not booked in advance, plan to attend the meeting with the concierge staff on your first afternoon to make reservations.

Suites have **hand-held blow dryers** in their vanity drawers.

While some lucky guests in the suites may be **invited to dine** with the Captain, this isn't a given.

Did you know? Suite guests have **gold Key to the World cards**, not blue/purple like others.

Category 1 Staterooms

(Walter E. and Roy O. Disney Suites—sleeps 7 guests)

The two **category 1 suites**, known as the Walter E. Disney Suite and the Roy O. Disney Suite, are the height of cruising. The 1,029 sq. ft. (95 sq. m.) suites luxuriate with warm, exotic woods, two bedrooms, 2 ½ bathrooms, whirlpool tub, a media library with a pull-down bed, a baby grand piano (Walter suite only), and a quadruple-wide verandah. Sleeps up to 7 guests.

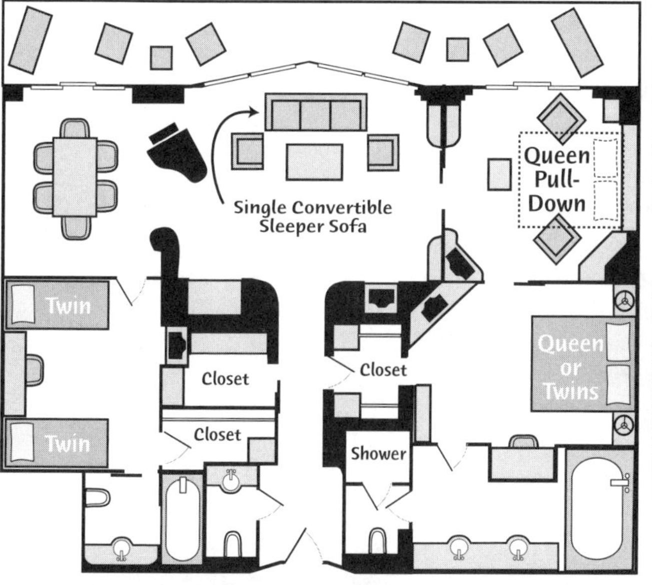

© MediaMarx, Inc.

Entryway

© MediaMarx, Inc.

The baby grand in the Walter E. Disney suite

© MediaMarx, Inc.

A view from the media library into the bedroom in the Walter E. Disney suite

© MediaMarx, Inc.

Jennifer enjoys the quadruple-wide verandah of a category 1 suite

Category 2 Staterooms

(Two-Bedroom Suite—sleeps 7 guests)

The **category 2** suites (at 945 sq. ft./88 sq. m.) have two bedrooms, 2 ½ baths, a whirlpool tub, and a triple-wide verandah. There are just two of these suites onboard, and both sleep up to seven.

Note: Categories 1 and 2 can sleep up to seven guests, but the sixth and seventh guests will require booking an additional resort hotel room at an extra cost (for those on land/sea packages).

Tip: Connecting rooms are great for larger groups. Many of the category 3 suites have connecting doors to a category 3 or 4, which holds four to five more guests. Alas, the category 1 and 2 suites do not have connecting staterooms.

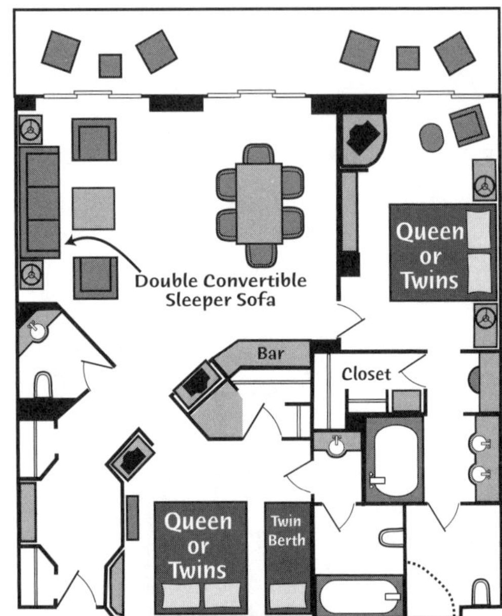

The triple-wide verandah of a category 2 suite

© MediaMarx, Inc.
A category 2 bedroom

© MediaMarx, Inc.
The entertainment center

© MediaMarx, Inc.

Category 3 Staterooms

(One Bedroom Suite–sleeps 4–5 guests)

The 18 stateroom suites in **category 3** (614 sq. ft./57 sq. m.) offer a bedroom separate from the living room and dining room, two baths, a double-size convertible sofa in the living room, and a double-wide verandah. Most category 3 suites have a pull-down twin bed in the bedroom (as shown on the layout). Four suites (#8032, #8034, #8532, and #8534) have a slightly different layout with a bit more floor space and feature the pull-down twin bed in the living room, which guests find more convenient–these four suites are under the Goofy Pool, however, and are noisier. Suites #8100, #8102, #8600, and #8602 are handicap-accessible and have deeper verandahs. Category 3 suites sleep four to five guests (see chart on pages 96–97 to see which suites sleep only four).

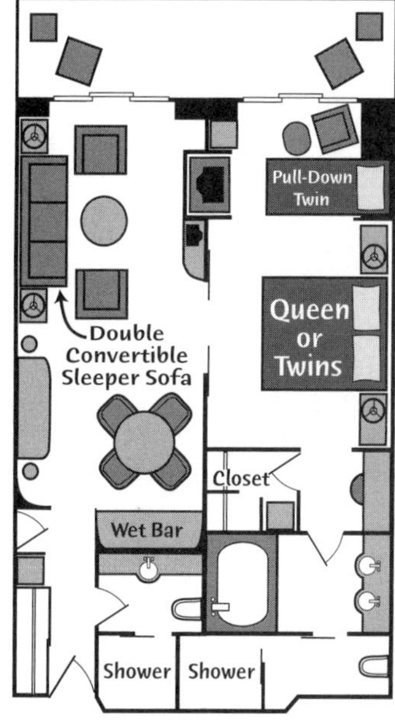

© MediaMarx, Inc.

A category 3 bedroom

© MediaMarx, Inc.

Dave relaxes in the living room of stateroom 8034 (different layout than pictured above)

Introduction | Reservations | Staterooms | Dining | Activities | Ports of Call | Magic | Index

Introduction Reservations Staterooms Dining Activities Ports of Call Magic Index

Outside Staterooms With Verandahs

(categories 4, 5, 6, and 7)

Welcome to the luxury of a private verandah at just a fraction of the cost of the higher categories! Staterooms with verandahs (categories 4–7) comprise the largest percentage of the ship's staterooms at a whopping 42%, and all have split baths (see page 88). All are located on decks 5–8.

AMENITIES

The main amenity in categories 4–7 is the verandah (balcony). Not only does the verandah offer fresh air and a gorgeous view, but it extends the space of your stateroom considerably. The option to sit outside and enjoy a sunset or read a book while someone else watches TV or sleeps inside is a huge bonus. Verandahs in categories 4–6 are open to the air, covered, and have privacy dividers. Category 7 staterooms (same size as categories 5 and 6) have either a slightly obstructed view from the verandah, or a Navigator's Verandah, which offers more privacy by hiding the verandah behind a large, glassless "porthole" (see photos on page 85). All verandahs have exterior lighting that is controlled by an on/off switch inside the stateroom. All the verandah staterooms can sleep at least three guests, and most category 4 rooms sleep up to five guests. See the chart on pages 96–97 for more specific room capacities.

© MediaMarx, Inc.

Verandah with plexiglass railing

© MediaMarx, Inc.

Verandah with metal railing

Most verandahs have a clear, plexiglass-covered railing (shown in the first photo). Others have a solid, metal railing (as shown in the second photo). There are fans of both styles, though we personally prefer the clear railings.

Which Staterooms Are Available for My Cruise?

Most guests let Disney or their travel agent select their stateroom. If you'd rather have a specific stateroom, find out which staterooms are available by calling Disney (888-325-2500). If you have Internet access, get online and visit Disney Cruise Line (http://www.disneycruise.com) or Travelocity.com (http://www.travelocity.com)—follow the directions to choose your cruise, then continue through the windows to check rates and to see any availabilities. If you have your heart set on a particular stateroom, call Disney or check the Internet to find a cruise with that room available. When you make your reservations, indicate the exact stateroom you want. Confirm that the stateroom you requested is printed in your travel booklet when it arrives.

Category 4 Staterooms

(Deluxe Family With Verandah—sleeps 4–5 guests)

Category 4 is the Deluxe Family Stateroom, which sleeps up to four or five guests (304 sq. ft./28 sq. m.). The room has a pull-down twin bed for the fifth guest, along with a convertible twin sofa bed, a pull-down twin berth, and a queen-size bed that can be separated into twin beds. The 80 **category 4** family staterooms are all on deck 8. Avoid staterooms directly below the Goofy Pool (#8036-8044 and #8536-8544) due to noise during deck parties. Note that staterooms #8092-8094 and #8596-8698 have a solid railing, rather than a plexiglass railing. Access to the verandah is limited when you have the twin bed pulled down.

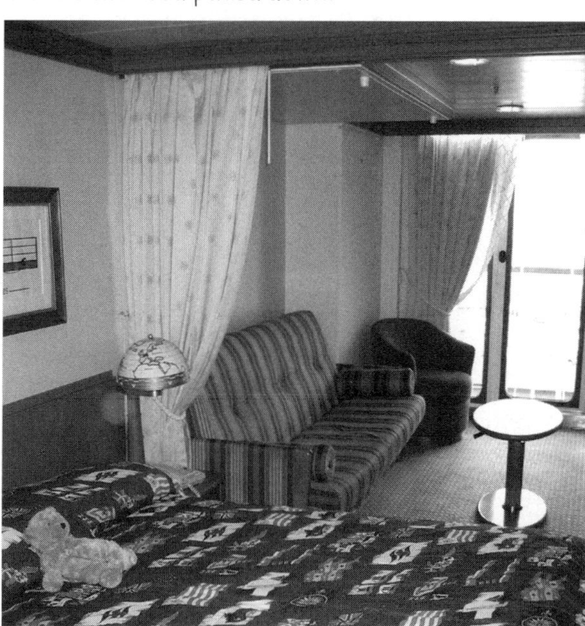

© Paul McGill

Squidgy the teddy bear naps in a category 4 stateroom (8544)

© Paul McGill

Desk/vanity area in category 4 stateroom

© Paul McGill

Another view of category 4

Introduction Reservations Staterooms Dining Activities Ports of Call Magic Index

Category 5 & 6 Staterooms

(Deluxe Stateroom With Verandah–sleeps 3-4 guests)

Categories 5 and 6 are the Deluxe Staterooms With Verandahs. These staterooms are identical to category 4 (see previous page) except they are 268 sq. ft. (25 sq. m.), sleep three to four guests, do not have the extra pull-down twin bed, and are missing a handy bench across from the bed. The 114 **category 5** staterooms are located on deck 7, mostly midship and aft. Staterooms to the aft have quick access to a secluded public deck. Staterooms #7130-7138 and #7630-7638 have a solid, four-foot metal railing (as opposed to the plexiglass railing on other verandahs), but the verandahs may be deeper and quieter, too. Avoid #7590 as it is across from a laundry room. **Category 6** staterooms number 138 and are situated on decks 5 and 6. We recommend deck 6 for its slightly larger verandahs. Avoid #6588 as it is across from a laundry room. Staterooms #5142-5150, #5642-5650, #6144-6154, and #6644-6654 have a solid railing.

© MediaMarx, Inc.

Verandah at sunset

© MediaMarx, Inc.

Jennifer enjoys the verandah in our category 5 stateroom (7618)

Category 7 Staterooms

(Navigator's Verandah—sleeps 3 guests)

There are only 30 **category 7** staterooms, of which 26 are Navigator's Verandahs (enclosed verandah with open-air porthole). All are located on the quietest decks: 5, 6, and 7. We recommend deck 7 for its easy access to the public deck to the aft. Note that the verandahs on deck 5 are a bit shallower at 42" (106 cm.) than those on upper decks at about 48" (122 cm.). We noticed this on our May 2002 cruise when we compared our verandah to that of a friend's. Note that four of the category 7 staterooms (#6134, #6634, #7120, and #7620) were originally category 5 and 6 staterooms—they have plexiglass railings and partially obstructed views due to the hull design, and their verandahs aren't enclosed like the other category 7 rooms.

Disney Magic Navigator's Verandah *Disney Wonder Navigator's Verandah*

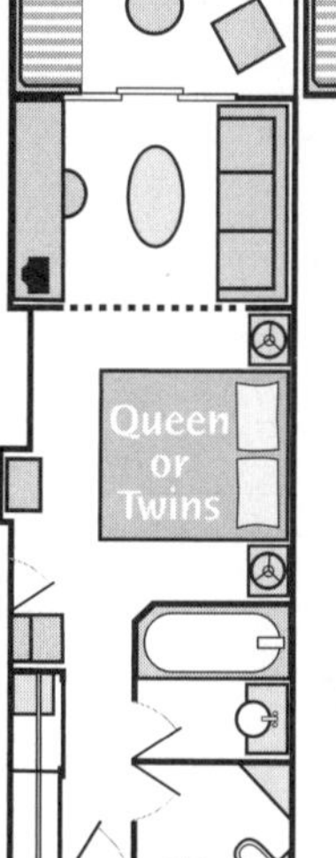

Note that the Navigator's Verandah on the Disney Wonder sports a larger porthole while the Magic's is a bit smaller. Both have a built-in, padded bench, a chair, and a small table.

Our category 7 stateroom was cozy and comfortable

The enclosed navigator's verandah

Dave loves the built-in bench

Outside Staterooms With Portholes

(categories 8 and 9)

Affordable elegance is yours if you choose a porthole over a verandah. As one of the most popular categories for cruisers, these rooms make up 27% of the staterooms onboard. They're located on decks 1, 2, 5, 6, and 7.

AMENITIES

The only real differences between these two categories are location and price—category 8 staterooms are on higher decks and cost more, while category 9 staterooms are lower in both regards. Their floor space and room layouts are identical. Both categories are considered "deluxe," which simply means they have the split bath (see page 88). Both are approximately 214 sq. ft. (20 sq. m.) and feature the sitting area in the rear of the stateroom. The natural light of the porthole is a real bonus over inside staterooms, especially for kids. We've included the layout for these staterooms on the next page.

© MediaMarx, Inc.

Baby Alexander enjoys our category 9 stateroom

Note that the portholes on deck 1 differ from those on the higher decks. Photographs of the two different styles of portholes are shown below. We've stayed in rooms with both types, and we prefer the larger porthole.

© MediaMarx, Inc.

Deck 1 portholes

© MediaMarx, Inc.

Deck 2 and up porthole

Category 8 and 9 Staterooms
(sleeps 2-4)

There are only 60 **category 8 staterooms**, scattered among decks 5-7 forward. This is due to the hull design of the ship, which features portholes rather than verandahs near the ship's bow. Staterooms on deck 5 are convenient to the kid's clubs. The fact that these staterooms are directly over the Walt Disney Theatre shouldn't be a problem—you aren't likely to be in your room during a show. Staterooms on decks 6 and 7 are excellent, by all accounts. Note that two category 8 rooms are handicap-accessible (#6000 and #6500). **Category 9 staterooms** are limited to decks 1 and 2. In general, we don't recommend deck 1 because it only has access to the forward and midship elevators and stairs, making it harder to get around. Additionally, staterooms #1030-1037 are fairly noisy on port days, which may be bothersome. Perhaps more importantly, the outside staterooms on deck 1 have two small portholes, rather than the one large porthole found on the other decks. We stayed in stateroom #1044 (deck 1) on our first cruise and liked it well enough, but we much prefer the staterooms we've had on deck 2. That said, there are certainly some staterooms which are better than others on deck 2. Due to fairly constant noise and vibration, we recommend you avoid these staterooms: #2000-2004, #2036-2044, #2078-2096, #2114-2129, #2140-2152, #2500-2508, #2586-2600, #2626, and #2630-2653. Unless you need connecting rooms, we recommend you avoid them (38 of the 177 category 9 staterooms are connecting) due to noise from the connecting stateroom. Our family stayed in rooms #2610-2616 on one cruise and we loved them—quiet and convenient (near the aft elevators and stairs).

© MediaMarx, Inc.

Relaxing in our category 8 stateroom with a porthole (#7514)

Inside Staterooms

(categories 10, 11, and 12)

Resplendent with the same luxurious decor found in the other staterooms, inside staterooms are smaller and more affordable versions of the higher-categories. Inside staterooms make up 29% of the staterooms onboard and are located on decks 1, 2, 5, 6, and 7 (all above the waterline).

AMENITIES

Inside staterooms come in three price categories, but in only two layouts—categories 11 and 12 have identical layouts. Category 10 is the Deluxe Inside Stateroom and is 214 sq. ft. (20 sq. m.) with a split bath (see below). Categories 11 and 12 are the Standard Inside Staterooms at 184 sq. ft. (17 sq. m.). Beyond the size and the split bath, there's little difference. All three categories of staterooms put the sitting area before the sleeping area, presumably because without a window there's no need to have the sitting area at the farthest end of the stateroom. One notable difference between category 10 and 11/12 is the orientation of the bed (see room layout diagrams on following pages). It is also important to note that none of the staterooms in categories 11/12 have connecting rooms, while many of the category 10 staterooms are connecting. The lack of a connecting door makes for a subtle difference in room layout.

The split bathroom found in category 10 (as well as 4-9) is convenient for families.

© MediaMarx, Inc.

The toilet/sink room

© MediaMarx, Inc.

The shower/tub/sink room

The one-room bathroom in categories 11 and 12 is much more compact. We show two views: a regular bathroom and a handicapped bathroom.

© MediaMarx, Inc.

A category 11/12 bathroom

© MediaMarx, Inc.

A cat. 11 handicapped bathroom

Category 10 Staterooms

(Deluxe Inside Stateroom–sleeps 4 guests)

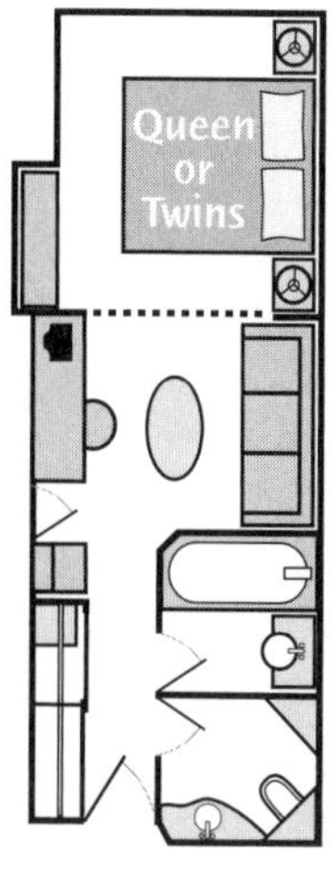

Inside staterooms are scattered over five decks of the ship. The 96 **category 10 staterooms** occupy four decks: 1, 2, 5, and 7. The staterooms on deck 1 are our least favorite because the corridor doesn't run the entire length of the deck, making it harder to reach destinations in the aft of the ship. Many of the staterooms on deck 2 are immediately below noisy places. To avoid noises from above, try for odd-numbered staterooms between #2071-2075, #2571-2575, #2101-2111, #2601-2611, #2629-2635, and #2129-2135. We also recommend the staterooms on deck 7. You should also note that almost half of the category 10 staterooms have connecting rooms, unlike the category 11 and 12 staterooms, which have none. Get a category 10 if you're traveling with a large family or friends and want connecting rooms. If you have booked only one stateroom, however, our advice is to avoid these connecting rooms. Many cruisers have reported that the connecting doors do not dampen noise well. Try to swing a category 10 on deck 5 (#5020, #5022, #5024, #5520, #5522, or #5524) with a partially obstructed, "secret" porthole–see the next page for details. All category 10 staterooms sleep up to four guests.

A cat. 10 inside stateroom with a round mirror on the far wall

Outside or Inside Stateroom?

There's no easy answer to this question. Each choice affects your cruise experience, but not necessarily in the ways you may think. First off, no matter where you sleep, it won't affect your status with fellow cruisers or staff-everyone receives the same quality of service. What does change is how much time you're likely to spend in your stateroom. Verandahs encourage folks to stay in their staterooms, while inside rooms push you out-of-doors to enjoy the sun, stars, and ocean breezes. With a ship full of attractive public spaces, there's nothing wrong with spending less time in your room. And a cheaper room can mean having more to spend on once-in-a-lifetime shore excursions, the deluxe wine package, or shopping in port. But then there are those magical, early morning moments in your bathrobe on the verandah while everyone else is asleep, reading a good novel and sipping room service coffee. We haven't made your choice any easier, have we? Maybe you can compromise with a picture window-sized porthole?

Special Category 10 Staterooms

("Secret Porthole"–sleeps 4 guests)

Six of the category 10 staterooms (see previous page) have a different layout–and a porthole! Now before you get too excited, the porthole has an obstructed view (see photo below), but most cruisers are delighted with these "secret porthole rooms." We've included the layout for these special staterooms below as well–they were once category 9 staterooms, but were later reclassified as category 10 because of the obstructions. These six special category 10 staterooms are all located on deck 5 (#5020, #5022, #5024, #5520, #5522, or #5524), and all sleep up to four guests.

Getting one of these special category 10 staterooms can be difficult. You can simply try checking with Disney Cruise Line or your travel agent to see if one of these staterooms are available for your cruise (use the stateroom numbers noted above). You can also use the Internet to find out which staterooms are still available for your cruise–then if you find that one of these coveted secret porthole staterooms is available, book that cruise before someone else books it. See page 82 to learn how to determine which staterooms are still available for your cruise.

Queen or Twins

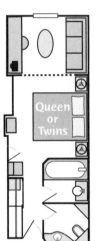

If you're considering a "secret porthole" stateroom but aren't sure how you feel about the obstructed view, we refer you to the excellent Platinum Castaway Club web site (http://www.castawayclub.com), which has photos of each of the six "secret portholes" so you can judge for yourself. Just click on the "Secret Porthole Rooms" link in the left column to get the photos and a list of pros and cons to help you make your decision.

© MediaMarx, Inc.

A "secret porthole" stateroom (#5024)

© MediaMarx, Inc.

Another view of this category

Category 11 and 12 Staterooms

(Standard Inside Stateroom—sleeps 3-4 guests)

The 147 **category 11 staterooms** are located on decks 5, 6, and 7, making them convenient to many destinations within the ship. We recommend the aft staterooms due to their convenience to food and relative quiet. Families with young children may prefer a stateroom on deck 5 for quick access to the movie theater and Oceaneer Club/Lab. Aft staterooms on deck7 are just down the hall from a secluded, public deck. Category 11 staterooms are also the only ones in this group to offer handicap-accessible rooms (#6147, #6647, #7131, and #7631—see photos below). Staterooms #6002, #6004, #6502, and #6504 are on the ship's outer side, but they have no portholes.

© MediaMarx, Inc.

A handicap-accessible, category 11 inside stateroom (6647)

© MediaMarx, Inc.

Another view of stateroom 6647, a handicap-accessible category 11 room

Category 12 staterooms (all 13 of them) are on deck 2 forward. While the staterooms closer to the elevators and stairs are convenient, they are also noisier (they are directly below Beat Street/Route 66). Request another stateroom for less noise.

© MediaMarx, Inc.

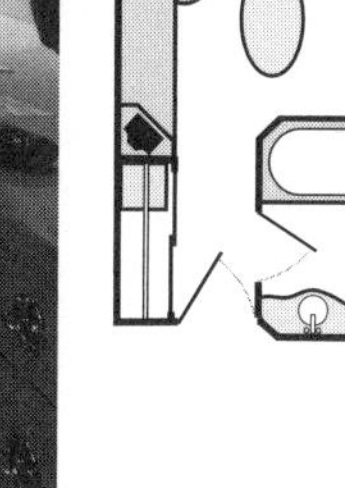

A standard category 11/12 inside stateroom

Stateroom Amenities and Services

Bathrooms—All staterooms have their own bathrooms, while categories 4–10 have innovative split bathrooms with a sink/toilet in one small room, and a second sink plus tub/shower in another room—see page 88. We love the split bathrooms—it makes getting ready much easier. Note that the light switches are located outside the bathrooms—you'll want to remember to turn them on before you enter!

Beds—Every room has a comfy queen-size bed that can be unlocked and separated into two twin-size beds by your stateroom host/hostess if needed. Most staterooms also have a twin-size, convertible sofa (72"/183 cm. long). Category 3 has a double-size convertible sofa instead. Some rooms have a pull-down, twin-size upper berth (72"/183 cm. long with a weight limit of 220 lbs./100 kg.) with safety rails. Category 4 has an extra twin-size bed.

Closets—Every stateroom has a roomy closet with a clothes rod, a dozen or so hangers, a set of drawers, a safe, your life jackets, and an overhead light (that turns on automatically when you open the closet). If you don't have enough hangers, ask your stateroom host/hostess for more.

Cribs—Portable, "pack-n-play" cribs are available, as are bed safety rails—request when reserving. High chairs are also provided in the dining areas.

A pack-n-play crib in a stateroom

Electrical Outlets—Staterooms are outfitted with four standard U.S. 110v, three-prong electrical outlets: two near the desk/vanity and two behind the TV. Two special outlets—one in each bathroom—are marked "for shavers only" and have a standard U.S. 110v, two-prong outlet along with a European 220v outlet (20 watts/20VA max.). You can't plug your hair dryer into these outlets, but electric toothbrushes should be OK. There's no outlet near the bed, so bring an extension cord or power strip if necessary.

Hair Dryers—Attached to the wall of the bathroom in each stateroom. They aren't terribly high-powered, though, so you may want to bring your own if you are particular about drying your hair.

Laundry—Self-service laundries are available, as is valet laundry service and dry cleaning. The three laundry rooms onboard are located across the hall from staterooms #2096, #6588, and #7590. Each laundry has several stacked washer/dryers ($1.00), two irons and boards (no charge), detergent vending machine ($1.00), change machine, and table. Estimate $3.00 for a full load of laundry. Use four quarters for the washer (38 minutes), and use eight quarters to get clothes fully dry (48 minutes for $2.00). If you plan to do laundry, pack some detergent and a mesh bag to tote your items. Plan to visit in the mornings—afternoons are very busy. You can bring your own iron or steamer to use in the laundry room, but their use is prohibited in the staterooms for safety reasons.

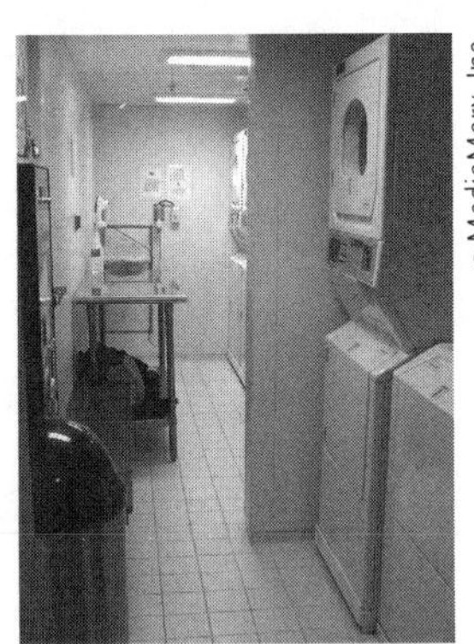

An onboard laundry (the iron is in the back)

Lights—The staterooms are well illuminated, but it can get pitch black in your room when you turn off the lights (especially the inside staterooms without a porthole). If you need it, bring a nightlight, leave the bathroom light on, or open your closet door a crack to trigger its automatic light.

Luggage—Once you've unpacked, you can store your empty luggage in the closet, slide it under the bed (it has a 9"/23 cm. clearance—lift up the bed and put the luggage underneath if you can't slide it), or ask your stateroom host/hostess if they can store your luggage (this is not always an option). You'll have plenty of drawers to unpack your belongings—we counted more than 20 drawers and shelves in our inside stateroom!

Messages—There are a variety of ways to leave and retrieve messages. First, the phone system allows you to call staterooms directly (dial 7 + the stateroom number) and leave voice mail messages. To check and retrieve your messages, just pick up the phone and press the "Messages" button. If you have messages, the light on your phone will blink until you listen to them. For a lower-tech message system, a decorative fish ornament outside your door serves as a message holder—you may find messages from crew members or fellow passengers. Third, we recommend you pack a pad of sticky notes—these are handy for messages to your cabinmates!

Phones—All staterooms have phones. For the most part, you'll use your phone to call other staterooms, room service, guest services, and other places on the ship. You can call locations off the ship for $6.95/minute at ship-to-shore rates (Disney uses the Maritime Telecommunications Network—http://www.mtnsat.com). You cannot call toll-free numbers from your stateroom phone, nor can you use calling cards. If someone needs to reach you while you're on the cruise, they can call toll-free 888-DC-ATSEA (callers from outside the U.S. can call +1-732-335-3281). Regardless of which number your caller uses, they will be prompted for a major credit card number. Your caller's card will be charged $6.95 for each minute the call is connected. Less expensive options include using your cell phone when in port and when sailing past islands with cell service (you'll need international roaming) or use a pay phone in port (bring calling cards). Castaway Cay has neither pay phones nor cellular coverage, however.

Refrigerator—While it may be best described as a beverage cooler, there is a small refrigerator in the sitting area of your stateroom. It's cool enough to chill your drinks (roughly 55° F/13° C). It is large enough (8"d x 12"w x 16.5"h, or 20.3cm x 30.5 x 50) to store several bottles of water, cans of soda/beer, and a bottle of wine or champagne. It seems to work best when it's 3/4 full. There's also an ice bucket in the room, and you may request ice for it.

© MediaMarx, Inc.
A stateroom refrigerator

Room Service—Free room service is available 24 hours a day for most of your cruise. For details, see page 117. When your food arrives, raise your coffee table (it adjusts like an office chair), and use it as a dining table.

© MediaMarx, Inc.
A stateroom safe

Safes—Every stateroom has its own safe—they are roughly shoebox-size (9"d x 6.5"h x 14"w, or 22.9cm x 16.5cm x 35.6cm) and located in the closet. To lock the safe, swipe your Key to the World card through the mechanism. Note that you must use the same card to unlock the safe. Tip: Use another card with a magnetic strip (any will work) to lock/unlock the safe, then hide the card in the room so anyone in your party can access the safe.

Stateroom Amenities and Services *(continued)*

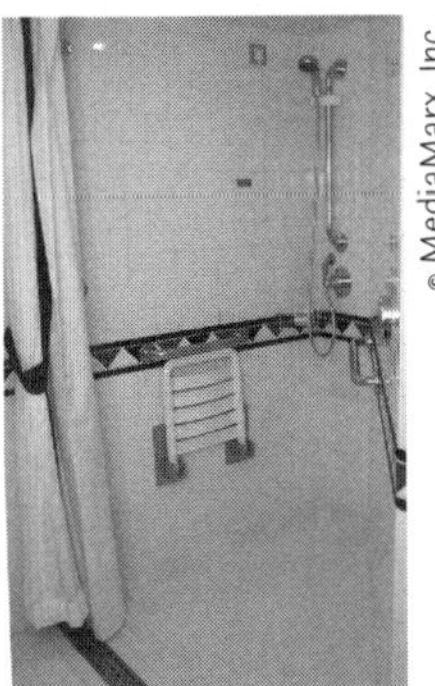

© MediaMarx, Inc.

A roll-in shower with rails, fold-down seat, and call button

Special Needs—Handicap-accessible, barrier-free staterooms (16 total available in categories 3, 5, 6, 8, and 11) are larger—see photos on page 91. Special features include open bed frames, ramped bathroom thresholds, fold-down shower seats, rails, emergency call buttons, and lowered bars. To reserve a handicap-accessible stateroom, call Disney and request the special medical form. Guests with young kids may request bed railings, pack-and-play cribs, and high chairs from the stateroom host/hostess. Strollers are available on a first-come, first-served basis from Guest Services, as are wheelchairs for emergencies. If you need a wheelchair while onboard or in ports, bring your own or rent one through Brevard Medical Equipment with delivery and pick-up right at the ship (866-416-7383 or http://www.brevardmedicalequip.com). Beach wheelchairs are available on a first-come basis at Castaway Cay.

Stateroom Host/Hostess—This crew member attends to all of your stateroom needs. See page 271 for details on gratuities.

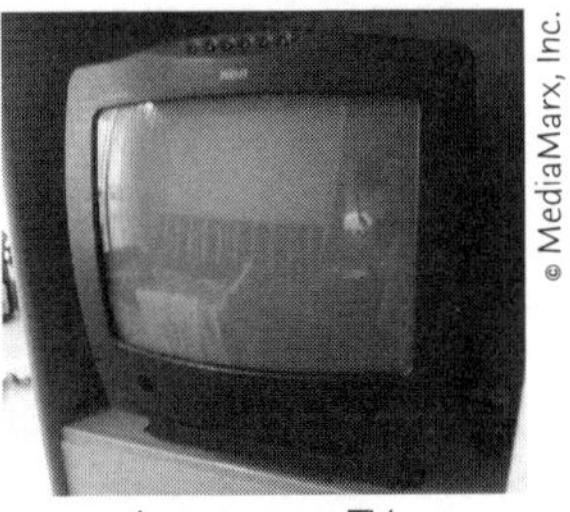

© MediaMarx, Inc.

A stateroom TV

Television—All staterooms have 13" televisions with remote control, and categories 1 and 2 have multiple televisions. A channel listing with movie schedules is provided in your stateroom upon arrival (see page 142 for a typical channel listing). Channels may change as you sail, especially when you're in port—expect to see some international networks show up on a channel or two. Special channels offer cruise details, such as "What's Afloat" and onboard shows. Recordings of the special talks on golf, shore excursions, shopping, and debarkation are also broadcast on your TV. Check channel 50 to trace your voyage's progress and channel 52 for bridge reports and views, including the current time, weather conditions, etc. You can use the TV as a wake-up "alarm" by setting it to turn on at a certain time—just be sure you set it to a channel that always has sound (avoid the movie channels). Here's how we set the alarm on our stateroom's television: menu → setup → alarm → use volume buttons to set time.

Temperature—Every stateroom has individual climate controls. The thermostat is normally located near the bed, high on the wall.

Toiletries—Your stateroom is stocked with basic bar soap, lotion, and a shampoo/conditioner combo. They are sufficient, but not luxurious. We recommend you bring your favorites from home instead. Tissues and toilet paper are also provided in your stateroom's bathroom. The suites offer upgraded toiletries, including bath/shower soap and a shower cap.

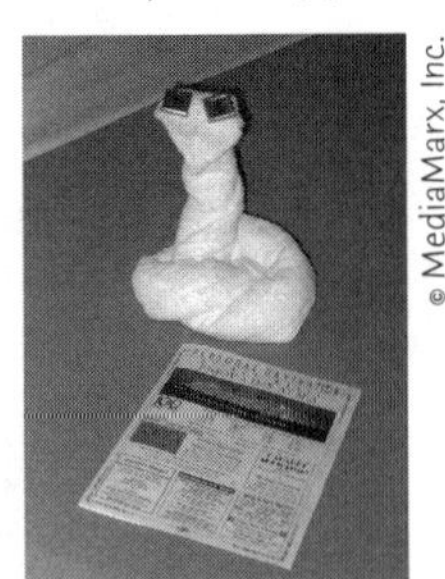

© MediaMarx, Inc.

A towel "snake"

Towel Animal—Don't be surprised to see a towel imaginatively folded and twisted into the shape of an animal on your bed at the end of the day. Disney's stateroom hosts and hostesses regularly create these "magical touches" for guests to discover in their staterooms. And if you have some props lying around, such as sunglasses, hats, or stuffed animals, your towel animal may become even more embellished. (Towel animal creation is up to the host or hostess, and there may be some that can't make them.)

Verandahs—All staterooms in categories 7 and up have a private verandah. A heavy, sliding glass door opens to reveal a deck as wide as your stateroom. Dividers offer privacy from your neighbors and the deck overhead protects you from most of the elements. The sliding door has a child-proof latch that can be difficult to open at first—the trick is to grasp the handle and pull hard without turning. Turn the handle horizontally to lock the sliding door. Two plastic/fabric chairs and a small table are on the verandah, along with an ashtray and two deck lights (the light switch is inside the stateroom, somewhat concealed by the curtains). The deck can be slippery, and the railing can be sticky from salty, moist air. Most verandahs have a clear plexiglass-and-metal railing which you can see through, while some staterooms in the aft have a solid railing—see photos on page 82. If you leave your verandah door open, your room will get warm and muggy quickly. Parents should supervise children when they're on the verandah. If you are concerned about kids climbing on the deck furniture, you may ask to have it removed.

Wake-Up Calls—A clock may be provided in your stateroom, but it does not have a lighted dial or numbers. You may prefer to set wake-up calls from your stateroom phone. Try it at least once—Mickey Mouse himself calls you! Alternatives to the wake-up call service are to bring a clock, set the alarm on your television (see page 94), or preorder room service for breakfast (a crew member may even give you a reminder call before delivery).

Will I Get a Free Upgrade?

Who wouldn't want a free upgrade to a "better" stateroom? It's the kind of perk that's bound to put a smile on your face, and plenty of cruisers look for ways to improve their chances of winning this particular lottery. Unfortunately, in all our time cruising, we've never discovered a foolproof "system." And since upgrades are so unpredictable, our most important advice is this: "Never, never book a room you won't be happy to spend your cruise in, should a hoped-for upgrade never materialize." • Most upgrades occur well in advance of your cruise, as Disney tries to maximize occupancy on the ship. In fact, those upgrades often go completely unheralded. Look closely at your cruise documents when they arrive—if those stateroom numbers don't match your earlier reservation documents, check our chart on the next two pages—you've probably been upgraded! Other cruisers have been delighted to learn they've been upgraded when they check in at the terminal, but don't expect to ask for a free upgrade when you check in (as folks sometimes do when they check into a hotel). We've never heard of someone getting a free upgrade that way. You may be able to purchase an upgrade at check-in, however. Either way, it never hurts to ask! • Disney sometimes offers "guaranteed" staterooms—you're guaranteed to receive a stateroom in a particular or better category, but you won't be able to reserve a specific stateroom number or location. In exchange for giving the cruise line the flexibility to locate you wherever they please, you may get an upgrade. • Disney may want to create vacancies in the lower-priced categories, which tend to sell better at the last minute than the higher-priced rooms. If someone is going to get that vacant verandah stateroom at a bargain price, it'll be someone who booked well in advance. • Some folks intentionally "under-book" in the lowest categories in hopes of an upgrade, but again, be sure you'll be happy in Cat. 12 if the upgrade never happens. • On longer cruises there's higher demand for verandah staterooms and less for inside staterooms, so your chances of an upgrade from inside to outside may be quite low. If they need to "clear space" at all, the upgrade may go from verandah to suite. • Off-season travelers may hope for an upgrade because there will be more vacancies aboard, but on the flip side, if Disney doesn't have to move someone to make room for someone else, then you won't be going anywhere. • So, best of luck, and if you do get an upgrade, do a happy dance for us!

Stateroom Details

Connecting Rooms

2038	or	2120
2039		**2122**
2040		**2124**

This chart lists every stateroom, organized by room number, with each room's category and its sleeping capacity. Handicap rooms are marked "H." Connecting rooms are in bold and bracketed. Even numbers are outside rooms; odds are inside. Capacity of rooms marked "3/4" could not be confirmed and may sleep either 3 or 4. Discrepancies exist between this and Disney's cruise brochure, but we've taken pains to make this more accurate. Due to ship capacity regulations, Disney may limit the number of guests in any room at the time of booking, regardless of the room's maximum capacity. However, if your party is booked into a particular room, you can rest assured that room will hold everyone in your party. In the event of confusion, call Disney at 888-DCL-2500.

Room #	Cat.	Sleeps
Deck 1		
1030	9	4
1032	9	4
1034	9	4
1036	9	4
1037	10	4
1038	9	4
1039	10	4
1040	9	4
1041	10	4
1042	9	4
1043	10	4
1044	9	4
1045	10	4
1046	9	4
1047	10	4
1048	9	4
1049	10	4
1050	**9**	**4**
1051	**10**	**4**
1052	**9**	**4**
1053	**10**	**4**
1054	9	4
1056	9	4
1058	9	4
1060	9	4
1062	9	4
1064	9	4
1065	10	4
1066	**9**	**4**
1067	**10**	**4**
1068	**9**	**4**
1069	**10**	**4**
1070	9	4
1071	**10**	**4**
1072	9	4
1073	**10**	**4**
1074	**9**	**4**
1075	**10**	**4**
1076	**9**	**4**
1077	**10**	**4**
1078	9	4
1079	10	4
Deck 2		
2000	9	4
2002	9	4
2004	9	4
2006	9	4
2008	9	4
2009	12	3
2010	9	4
2011	12	3
2012	9	4
2013	12	3
2014	9	4
2015	12	3
2016	9	4
2017	12	3
2018	**9**	**4**
2019	12	3
2020	**9**	**4**
2021	12	3
2022	9	4
2024	9	4
2026	9	4

Room #	Cat.	Sleeps
2028	9	4
2030	**9**	**4**
2032	**9**	**4**
2034	9	4
2035	10	4
2036	9	4
2037	10	4
2038	**9**	**4**
2039	10	4
2040	**9**	**3/4**
2041	10	4
2042	9	3
2043	10	4
2044	9	3/4
2045	10	4
2046	9	3
2047	10	4
2048	9	3
2050	9	3
2052	9	3
2054	9	3
2056	9	3
2058	9	3
2060	9	3
2062	9	3
2064	9	3
2066	9	3
2068	9	3
2070	9	3
2071	**10**	**4**
2072	9	3
2073	**10**	**4**
2074	9	3
2075	**10**	**4**
2076	9	3
2077	**10**	**4**
2078	9	3
2079	**10**	**4**
2080	9	3
2081	**10**	**4**
2082	9	3
2083	**10**	**4**
2084	9	3
2085	**10**	**4**
2086	9	3
2088	9	3
2090	9	3
2092	9	3
2094	**9**	**4**
2096	**9**	**3**
2098	9	3
2100	9	3
2101	10	4
2102	**9**	**3**
2103	10	4
2104	**9**	**4**
2105	10	4
2106	9	4
2107	**10**	**4**
2108	9	4
2109	**10**	**4**
2110	9	4
2111	10	4
2112	9	4
2114	9	4

Room #	Cat.	Sleeps
2116	9	4
2118	9	4
2120	9	3
2122	**9**	**4**
2124	**9**	**4**
2126	9	4
2128	9	4
2129	10	4
2130	9	4
2131	10	4
2132	9	4
2133	10	4
2134	9	4
2135	**10**	**4**
2136	9	4
2137	**10**	**4**
2138	**9**	**4**
2139	10	4
2140	**9**	**4**
2141	10	4
2142	9	4
2143	**10**	**4**
2144	9	4
2145	**10**	**4**
2146	**9**	**4**
2147	10	4
2148	**9**	**4**
2150	9	4
2152	9	4
2153	10	4
2500	9	4
2502	9	4
2504	9	4
2506	9	4
2508	9	4
2509	12	3
2510	9	4
2511	12	3
2512	9	4
2513	12	3
2514	9	4
2515	12	3
2516	9	4
2517	12	3
2518	**9**	**4**
2519	12	3
2520	**9**	**3/4**
2521	12	3
2522	9	4
2524	9	4
2526	9	4
2528	9	4
2530	**9**	**4**
2532	**9**	**4**
2534	9	4
2535	10	4
2536	9	3/4
2537	10	4
2538	**9**	**4**
2539	10	4
2540	**9**	**3/4**
2541	10	4
2542	9	3/4
2543	10	4
2544	9	3

Room #	Cat.	Sleeps
2545	10	4
2546	9	3
2547	10	4
2548	9	3
2550	9	3
2552	9	3
2554	9	3
2556	9	3
2558	9	3
2560	9	3
2562	9	3
2564	9	3
2566	9	3
2568	9	3
2570	9	3
2571	**10**	**4**
2572	9	3
2573	**10**	**4**
2574	9	3
2575	**10**	**4**
2576	9	3
2577	**10**	**4**
2578	9	3
2579	**10**	**4**
2580	9	3
2581	**10**	**4**
2582	9	3
2583	**10**	**4**
2584	9	3
2585	**10**	**4**
2586	9	3
2588	9	3
2590	9	3
2592	9	3
2594	**9**	**3**
2596	**9**	**3**
2598	9	3
2600	9	3
2601	10	4
2602	**9**	**3**
2603	10	4
2604	**9**	**4**
2605	10	4
2606	9	4
2607	**10**	**4**
2608	9	4
2609	**10**	**4**
2610	9	4
2611	10	4
2612	9	4
2614	9	4
2616	9	4
2618	9	4
2620	9	4
2622	**9**	**4**
2624	**9**	**4**
2626	9	4
2628	9	4
2629	10	4
2630	9	4
2631	10	4
2632	9	4
2633	10	4
2635	**10**	**4**
2637	**10**	**4**

Room #	Cat.	Sleeps
2638	**9**	**4**
2639	10	4
2640	**9**	**4**
2641	10	4
2642	9	4
2643	**10**	**4**
2644	9	4
2645	**10**	**4**
2646	**9**	**4**
2647	10	4
2648	**9**	**4**
2650	9	4
2652	9	4
2653	10	4
Deck 5		
5000	8	4
5001	11	4
5002	8	4
5004	8	4
5005	11	4
5006	8	4
5008	8	4
5009	11	4
5010	8	4
5012	8	4
5013	11	4
5014	8	4
5016	8	4
5018	8	4
5020	10	4
5022	**10**	**4**
5024	**10**	**4**
5122	6	3
5124	6	3
5126	6	3
5127	11	3
5128	6	3
5129	11	3
5130	6	3
5131	11	3
5132	7	3
5133	11	3
5134	7	3
5135	11	3
5136	7	3
5137	11	3
5138	7	3
5139	11	3
5140	7	3
5142	6	3
5144	6	3
5146	6	3
5148	6	3
5150	6	3
5500	8	4
5501	11	4
5502	8	4
5504	8	4
5505	11	4
5506	8	4
5508	8	4
5509	11	4
5510	8	4
5512	8	4
5513	11	4

Room #	Cat.	Sleeps
5514	8	4
5516	8	4
5518	8	4
5520	10	4
5522	**10**	**4**
5524	**10**	**4**
5622	6	3
5624	6	3
5626	6	3
5627	11	3
5628	6	3
5629	11	3
5630	6	3
5631	11	3
5632	7	3
5633	11	3
5634	7	3
5635	11	3
5636	7	3
5637	11	3
5638	7	3
5639	11	3
5640	7	3
5642	6	3
5644	6	3
5646	6	3
5648	6	3
5650	6	3
Deck 6		
6000	8	2H
6002	11	4
6003	11	3
6004	11	4
6006	8	4
6007	11	3
6008	8	4
6010	8	4
6011	11	3
6012	8	4
6014	8	4
6015	11	3
6016	**8**	**4**
6018	**8**	**3/4**
6019	11	3
6020	8	4
6022	8	4
6024	**8**	**4**
6026	**8**	**4**
6028	**6**	**4**
6030	**6**	**4**
6032	6	4
6034	6	4
6036	**6**	**4**
6037	11	4
6038	**6**	**3/4**
6039	11	4
6040	6	4
6041	11	4
6042	6	4
6043	11	4
6044	**6**	**4**
6045	11	4
6046	**6**	**3/4**
6047	11	4
6048	6	4

For recent updates to this chart, visit http://www.passporter.com/dcl/stateroomdetailchart.htm

Room #	Cat.	Sleeps
Deck 6 (continued)		
6049	11	4
6050	6	4
6051	11	4
6052	**6**	**4**
6053	11	4
6054	**6**	**4**
6055	11	4
6056	6	4
6058	6	4
6060	6	4
6062	6	4
6064	**6**	**4**
6066	**6**	**4**
6067	11	4
6068	**6**	**4**
6069	11	4
6070	**6**	**3/4**
6071	11	4
6072	**6**	**3**
6074	**6**	**3/4**
6076	6	3
6078	6	3
6080	6	3
6081	11	4
6082	6	3
6083	11	3/4
6084	6	3
6085	11	3
6086	6	3
6087	11	3/4
6088	6	3
6089	11	3
6090	6	3
6092	6	3
6094	6	3
6096	6	3
6098	6	3
6099	11	4
6100	**6**	**3/4**
6101	11	4
6102	**6**	**3/4**
6103	11	4
6104	**6**	**3**
6105	11	4
6106	**6**	**4**
6107	11	4
6108	6	4
6109	11	4
6110	6	4
6111	11	4
6112	**6**	**4**
6113	11	4
6114	**6**	**4**
6116	6	4
6118	6	4
6120	**6**	**4**
6122	**6**	**4**
6124	6	3
6126	6	3
6128	6	3
6130	6	3
6131	11	3
6132	6	3
6133	11	3
6134	7	3
6135	11	3
6136	7	3
6137	11	3
6138	7	3
6139	11	3
6140	**7**	**3**
6141	11	3
6142	**7**	**3**
6143	11	3
6144	6	3
6145	11	3
6146	6	3
6147	11	3H
6148	6	3
6150	6	3
6152	6	3
6154	6	3H
6303	11	3
6305	11	3
6307	11	3
6309	11	3
6311	11	3
6313	11	3
6315	11	3
6317	11	3
6319	11	3
6321	11	3
6323	11	3
6500	8	2H
6502	11	4
6503	11	3
6504	11	3
6506	8	4
6507	11	3/4
6508	8	4
6510	8	4
6511	11	3
6512	8	4
6514	8	4
6515	11	3
6516	**8**	**4**
6518	**8**	**4**
6520	8	4
6521	11	3
6522	8	4
6524	**8**	**4**
6526	**8**	**4**
6528	**6**	**4**
6530	**6**	**4**
6532	6	4
6534	6	4
6536	**6**	**4**
6537	11	4
6538	**6**	**4**
6539	11	4
6540	6	4
6541	11	4
6542	6	4
6543	11	4
6544	**6**	**4**
6545	11	4
6546	**6**	**3/4**
6547	11	4
6548	6	4
6549	11	4
6550	6	4
6551	11	4
6552	**6**	**4**
6553	11	4
6554	**6**	**4**
6555	11	4
6556	6	4
6558	6	4
6560	6	4
6562	6	4
6564	**6**	**4**
6566	**6**	**3/4**
6567	11	4
6568	**6**	**4**
6569	11	4
6570	**6**	**3/4**
6571	11	4
6572	**6**	**3**
6574	**6**	**3**
6576	6	3
6578	6	3
6580	6	3
6581	11	4
6582	6	3
6583	11	3
6584	6	3
6585	11	3
6586	6	3
6587	11	3
6588	6	3
6590	6	3
6592	6	3
6594	6	3
6596	6	3
6598	6	3
6599	11	4
6600	**6**	**3**
6601	11	4
6602	**6**	**3/4**
6603	11	4
6604	**6**	**3/4**
6605	11	4
6606	**6**	**4**
6607	11	4
6608	6	4
6609	11	4
6610	6	4
6611	11	4
6612	**6**	**4**
6613	11	4
6614	**6**	**4**
6616	6	4
6618	6	4
6620	**6**	**4**
6622	**6**	**4**
6624	6	3
6626	6	3
6628	6	3
6630	6	3
6631	11	3
6632	6	3
6633	11	3
6634	7	3
6635	11	3
6636	7	3
6637	11	3
6638	7	3
6639	11	3
6640	**7**	**3**
6641	11	3
6642	**7**	**3**
6643	11	3
6644	6	3
6645	11	3
6646	6	3
6647	11	3H
6648	6	3
6650	6	3
6652	6	3
6654	6	3H
Deck 7		
7000	8	4
7001	10	4
7002	8	4
7003	10	4
7004	**8**	**4**
7005	**10**	**4**
7006	**8**	**3/4**
7007	**10**	**4**
7008	8	4
7009	11	3
7010	8	4
7012	8	4
7014	8	4
7016	**5**	**4**
7018	**5**	**4**
7020	5	4
7022	5	4
7024	5	4
7026	5	4
7028	**5**	**4**
7030	**5**	**3/4**
7032	5	4
7034	5	4
7035	11	4
7036	5	4
7037	11	4
7038	5	4
7039	11	4
7040	**5**	**4**
7041	11	4
7042	**5**	**4**
7043	11	4
7044	5	4
7046	5	4
7048	5	4
7050	5	4
7052	5	4
7054	5	4
7056	5	4
7058	5	4
7060	5	4
7062	5	4
7063	11	4
7064	5	4
7065	11	4
7066	5	3
7067	11	3
7068	5	3
7070	5	3
7072	5	3
7074	5	4
7076	5	4
7078	5	4
7080	**5**	**4**
7082	**5**	**3/4**
7084	5	4
7086	5	4
7088	**5**	**4**
7090	**5**	**4**
7092	5	4
7094	5	4
7096	5	4
7098	5	4
7100	**5**	**4**
7102	**5**	**4**
7104	5	4
7106	5	4
7108	**5**	**4**
7110	**5**	**4**
7112	5	3
7114	5	3
7116	5	3
7118	5	3
7119	11	3
7120	7	3
7121	11	3
7122	7	3
7123	11	3
7124	7	3
7125	11	3
7126	7	3
7127	11	3
7128	7	3
7129	11	3
7130	5	3
7131	11	3H
7132	5	3
7134	5	3
7136	5	4H
7138	5	4H
7500	8	4
7501	10	4
7502	8	4
7503	10	4
7504	**8**	**3/4**
7505	**10**	**4**
7506	**8**	**3/4**
7507	**10**	**4**
7508	8	4
7509	10	4
7510	8	4
7512	8	4
7514	8	4
7516	**5**	**4**
7518	**5**	**4**
7520	5	4
7522	5	4
7524	5	4
7526	5	4
7528	**5**	**4**
7530	**5**	**3/4**
7532	5	4
7534	5	4
7535	11	4
7536	5	4
7537	11	4
7538	5	4
7539	11	4
7540	**5**	**4**
7541	11	4
7542	**5**	**3/4**
7543	11	4
7544	5	4
7546	5	4
7548	5	4
7550	5	4
7552	5	4
7554	5	4
7556	5	4
7558	5	4
7560	5	4
7562	5	4
7563	11	3
7564	5	4
7565	11	4
7566	5	3
7567	11	3
7568	5	3
7570	5	3
7572	5	3
7574	5	4
7576	5	4
7578	5	4
7580	**5**	**4**
7582	**5**	**3/4**
7584	5	4
7586	5	4
7588	**5**	**4**
7590	**5**	**4**
7592	5	4
7594	5	4
7596	5	4
7598	5	4
7600	**5**	**4**
7602	**5**	**4**
7604	5	4
7606	5	4
7608	**5**	**4**
7610	**5**	**4**
7612	5	3
7614	5	3
7616	5	3
7618	5	3
7619	11	3
7620	7	3
7621	11	3
7622	7	3
7623	11	3
7624	7	3
7625	11	3
7626	7	3
7627	11	3
7628	7	3
7629	11	3
7630	5	3
7631	11	3H
7632	5	3
7634	5	3
7636	5	4H
7638	5	4H
Deck 8		
8000	4	5
8002	4	5
8004	**4**	**5**
8006	**4**	**4**
8008	4	5
8010	4	5
8012	4	5
8014	4	5
8016	2	7
8018	4	5
8020	4	5
8022	**3**	**5**
8024	**4**	**4**
8026	4	5
8028	4	5
8030	1	7
8032	**3**	**5**
8034	**3**	**5**
8036	4	5
8038	4	5
8040	4	5
8042	4	5
8044	4	5
8046	3	5
8048	3	5
8050	4	5
8052	4	5
8054	4	5
8056	4	5
8058	4	5
8060	4	5
8062	4	5
8064	4	5
8066	4	5
8068	**4**	**5**
8070	**4**	**5**
8072	4	5
8074	4	5
8076	4	5
8078	3	5
8080	**3**	**5**
8082	**4**	**5**
8084	4	5
8086	3	5
8088	4	5
8090	**4**	**5**
8092	**4**	**5**
8094	4	5
8100	**3**	**4H**
8102	**3**	**4H**
8500	4	5
8502	4	5
8504	**4**	**5**
8506	**4**	**5**
8508	4	5
8510	4	5
8512	4	5
8514	4	5
8516	2	7
8518	4	5
8520	4	5
8522	**3**	**5**
8524	**4**	**5**
8526	4	5
8528	4	5
8530	1	7
8532	**3**	**5**
8534	**3**	**5**
8536	4	5
8538	4	5
8540	4	5
8542	4	5
8544	4	5
8546	3	5
8548	3	5
8550	4	5
8552	4	5
8554	4	5
8556	4	5
8558	4	5
8560	4	5
8562	4	5
8564	4	5
8566	4	5
8568	**4**	**5**
8570	**4**	**5**
8572	4	5
8574	4	5
8576	4	5
8578	4	5
8580	4	5
8582	**3**	**5**
8584	**4**	**5**
8586	4	5
8588	4	5
8590	4	5
8592	4	5
8594	**4**	**5**
8596	**4**	**5**
8598	4	5
8600	**3**	**4H**
8602	**3**	**4H**

Rocking to Sleep

Sleeping on a moving vessel can be a magical experience. Make more magic in your stateroom with these tips:

- "If you are **prone to motion/sea sickness**, the best stateroom location for you is on a lower deck in the middle of the ship, midway between the bow and the stern. Pitch, roll, and yaw—the movements made by a ship—will be less noticeable than in other ship areas."
  – contributed by Disney cruiser Angie J.

- Bring something from home to **personalize your stateroom**, like a photo in a frame, a bouquet of silk flowers, or a radio or CD player. You can also decorate your stateroom door (see page 264).

- **Make every bit of space count!** After you unpack, stash your empty luggage under the bed and use one (or more) bags for your dirty laundry and another for souvenirs.

- Consider bringing a **clear shoe organizer** and hanging it up in your closet or on the back of your bathroom door. It keeps all those little items that can clutter your stateroom organized.

- "I found a **hanging mesh laundry bag** at Linens & Things before our trip. The bag hooked over the clothes rod in our stateroom closet, just over the safe. It came folded flat and small (maybe 5" x 5") and then popped open into a large mesh bag with a metal ring built in to keep it open when hanging. It was great to just throw dirty laundry in there during the cruise. The bag also made it easy to repack all the dirty stuff into one suitcase on the last night of the cruise, leaving the clean clothes for a separate bag."
  – contributed by Disney cruiser Jeanne Sacks

Magical Memory

- *"We had a group of seven on our cruise to celebrate a college and 8th grade graduation. We booked one category 5 and two category 11 staterooms, which were across the hall from each other. To make our rooms more festive, I ordered inflatable parrots and flamingos from Oriental Trading catalog—they pack so nice deflated! After we boarded, I went into all the staterooms and hung the inflatables with chenille stems from various parts of the staterooms. We also had magnetic message boards on our front doors where we left messages of where we could be located for each other. On the night of Pirates in the Caribbean party, everyone drew pirates on their boards, writing things such as "Out doing pirate things" and "Happiness is being a pirate." We loved that last one so much we never erased it and brought it home with the message still intact to remind us of what fun we had."*

...as told by Disney cruiser Joan Welch

LEARN
the basics of
rotation
dining
DECIDE
how and
when to
dress for
dinner

Dining on the High Seas

FIND
your
dining
options
EXPLORE
the various
restaurant
menus

Cruises are famous for food—buffet breakfasts, brunches, snacks, pool-side lunches, high tea, elegant dinners, dessert buffets, and room service! You won't be disappointed by the food on the Disney Cruise Line. Sure, there's plenty of it—we like to say, "If you're hungry, you're not trying hard enough." More important, in our opinion, is the quality of the food. As restaurant critics, we pay attention to food—presentation, preparation, quality, and taste. We would grade virtually every dish we tried during our cruises as a B or B+. There were some disappointments, sure, but in general we've been very happy cruisers with no rumblies in our tummies.

In all fairness, we have heard a few complaints about the food from other cruisers. Some feel there should be even more food offered, like on some other cruise lines. (Our poor waistlines!) Others feel the food options are too exotic for their tastes (and Disney has since added some simpler choices to the menus). Yet others say the food isn't as "gourmet" as some European lines. Most cruisers, however, rave about the food onboard.

Dining options abound during your cruise. For **breakfast**, try room service (available for virtually all meals, plus snacks—see page 117), Topsider's/Beach Blanket Buffet (page 112), Lumière's/Triton's (pages 103–104), Parrot Cay (pages 107–108), or Palo's Champagne Brunch (pages 109–110). For **lunch**, try Topsider's/Beach Blanket Buffet (page 112), Pluto's Dog House (page 113), Pinocchio's Pizzeria (page 113), Lumière's/Triton's (pages 103–104), or Parrot Cay (pages 107–108). For **snacks**, try Goofy's Galley on the Magic or Scoops and Fruit Station on the Wonder (page 113), Pluto's Dog House (page 113), or Pinocchio's Pizzeria (page 113). For **dinner**, you may eat in Lumière's/Triton's (pages 103–104), Animator's Palate (pages 105–106), Parrot Cay (pages 107–108), and Palo (pages 109–110). Topsider's/Beach Blanket Buffet (page 112) may also be open for dinner. Theme dinners and dessert buffets are held on special nights (see page 104 and 111). Whew! Read on to learn about Disney's innovative dining rotations and your delicious choices.

Bon appetit!

Introduction | Reservations | Staterooms | Dining | Activities | Ports of Call | Magic | Index

Rotation Dining

Unlike other ships that stick you in one dining room throughout your cruise, the Disney ships offer **three uniquely themed dining rooms** for all. Your family rotates together through these dining rooms during your cruise, enjoying a different menu each evening. Best of all, your tablemates and servers rotate with you. You can bypass the regular rotation and choose an adults-only restaurant, one of several snack counters, or room service—a buffet restaurant may also be open. You'll find it hard to do them all!

You learn your **dining room rotation** on your first day—look for a set of "tickets" in your stateroom indicating which dining rooms your party is assigned to for dinner on each day. The tickets are not required to dine, but they do help the servers direct you to your table. To learn your dining rotation a bit earlier, check your Key to the World card for a code (i.e., "APT," "PPTA," or "LAPLAPL"), like the one on page 68. This code indicates your rotation: L or T = Lumière's/Triton's, A = Animator's Palate, and P = Parrot Cay. Your rotation is sometimes based on the ages of guests in your party. On the first night, you'll may find more kids in Animator's Palate, families in Parrot Cay, and adults in Lumière's/Triton's. Rotation dining only applies to dinner and breakfast on debarkation day—see page 107 for breakfast and lunch.

There are **two dinner seatings**: main (first) seating and late (second) seating. Your seating is noted in your cruise documents. Main seating is typically at 5:30 pm, 5:45 pm, 6:00 pm, or 6:15 pm. Late seating is at 8:00 pm, 8:15 pm, or 8:30 pm. Check your dining tickets for your assigned time, which will remain constant during your cruise. Dinner takes from 1 ½ to 2 hours to complete. Guests with main seating watch the evening show after dinner, while guests with late seating see the show first. If you have a seating preference (see page 119 for tips), have it noted on your reservation prior to cruising. Parties with kids tend to get assigned the early seating.

Your **assigned table number** is printed on your dinner tickets and your Key to the World card. Your party has the same table number at dinner in all three of the main dining rooms. Like the dining room assignment, table assignments are determined by factors like age and association (i.e., Disney Vacation Club members may be seated together); your stateroom category does not affect your table assignment. You can request to be seated with your traveling companions—call the Disney Cruise Line well ahead of your departure date and have it noted on your reservation. Table sizes range from four to twenty guests, though most tables seat eight guests. If you want to switch to another table or feel uncomfortable with your assigned tablemates, check your *Personal Navigator* for a Dining Assignment Change session (held on your first afternoon) or see your head server.

Dressing for Dinner

"How should I dress for dinner?" If we had a nickel for everyone who asked! Whether you itch to relive the elegance of days gone by, or can't stand the thought of being bound into a "penguin suit," you'll find a happy welcome on your Disney cruise. Different itineraries call for slightly different wardrobes, as we describe below, and once you're aboard, you can also refer to your Personal Navigator for the evening's suggested dress.

In keeping with its **guest-friendly policies**, Disney doesn't strictly enforce dress codes for the most part. They won't deny you access if you don't have a jacket, though they will ask you to put on shoes or a shirt. Disney requests that you wear shoes and shirts and refrain from wearing bathing attire in the dining rooms. You should also refrain from wearing shorts at dinner, though even jeans are acceptable now everywhere but at Palo and formal night.

Three- and Four-Night Itineraries—In Lumière's/Triton's, Animator's Palate, and Parrot Cay in the evening, men wear casual, open-collared shirts (such as polo or camp shirts) and slacks (such as khakis or Dockers), and women wear a blouse and skirt or casual dress. In the elegant setting of Palo, jackets and ties are preferred for men, and the ladies are encouraged to don dresses or pantsuits.

Seven-Night and up Itineraries—Dress code for longer itineraries is the same as for the three- and four-night cruises with the exception of the formal nights. There is one formal and one semi-formal night on the seven-night itineraries—see page 262 for details and tips on formal nights.

All Itineraries—On at least one evening, Disney suggests Pirate or Caribbean style dress for its Pirates of the Caribbean night (see page 111). You'll probably find it easiest to dress in a tropical shirt or dress. If you really want to get into the spirit of the occasion, try picking up Pirate gear at one of the parks before your cruise. Other things you could do include eyepatches, temporary tattoos, or a costume like Captain Hook.

The Disney Cruise Line requests that guests dress for dinner because they are trying to set a **special atmosphere** in the evenings. The Disney Magic and the Disney Wonder are elegant ships—dressing for dinner shows respect for the occasion, the atmosphere, and your fellow guests. We understand that some guests aren't comfortable in a jacket or suit, and that's okay, too—you'll see a wide range of dress, even on formal night. Don't want to change out of those shorts? Snacks are available on deck 9 (see Casual Dining on page 113). Topsider's Buffet (deck 9 aft) on the Magic may be open for an early dinner on some evenings (never the first or last nights) for those guests who don't wish to get dressed up.

Special Diets

Guests with **special dietary requirements** of virtually any type (i.e., kosher, low-sodium, allergies, etc.) are accommodated. When you make your reservation, let the representative know about any requirements. The representative notes the information with your reservation and may instruct you to meet with the Food/Beverage team after you board—they are usually available in Sessions/Cadillac's (deck 3 fwd) from 12:00 pm to 3:30 pm on your first day—check your *Personal Navigator*. The Food/Beverage team gets details from you and passes it on to your servers. We recommend you remind your server of your requests at your first meal. Jennifer is lactose-intolerant and requests soy milk with her meals—the attention to her request is impressive and she is always offered soy milk.

While Disney excels at these special, pre-cruise requests, we found it **more difficult to get a special dish or variant** ordered at meal time. For example, it generally isn't possible to order a dish from the menu and have sauces or dressings kept on the side. This is because the dishes are prepared *en masse* in the kitchen. However, you can order a plain salad or simple entrée (vegetarian, grilled chicken, etc.) without the highfalutin' extras—ask your server. We note the vegetarian items in the menus later in the chapter. Kosher is only available in the table-service restaurants.

Will I Gain Weight on My Cruise?

Short answer: No, you don't have to gain weight on your Disney cruise! Long answer: Cruises are renowned for their ability to add inches to your waistline. All that scrumptious, "free" food can send your diet overboard. But if you're determined to maintain your weight and healthy eating habits, it's not at all difficult to do. Your authors successfully maintain their weight on cruises while still enjoying treats. The first key is **moderation**. Eat well—don't restrict yourself too severely and don't overeat. Not only is it okay to sample a little of everything, it's a good idea—if you deny yourself, you'll likely break down halfway through your cruise and eat everything in sight. Remember that just because the food is included with your cruise doesn't mean you have to overindulge. If the temptation seems too great, grab some of the delicious fruit available at Scoops (deck 9 aft). If you just can't resist that chocolate ice cream cone, order one, eat half, and ditch the rest. You'll also find that buffet meals may actually be easier for you—there are more food choices. The second key to maintaining your weight is **activity**. Most of you will be more active than usual on your cruise—swimming, snorkeling, biking, and walking around the ports. Take advantage of every opportunity to move your body! You can walk a mile every morning around deck 4 (it takes four laps), take the stairs instead of the elevator, and enjoy free exercise classes at the Vista Spa (deck 9 forward). Check your *Personal Navigator* for a session at the Vista Spa that shows you how to lose weight on your cruise, too.

For more tips, surf to: http://www.passporter.com/wdw/healthyeating.htm

Lumière's/Triton's

Have you ever yearned to dine elegantly in a gorgeous, grand dining room aboard a majestic ocean liner? This is your chance. On the Disney Magic, the grandest dining room is known as Lumière's; on the Disney Wonder, it's called Triton's. Both are located next to the ships' breathtaking lobby atriums on deck 3 midship and serve breakfast, lunch, and dinner. Breakfast and lunch have open seating—just show up when and where you like.

Decor—Lumière's (Magic) has a decidedly French flair, just like its namesake, the saucy candelabra in Disney's *Beauty and the Beast*. Rose-petal chandeliers, inlaid marble floors, and graceful columns set the mood for elegance and romance. Large portholes look out to the sea on one side of the restaurant. A mural depicting a waltzing Beauty and her Beast adorns the back wall. Look for the glass domes suspended from the ceiling—inside each is Beast's red rose. Triton's (Wonder) takes you "under the sea" with Ariel's father from Disney's *The Little Mermaid*. The Art Nouveau-inspired dining room is decorated in soft colors with blue glass-and-iron "lilypads" floating on the ceiling. A breathtaking Italian glass mosaic of Triton and Ariel graces the back wall. The lighting changes during the dinner, casting an "under the sea" effect.

Dinner Dress—Unless the evening is formal, semi-formal, or "pirate" (see 101 and 262), dress is upscale casual: jackets are appropriate (but not required) for men and dresses/pantsuits for women. No shorts, please.

Our Review—The very elegant surroundings are the restaurants' best feature. These are the only restaurants offering full table service at breakfast and lunch. The extra attention and elegance at dinner is a treat. Breakfast here is good, but service is slow and the selection is more limited than at Parrot Cay or at Topsider's/Beach Blanket Buffet. Lunch is enjoyable, though portions may be a bit smaller than you'd expect. Dinner is very elegant and the food is finely prepared. We highly recommend this restaurant over Parrot Cay and Animator's Palate. Jennifer and Dave's rating: 8/10.

Chatting with Chef Levi at Triton's

Lumière's/Triton's Sample Menus

While we can't predict exactly what you'll be offered at Lumière's or Triton's, we can share the menus from past cruises. Below are typical breakfast, lunch, and dinner menus. We've underlined those menu items we and our fellow cruisers have enjoyed and recommend that you try.

Breakfast at Lumière's/Triton's *(menu does not change day-to-day)*
chilled juices (orange, grapefruit, cranberry, prune, V-8, apple, tomato); **fresh fruit** (grapefruit, melon, banana, fruit cocktail); **yogurt** (fruit and plain yogurt, assorted low-fat yogurt); **hot cereal** (oatmeal, Cream of Wheat); **cold cereal** (Corn Flakes, Raisin Bran, KO's, Rice Krispies, Frosted Flakes, low-fat granola, Froot Loops); **Mueslix** (mixture of toasted whole grain flakes, sun-dried raisins, dates, almonds, and brown sugar); **lox and bagel** (served with cream cheese); **pastries** (Danish pastries, muffins, croissants, bagels, donuts, English muffins, toast—white, wheat, or rye); **preserves** (assorted jellies, jams, marmalades); **Express Breakfast** (scrambled eggs, bacon, link sausage, oven-roasted potatoes); **Eggs Benedict**, **eggs to order** (scrambled, fried, poached, or boiled—with oven-roasted potatoes and your choice of breakfast meat: link sausage, grilled ham, or bacon); **omelets** (Denver, ham and cheese, plain, Egg Beaters—with oven-roasted potatoes); **hot off the griddle** (buttermilk pancakes, blueberry pancakes, French toast, waffles); **daily skillets** (American beef hash with fried eggs, scrambled eggs and smoked salmon, or creamed chicken with biscuit); **beverages** (coffee—regular or decaf, assorted teas, hot chocolate, milk—whole, low-fat, skim, or chocolate).

Lunch at Lumière's/Triton's *(menu changes daily)*
starters (shrimp cocktail, chips and salsa, roasted vegetable tart, hummus "chickpea" dip, curried pumpkin soup, mixed greens and arugula, or niçoise salad); **main courses** (mushroom risotto, classic Reuben sandwich, traditional American meatloaf; broiled filet of tilapia, roasted chicken, or traditional hamburger); **desserts** (banana cream pie, carmelized rice pudding, double chocolate cake, key lime pie, or chef's sugar-free dessert).

Dinner at Lumière's/Triton's *(for your first rotational visit only)*
appetizers (deep-fried camembert fritters, shrimp medley, pearls of seasonal melon, baked escargot); **soups and salads** (cauliflower soup, chilled vichyssoise soup, mixed garden salad, tossed field greens, Boston bib lettuce); **main courses** (rigatoni pasta, garlic-roasted beef tenderloin, herb-crusted prime fillet of cod, braised lamb shank, roasted duck breast, sirloin steak, grilled chicken breast, salmon steak, or vegetarian selections—potato and cauliflower curry and stack of vegetables); **desserts** (apple tart, cherries jubilee, Grand Marnier souffle, crème brûlée, white chocolate domes, ice cream sundae, or sugar-free dessert—seasonal fruits, chocolate cheesecake, or sugar-free ice cream).

Tip: No matter where you dine, you can request a simpler, off-menu item like steak, roasted or grilled chicken, or plain broiled fish.

Dessert Buffets
You've saved room for dessert, right? On select nights of your cruise (any length), a fruit and dessert spread of monumental proportions is laid out for your gastronomic pleasure. Check your *Personal Navigator* for days, times, and locations. A "midnight" dessert buffet is generally held from 11:00 pm to midnight on deck 9 on one night of most cruises. The seven-night cruises may feature a Gala Dessert Buffet in Lumière's, typically held from 11:30 pm to 12:30 am on an at-sea day. The line can get long at the dessert buffets—to avoid a long wait, arrive just as it begins. Desserts vary, but typical treats include crepes, cheesecakes, tortes, pies, cookies, and pastries.

Animator's Palate

Disney's true colors shine in this imaginative, $4.3 million restaurant. Animator's Palate—which serves dinner only—is located on deck 4 aft.

Decor—Entering the large, windowless restaurant feels a bit like walking into a black-and-white sketchpad. The tables and chairs are black and white, and the walls are covered in line drawings of classic Disney animated characters. Where's all the color? Don't worry—it's coming, along with your food. As each course is served, color is added to the walls and ceilings, and the characters come to life in full color. There's a colorful surprise at the end, but we won't give it away. This production is limited to the first, second, and third nights; on subsequent evenings, the room remains black and white (this is a good time to visit Palo—see page 109).

Dress—Unless the evening is formal, semi-formal, or "pirate" (see page 101 and 262), dress is resort casual. Polo and camp shirts are fine, but please don't wear shorts in this dining room.

Animator's Palate on formal night

Our Review—Animator's Palate is a fun place for all ages. The "show" is breathtaking and food is decent. Inventive dishes have an Italian flavor and offer enough choices to please most. Service is fine, though you may feel rushed or stymied as servers need to keep pace with the show. When you arrive at the table, try to pick a seat with a view of one of the video screens on the walls. Jennifer and Dave's rating: 7/10.

Dining Room Etiquette

Don't worry—thanks to Disney's family atmosphere, there's no finicky, starched-up rule of etiquette here. Just remember to arrive on time for dinner, greet your tablemates and servers with a smile, place your napkin in your lap, and have your meal and beverage orders ready for your servers. If the elegant table confuses you, keep in mind that your bread plate is always on the left, your glasses are always on the right, utensils are used from the outside in, and wine glasses are held by the stem for white wine and by the base for red wine. When you get up from the table before you've finished eating, place your napkin on your chair to indicate you will be returning again. At the end of your meal, place your unfolded napkin on the table.

Animator's Palate Sample Menu

Dinner at Animator's Palate *(for your first rotational visit only)*

appetizers (seafood and avocado wrapper, duck and goat cheese flatbread, smoked salmon, baked stuffed tomato); **soups and salads** (chilled gazpacho, creamy butternut squash soup, confetti tomato salad, Caesar salad, Boston bib lettuce); **main courses** (cheese cannelloni, maple-glazed salmon, pan-fried veal chop, roasted chicken breast, grilled sirloin, sirloin steak, grilled chicken breast, salmon steak, or vegetarian selection—vegetable curry, pasta marinara); **desserts** (strawberry shortcake, Boston cream pie, New York-style cheesecake, double-fudge chocolate dessert, ice cream sundae, or sugar-free dessert—seasonal fruits, pound cake, or sugar-free ice cream).

An Armchair Galley Tour

Ever wonder how they prepare all this food and for so many people? Cruisers on itineraries with at-sea days (four-night and up) usually have the opportunity to take a galley (kitchen) tour. The 30-minute walking tour starts in Lumiere's/Triton's, walks through the galley, and ends up on the other side at Parrot Cay. If you won't have the opportunity to experience this behind-the-scenes glimpse into the inner workings of the Disney Cruise Line, here's a short, armchair version of the galley tour!

The Disney Cruise Line galleys are big, immaculately clean, stainless steel kitchens that gleam with organization. There are six galleys onboard—three main banqueting kitchens, a crew kitchen, Topsider's/Beach Blanket Buffet, and Palo. In these galleys are 9 chefs, 120 cooks, 88 stewards, 12 provision masters, and 150 servers and assistant servers. Galleys are inspected constantly for cleanliness, safety, and temperature requirements—the Captain himself performs inspections. Disney has a shopping list of 30,000 food items for each cruise! When you consider that more than 8,000 cups of coffee and more than 5,000 eggs are served every day, you can imagine how big that grocery bill must be! And all food for your voyage is brought on in your embarkation port—the cruise line is not allowed to take food on in other ports due to FDA regulations.

The first thing you see upon entering the galley are the beverage dispensers—this is how your servers get your drink refills so quickly. Then comes the kids food station—it's separated from other food prep areas to allow servers to get kids meals out to the hungry munchkins as soon as possible.

Next we come to the hot food preparation areas of the galley. Did you know that nothing is prepared ahead of time (with the exception of some veggies)? There's a butcher room with four cooks and a fish room with two cooks below decks where the meats are prepared and portioned. The meats are then sent up to the galley to be seasoned and cooked based on each guest's preferences. Once cooked, the plates are cleaned and garnished based on photographs of how each dish should appear (and below each photograph is a list of the dish's ingredients, allowing the servers to spot potential allergens for guests). The servers then come in to pick up the various plates they "ordered" earlier, covering each dish with a warming lid to keep it toasty during its trip to your table. It's quite a production that goes on behind the scenes.

Beyond the hot food prep areas is the pastry prep area. There are four pastry chefs onboard. There's even a 24-hour bakery below decks that keeps churning out fresh baked goods throughout your cruise. And the tour comes to a sweet ending with a chocolate chip cookie for everyone!

© MediaMarx, Inc.

A pastry chef at work

Parrot Cay

This breezy, island-inspired restaurant is the most casual of the three main dining rooms. Parrot Cay (pronounced "key") is on deck 3 aft. The restaurant serves breakfast (buffet and character) and lunch, plus dinner with a grillhouse flair. The buffet breakfast and lunch have open seating.

Decor—The first thing you may notice is the sound of parrots—they're not real, but they sound like it as you walk through the breezeway and into the restaurant. Inside is a cacophony of colors and sounds, with parrot chandeliers that evoke the Enchanted Tiki Room at Disney's theme parks and lush tropical greens and oranges on the walls and floors. Large portholes line two sides of the restaurant, affording beautiful views.

Dinner Dress—Unless the evening is formal , semi-formal, or "pirate" (see page 101 and 262), dress is resort casual. No shorts at dinner.

Our Review—The grillhouse-inspired menu here is very good and a vast improvement over the old menu. Breakfast and lunch are buffet-style, which just doesn't afford the same elegance you get in Lumière's/Triton's. The food is great, with some stand-out items, and the food variety at the buffet is generous. Most outstanding still, there always seems to be one or two delightful surprises for adventurous diners. They do a good job of keeping the buffet fresh and appealing. A "show" by the servers livens things up at dinner. Alas, Parrot Cay is the noisiest dining room. Jennifer and Dave's rating: 7/10. (This is often the restaurant we skip for Palo.)

© MediaMarx, Inc.

Jennifer enjoys the breakfast buffet at Parrot Cay

Open Seating at Breakfast and Lunch

Breakfast and lunch are usually open seating, meaning you dine where and when you please, and you don't sit at your assigned table—you are seated by a crew member. If you'd like your regular servers at breakfast or lunch, just ask to be seated at their table (if it's available and if they're on duty). Better yet, ask your servers at dinner where they are serving the following day and follow them to that restaurant.

Parrot Cay Sample Menus

Buffet Breakfast at Parrot Cay

You can usually find fresh fruit, cereals (hot and cold), yogurt, smoked salmon, assorted pastries, scrambled eggs, bacon, link sausage, ham, hash browns, pancakes, waffles, or French toast. A made-to-order omelet station is often available.

Character Breakfast at Parrot Cay *(seven-night cruises only; seating at 8:00 or 8:15 am for main seating guests and 9:30 or 9:45 am for those with late seating)*

Special Goofy combination plate for children (scrambled eggs, chocolate pancake, Mickey waffle, and Canadian bacon); **chilled juices** (orange, grapefruit, and cranberry); **fresh fruit and yogurt** (sliced fruit, grapefruit, plain and fruit yogurt, and low-fat yogurt); **cereals** (Cream of Wheat, Corn Flakes, Raisin Bran, KO's, Rice Krispie, and Frosted Flakes); **lox and bagel** (served with cream cheese); **pastries** (Danish pastries, muffins, croissants, donuts, and toast–white, wheat, or rye); **express breakfast** (scrambled eggs, bacon, link sausage, and hash browns); **breakfast classics** (scrambled or fried eggs served with hash browns and your choice of bacon, link sausage, or ham); **omelets** (plain or ham and cheese–served with hash browns, Egg Beaters available); **hot off the griddle** (buttermilk pancakes or blueberry pancakes); **beverages** (coffee–regular or decaf, assorted teas, hot chocolate, milk–whole, low-fat, skim, or chocolate); **preserves** (assorted jellies, jams, and marmalades).

Lunch Buffet at Parrot Cay

The buffet on the seven-night cruises changes daily: day one–welcome aboard buffet; day two–Italian buffet; day three–Asian buffet; day four–Mexican buffet; day five–American buffet; and day six–seafood buffet. On the Disney Wonder, brunch is served until noon on day two and, on the four-night itinerary with a sea day, the Oriental buffet is served on day three. On the last day, the menu that is offered at Cookie's BBQ on Castaway Cay is also offered at Parrot Cay onboard the ship (all itineraries).

Dinner at Parrot Cay *(for your first rotational visit only)*

appetizers (quinoa and grilled vegetables, spice island chicken wings, baked crab Martinique, trio of salmon); **soups and salads** (cold cream of mango and papaya soup, cream of sweet onion soup, Parrot Cay salad, mixed island greens, tropical style fruit salad); **main courses** (roasted rib-eye of beef, mixed grill, pan-seared grouper, Caribbean roast chicken, baby back pork ribs, sirloin steak, grilled chicken breast, salmon steak, or vegetarian selections–gnocchi au gratin with spinach or vegetable strudel); **desserts** (crème brûlée cheesecake, banana bread pudding, lemon meringue pie, chocolate-espresso walnut cake, ice cream sundae, or sugar-free dessert–fresh berries in Jello, cheesecake, or sugar-free ice cream)

Character Breakfast

Seven-night and up cruisers have a special treat–an invitation to a character breakfast in Parrot Cay (see menu above). Typically Mickey, Minnie, Goofy, Pluto, Chip, and Dale show up in tropical garb. Each character makes an effort to visit each table, and it's not uncommon for a Disney's photographer to snap your picture while Goofy gives you a hug. Expect lots of energy, napkin-waving, character dancing, and loud music. This character meal reminds us of Chef Mickey's at the Contemporary in Walt Disney World. Character breakfasts are offered at two seatings (guests with earlier seating at dinner will have the earlier seating at breakfast). If your dining rotation starts in Animator's Palate, your character breakfast will probably be Sunday morning (Lumière's=Monday morning and Parrot Cay=Thursday morning). Your server may present your tickets on the evening before, or they may be left in your stateroom–bring them with you to breakfast. Your character breakfast's date and time are noted on the tickets.

Palo

Palo is the adults-only restaurant offering Northern Italian cuisine, an intimate setting, phenomenal service, and a 270° view. Unlike the three main dining rooms, adults must secure reservations to dine here and there is a nominal, per-person service charge ($10 for dinner or brunch, $5 for high tea). Palo has its own servers, so be prepared to part with your regular servers for the meal. Palo is on deck 10 aft and serves dinner nightly from 6:00 pm until 9:00 or 10:00 pm. A wine tasting seminar may also be offered here (see page 149), as well as a champagne brunch (four-night and up cruises) and a high tea (seven-night and up cruises—see page 110).

Reservations—Reservations for all Palo meals can and should be made in advance at http://www.disneycruise.com once your cruise is paid in full. Palo reservations can be made from 2 to 70 days in advance for guests in stateroom categories 4–12, from 2 to 90 days in advance for Castaway Club members, and from 2 to 105 days in advance for concierge guests in stateroom categories 1–3 and guests who have reserved the Romantic Escape at Sea package (see page 43). Only one reservation per stateroom is allowed—we should note this policy may vary from cruise to cruise as some guests report being able to make a reservation for dinner, brunch, and tea while others (including ourselves) had to choose just one. While you may dine with guests from another stateroom by reserving a larger table size, Disney may have already associated you with your friends and may block your friends from making their own Palo reservation (this happened to us in August 2005). You may also make reservations and changes on your first afternoon aboard—check the *Personal Navigator* for the time and place. We recommend you send just one person from your party and arrive early—Palo reservations are extremely popular and they go quickly. Know the day(s) you prefer to dine at Palo before arriving (use our worksheet on page 121). Cancel at least six hours before your meal to avoid the charge. If you can't get reservations, get on the wait list and check for cancellations. Guests in suites (cat. 1–3) can ask their concierge to make reservations for them.

Decor—The most striking feature of Palo is its sweeping ocean views—we have fond memories of a meal served just as the sun set. Warm wood paneling, Venetian glass, and smaller tables (yes, you can get a table for two here!) make this the most romantic spot onboard. An exhibition kitchen and wine displays set the stage for a special dining experience. The restaurant also has a private room tucked in the corner for groups.

Dress—Men should wear jackets and ties; women should wear dresses or pantsuits. Formal attire is also welcome. No jeans (this rule is enforced).

Our Review—We simply adore Palo! The servers are friendly, engaging, and incredibly attentive. The restaurant itself is quiet and mellow. The best part of dining at Palo, however, is the food—it's simply outstanding, as items are made or finished to order. We also recommend brunch and high tea. While the service charge is intended to replace the gratuity, an extra tip may be justified. Jennifer and Dave's rating: 9/10.

© MediaMarx, Inc.

Jennifer and Dave dress up for Palo

Palo Sample Menus

Dinner at Palo *($10/person service charge; menu doesn't change on repeat visits, but the chefs do try to offer different specials each evening).*

pizzas (pizza prosciutto, pizza margherita, pizza lucana, pizza del lavante, or chef's specialty pizza of the day); **starters and salads** (grilled eggplant, buffalo mozzarella and plum tomatoes, warm shrimp salad, grilled portobello mushroom and polenta, lightly-fried calamari, or fresh mixed salad; **soup** (minestrone or traditional fish and seafood soup); **main courses** (grilled salmon, pan-fried tuna, rack of lamb, chicken breast, grilled filet mignon, tortelloni stuffed with crabmeat, penne arrabbiata, spaghetti capone, linguini carbonara, gnocchi fiorentina, seafood risotto, or wild mushroom risotto); **desserts** (tiramisu, chocolate and hazelnut soufflé with vanilla bean sauce, panna cotta, pistachio torte, sweet pizza, cappuccino cheesecake, or assorted gelato).

Special Meals at Palo

In addition to the nightly dinners, Palo hosts two special, adults-only events, primarily on the seven-night cruises. These popular events are by reservation only (see details on making reservations on previous page) and are generally held only on days at sea.

Champagne Brunch *($10/person charge) – also available on the 4-night cruise*
Buffet of assorted traditional breakfast and lunch items: **breakfast items** (cereals, breakfast breads, Danish pastries, specialty eggs, and pancakes); **lunch items** (shrimp, grilled marinated vegetables, Alaskan King Crab legs, smoked salmon & mixed greens, selection of cheeses and meats, pizzas, and garlic roasted tenderloin); and **desserts** (fresh fruit and berries, tiramisu, lemon meringue pie, and cappuccino mousse). One glass of champagne is complimentary, as is fresh-squeezed orange juice. (Tip: If you don't drink, ask for sparkling juice.) Champagne specialty drinks are available for $5.25.

High Tea *($5/person charge)*
traditional teas (Darjeeling, Yunnan Top Grade, Ceylon and Yalta, Lapsaung Souchong); **flavored teas** (California Fields and Black Currant); **herbal & caffeine free** (Chamomile Citrus, Rainforest Mint, African Nectar); **finger sandwiches** (cream cheese and cucumber, smoked salmon and sour cream, chicken and curry, and egg salad); **scones** (available with apricot jam, raspberry jam, or Devonshire cream); **desserts** (English trifle or chocolate eclairs). Specialty coffees, full bar, and extensive wine list also available.

Beverages at Dinner *(all restaurants)*

Don't be surprised if your server learns your drink preferences. We are always impressed when our server remembers what we like after our first dinner. Complimentary beverages include soda (fountain drinks), iced tea, juice, milk, coffee, tea, and tap water. Sparkling water (Perrier or San Pellegrino) is $3.50 for a large bottle. A full bar and wine list is available. If you need suggestions, each menu has a selection of specialty drinks/apéritifs ($4.75) and featured wines ($5.25-$8.25/glass). Each menu also features a themed drink, such as Lumière's French Flag (grenadine, créme de cacao, and blue curaçao), Animator's Palate's Black and White (Kahlúa and layered cream), and Parrot Cay's Island Kiss (Amaretto, Bailey's, and créme de cacao). Specialty drinks are also available without alcohol—just ask your server. If you're a wine drinker, you may be intersted in the wine package—see page 116.

Special Dining Themes and Menus

All Disney cruises offer at least one dining theme night, and the longer cruises add in several more. These theme nights have their own menus. and take place on different nights, depending upon your cruise length and destination. For tips on figuring out which night of your cruise you can expect these themed dinners, see pages 120–121. Here are the menus (as of January 2006) for each theme night:

Pirates of the Caribbean *(theme night all cruises; menu on 4+ night cruises)*
This recently added theme night is enjoyed by all Disney cruisers, and all but the three-night cruises have a special menu (guests on the three-night cruises have their regular rotational menu). The special menu is presented on a rolled "treasure map" and all diners are presented with glow-in-the-dark bandanas. For more information, see page 141: **appetizers** (Blackbeard's jumbo crab cake, cannon smoked barbecue chicken drumsticks, buccaneer's sun-ripened pineapple, or pearls of the Caribbean); **soups and salads** (chilled-to-the-bone honeydew melon and mango soup, Caribbean-style vegetable gumbo soup, Hideaway Bay salad, jerk chicken salad, or Mr. Smee's Bib Lettuce); **main courses** (treasure-of-the-seas grilled shrimp and seared scallops, Jack Sparrow's fruit marinated roasted loin of pork, Castaway Cay's chicken breast rubbed with pirate island spice, Captain Hook's coconut crusted oven-baked snapper, The Black Pearl's oven-roasted beef tenderloin, roasted chicken breast, grilled sirloin steak, baked salmon steak, or vegetarian selections–baked bell pepper or Tiger Lily's grilled eggplant); **desserts** (shiver-me-timbers white chocolate cheesecake, floating island of tropical fruit treasures, walk the triple layered chocolate gangplank cake, The Lost Boys treasure, The Calypso ice cream sundae, or sugar-free dessert).

Master Chef *(all 7+ night cruises)*
appetizers (shrimp and crabmeat Andalusia, cheddar cheese tartlet, tropical fruit cup, mussels on the half shell); **soups and salads** (chilled potato and dill cream, Tuscan tomato soup, beefsteak tomatoes and baby mozzarella, leaves of Boston bib & radicchio); **main courses** (orange roughy, angel hair pasta, venison medallions in stilton and red currant jus, roasted half chicken, rib of beef, roasted chickent breast, grilled sirloin steak, baked salmon steak, vegetarian selections–lasagna or vegetable strudel); **desserts** (triple chocolate terrine, apple cheesecake, peach flambe, brioche pudding, citrus sundae, or no sugar added dessert).

Captain's Gala *(all 7+ night cruises)*
appetizers (baked clams, grilled shrimp, grilled vegetables and beef prosciutto, or fresh fruit cocktail); **soups and salads** (wild forest mushroom soup, chilled tomato consommé, garden fresh salad, or Californian mixed salad leaves); **main courses** (baked lobster tail, roasted turkey, pan-fried halibut, grain-fed chicken breast, fettuccine with seared sea scallops, roasted chicken breast, sirloin steak, salmon steak, or vegetarian selection–eggplant parmigiana or blue cheese and asparagus risotto); **desserts** (amaretto cheesecake, cherries jubilee, warm chocolate lava cake, lingonberry cheese pudding, ice cream sundae, or sugar-free dessert).

Til We Meet Again *(all 7+ night cruises)*
appetizers (artichoke and garlic dip, California roll with caviar, seafood medley, or honey-mustard chicken tenderloins); **soups and salads** (crawfish and lobster bisque, chilled split pea soup, romaine salad, Florida citrus and baby spinach, or bib lettuce); **main courses** (grilled beef tenderloin, Kentucky Bourbon and maple-glazed pork tenderloin, roasted lamb filet, seafood pappardelle pasta, roasted red snapper, sirloin steak, grilled chicken breast, grilled salmon, or vegetarian selections–vegetable curry, risotto with black-eyed peas, or steamed vegetables); **desserts** (banana crème brûlée Napoleon, chocolate decadence, celebration cake, deep-dish apple-cranberry pie, baked Alaska, ice cream sundae, or sugar-free dessert).

Topsider's/Beach Blanket Buffet

This casual buffet restaurant (deck 9 aft) is a pleasing alternative to the formal dining rooms. Choices are plentiful and varied, with themes such as seafood, Italian, Mexican, and Asian. The welcome aboard buffet (first afternoon) offers peel-and-eat shrimp, a popular offering with cruisers. Salad and dessert buffets are expansive, and kid-friendly food is always offered. Breakfast offerings are excellent, with hot and cold selections, omelet bar, and a cereal bar—note that breakfast here on the last day is very busy. It's usually open for breakfast (7:30 am to 10:30 am) and lunch (noon to 2:00 pm). Occasionally early-morning pastries, dinner (6:30 pm to 8:30 pm), and a late-night buffet are offered. Seating indoors and outdoors. Drinks include soda, water, fruit punch, iced tea, coffee, milk, and juice.

Decor—Topsider's (Magic) is nautically themed, with bright, nautical flags, teakwood tables, and glass etchings of maritime scenes. Beach Blanket Buffet (Wonder) has a surf's-up feel, with colorful surfboards, beach towels, and beach balls decorating the floors, walls, and ceilings. Both offer indoor and outdoor seating (with and without shade).

Dress—Casual resort wear. You can wear shorts and tank tops for any meal, and dressier clothes are welcome, too. For the sake of other guests, however, do cover up that swimsuit.

Dinner—Dinner works differently than breakfast and lunch—you go to the buffet for your salads and some desserts, but your drinks and others courses are brought to your table by servers. In fact, your main course entrees will probably be the same as those offered in one of the regular restuarants that evening. Note that dinner here may only be offered on select nights of your cruise.

Our Review—An excellent place for a fast yet satisfying breakfast. We generally prefer the other restaurants for lunch and dinner (better food, better service, and alcohol can be purchased), but when we've stopped by for a casual meal we've always been pleased. It's a great place to feed kids before they go to Flounder's or Oceaneers. As to whether it's best to eat lunch here or at Parrot Cay on embarkation day, we really prefer Parrot Cay for its service and slightly less crowded atmosphere. Jennifer and Dave's rating: 6/10.

Dave enjoys lunch at Beach Blanket Buffet

Casual Dining

Need to grab a bite on your way to a movie? Want to avoid the dining room at dinner? Casual dining is your ticket. Disney offers several quick-service options throughout the ship at various times during the day, all at no extra charge. All times noted below are based on previous cruises.

Topsider's Buffet/Beach Blanket Buffet — Deck 9 Aft

See previous page for a full description and photo.

Pluto's Dog House — Deck 9 Aft

Your basic burger stand. The menu includes hamburgers, hot dogs, veggie burgers, chicken sandwiches, tacos, bratwurst, chicken tenders, and fish burgers. All are served with fries. A toppings bar offers standard bun veggies (lettuce, tomatoes, onions, pickles) and condiments. Pluto's may also offer an express breakfast or treats like cheese fries and nachos on select days. Patio tables nearby. Hours vary—usually open from lunch until 8:00 pm or midnight.

Goofy's Galley [Disney Magic] — Deck 9 Aft

Scoops (see below) was renovated into Goofy's Galley in October 2005. Offerings include soft serve ice cream, salads, fresh fruit, deli sandwiches, panini, and wraps. In the morning (7:00-9:30 or 10:00 am), you'll find a selection of pastries, cereal, and fruit. Open daily from 11:00 am to 6:00 or 7:00 pm (ice cream may be available until 11:00 pm).

Scoops and Fruit Station [Disney Wonder] — Deck 9 Aft

Vanilla and chocolate frozen yogurt (soft serve) with a variety of toppings and sprinkles. You can get your frozen yogurt in a cone or a cup. Open daily from 11:00 am to 8:00 pm. Wraps (chicken, veggie, or seafood) may also be served here on select days. Fruit (bananas, apples, etc.) from 12:00 pm to 6:00 pm. May change to Goofy's Galley (see above) in October 2006.

Pinocchio's Pizzeria — Deck 9 Mid

Pizza, pizza, pizza! Get your slice in traditional cheese or pepperoni. Special pizzas like veggie and Hawaiian may also be served at times. Beverages also available here. Generally open from 11:00 am to 6:00 pm, then again from 10:00 pm to midnight. Seating is at patio tables. (Tip: You can order more pizza types from room service—see page 117).

© MediaMarx, Inc.

Outlook Bar — Deck 10 Fwd

Chicken wings and panini sandwiches are offered here around lunchtime on select days. Check your Personal Navigator *or stop up for a visit.*

Beverage Station — Deck 9 Aft

Breakfast pastries available early morning (6:30-7:30 am). Cookies may also be served on select days—look for them on the counters to the aft of the beverage station. Complimentary beverages, including soda, are available 24 hours/day—for more details, see page 116.

Snacks and desserts are liberally sprinkled in other places, too. You'll find snacks in the Cove Café and Promenade Lounge, as well as in Beat Street/Route 66 from 11:00 pm to midnight. Dessert buffets are available (see page 104).

Castaway Cay Dining

Jennifer's nieces, Megan and Natalie, discuss the nutritional merits of hot dogs vs. burgers at Cookie's BBQ on Castaway Cay

© MediaMarx, Inc.

Two more dining opportunities bear mention, even though they are located off-ship. All itineraries visit Disney's private island, Castaway Cay, and you'll be happy to learn your food is included in the price of your cruise! The main place to eat is **Cookie's BBQ**, located directly across from the family beach (see island map on page 247). Cookie's typically serves from 11:30 am to 2:00 pm and offers the best selection with burgers, BBQ ribs, grilled chicken sandwiches, lobster burgers, hot dogs, potato salad, fruit, frozen yogurt, and big chocolate chip cookies. Food is served buffet-style. Plenty of covered seating is nearby (see photo above). Beverages are also provided (you can get free sodas at the dispensers), or purchase alcoholic beverages across the way at the Conched Out Bar.

Adults 18 and over can eat at the **Castaway Cay Air Bar-B-Q** (see photo below) located at Serenity Bay, the adults-only beach, from about 11:30 am to 2:00 pm. Offerings include burgers, salmon, grilled chicken, steak sandwiches, lobster burgers (not always offered), potato salad, fresh fruit, and fat-free yogurt. Water, soda, and juice is provided, or you can purchase alcoholic beverages at the bar nearby. A half-dozen umbrella-shaded tables are located to the left of the food hut, or take your tray down to the beach.

Relax at the Castaway Cay Air Bar-B-Q at Serenity Bay

© MediaMarx, Inc.

In addition to the two bars already mentioned, there's a third—the Heads Up Bar—at the far end of the family beach. All bars close around 3:30–4:00 pm.

Tip: If you choose not to visit Castaway Cay, a buffet is served in Parrot Cay, usually from about 8:00–10:30 am and 12:00–1:30 pm.

Kids' Dining

We don't know about your kids, but Jennifer's nieces, Megan and Natalie, won't touch pepper-seared grouper or seafood Creole with a ten-foot pole. Megan, Natalie, and many other kids prefer the kids' menus available at each table-service restaurant (and adults can order from these menus, too!). The **menus vary slightly** and are kid-friendly. Here is a typical menu:

appetizers (chicken noodle soup or honeydew melon boat); **main courses** (Mickey's macaroni and cheese, Minnie's mini burger, crusty cheese pizza, chicken strips, Mickey pasta, roasted chicken, or vegetable croquettes); **desserts** (Mickey ice cream bar, chocolate pudding, caramel custard, or assorted ice cream); **drinks** (milk–whole, low-fat, skim, or chocolate; soda, juice, water). Smoothies are $3.50 each.

And, yes, the menus come with **kid-pleasin' activities**, like word searches and connect-the-dots. Crayons are also provided with meals (see photo).

© MediaMarx, Inc.

Megan discovers that kids are pampered on Disney cruises, too

If you are the lucky parent of children who will try anything, rest assured that your **kids can choose from the regular menu** if they wish.

Kid-friendly items are **offered elsewhere** outside of the restaurants, too. Pluto's and Pinocchio's are favorites, naturally, and Topsider's/Beach Blanket Buffet has plenty of kids' food.

If your child is checked into **Oceaneer's Club or Lab** at dinnertime, crew members take kids up to Topsider's/Beach Blanket Buffet before or at the start of the first dinner seating. The eatery reserves one buffet line just for kids. Checking your kids into the Oceaneer's Club or Lab just before dinnertime may be a good idea if you're hoping for a quiet dinner alone some evening.

While lunch and dinner are provided for kids checked into the Oceaneer's at mealtimes, **no snacks** are made available. You can check them out and take them to get a snack.

Younger children may find it **hard to sit through a meal** in a table-service restaurant. If you ask your server, you can have your child's meal served at the same time as your appetizers to curb their impatience. And the servers are typically great at entertaining the kids. Of course, you may prefer to do casual dining or room service on some nights.

Babies in **Flounder's Reef** are given apple juice and saltine crackers, as appropriate for their ages—you may also bring food for them. The dining rooms don't have pre-made baby food—you may want to bring a small food grinder to prepare foods for your infant. Formula for infants (Similac and Isomil) is available for purchase in Treasure Ketch (deck 4 mid), but supplied are limited. Disposable bottles are also sold in Treasure Ketch. For older babies, whole milk is available from room service and from the beverage station on deck 9 aft.

Beverages

Your food onboard is included in your fare, but **some drinks are not free**. Sure, you can get tap water, coffee, tea, milk, and juice with your meals and at select locations onboard. Sodas (fountain drinks) are also available for free everywhere except bars and room service. But bottled water, specialty drinks, smoothies, and alcohol come at a price.

- ✔ **Soda**—Disney offers complimentary soda at all meals, at the Beverage Station (deck 9 aft), and on Castaway Cay. Selection is limited to Coke, Diet Coke, Sprite, Diet Sprite (not available everywhere), and ginger ale. Soda purchased at bars and from room service are priced at about $1.50 each.
- ✔ **Beers** range from about $3.25 to $4.00 and include tap beers (Bud, Miller Lite, Heineken), canned beers (Bud, Bud Lite, Coors Light, Icehouse, Miller Draft, Miller Lite, Beck's, Guinness, Heineken), and bottled beers (Amstell Light, Bass, Corona). Mixed drinks are $3.00 to $6.00 each, wine is $4.25 and up, and smoothies are $3.50.
- ✔ A 15% **gratuity is automatically added** to all beverage purchases. There's no need to give another tip, even though there is a space provided for it on your receipt.
- ✔ **Bring Your Own**—Many guests opt to "BYOB." Pick up some bottled water, beer, wine, and/or liquor and stow it in your luggage. If you run out, pick up more at a port. Unlike other cruise lines, there are no restrictions on bringing beverages aboard, but you can only take home one liter duty-free per person and it must be unopened. (Warning: Don't expect to restock at the onboard liquor shop—you won't get your booze until the night before you disembark.) The stateroom "refrigerators" keep your beverages chilled (see page 93). If you bring your own wine to the dinner table, expect to pay $17.25 per bottle ($15 corkage fee + 15% gratuity)—ouch! You may, however, bring a glass of poured wine to the dinner table, but we suggest you do this only occasionally.
- ✔ **Beer Mug**—Check the lounges for a 22 oz. refillable, glass beer mug. Cost $15 for the mug. Get 22 oz. refills at the 16 oz. price. Note: You'd need 10 to 12 refills to break even.
- ✔ **Beverage Station**—Visit the beverage station on deck 9 aft for complimentary soda, water, coffee, hot tea, iced tea, hot cocoa, whole milk, fruit punch, and lemonade—available 24 hours a day. Orange juice may also be available in the mornings.
- ✔ **Topsider's Buffet/Beach Blanket Buffet**—Soda, fruit punch, and iced tea are complimentary when the restaurant is open for lunch or dinner. If you want lemonade, milk, hot tea, or coffee, the Beverage Station is nearby.
- ✔ **Wine Package**—Commit to a bottle of wine for each night of your cruise and save more than 25% off the list prices. You can choose your wine from a list at each meal. The seven-night cruise's classic wine package is $145 and the premium package is $265. If you don't finish an entire bottle of wine at dinner, you can take it back to your stateroom or ask your assistant server to keep it for you until your next meal. Unopened bottles may be taken home, but they count towards your customs allowance.
- ✔ **Fairy Tale Cuvée**—This champagne—available for purchase in the dining rooms—was created just for Disney by Iron Horse Vineyard (the White House's purveyor).
- ✔ **Drinks Come to You**—Servers on Castaway Cay and at the Walt Disney Theatre bring specialty drinks around on trays for purchase so you don't have to get up for them.

Stateroom Dining
(Room Service)

There are no other three words that say "luxury" more than "Hello, Room Service?" It's a sinful extravagance for the filthy rich and people too pooped or love-struck to creep from their rooms. But why feel guilty, when **the cost of room service is included** in the price of your cruise? You want real luxury? Keep your stateroom stocked with oversized chocolate chip cookies from room service throughout your cruise!

Room service is available **24 hours/day** (though it's closed the morning of disembarkation for most guests). Service is quick and punctual—food usually arrives in 20 to 30 minutes or less. You'll find room service menus in your stateroom, and we've included sample menus at the bottom of this page—please note that menu items and beverage prices may change. Food and basic drinks (coffee, tea, milk, juice) are free, but all other beverages carry an extra charge.

To place an order for room service, fill out the breakfast menu in your stateroom and hang it on your door handle, or simply **press the dining button on your stateroom phone** and relay the items you want. You can also specify a time for delivery if you are ordering in advance, as with the breakfast menu. Coffee drinkers may find it convenient to order a pot of coffee before going to bed—have it delivered immediately (it may stay warm in its thermal carafe) or request it for a particular time in the morning (its arrival works as a wake-up call). Don't forget to tip your room service steward on delivery. They don't get automatic tips for the food, just the drinks. $1-$2 dollars/person is fine.

Tip: Guests going on all-day excursions have been known to order a couple of sandwiches, have them delivered before departing, keep them cool in the refrigerator, and pack them in resealable bags for a midday snack. Be aware that the Disney Cruise Line does not encourage this, it **may be illegal to bring food offboard** in some ports, and you are not allowed to bring cooked/opened food back onboard. We do not recommend it.

Breakfast Menu (7:00 am to 10:00 am) Note: Guests in suites may order full breakfasts (see page 78). ***Juices*** *(orange, apple, grapefruit);* ***Cold Cereal****, served with whole or skim milk (Corn Flakes, Raisin Bran, Rice Krispies, Froot Loops, KO's, Frosted Flakes, low-fat granola);* ***Breads and Pastries*** *(Danish pastries, fruit and bran muffins, croissants, donuts, toast, English muffins, bagel);* ***Condiments*** *(selection of jams and honey, butter, margarine);* ***Beverages*** *(whole milk, skim milk, chocolate milk, 100% Colombian Coffee, 100% Colombian Decaffeinated Coffee, selection of teas); and* ***Cocktails*** *- $4.25 (Mimosa, Screwdriver, Bloody Mary)*

All-Day Menu Note: Guests in suites may order from the main dining room menus (see page 78). ***Appetizers*** *(Port of Salad—iceberg lettuce, tomato, red onion, roasted corn, bacon, turkey, blue cheese, herb croutons, and pesto vinaigrette; Ship's Kettle—creamy tomato soup with oregano and croutons; Chili Tricolore—spicy chili con carne with shredded lettuce, tomato, cheddar cheese, and sour cream; and All Hands on Deck—a special selection of international cheeses served with crackers);* ***Sandwiches****, served with coleslaw and potato chips (tuna sandwich, roasted turkey sandwich, or grilled ham and cheese sandwich);* ***All-American Fare*** *(cheeseburger with fries and cole slaw, hot dog with fries, and macaroni & cheese);* ***Chef's Specialities*** *(triple cheese pizza, Mexican fiesta pizza, vegetarian delight pizza, and manicotti al forno);* ***Desserts*** *(daily cake selection or an extra large chocolate chip cookie);* ***Kid's Meals*** *(Captain Hook's chicken tenders with potato chips or Catch a Wave PB&J with potato chips).* ***Beverage Packages*** *(6 domestic beers for $19.50, 6 imported beers for $22.50, 3 imported and 3 domestic beers for $21, 6 Coca Cola or other sodas for $7.50, or 6 bottled waters for $7.50). Milk is free.*

Our Recommendations

Your first hours on board can be very chaotic, and it's tough to arrange a proper family meal. We suggest you split up and **grab quick bites** whenever you can—the buffets close before the ship sets sail.

Are you still uncomfortable about wearing a jacket or a suit? Other than formal nights, **a nice shirt and slacks will be fine** at Triton's/Lumière's.

Presuming you love **Disney music** (a fair guess, we think), the soundtrack at Animator's Palate and Lumière's/Triton's takes your meal to a high "sea." You don't get a 16-piece, live, be-tuxed orchestra, but the prerecorded scores are a feast for the ears. This is especially true at Animator's Palate, where the visual extravaganza is choreographed to the music.

You can't keep Dave away from **smoked salmon**, even under "lox and cay." Alas, Disney's smoked salmon is not quite the stuff of dream cruises. It's fine on a bagel with cream cheese, but it's not that firm-but-buttery/velvety, smoky-sweet stuff of his dreams. The salmon at Palo is a bit better (as is their fresh-squeezed OJ!).

We love **seafood** (especially Dave), and you'll notice that many of our choices in this chapter (all those dishes we've underlined) are seafood-based. We know there are many of you who don't share our love for it, so please rest assured that virtually all the dishes are good—it's just that we've tried the seafood the most often.

The **seating and traffic flow** for Topsider's/Beach Blanket Buffet is the most chaotic on board. It's far better, though, when you enter the buffet using the right-hand doors (port). The indoor seating on that side is also more spacious and relaxing. When the weather's right, we prefer the outdoor tables aft—they're a glorious relief from the indoor chaos.

© MediaMarx, Inc.

Eating outdoors on deck 9 aft

Get to Know Your Dining Room Servers

If you've never had the chance to bond with a good server, try it! Great servers resemble stage actors—they come alive for a good audience. Be generous with your attention and thanks throughout the cruise—don't save it all for the tip. From the start, help them understand your tastes and interests. Listen attentively when they describe dishes, ask for their recommendations (they know what's good), and ask questions while ordering—you may save them several trips to the kitchen. If something disappoints you, break the news gently—but don't suffer in silence, either. Your server likes happy guests, and you'll be even happier with a happy server. You have three crew members on your dinner service staff, all of whom should be tipped at cruise end (see page 271). Your Head Server oversees many tables, supervises your special needs (and celebrations), and should visit your table once per meal. Your Server guides you through your meal, takes your orders, and (hopefully) pampers you beyond belief. Your quiet Assistant Server helps keep your food coming, serves wine and other beverages, and clears the table.

A Melting Pot of Notes

If you're thinking of **bringing any food onboard**, please note that it is against U.S. Public Health regulations to bring aboard any food that is cooked or partially cooked or packaged food that has already been opened. Unopened, commercially packaged foods are fine.

It's a good idea to **pack a change of clothes** for your first night's dinner in your carry-on. While it doesn't happen often, checked luggage may arrive in your stateroom too late to allow an unhurried change for an early dinner seating.

Even parents with **young children may appreciate the late seating**—the kids will be more alert for the early show.

Trying to decide between the **earlier or later seating?** The earlier seating is most popular with families and young children. The earlier seating is also preferred by those who like to get to sleep earlier. Early seating takes about 1 ½ hours to complete your meal, while late seating can take as long as 2 hours. As you might have guessed, the later seating is comprised of mostly adults and some older children. The later seating gives you more time on your port days, as you don't need to rush back for an early dinner. Keep in mind that guests with late seating see the show before dinner, so you may need a snack before the show. We prefer the late seating ourselves.

Just can't **finish your meal**? Ask your server if you can take it back to your room. Most servers are happy to accommodate you. Don't be shy about asking for another dish or for seconds, either.

If you are **seated with other guests**, which is likely if you aren't traveling in a large group, enjoy their company and swap tales of your adventures! Most cruisers find it more enjoyable to share a table!

On the **second night** of the four-night cruises, guests return to the restaurant where they dined on the first night of their cruise. Regardless of what restaurant you're in, you will enjoy the "Pirates in the Caribbean" menu (see page 111) on this evening.

Jennifer's brother-in-law, Chad, enjoys two main entrees

Not sure what evening to **experience Palo**? Personally, we think Parrot Cay is the least interesting of the three dining rooms and the evening we're in Parrot Cay is generally the evening we prefer to spend in Palo. Be careful, however, that you don't accidentally overlook the "Pirates of the Caribbean" theme night (see next page).

If you want to try **Palo on more than one evening** and you have friends onboard, ask them to include your party in their reservation for one evening while you do the same for them on the other evening.

Breakfast on disembarkation day is in the same restaurant you were assigned to the evening before (so if you ate in Palo, you need to go the restaurant you would have eaten in if you hadn't gone to Palo). A special "Welcome Home" menu is served—it's virtually identical to the Character Breakfast menu (page 108).

Determining Dining Schedules

Before you read any further, know this: you don't have to figure out your dining schedule ahead of time. If you want to just kick back and relax, all you need to pay attention to is the dining "tickets" left in your stateroom on your embarkation day and the Personal Navigators (the daily schedules left in your stateroom every evening). This approach may make it difficult to decide which night to dine at Palo, however. Should you really want to have a good idea of the what, where, when of your dinners, then read on!

At the time of writing, these are the dining schedules for the various regularly scheduled cruises. If you're on a special cruise, check the bottom of this page for our thoughts on likely-sounding schedules. It's very important to remember, however, that <u>Disney can and does change these schedules at the drop of a hat</u>. Always, always check your Personal Navigators to determine what's really going on for your cruise.

3-Night Cruise Dining Schedule

Day 1	Day 2	Day 3
regular rotation menu	Pirates of the Caribbean	regular rotation menu

4-Night Cruise Dining Schedule

Day 1	Day 2	Day 3	Day 4
regular rotation menu	Pirates of the Caribbean	regular rotation menu	regular rotation menu

7-Night Eastern Caribbean Dining Cruise Schedule

Day 1	Day 2	Day 3	Day 4	Day 5	Day 6	Day 7
regular rotation menu	reg. rotation menu ***(Formal Attire)***	regular rotation menu	Pirates of the Carribean ***(Pirate Attire)***	Master Chef	Captain's Gala ***(Semi-Formal Attire)***	'Til We Meet Again
	Palo Brunch/ High Tea	Palo Brunch/ High Tea			Palo Brunch/ High Tea	

7-Night Western Caribbean Dining Cruise Schedule

Day 1	Day 2	Day 3	Day 4	Day 5	Day 6	Day 7
regular rotation menu	regular rotation menu	reg. rotation menu ***(Formal Attire)***	Master Chef	Pirates of the Carribean ***(Pirate Attire)***	Captain's Gala ***(Semi-Formal Attire)***	'Til We Meet Again
	Palo Brunch	Palo Brunch/ High Tea			Palo Brunch/ High Tea	

Note: The character breakfast on the 7-night cruises is on day 2 if your dining rotation starts with Animator's Palate, day 3 if you start with Lumière's/Triton's, and day 6 if you start with Parrot Cay.

The 10-night cruises historically have two formal attire evenings (day 3 and day 7) and one semi-formal attire evening (day 9).

Dining Worksheet

Use this worksheet to note your dining preferences and be sure to keep it with you on your first day aboard.

Fill in/circle the following:
We have the **main seating** / **late seating** *(circle the appropriate choice—if you're not sure of your seating, call the Disney Cruise Line and inquire)*

Our Anticipated Dining Rotation: While this rule doesn't work for everyone, in general you can anticipate the following rotations if the occupants of your stateroom include:
All adults—day 1: **Lumière's/Triton's**, day 2: Animator's Palate, day 3: Parrot Cay, etc.
Young kids—day 1: **Animator's Palate**, day 2: Parrot Cay, day 3: Lumière's/Triton's, etc.
Older kids—day 1: **Parrot Cay**, day 2: Lumière's/Triton's, day 3: Animator's Palate, etc.
Note: The exception to the above rotation rule is on 4-night cruises, which repeat the first restaurant on the second night, then continue on. See page 119 for details.

Now write in the restaurants you anticipate being assigned to on each day. You may also want to add in ports or other notes such as formal/semi-formal nights.

Day 1	Day 2	Day 3	Day 4	Day 5	`Day 6	Day 7

Day 8	Day 9	Day 10	Day 11	Day 12	Day 13	Day 14

Now pencil in your first and second preferences for a dinner at Palo, keeping in mind which restaurants/meals you really want to try and which you are less interested in. Guests on the seven-night cruise: add in your preferences for the champagne brunch and/or high tea, if those interest you. Also note your preferences below for easy reference:

My first Palo preference is for ____________________ at ____________________ pm
My second Palo preference is for ____________________ at ____________________ pm

My Palo brunch preference is for ____________________
My Palo high tea preference is for ____________________

You can fill in this worksheet before you leave for your cruise or once you're aboard and are confident about your dining rotation—just be sure to bring this worksheet with you!

A Recipe for Fun

Make the most of your dining experience with these delicious tips:

- Can't decide between the lamb and the cod? Tell your server you'd like to **try both dishes**! You can also order multiple appetizers and desserts if you wish. But take our advice and don't say you want "nothing" for dessert—that's just what you may get (a plate with the word "Nothing" written in chocolate syrup, for example).
- How do you **choose between four full-service restaurants** on a three-night cruise? If you can't bear to miss the pleasures of Triton's, Animator's Palate, Parrot Cay, and Palo, try this: Make a late-night reservation at Palo and just have appetizers and/or dessert. Or, eat an early, light meal in your regular restaurant before having a late, full dinner at Palo.
- For easy **room service tipping**, bring an envelope full of $1 bills and leave it by the door in your stateroom.
- Picky eater? Ask your server to **mix and match menu items** so you can get just the meal you want.
- If you've **brought your own wine** or picked up a bottle at a port, you can request a "wine opener" (corkscrew) from room service.

Magical Memories

- *"With all of the exciting things for families to do apart on the ship, the dining rooms were the perfect place for me to reconnect with my children. The teenager came down from Aloft, the 9-year-old made it away from Oceaneer Lab, the 7-year-old left Oceaneer Club, and we all gathered every evening to relax, reconnect, laugh, and share the day's stories. We all enjoyed being treated like the Princesses we are, but the children especially loved that special time to dress up a bit and unwind. The teen dramas were all played out again, and the little pirates could tell their tales, too. We shared a pause of good food and good company before going our separate ways again for the evening. Those times together were the highlight of our cruise."*

  ...as told by Disney cruiser Dawn Dobson

- *"We had our five-year-old son bring his pirate costume from Halloween on the cruise for the 'Pirates in the Caribbean' night. He wore his costume to dinner and the evening show and was very proud and excited. Many guests and cast members gave him attention as we walked down the halls, and our pictures from that night turned out great!"*

  ...as told by Disney cruiser Stacy G.

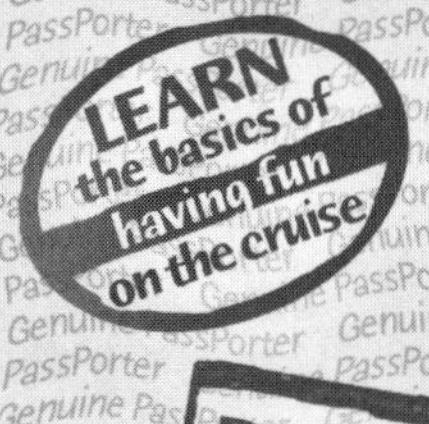
LEARN
the basics of
having fun
on the cruise

Playing and Relaxing Onboard

READ
your
Personal
Navigator

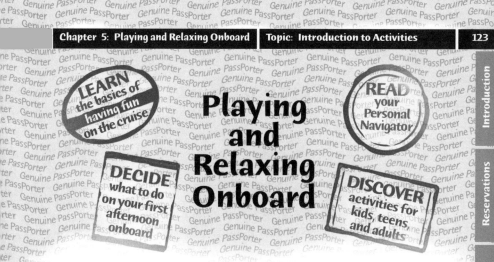

DECIDE what to do on your first afternoon onboard

DISCOVER activities for kids, teens, and adults

Cruise ships are often called floating hotels, but "mobile resort" is much closer to the truth. Like the legendary "Borscht Belt" hotels of New York's Catskill Mountains, the Disney cruise offers a bewildering array of entertainment, recreation, and enrichment opportunities from sun up way into the wee hours.

The Disney Cruise Line has become legendary for its pacesetting children's and teens' programs, and it may seem like an ocean-going summer camp. With the kids' programs open all day and well into the night, even Mom and Dad get a vacation.

Despite its emphasis on family travel, the Disney cruises are a summer camp for all ages, boasting a full range of adult-oriented activities. The single most obvious omission is the lack of a gambling casino—you'll have to be satisfied with onboard bingo and in-port casinos.

Leave time for relaxation as well as playing. On a cruise, it's just as easy to overplay as it is to over-eat. You'll be tempted to fill every available hour with shipboard fun, but you'll have a far more enjoyable cruise by picking only the most tempting morsels. If you shop 'til you drop in port and play 'til you plotz (collapse) onboard, you'll be one very weary vacationer.

We start this chapter with an introduction to the *Personal Navigator*, your cruise's four-page daily gazette. Then it's time to prep you for your first day onboard. There's a lot to do, and it's particularly hectic for first-time cruisers. From there, we move on to describe shipboard activities for families, teens, kids, and adults—this is where you learn about the famous kids' program and adult entertainment offerings. Next, in-depth details are in order—the swimming pools, deck parties, films, stateroom TV, live entertainment, surfing (the World Wide Web), the spa, and lounges all get their moment in the limelight. Finally, now that you're completely exhausted, we help you kick back and relax, and share some insider tips. Shuffleboard, anyone?

Your Personal Navigator

We hope this field guide has become your "first mate." If so, we predict the *Personal Navigator* will seem like your very own "cruise director." The *Personal Navigator* is a folded, **4-page sheet** that lists the day's activities. A new *Personal Navigator* is placed in your stateroom daily, and there are special versions for kids and teens, too. While we don't have room to print the full text of *Personal Navigators* here, you can get a peek at previous edition *Personal Navigators* by visiting http://www.castawayclub.com—this site maintains collections from previous cruisers, and they'll give you an excellent idea of what to expect.

The first time you see a *Personal Navigator*, you may feel overwhelmed. They pack in a lot of details! Here's a **capsule review** of what you'll find:

Page 1—Date, day's destination, suggested dress, sunrise/sunset times, day's highlights
Page 2—Morning/afternoon activities, character appearances, movies, family activities
Page 3—Afternoon/evening activities, adult activities, tips, notes
Page 4—Meal times/hours, lounge hours, important numbers, policies, specials, etc.

Pay attention to the **small symbols** in the margins—these indicate which activities feature Disney character appearances, are for guests 18 and older, families, etc. You'll find the symbol key at the bottom of page 3.

We highly recommend you keep **highlighters** handy (a different color for each person) to mark appealing activities. Finding activities in your *Personal Navigator* later can be tricky—on some days, there are more than 80 activities listed! Obviously, you can't do everything, and that's where this chapter comes in—we introduce many of the activities here, so you'll be better informed when it comes to deciding among all of your choices.

We find that life is much easier when we each have a copy of the *Personal Navigator* with us at all times. Only one copy is left in your stateroom, so stop at Guest Services (deck 3 mid) and **pick up more copies**. (The kids versions are in Oceaneer Club/Lab and the teen version is in The Stack/Aloft.) How do you keep it with you if you don't have pockets? We fold it and tuck it into a PassHolder Pouch, which also holds our Key to the World card and other small items. See page 299 for details.

In addition to the *Personal Navigator*, you may receive a highlights sheet covering the entire cruise, a listing of movie showtimes and TV channels, and a daily onboard shopping flyer. **Port and shopping guides** are distributed when you visit a port—they contain historical overviews, maps, shopping and dining ideas, basic information, and hours.

Your First Day Aboard

At last! Are you excited? Many cruisers report feeling overwhelmed and even a little nervous on their first afternoon. The good news is that your first day aboard can now be far more relaxing. The Disney Cruise Line web site (http://www.disneycruise.com) now lets you make Palo, Vista Spa, Flounder's Reef childcare, and shore excursion reservations online—you can even pre-register for the Oceaneer Club and Lab. Reservations can be made online from 2 to 75 days in advance (up to 90 days for Castaway Club members and up to 105 days in advance for guests in stateroom categories 1–3), assuming your cruise is paid in full. Look for the "My Disney Cruise" links on the web site. Note that online bookings are limited to one Palo reservation and no more than 8–10 hours per child in Flounder's Reef, and some Spa treatments (such as haircare and the Rainforest) are not listed. Additional reservations may be available after boarding.

To give you an idea of what to expect on your first afternoon onboard, we've made up a **sample "touring plan."** You probably won't want to do everything in our touring plan, and remember that times/locations may differ. Modify it as needed and use the worksheet on page 127 to record your own plans!

As soon as you can—Smile for the photographer, walk the gangway, and board the ship. Go to Topsider's/Beach Blanket Buffet (deck 9 aft) or Parrot Cay (deck 3 aft) for a seafood buffet. Relax and enjoy—it may get a bit hectic over the next few hours.
12:00 pm (or so)—Send one adult from your party for Palo reservations, if you didn't reserve in advance (be sure to check your *Personal Navigator* for exact time and place).
12:00 pm (or so)—Send one adult to get Vista Spa bookings (including massages on Castaway Cay), if not done in advance. Send another person to your stateroom (usually ready at 1:00 pm). This is also the time to confirm any special needs requests you made (visit Guest Relations).
Tip: If you've got kids, they may be getting antsy by now. Let them explore your stateroom, or, if they're old enough, introduce them to the pools and meet up with them later.
1:30 pm—Go to Flounder's Reef Nursery (deck 5 aft), if not reserved in advance.
1:30 pm—Send someone to the Shore Excursions Desk (deck 3 midship) to fill out and drop off order forms, if not reserved in advance. Decide which excursions you'd like in advance.
Lunch—Take a deep breath and slow down. If you haven't eaten or visited your stateroom yet, do so now. The buffet typically closes at 3:30 pm, so don't miss it!
2:30 pm—Make dining assignment changes or special dietary requests, if needed.
2:45 pm—Take kids 3–12 to Oceaneer Club/Lab (deck 5 midship), if not pre-registered.
3:15 pm—Return to your stateroom and get acquainted with it. If you're in need of anything (extra pillows, bed safety rail), request it from your stateroom host/hostess.
3:45 pm—Make sure everyone meets back in the room for the mandatory assembly drill.
4:00 pm—Don your life jackets and walk to your assembly station (see next page).
4:30 pm—After returning your life jackets to your room, go up to deck 9 midship and have fun at the sailaway deck party, and/or explore the ship until it is time to get ready for dinner or the evening's show.
5:30 pm/5:45 pm/6:00 pm/6:15 pm/6:30 pm—Enjoy dinner (main seating guests) or the stage show at 6:30 pm (late seating guests).
7:00 pm—The Stack/Aloft (teens) and Oceaneer Club/Lab (kids 3–12) are now officially open. If you haven't yet registered your children, do this now.
8:00 pm/8:15 pm/8:30 pm—Enjoy the show (main seating) or dinner (late seating)

Whew! What a day! Rest assured that it all gets much, much easier from this point forward.

First Day Tips

Having a plan is the key to staying on course and feeling good. Here are a few helpful tips for your first day:

Check and double-check your ***Personal Navigator*** as soon as you get it (either at check-in or when you visit your stateroom). Places and times often change, and new activities and opportunities may be available.

Don't forget to eat! It can be hard to sit down together to one big family meal on your first afternoon. It's okay to split up and/or get **nibbles and bites** here and there.

Of course, you can always **kick back and do nothing** on your first day but eat, drink, be merry, and attend the boat drill. If you prefer this tactic, you can try to get those Palo and spa reservations later, and you may get lucky with cancellations. If you've got someone in your family who just wants to relax once they're onboard, arrange to go your separate ways on this first afternoon—you'll all be much happier.

Lucky guests with **concierge service** only need to attend one meeting to make the various reservations. You'll be told when and where to meet.

Be **flexible**. Make a plan, but then be willing to change it when needed.

Mandatory Boat Drills

It's inevitable that just as you're settling in or about to leave your stateroom for an exploration of the ship, a disembodied voice from the bridge announces the mandatory boat drill. But thanks to this guide, you now know that the drill happens at 4:00 pm on departure day, and all ship services are suspended from 3:30 to 4:30 pm. You'll find bright-orange life jackets on the top shelf of your stateroom closet (if you need a different size, such as an infant jacket, ask your stateroom host/hostess). The life jackets, by the way, were recently replaced with significantly more comfortable models. They have a water-activated light and a whistle—please remind your kids not to blow the whistles. Your Assembly Station location is mapped on the back of your stateroom door. Assembly stations are all on deck 4, but may be outside on deck or inside. If you forget your assembly station designation, it's printed on your life jacket (see the "M" on Dave's jacket in the photo). When you hear the loud emergency signal, put on your life jackets and walk to the assembly station—your attendance is mandatory. Be sure to bring your Key to the World card(s) with you, but leave cameras and other things behind. The life jackets are uncomfortable, but now is the time for everyone (including young kids) to get used to them. Crew members in the hallways will direct you to your assembly station (disabled guests should ask crew members for special instructions on attending drills). Once there, a crew member takes attendance and displays the correct way to wear and use the life jacket. If you miss the drill, you'll receive a sternly worded letter indicating where and when to meet to go over the assembly procedures—don't miss it! When the drill is over, the captain releases everyone back to their staterooms. The drill lasts from 15 to 30 minutes. Keep your life jacket on until you return to your stateroom.

"Hey, these life jackets aren't half bad!"

First Things First Worksheet

Use this worksheet to plan those crucial activities that occur during your first day aboard. The chart below includes times (spanning the time period with the most important activities) and two columns each for activities and decks/locations. You may wish to list activities for other members of your party in the second column to coordinate and organize your day, or use the second column for notes or alternate activities.

Time	Activity	Deck	Activity	Deck
10:00 am				
10:15 am				
10:30 am				
10:45 am				
11:00 am				
11:15 am				
11:30 am				
11:45 am				
12:00 pm				
12:15 pm				
12:30 pm				
12:45 pm				
1:00 pm				
1:15 pm				
1:30 pm				
1:45 pm				
2:00 pm				
2:15 pm				
2:30 pm				
2:45 pm				
3:00 pm				
3:15 pm				
3:30 pm				
3:45 pm				
4:00 pm	Mandatory Boat Drill ↓	Deck 4	Mandatory Boat Drill ↓	Deck 4
4:15 pm				
4:30 pm				
4:45 pm				
5:00 pm				
5:15 pm				
5:30 pm				
5:45 pm				
6:00 pm				
6:15 pm				
6:30 pm				
6:45 pm				
7:00 pm				
7:15 pm				
7:30 pm				
7:45 pm				
8:00 pm				
8:30 pm				

Activities for Families

When Walt Disney was asked why he created Disneyland, he replied, "I felt that there should be something built where the parents and the children could have fun together." And that's exactly what Disney does for cruising. Family activities outnumber all other activities onboard, helping families have a great time when they're together. By "family" we mean groups of all ages, including all-adult families! Here's a list of what you can expect:

Deck Parties—Celebrate with music and dancing on deck 9 midship (see page 141).

Stage Shows—Disney puts on a different stage show each night of your cruise, and all shows are designed to please both adults and kids. See page 143 for more information.

Movies—Most of the movies playing in the Buena Vista Theatre and at the "Dive-In" outdoor screen (Magic only) are rated G or PG, making them ideal for families. Special matinees may be held in the huge Walt Disney Theatre, too! See page 142 for movie details.

Studio Sea—This "family nightclub" (deck 4 midship) is a working TV studio. The club hosts family dance parties, family karaoke, theme parties, Tea with Wendy (see page 270), and game shows like Mickey Mania (Disney trivia) and Seafarer's Saga (guess the fibber). Game shows are oriented towards families with young children, and generally contestant teams include both a parent and a child (see photo to right). Note that in the late evening Studio Sea may be reserved for teens only.

© Disney

Walk the Plank game show at StudioSea

Cabaret Shows—Shows for all ages may be held in Rockin' Bar D/WaveBands in the early evening. See page 138 for details.

Promenade Lounge—We think of this as the "family lounge"—it's non-smoking and families can relax together here in the afternoon and early evening. Watch for many family-friendly events, hosted in the Promenade Lounge. Located on deck 3 aft.

Oceaneer Club/Lab—At special times, families can explore these areas together.

Swimming—Families can swim together in the Goofy Pool (deck 9 midship), where pool games are also occasionally held. See page 140 for more information on the pools.

Games—Board games, shuffleboard, Ping-Pong, and basketball. A special Family Mini Olympics may also be held on deck 10 forward.

Pin Trading—Trading cloisonne pins is a very popular activity for kids and adults alike! Attend one of the trading sessions in the Atrium Lobby or trade casually with other cruisers and cast members. See page 151.

Character Meet & Greets—Plenty of opportunities for kids (or kids-at-heart) to get autographs and for parents to get photos. See page 270 for more information.

Shore Excursions—Most of Disney's shore excursions are great for families with kids ages 12 and up, and a good number of these work for families with kids ages six and up. Quite a few are open to all ages, as well. See chapter 6 for all the details.

Special Events—Try your hand at drawing Disney characters, or compete in a talent show or the "Mickey 200" veggie race—check your *Personal Navigator*.

Tip: Check your *Personal Navigator* for a special section titled "Family Activities," which lists the family-oriented highlights for the day. Also, there's usually some family-oriented entertainment between dinner and the show, such as the cabaret shows and game shows. Here is a sample of activities taken from recent *Personal Navigators* (keep in mind that not all these activities may be available on your cruise):

- ✔ Fun in the Sun Pool Party
- ✔ Pictionary or Scattergories—test your skills against the crew members'
- ✔ Family Line Dancing in Studio Sea
- ✔ Disney and Family Team Trivia
- ✔ Talent Show—show-off time!
- ✔ Mr. Toad's Wild Race (limited to 16 teams)
- ✔ Family SPY Party—fun for all "secret agents"
- ✔ Arcade Tournament
- ✔ Family Rock 'n' Roll Sock Hop
- ✔ Father and Daughter Dance
- ✔ Family Golf Putting Contest
- ✔ The Best Disney Legs Contest
- ✔ Walk the Plank Game Show
- ✔ Ping Pong Tournament
- ✔ Family Magic/Wonder Quest Game Show
- ✔ Family Animation Lesson
- ✔ Kite Making and Decorating
- ✔ "So You Think You Know Your Family?" Game

Kim and daughter Natalie dance on deck 10

Families That Play Together Don't Always Have to Stay Together

One of the wonderful benefits of a cruise is that each member of your family can do entirely different things, all while staying within the general vicinity of one another—a cruise ship is not a big place like Walt Disney World. With all the activities on your cruise, you're going to want to go in different directions at times... and you should feel free to do it! It only makes the time you spend together that much more valuable. When we sail alone, we often split up—one goes to the pool with Alexander, the other to the spa—and we agree on a time and place to meet again. With larger families, including extended families, you can do your own thing in small groups while still feeling like you're "together." The key to making this work is to communicate with one another and set meeting places/times for the next group get-together. Some families bring along two-way radios, which do work to keep one another in touch—keep in mind, however, that the metal bulkheads of the ship can interfere with reception. A much less expensive, low-tech way to stay in touch is by leaving one another notes in your stateroom—or if you're staying in multiple staterooms, leaving them on one another's doors or voice mail. You can keep tabs on one another with a notepad—everyone in your family/group signs in each time they pass through the stateroom. On our last group cruise (MouseFest—see page 265 for details), we made up our own versions of *Personal Navigators* and left them on each other's stateroom doors. During the cruise, folks were able to add new events/times/places to the list by noting them on the "master Navigator" on one stateroom door. Sometimes it's as simple as picking up a phone somewhere on the ship (they're everywhere) and letting a family member know where you are (live or via voice mail). So feel free to go your separate ways—just be sure to save some special time to spend together as a family, too!

Activities for Teens

Teens are perhaps the hardest to please onboard, given their widely varying interests and levels of maturity. Some are perfectly happy to swim all day or play in the arcade. Others prefer to hang out with the adults. Still others want to socialize with other teens and party. If your teen prefers more family-oriented activities, we refer you to the previous page. Read on for Disney's teen-oriented places and events:

Note: Disney defines a teen as a 13- to 17-year-old. Older teens (18 and 19) are considered adults (although drinking age is still 21 and up).

Personal Navigators—Teens can pick up their own version of the daily schedule in the teen club (see below). The teen version lists teen activities for the day and what's coming up.

Teens-Only Club—A teens-only (ages 13 to 17) hangout is located on both ships, but with some decor differences. The Stack (Disney Magic) and Aloft (Disney Wonder) are each located on deck 11 midship (in the spot of the former ESPN Skybox)—they're actually inside one of the ship's stacks! Both clubs are hip and trendy. The Stack has huge windows dominating the large dance floor, flanked by chairs, tables, and a bar. Aloft has more of a big city loft feel to it, with lots of comfy couches, brick walls, and a big table. Both clubs serve smoothies and non-alcoholic drinks at their bars. Tucked in the corner are three Internet terminals (same rates apply—see pages 144–145). Flat-panel screens are scattered throughout the clubs, offering a playlist of music videos which are shown on state-of-the-art TVs (including one giant-screen TV). In the back behind glass doors is an intimate little area with more comfy chairs, video screens, and a great view. Both clubs schedule plenty of parties, games, trivia, and karaoke during the cruise—the *Personal Navigators* list activities and times. The teen-only clubs also serve as an assembly spot for teen activities elsewhere on the ship, such as group events at the pool, group lunches, or a dance at Studio Sea.

© MediaMarx, Inc.

The Stack on the Disney Magic

© MediaMarx, Inc.

Allie at Aloft on the Disney Wonder

Arcade—Quarter Masters is a favorite teen hangout located on deck 9 midship, near Cove Café. There are also a few video arcade games on deck 10 midship, just below the teens-only club. See page 132.

Wide World of Sports Deck—Shoot some hoops alone or with friends on deck 10 forward.

Internet Cafe—Sure, there are Internet terminals in The Stack/Aloft, but sometimes it's just more convenient to come down to deck 3. See pages 144–145.

Ocean Quest (Magic only)—This new interactive area on deck 2 midship appeals to younger teens—see page 133 for details on this area.

Vista Spa—Normally off-limits to anyone under 18, teens may be able to sign up for facials/manicures on port days. $69/hour treatment. See pages 146–148.

Buena Vista Theatre—Teens love free movies! See page 142 for details.

Teen Parties—On special evenings, teens get dance parties, held either in The Stack/Aloft or in Studio Sea.

Teen "Deck"—Deck 10 (port side) next to the Outlook Bar is designated as a teens only deck. Hangout with friends or just worship the sun.

Teen Shore Excursions—Special teen-only excursions are available at certain ports, such as the "Wild Side" on Castaway Cay. See chapter 6 for details.

Teen Beach—On Castaway Cay, teens get their own beach with activities.

Other Teen Activities—Here is a sample of activities taken from recent teen *Personal Navigators* (keep in mind that not all these activities may be available on your cruise):

- ✔ Teen Tribal Challenge—Earn points for your "tribe"
- ✔ Wide World of Sports Trivia
- ✔ Hidden Mickey Challenge
- ✔ Pump It Up—weight training in the Vista Spa
- ✔ Gotcha!—A day-long game of elimination
- ✔ Teen Karaoke
- ✔ Power Lunch in Parrot Cay
- ✔ Go Fetch—Race against each other to get all your stuff
- ✔ Animation—Learn to draw your favorite Disney characters
- ✔ Gender Wars—Girls vs. Boys
- ✔ Bring It—trivia game show
- ✔ Celebrity Heads—Can you figure out which star is which?
- ✔ H20 Splashdown in the Goofy Pool
- ✔ Make a Mousepad
- ✔ Amazing Race—Race from location to location, following clues
- ✔ Invade the Lab—Find out what's cool in Oceaneer Lab
- ✔ Beach Bonanza on Castaway Cay—compete in challenging and daring obstacles
- ✔ Ultimate Teen Scavenger Hunt

Tip: Even if you're not sure about all these activities, we highly recommend teens visit the club on the first evening to meet other teens and see what it's all about. This first evening is when many onboard friendships are formed.

Note to Parents of Teens

Teens have virtually the run of the ship, and aside from the times they're with you, in The Stack/Aloft, or at a structured teen activity, they're not chaperoned. Teens may make friends with others from around the country and the world—their new friends' values may be incompatible with your own standards. It's a good idea to know where they are and who they're spending their time with, and agree on what time they should return to the stateroom (some teen activities go late into the night). Talk before you go and remind them that being on vacation is not an excuse to throw out rules about drinking, drugs, or dating. U.S. Customs does not take drug possession lightly and penalties can be severe in other countries, too. Note also that any underage person caught with alcohol on the ship is fined $250 and could get up to three days of "stateroom arrest."

Activities for Kids

A whopping 15,000 sq. ft. (1394 sq. m.) are devoted to activities just for kids. And there are a lot of kid-oriented activities on these ships. What else would you expect from Disney?

Oceaneer Club/Lab—A fantastic program for kids ages 3 to 12 with activities available daily from 9:00 am to midnight or 1:00 am. We highly recommend you encourage your kids to give these programs a try on the first day aboard. See pages 134–136 for more details.

Celebrate the Journey Farewell Show—Kids registered for the Oceaneer Club/Lab have the opportunity to participate in a special show on the last day of the cruise. All participants get to sing on stage with Mickey and receive a T-shirt! Held in the Walt Disney Theatre.

Swimming—We dare you to keep them out of the water! See page 140 for details.

Arcade—Located on deck 9 midship, Quarter Masters is a small arcade offering about 20 video games, plus air hockey and a prize "claw" game. These are straight games, though—no award tickets and no prize redemption. Most games are 50 cents to $1 each and you must use an arcade card to play. An "arcade debit card teller" machine dispenses $10 arcade cards—just use your Key to the World card to purchase. You can also purchase arcade cards at Guest Services. (Note: Keep your arcade card separate from your Key to the World card as they'll demagnetize if they come into contact.) If you're worried about your kids racking up huge charges for arcade cards, disable the charging privileges on their cards at Guest Services and purchase arcade cards for them. Hours: 8:00 am to midnight (last game at 11:50 pm).

© MediaMarx, Inc.

Allie enjoys a game in Quarter Masters

Games—In addition to the arcade, there are often pool games and Ping-Pong on deck 9, board games in the Oceaneer Club/Lab, basketball on deck 10, and shuffleboard on deck 4. There is no charge for these games.

Movies and Shows—Most of the movies playing are kid-friendly! And the stage shows in the Walt Disney Theatre are well-liked by kids, especially "Disney Dreams." See page 143 for details.

Sports—The sports deck on deck 10 forward may be just the thing for your young sport.

Deck Parties—The deck parties are very popular with kids! See page 141 for details.

Snacks—The opportunity to eat ice cream and hot dogs without forking over money is a real treat for kids! We don't think it's a coincidence that Goofy's Galley (Magic), Scoops (Wonder), Pluto's Dog House, and Pinocchio's Pizzeria are right next to the kids' pools. See page 113 for details.

Character Meet & Greets—Disney friends come out for autographs and photos many times during your cruise. For details, see page 270.

Ocean Quest (Magic only)—Did you know that there's a second bridge tucked away on deck 2 midship of the Disney Magic? It's called Ocean Quest! And while the bridge isn't real, it is a very fun—albeit scaled down—replica of the real thing, complete with a traditional captain's chair and LCD viewscreens with live video feeds. Kids can pretend they are steering the ship in and out of various ports in a simulator game. There are also computer and video game stations, movies on one of several plasma screen TVs, and arts and crafts. A sitting area with books, magazines, and board games is also here. All ages are welcome, but the area is really geared toward "tweens"—that's kids ages 10-14. Guests ages 8 and up are welcome to participate unaccompanied; kids under 8 may participate with their kids program (Oceaneer Club/Lab) and/or with a parent. Do note, however, that the area isn't always open to anyone—a posted schedule will let you know when there's an "Open House" (open to all) or when the area is reserved for certain age groups (usually kids 10-14) or for organized children's or teen's programming visits (kids participating in Oceaneer Club or Lab, as well as The Stack, venture down here as part of their regular programming). There's typically an Open House every day. Ocean Quest's hours of operation vary from day to day, with longer hours on days the ship is at sea. There is no extra cost to use this area, the area is always staffed by at least one crew member, and adults are welcome to try out their navigation skills during Open Houses. Also note that while kids do not need to formally check in, the on-duty crew member does have access to the kids programming computer and paging system. *(Wondering why Ocean Quest isn't on the Disney Wonder? It may be added when the Wonder goes into drydock in October 2006.)*

Here is a sample of kid-pleasin' activities taken from recent *Personal Navigators* (keep in mind that not all these activities may be available on your cruise):

- ✔ Kite Making Activity—make your own kite for Castaway Cay (no extra charge)
- ✔ Paper Plane Making
- ✔ Goofy's Fun Fitness Pool Party
- ✔ Board Games in the Promenade Lounge

Wondering about letting your **kids roam free** onboard? It depends on their age and maturity. A general guideline is kids 8-9 may be given some onboard freedom, while kids 10 and up can move about independently. These are in line with Disney's policies at the Oceaneer Club and Lab. If you let your kids loose, set down ground rules, such as no playing in elevators, keeping in touch, and set meeting times for meals, shows, and family activities.

Activities for Toddlers

While the rate for your toddler to cruise with you is a great deal, the variety of toddler-friendly activities onboard isn't as favorable. We've spent over 2 $1/2$ weeks onboard with a toddler (our son Alexander) in the last year alone, and here's what we've found to do: Go "swimming" in the shallow Mickey ear wading pool (see page 140). Take your toddler to Oceaneer Club (see pages 134-136) to play on the climbing toys or even participate in activities—your toddler is always welcome so long as a parent remains with the child (just check in at the desk for nametags). Watch a movie (see page 142)—you may want to sit in the back of the theater near the aisle for easy escapes, however. Go for supervised treks down the hallways and up and down staircases—our son Alexander learned to walk independently while exploring the ship this way. Your toddler may or may not sit through stage shows (Alexander doesn't yet), and may or may not enjoy Flounder's Reef (Alexander loves it so far), but both are worth trying.

Playing at Oceaneer Club/Lab

Oceaneer Club and Oceaneer Lab are special areas on deck 5 midship **designed just for kids**. The Oceaneer Club is for potty-trained kids ages 3 to 4 and 5 to 7, while the Oceaneer Lab is for older kids ages 8 to 9 and 10 to 12. The four age groups primarily play independently. Kids may participate in an older age group if they are within one month of the minimum age for that group, but older kids cannot join younger groups (though exceptions may be made for children with special needs). Participation in the Club and Lab is included in your cruise fare.

The Club and Lab provides fun, **age-appropriate activities** throughout the day and into the evening. Some kids spend virtually their entire cruise in these areas, while others drop in now and then. Some prefer to spend their time with their families or just playing with other kids elsewhere. Typically, the kids that visit the Club or Lab on their first evening (when friendships are being formed) are more likely to enjoy the experience.

To participate in the Club or Lab, **register on the first day** of your cruise. You can now register children online (see page 125). This saves you some time when you board, but you'll still need to visit the club open house on embarkation day. If you don't pre-register, drop by the Club or Lab on your first afternoon to take a look around and register your kid(s). To register, you'll need to fill out a participation form indicating name(s), birthday(s), age(s), special considerations (such as allergies, fears, and/or any special needs), and give your authorization for first aid if necessary. While there are maximum occupancy limits for the Club and Lab, Disney Cruise Line is very careful about booking and ratios—it's extremely rare that the Club or Lab fills up.

Once registered, your kids may **partake of Club/Lab activities as often as desired**—there's no need to sign up for blocks of time, no reservations for activities, and no worries. Kids ages 3 to 7 must have their parents sign them in when they enter the Club and the parents must return to sign them out later. Parents of kids 8 to 9 can indicate whether their kids can sign themselves in and out of the Lab or if the parents must sign them in and out. Kids ages 10 to 12 can sign themselves in and out by default. Each family is given one pager for the duration of the cruise. Each child gets a wristband and a name tag—they should keep the wristband on and bring the name tag with them when they go to the Club/Lab. Parents are welcome to drop in and observe at any time.

The **Oceaneer Club** (see photo to right) looks like a big, fanciful playroom with a pirate ship to climb on and slide down and computers to play games on—it's also equipped with tables and chairs, a dress-up room, and a stage. Floors and furniture are kid-friendly. It's a big hit with the 3 to 7 crowd. During a visit here, Jennifer's niece Megan (age 3) fell in love with it at first glance.

Megan and Natalie at the Oceaneer Club

The **Oceaneer Lab** (see photo on right) looks just like it sounds—a kids' lab! It has lots of tables and cupboards, along with computer game stations, activity stations, and board games. Allie's visit here (at age 9) is one of her best memories of the cruise—she loved making "Flubber"! Allie at age 12, however, felt it was too young for her and she refused to go. (Your mileage may vary!)

The computer game stations at the Oceaneer Lab

Pick up a ***Personal Navigator*** at the Club or Lab for the appropriate age group(s)—you'll find a great number of group activities planned, including games, crafts, movies, dancing, and theme parties (see sample activities below). Here is a sample of activities taken from recent kids' *Personal Navigators* (keep in mind that not all these activities may be available on your cruise):

Sample Activities for Ages 3-4

- ✔ Stormin' the Club—arts & crafts and playtime with new friends
- ✔ Nemo's Coral Reef Adventures—join Nemo for a magical puppet show!
- ✔ Do-Si-Do with Snow White—learn the "Dance of the Seven Little Dwarves"

Sample Activities for Ages 5-7

- ✔ Professor Goo's Magical Experiments—make your own Flubber!
- ✔ So You Want To Be a Pirate?—learn how to play pirate with Captain Hook!
- ✔ Animation Antics—learn how to draw Mickey Mouse

Sample Activities for Ages 8-9

- ✔ Bridge Tour—get a tour of the ship's control center
- ✔ Disney Game Show—test your Disney knowledge
- ✔ Goofy Files—enter the invisible world of forensics and crack a case

Sample Activities for Ages 10-12

- ✔ Animation Hour—write and create your very own commercial
- ✔ Mysterious Islands—share scary stories of lost ships and vanishing islands
- ✔ Cranium Crunchers—test your knowledge and bring your team to victory

Fanciful climbing toys at Oceaneer Club

A huge video game station at Oceaneer Club

Oceaneer Club and Lab *(continued)*

Tips and Notes

The **first activity** on the Disney Wonder typically starts at 6:30 pm or 7:00 pm on your first night aboard. On the Disney Magic, the entire first night is now "family night" and if children want to visit this evening, a parent must accompany their child in the Club/Lab (kids who can check themselves in and out do not need to be accompanied by a parent). Family night gives kids a chance to acclimate to the new surroundings with the security of parents nearby.

Trained **counselors** keep kids active and safe while checked in. The counselor-to-kid ratio is 1:15 (ages 3 to 4) and 1:25 (ages 5 to 12). Counselors are mostly female, college grads, and from English-speaking countries (Canada and the United Kingdom are popular). You may rest assured that counselors are trained in how to evacuate children in the event of an emergency.

If your kids are checked in during **mealtimes**, they'll generally be taken up as a group to Topsider's/Beach Blanket Buffet for a trip through a special kid-friendly buffet. At times, younger children may remain in the Club for meals, at the discretion of the counselors. Other than that, no food or drink (other than a water fountain) is provided here.

If your child is very **recently potty-trained**, have a special talk with them before leaving them alone at the Club. All that first-day excitement may give them upset tummies, and they may not know what to do without you there to help. Show them where the toilet is, explain to them that they will need to use the toilet by themselves (the crew members cannot help them nor will they regularly prompt them to use the toilet), and remind them that they can ask a counselor to contact you if they have a problem. Rest assured that the toilets and sinks in the Oceaneer Club are kid-sized, not adult-sized. If a child has an accident, you will be paged and they may be asked not to re-visit the Club for 24 to 48 hours in the event their accident was the result of an illness. Pull-up diapers are not allowed unless you are dropping off your child in their pajamas in the evening hours, as it is understood that young children may sleep in pull-up type diapers at night and will probably be sleeping when you pick them up.

Do you have a **toddler under three** who is already potty trained? If so, the counselors may allow your child to join the Oceaneer Club on a trial basis. Your child must be fully potty-trained however, from deciding when to go, finding the toilet, closing the door, removing clothing, going potty, wiping, redressing, and washing up. If you have a fully potty-trained child, and you feel your child is ready for this type of environment, talk to the counselors and politely inquire if your child can be accommodated.

Kids may stay in the Club or Lab while you go **play in port**. Just be sure to let the counselors know where you are, and be aware that your pager won't work if you go too far afield. Also check that the Club/Lab opens early enough for your shore excursion meeting time.

If a child gets **sleepy** while at the Club, they can nap on a sleep mat, which is usually placed near the check-in desk or in a quiet corner. If kids are still in the Club around 10:00 pm, counselors will bring out sleep mats to rest on while watching movies.

When Allie cruised at age 9, her 10-year-old cousin Nina was also along. Alas, the 8 to 9 group and the 10 to 12 group have different activities. Allie and Nina found it frustrating that they couldn't stay together. Allie asked us to remind you that if you have siblings or cousins in these **different age groups**, let them know in advance that they may be separated so it's not such a huge disappointment.

Activities for Adults

Kids, keep out—this page is just for grown-ups! Disney may be family-focused, but rest assured Disney hasn't forgotten your adult needs. There are **plenty of adult-oriented and adult-only activities** onboard, including an entire entertainment district (see next page). If you're worried you'll be bored, it's unlikely—we never have enough time to do what we want, with or without kids. Here's a list of specifically adult-oriented activities:

Bingo—If you're not a bingo person you may want to pass this one up, but it is surprisingly popular and fun! Bingo is the only gambling onboard and attracts mostly adults. (Kids often attend and play, but you must be 18 or older to claim any winnings.) Bingo is held once a day in Rockin' Bar D/WaveBands (and occasionally in the Promenade Lounge) and a special "Snowball" jackpot rolls over each day until won. Cards are about $10 for a single pack (5 cards, one per game), $25 for a value pack (15 cards, three per game), or $35 for a super pack (30 cards). Your odds of winning are higher earlier in the cruise, when fewer people are playing. Prizes (cash and gifts) are awarded daily at each game. Yeah, baby!

Dance Lessons—Learn the basics of ballroom dancing—check your *Personal Navigator*.

Beer and Wine Tastings—There are beer tastings in Diversions (check your *Navigator*). There's also a wine tasting seminar (about $12)—only adults can participate. Make reservations at Guest Services.

Captain's Receptions—Meet the captain at various functions, including receptions and Disney Navigator Series seminars (see page 149).

Sports—Shoot hoops or play volleyball on the Wide World of Sports deck (deck 10 forward), play shuffleboard or run laps on deck 4, or try your hand at Ping-Pong (deck 9 mid). And don't forget the exercise classes in the Vista Spa (see pages 146–148).

Pin Trading—Bring along your pins and trade with others. Special pin trading sessions are generally held in the Atrium Lobby—check your *Personal Navigator*.

Games—Play chess or backgammon in Diversions or start up a Scrabble game in Sessions/Cadillac Lounge. There may also be pool games at the Quiet Cove pool. Check your *Personal Navigator* for details.

Live Auctions At Sea—Fun to bid or just watch others bid! See page 151 for details.

Cocktail Hours—Held in the Atrium (deck 3 midship) or in Sessions/Cadillac Lounge (deck 3 forward) on certain days. Alas, the beverages—alcoholic or not—aren't complimentary, with the possible exception of the Captain's Reception.

Seminars and Tours—Get the low-down on shopping, shore excursions, and debarkation procedures with talks held in the Buena Vista Theatre (note that these talks are broadcast on your stateroom TV if you can't make it). And on the 7-night cruises, adults can learn the art of entertaining, get behind-the-scenes peeks, and more. See page 148.

In addition to the above, you'll also enjoy these **adult-only places**: Palo restaurant (see pages 109–110), Vista Spa (see pages 146–148), the Quiet Cove pool (see page 140), the Cove Café (see page 139), Signals bar (deck 9 forward), the adult entertainment district (see next page), and Serenity Bay Beach on Castaway Cay (see page 250). And while it's not adults-only, the Buena Vista movie theater in the late evenings is mostly adults (see page 142).

Tip: Check your *Personal Navigator* for a special section titled "Adult Activities."

Adult Entertainment District (Beat Street/Route 66)

After all those adults-only activities, you may want an adults-only place to wind down the day, too. Beat Street (on the Disney Magic) and Route 66 (on the Disney Wonder), both on deck 3 forward, are exclusively for adults 18 and older after 9:00 pm. The names and decor of the clubs and lounges may differ a bit on the two ships, but after a recent renovation on the Wonder they offer essentially the same venues. On both ships you can expect to find a dance club; a relaxing, adult lounge; a pub; and the ship's duty-free liquor shop. Here is a description of each club:

Dance Club—Rockin' Bar D (Magic) and WaveBands (Wonder) are the ships' largest clubs, offering Top 40 and Golden Oldies dance music, DJs, karaoke hours, and cabaret acts featuring entertainers from the stage shows. Typically, a special event is held each evening around 10:30 pm or 11:00 pm, such as the Match Your Mate game show, Rock and Roll Night, 60s Night, 70s Disco Night, and 80s Night. Many cruisers report a preference for the 70s night, and would pass up the 80s night. Guests are selected from the dance floor to participate in some shows—if you want to be picked, get up and be wild! The Match Your Mate game show works like the Newlywed Game. They choose three couples who've been married for various durations as contestants. Unmarried couples will enjoy watching it, but only married couples can participate. A DJ or live band generally precedes and follows these events. Hours are usually from 7:30 pm to 2:00 am. Smoking is allowed in the rear, but poor ventilation can make the entire club smoky.

Dave gets drafted to play one of the Village People during 70s Disco Night

Smoking Onboard

Unlike most other cruise ships, Disney restricts smoking to limited areas on the ship, and enforces their rules. Smoking is allowed in the dance club, part of the adults-only lounge, Diversions, and open-air guest areas such as decks 9 and 10 and stateroom verandahs. The Mickey Pool area is an exception, as it is all non-smoking. No smoking is allowed in any of the staterooms. We've had no problems with smoke on our cruises. And smokers report that the accessibility of smoking areas meets their needs, though it is sometimes tough to find an ashtray (try deck 10). You can purchase cigarettes ($16/carton) in the liquor shop on deck 3 forward. For those interested in Cuban cigars, you can purchase them in virtually all of the ports except Key West. At the time of writing, cigar smoking was allowed only in the usual open-air guest areas (decks 9, 10, and stateroom verandahs). Sometimes there is a cigar and cognac night at the adult pool. Keep in mind that you cannot bring Cuban cigars back into the U.S., so smoke 'em while you can.

Adult Lounge—This lounge is always adults-only. On the Disney Magic, it's called Sessions and it has a jazzy feel. On the Disney Wonder, it's called Cadillac Lounge and has a vintage auto theme. Relax in low, comfy chairs, listen to the pianist or recorded music, and get mellow. Music listening stations are available along the wall with the large portholes if you want to listen to something different (though cruisers report they aren't always functioning). This is a dim, mellow lounge—perfect for pre-dinner or pre-show drinks and romantic interludes. It's not uncommon to find fruit and cheese platters in here between 7:30 pm and 8:30 pm. Hours are usually from 4:30 pm to midnight or 1:00 am. Smoking is permitted at the bar and in the rear of the lounge only, but it can still get smoky.

Diversions—Formerly a dueling piano club, renovations in September 2003 on the Magic and October 2004 on the Wonder opened the space up into Diversions, an all-purpose pub and sports bar. The lounge now has huge portholes, spilling light into a clubby room filled with comfy chairs. Warm wood tones create a relaxing atmosphere, as do large chess/backgammon tables in the center of the room. The lounge still has a piano off to the side, as well as a long bar in the back of the room. A small selection of books and magazines are available for those who want a quiet respite during the day. What can you do here besides drink and relax? Check your *Personal Navigator* for sporting event broadcasts (shown on the numerous televisions in the back), beer tastings and trivia, and a British Pub Night. Smoking is allowed at the bar only.

Diversions on the Wonder

Beverages of all kinds are served at all clubs. See page 116 for details on availability and prices. Snacks may be available out in the hallway from 11:00 pm–midnight. There's a duty-free liquor shop (see page 261), but purchases cannot be consumed onboard.

Cove Café

A new adults-only area has recently appeared on both the Disney Magic and Disney Wonder: Cove Café on deck 9, beside the adults-only pool. It took the place of the Common Grounds teen club, which moved up to deck 11 at the same time. Cove Café is a cozy coffeehouse, lined with books and magazines and filled with light from huge, new portholes and sliding glass doors. Four Internet terminals are here (see pages 144–145 for rates), as are several music listening stations. An extensive specialty coffee menu is available—expect to pay $2.00 for espresso, $2.50 for cappuccino and café mocha, and $4.75 for coffee drinks laced with liquors. Teas ($3.75) are also available, as is champagne, wine, port, martinis, and a full bar. Light snacks such as pastries and sandwiches may be available, too. Open until midnight. This is an delightful expansion of the ship's adults-only territory.

Cove Café

Swimming in the Pools

Cruise ship pools aren't exactly sized for Olympic competition, but while your ship's three pools are best described as "cozy," it doesn't stop them from being some of the busiest places onboard. What makes Disney's pools especially nice is that they're fresh water, not salt; that kids, families, and adults each get their own pool; and that they have a little extra magic.

Quiet Cove Adult Pool—the largest pool onboard—is on deck 9 forward. This is one of the five areas on the cruise that adults can go to for child-free relaxation. Pool depth is 48" (122 cm). No jumping or diving is permitted. Adjacent are two whirlpools (caution: the water can be hot!), Vista Spa, Cove Café, an open shower, and the Signals pool bar.

Amidship is **Goofy's Family Pool** featuring an image of Goofy snorkeling at the bottom of the pool. Alongside Goofy's pool are two whirlpools, an open shower, and Pinocchio's Pizzeria (see page 113). Pool depth is 48" (122 cm). No jumping or diving is permitted. At the other end of the pool is a stage where the crew and Disney characters join the guests for the deck parties (see next page). A hideaway deck may be pulled out to completely cover the pool during deck parties.

The sight to see on deck 9 is **Mickey's Kid's Pool** (see photo below). True to Disney style, a regular wading pool and slide is transformed into Mickey Mouse. His face is the main part of the pool with a depth of 18" (46 cm). Mickey's ears (with a depth of 11"/28 cm) are for the very little ones. This is a very busy place on sea days. The centerpiece of Mickey's Kid's Pool is the water slide supported by Mickey's gloved hand. To use the slide, the kids must be between ages 4 to 14 and between 32" and 64" tall (81 to 162 cm). The slide is staffed by crew members, but there are no lifeguards. Health regulations require that kids be potty-trained—swim diapers are not allowed in the pools. Infants with swim diapers are allowed in the starboard "ear," which is a fountain play area. Pluto's Dog House as well as Goofy's Galley/Scoops (see page 113) are nearby.

© MediaMarx, Inc.

A quiet, lazy day at the Mickey Pool

Typical **pool hours** are from 6:00 am to 10:00 pm for Mickey's Pool and 6:00 am to midnight for the other two pools. Goofy's pool closes during deck parties and other events that use the extending deck. Mickey's slide is only open when the pool is busy (usually 9:00 am to 6:30 pm).

Tip: When is a good time to use the pools? With a lot of guests and small pools, they can get very crowded. This is especially true on hot afternoons at sea. The trick is to think differently—go when your fellow guests are busy elsewhere, like in port or during meals. Immediately after you embark is a good time, but be ready to make it to your assembly station by 4:00 pm. Other good times are in the evenings and early in the morning, as the pools open at 6:00 am.

Living It Up at Deck Parties

Every Disney cruise, regardless of its length, has at least one of Disney's famous deck parties. These high-energy parties are held on and around the family Goofy Pool on deck 9 midship. No, you don't have to dance on water—the pool is covered by a large, retractable dance floor during the parties. You can expect to be entertained by some or all of the following: a live band, DJ, dancers, fireworks, a dessert buffet, big video screen (Magic), and "party animals" (Disney characters). Here are descriptions:

Bon Voyage Sailaway Celebration—Every cruise enjoys this celebration, held as your ship pulls away from the dock. This is probably the first time you'll meet your cruise director, who is joined by Disney characters and either a live band or a DJ. As the ship gets underway, the ship's whistle plays the first seven notes of "When You Wish Upon a Star." We highly recommend this party—it really gets you in the mood (see the photo on page 19). Tip: Celebrate your sailaway by bringing bubbles to blow or a small flag to wave! (Party typically starts at 4:30 pm or 4:45 pm and lasts for about 30 minutes.)

Pirates in the Caribbean Party—Ahoy, ye landlubbers! This new deck party is offered to all Disney cruisers, regardless of cruise length. On the three- and four-night cruises, it's held on the evening you're in Nassau; on the seven-night cruises, it's held on day 4 or 5 (see page 120 for schedule). The party starts around 9:45 pm on deck 9 midship, after the Pirate-themed dinner earlier that evening (see page 111). Expect lots of infectious music, dancing, and visits from crew members and Disney characters (watch out for Jack Sparrow and Captain Hook!). You are treated to a Pirate buffet around 11:00 pm with desserts and "pirate fare" such as chili, fajitas, and turkey legs. You may even get fireworks! We've experienced this party twice ourselves and it's a not-to-be-missed experience—it's better than the Tropical deck party it replaced. Pirate or Caribbean dress is encouraged (we dressed up and loved it!). The party lasts until about 11:30 pm.

Pirates!

The **music** at the deck parties is quite loud and is geared towards older kids, teens, and young adults. If you don't want to be in the thick of things, you may enjoy watching from deck 10 midship. We recommend you visit deck 10 during the sailaway party—it's the best place to enjoy the party while watching the ship pull away (see sidebar below).

To find out exactly what deck parties are offered, check the ***Personal Navigator*** upon arrival. Note: In inclement weather, the deck parties are held in the atrium (deck 3 mid).

Sailing Away From Port Canaveral

One of the most exciting experiences of your cruise is when your ship pulls away from the pier and makes its way down the channel, heading for the ocean. You don't want to miss it. Make time to go up to deck 10 around 5:00 pm and watch the scenery slide by as you leave port. Look for the crew members at the terminal—they don huge Mickey gloves and wave the ship off. One of the best places to watch your ship's progress is from deck 10 forward, near the Wide World of Sports courts. Or visit deck 9 forward to watch the bridge crew on the wing. Look for the escort of security boats as your ship moves through the channel, too!

Watching Movies and TV

The Buena Vista Theatre on deck 5 aft is not your typical, boxy movie theater. This is a **gorgeous, sumptuous theater** with 268 stadium-style seats, a large, two-story screen, and a state-of-the-art sound system. The only thing missing are drink holders on the armrests of the seats. And on the Disney Magic, the new "Dive-In" theater offers fresh-air movies.

You can expect to see recent Disney animated classics and first-run movies from Disney's motion picture divisions. You may also see some popular, non-Disney movies a few months after they've been released—we were treated to "Harry Potter" on our May 2002 cruise. Films are rated G and PG (with some PG-13 and R in the Buena Vista Theatre only) and are shown in that order throughout the day. Movies are free, there's no need to reserve seats, and they start as early as 9:30 am—the last show usually starts between 10:00 pm and 11:00 pm. Check your *Personal Navigator* or the theater for a **list of movies** during your cruise. Matinees on at-sea days are popular—arrive early for a good seat. Wondering what will be playing on your cruise? About a week before you cruise, you can call 888-325-2500, choose the "reservations" option, then ask the representative what movies will be showing. Tip: If you like to snack during your movies, a stand outside the theater sells packaged snacks, bagged popcorn, and beverages. To save money, order room service and bring it with you or take a detour up to deck 9's snack counters.

© MediaMarx, Inc.

Buena Vista Theatre

The new **"Dive-In" outdoor movies** on the Disney Magic are always rated G or PG and have recently included favorites like "Mary Poppins" and "Pirates of the Caribbean." Movies are displayed on a large, bright Jumbotron screen affixed to the stack above the Goofy Pool (deck 9 midship). Movies play in afternoons and evenings, but are generally limited to one or two showings per day. These outdoor movies are currently available only on the Magic, but we're hopeful the Wonder will get them after its renovations in October 2006.

Your **stateroom TV** has plenty to watch, too! Below is a recent channel guide (channels and stations may vary). Use the TV for Disney background music while you're in the stateroom. Jennifer and Dave enjoy watching movies on it at the end of the day. Check your stateroom for a movie list. Anticipate about 12–15 distinct movies to be showing on TV—movies repeat frequently. The "all movies, all the time" channel (42) starts a new movie every two hours, beginning at midnight. The Disney Classics channel (40) also starts a Disney animated movie every two hours, beginning at 1:00 am. Both movie channels go around the clock. Tip: You may be able to watch taped performances of the stage shows like *Golden Mickeys* and *Disney Dreams* on your stateroom TV—look between 6:30 pm and 10:30 pm on show nights.

16 What's Afloat	26 CNN Headline News	36 Disney Channel	46 Shopping, Etc.
18 Disney on Land	28 CNN	38 Toon Disney	48 Voyage Info (or DVC Info)
20 ABC	30 Golf/Shore Excursions	40 Disney Classics	
22 Entertainment	32 ESPN	42 24-Hour Movies	50 Ship Information
24 Channel Guide	34 ESPN2	44 CBS	52 Bridge Report

Introduction Reservations Staterooms Dining Activities Ports of Call Magic Index

Enjoying the Shows

Depend on the world's greatest entertainment company to deliver the **best live shows** on the seven seas. Disney turned to Broadway and Hollywood for inspiration (rather than Las Vegas), and delivers shows that the whole family enjoys. Live shows are presented in the Walt Disney Theatre on deck 4 forward, a 975-seat theater that fills the ship from deck 3 to 7. State-of-the-art sound and lighting systems (there are nearly 400 stage lights!) and a very talented cast combine to entertain you.

On all of the cruise itineraries, you can expect to see three shows: *Golden Mickeys, Disney Dreams*, and either *Twice Charmed* (Disney Magic) or *Hercules, the Muse-ical* (Disney Wonder). The 4-night cruises add a Variety Show. The 7+-night cruises add the *Welcome Aboard Variety Show*, a first-release film, an entertainer (such as a juggler or magician), and the *Farewell Variety Show*. Shows are held **twice nightly** at roughly the same times as the dinner seatings (see page 100), so if you have the early seating, you'll see the "late" show (and vice versa). Shows are 50 to 55 minutes long. Arrive about 15 to 30 minutes before showtime to get a good seat. Disney doesn't allow videotaping, flash photography, or the saving of seats in the theater. Preludes Lounge (located just in front of the theater) sells beverages and snacks (such as candy bars), or you can bring your own. Smoothies and beverages are sold in the theater before the show.

Hercules the Muse-ical (Disney Wonder)—A whimsical show that follows the adventures of Hercules as he goes from zero to hero with lots of puns, singing, dancing, and gags.

Twice Charmed—An Original Twist on the Cinderella Story (Disney Magic)—This creative show picks up where the traditional Cinderella story ended. What would happen if an Evil Fairy Godfather turned back time to stop Cinderella from fitting into the glass slipper?

Golden Mickeys—This delightful, Hollywood-style award show features favorite musical scenes from Disney films, just as you might see at the Oscars or Tonys. Flanking the stage are two movie screens that show a wide range of documentary film clips, presentations by celebrities like Roy Disney and Angela Lansbury, and excerpts from the animated films.

Disney Dreams—The must-see show for Disney fans! Anne-Marie is visited in her dreams by characters from her favorite Disney stories. It's wonderfully sentimental and the special effects at the end are not to be missed. Every Disney fan will be at least a little misty-eyed by the end of this "bedtime story." Being the most popular show aboard, Disney Dreams is often crowded. Check your *Personal Navigator* for an extra performance in the afternoon.

Variety and Cabaret Shows—Featuring guest performers who do a short sampling of the shows they'll perform later in the Rockin' Bar D/WaveBands club. Because Disney switches guest entertainers mid-cruise on the 7-night itinerary, the Farewell Variety Show features different performers than the Welcome Aboard Variety Show.

Notes: The ***Who Wants to be a Mouseketeer?*** show which was previously held in the Walt Disney Theatre now only appears in Studio Sea (if it all). In this game show (based on the popular show "Who Wants to be a Millionaire?"), contestants are selected at random from the audience and the "phone a friend" panel is also selected from the guests. Prizes are limited edition Disney merchandise, much smaller than the one million dollars offered on television. No longer is a free cruise offered as a prize, either. It's still fun to play, though!

Introduction Reservations Staterooms Dining Activities Ports of Call Magic Index

Surfing the Internet

While it isn't as fun as a message in a bottle, the Internet is an easy, quick way to keep in touch with family, friends, and clients while you're cruising. Internet access is available on both the Magic and Wonder at computer terminals and as wireless access (wi-fi) in select areas of the ships.

Terminal Access—Computer terminals are available to guests in three locations onboard: Internet Cafe (main location, eight terminals, open to everyone), Cove Cafe (four terminals, adults only), and The Stack/Aloft (two terminals, teens only). The Internet Cafe (located at the aft end of the Promendade Lounge on deck 3 midship) is open 24 hours a day and boasts about 8 terminals (flat panel screens, keyboards, mice, headphones, and video cameras) with reasonably comfortable chairs. Typically at least one, if not several, terminals are available at any given time. All terminals are installed with Web browsers and America Online. Your e-mail provider may offer a Web-based interface to check your e-mail—inquire about this before you leave home and bring any necessary web site addresses, login names, and passwords with you (see worksheet on the next page). Note that if you can access your e-mail through America Online (AOL) or the web, you avoid the CruisEmail rates noted later (see Pricing on the next page)—just be sure not to send e-mail through the "E-Mail" option on the terminal and use AOL or the web instead. AOL Instant Messenger users can use the AOL application to access their buddy list and send Instant Messages. Note that if you login to any e-mail, message boards, or other sites that require a login name and password during your time on the cruise, be sure to logoff before you leave the terminal. If you do not, the next person who uses those same sites could find themselves able to access your account or post under your user name on a message board. Digital Seas (http://www.digitalseas.com) provides reliable Internet access. If you have questions once you are onboard, you can check with one of the Internet Cafe managers, who are on duty during the day and early evening. There may be a printer available, though it may also incur an additional, per-page fee—inquire with the manager on duty. Note that the Internet Cafe is not always open the morning of disembarkation.

One of Jennifer's hangouts, the Internet Cafe

Wireless Access—At last! Wireless Internet access arrived on both the Magic and the Wonder in 2005 in select locations on the ship. To use it, you'll need to bring your own laptop (which must be wireless-ready) and power cables. Once onboard, visit Guest Services (deck 3 midship) and request the Wireless Internet Information. Next go to a wireless "hot spot" on the ship—at press time, the ten "hot spots" are the Promenade Lounge, Lobby Atrium (decks 3-5), open decks (9 and 10), Cove Cafe, Studio Sea, Sessions/Cadillac Lounge, and Rockin' Bar D/Wavebands. The wireless access does not reach to staterooms, unfortunately. We preferred to use our laptop while sitting in the comfortable chairs on deck 4 or 5, overlooking the atrium. As for ease of use, we had to fiddle a bit with our settings at first but after that, it worked fine. Instructions for both PC and Mac users were provided on the information sheet from Guest Services. Note that printing is not available with wireless access. Tip: If you plan to use wireless, you may want to investigate using a VOIP service (Voice Over Internet Protocol) such as Skype (http://www.skype.com) to make cheaper outgoing phone calls at sea. We haven't tried Skype ourselves, but we've witnessed other cruisers using it successfully.

Pricing—Alas, Internet usage is not free. Expect to pay about 75 cents a minute for access (either terminal access or wireless access). If you expect to surf for more than an hour total, you can purchase 100 minutes for $55. Unfortunately, your minutes only work for either terminal access or wireless access, but not both. While there is no unlimited minutes package offered for wireless access, you may be able to get unlimited terminal access at $39.99 (3- and 4-night cruises), $89.99 (7-night cruises), or $129.99 (10-night cruises). Everyone in your stateroom can use the unlimited package, but only one person can be online at a time. Look for a free access period on your first night and again on the last day (typically five free minutes), but the terminals will be very popular during this time. Also note that you are "on the meter" from the moment you login until you logoff, and you cannot use the terminal without being logged in. You can send special "CruisEmail" ($3.95 each) or "Video Email" ($4.95 each), but note that the basic Internet usage fees are tacked on top of these rates. "CruisEmail" is an unnecessary expense—save money by using a free e-mail service such as Hotmail (http://www.hotmail.com) or Yahoo! Mail (http://mail.yahoo.com). All Internet usage fees are automatically billed to your onboard account. Parents who don't want their kids to use the Internet can contact Guest Services to disable their Internet accounts. Note that no credit is given for unused time plan minutes.

Logging In—Expect to enter a login name—it's typically the first initial and last name of the person under whose name the cruise reservation was made, plus the stateroom number (e.g., jmarx2612). Passwords are also required, and may initially be the birthdate of person who made the cruise reservation.

Access—If you've purchased a time plan package, only one member of your family/group can be online at any one time. Note that if another family member is online somewhere else, you won't be able to get online until they log off. While there are computers in the Oceaneer Club and Lab and Ocean Quest, the kids can not surf the Internet from them.

Off-Board Internet Access—There are Internet Cafes offering lower rates in various ports of call. In Nassau, "Tikal Tees & Tokens" has Internet access at 10 cents/min. In St. Maarten, there's an Internet Cafe at the end of the pier for 20 cents a minute. In St. Thomas, "Soapy's Station" in front of the Havensight Mall offers access at 10 cents/min. In Key West, check out the "Internet Isle Cafe" on 118 Duval Street for 25 cents/min. In Cozumel, the "C@fe Internet" near Ave. 10 and Calle 1 has access at 10 cents/min. You can usually find Internet Cafes very near the pier—just browse or ask around.

Web Site Addresses—E-mail your favorite web site addresses to yourself before you cruise or visit http://www.passporter.com/dcl/porthole.htm once onboard for helpful links.

My E-Mail: ______________________________

Account	Login Name	Password	Notes

Tip: Use some system to disguise your passwords here, just in case your PassPorter is seen by someone else.

Rejuvenating at the Spa

The Vista Spa & Salon on deck 9 forward offers world-class spa treatments, a hair salon, an aerobics studio, and a fitness room. The large spa is **exclusively for adults** (with the exception of special teen days—see your *Personal Navigator*). The newly expanded spa on the Disney Magic measures in at an astounding 10,700 sq. ft., while the spa on the Disney Wonder is a "mere" 8,500 sq. ft. Like most ship spas, the facility is operated by Steiner (http://www.steinerleisure.com) and the spa staff tends to be female and young. The spa is typically open from 8:00 am to 10:00 pm. Spa reservations can now be made in advance online (see page 125).

If the spa interests you, we recommend you visit during the **open house** on your first afternoon (check your *Personal Navigator* for specific start times). This is also the best time to make reservations for spa treatments, which can go very quickly. Read this section well so you have a good idea of what spa treatments you may want to reserve (see next page). Reservations must be cancelled at least 24 hours in advance to avoid a 50% fee.

The **hair salon** offers a variety of services—reservations are necessary and they fill up quickly for formal and semi-formal evenings. The hair stylists specialize in European styles and all the basics. Prices: blow dry ($30 to $45); woman's hair cut with wash, cut, and style—$52 to $70 (depends on hair length); man's cut and style—$29; highlights ($79 to $99); permanent color (roots)—$64 to $79; and permanent color (full head)—$84 to $104. You can also get nail services: A 40-minute manicure is $40 and a 55-minute pedicure is $55.

The **aerobics studio** is where many of the fitness classes and seminars are offered. Activities are listed in the *Personal Navigator* as well as on a schedule available in the Vista Spa. Expect complimentary hair consultations, metabolism seminars, fatburner aerobics, detoxification seminars, skin care clinics, introduction to Pilates, de-stress techniques, Step Magic, and cardio kickbox. You are encouraged to sign up in advance for the free classes and seminars, which last about 30 to 45 minutes each. Group personal training may be offered on your cruise for $75/60 minutes. Or get a Body Composition Analysis to measure your body's metabolic rate, water, fat, and lean tissue—price is $30 and includes analysis from a fitness instructor. Zone diet consultation (which includes the body composition analysis) is available for $75/45 min. Pre-registration is required for the personal training sessions, body composition analysis, and diet consultations.

The **fitness room** has a panoramic overlook on both ships. On the Disney Magic, the fitness room recently doubled in size by expanding over the bridge, and it now overlooks the ship's bow. Disney Magic's expansion also brings more fitness equipment, an area for spinning classes, and private salons for Pilates instruction. On the Disney Wonder, the fitness room still overlooks the bridge—in fact, it's the only place on the ship where you can peek into the bridge. On both ships, the fitness rooms offers guests the use of free weights, Cybex weight machines, treadmills, stair-steppers, ab-rollers, and stationary bikes. No fees or reservations are needed to use the fitness room, though there may be a waitlist for a treadmill during peak times. The fitness room is more crowded on at-sea days. Open from 7:00 am to 8:00 pm.

Tip: Walk (or jog) all around the perimeter of deck 4—the "promenade" deck. One lap around the deck is 1/3 of a mile (535 m.); three laps is one mile (1.6 km). Want to walk with others? Check your *Personal Navigator* for instructor-led "Walk a Mile" morning sessions.

Spa treatments are given in one of twelve private treatment rooms or in the private "spa villas" on the Disney Magic. Separate men's and women's locker rooms are available with restrooms, delightful showers, saunas, steamrooms, and lockers. Some people prefer the showers at the spa to the showers in their staterooms—there's more room, the water pressure's better, and the showerhead is luxurious. Present your Key to the World card at the check-in desk to get a robe and locker key at no charge.

Spa Treatments—A variety of treatments are available at prices ranging from $26 to $288. We've underlined the spa treatments we've tried and would do again! A menu of treatments is available in the spa, but here's a sneak peek: Spa Taster (massage and facial for $109/50 min. total or $242 for couples massage); Aromaspa Ocean Wrap with Well Being Back Massage ($176/75 min.); Ionithermie Algae Super-Detox ($145/55 min.); Aromastone Therapy ($175/75 min.); LT Oxygen Lifting Facial ($109/55 min.); Elemis Pro Collagen Facial ($130/50 min.); Well Being Massage ($109/50 min. total or $242 for couples massage); Lime & Ginger Salt Glow ($178/75 min.); Gentle Touch Teeth Whitening ($199/45 min.); and Cabana Massage at Castaway Cay ($139/50 min. or $278 for couples massage). Let's not forget the Tropical Rainforest , the Exotic Rasul, and new Spa Villas—read on for more details!

Tropical Rainforest—An innovative, relaxing "thermal suite" with a dry sauna, a chamomile-essence sauna, a eucalyptus steam room, and special showers that spray water overhead and on the sides. The main room has four heated, tiled loungers (see photo on right)—loll about on one then cool off in a fog shower. Jennifer loves this! The Tropical Rainforest is open from 8:00 am to 10:00 pm. It's very popular and can host upwards of two dozen people—men and women—at any one time. Quietest times are on the first day of the cruise and on port days. On busy days, the four tiled loungers are usually occupied and waiting for one to open can be frustrating. Swimsuits are required. Cost is $15/day (just $8 if you're having a "hands-on" spa treatment) or $35/3 days, $75/week, or $120/10 days.

© MediaMarx, Inc.

Jennifer's mother Carolyn relaxes in the Tropical Rainforest

Exotic Rasul (formerly known as Surial Ritual Chamber)—This unique treatment is inspired by the Rasul cleansing rituals performed in the Sultan's harems during the Ottoman Empire. You are escorted to the tile-lined ritual chamber, which is a suite with a sitting area, steam room, and shower. Exfoliating mud is in a small bowl—smear the mud on yourself or on each other (if you're with a friend) and relax in the steam room to absorb the minerals and trace elements from the mud. Afterward, shower off and apply complimentary lotions and scrubs. This is very popular with couples. We loved it ourselves! Be warned that it does get very hot. Bring some bottled water—you'll probably get quite thirsty—and extra towels. Cost is $83 for 1 to 3 people for 60 minutes.

Rejuvenating at the Spa *(continued)*

Spa Villas (Disney Magic)—The Disney Magic's spa expansion included the creation of singles and couples spa "villas" with special spa treatments. The villas are private, Mediterranean-themed treatment rooms with their own verandahs, complete with whirlpool tubs, open-air showers, and luxurious lounge "beds." All spa treatments in the villas include a tea ceremony, a bathing ritual of your choice, and foot cleansing ceremony—and you can spring for a bottle of champagne and strawberries or even add on an extra spa treatment. Treatments available in the single villas (for one person) include Alone Time (50 min. spa treatment of your choice—$199/105 min.); Body Purifying (100 min. body wrap with full body massage and dry float bed—$245/155 min.); and Sensory Awakening (facial and deep tissue massage—$295/155 min.). Treatments in the couples villa include Romantic Hideaway (50 min. spa treatment of your choice—$449/120 min.); Couples Choice (75 min. spa treatment of your choice—$475/130 min.); and Ultimate Indulgence (facial and deep tissue massage—$589/130 min.). If you do the math, you'll see that each of these treatments has 55-70 minutes of extra time included so you can enjoy your spa villa's amenities in privacy, though we should note that this extra time is not in one uninterrupted block but rather a bit before your treatment and the rest after. And if you need more privacy than the open-air verandah provides (remember, that is where your whirlpool tub and shower are located), there are two curtains you can use—one offers privacy for the shower, the other offers privacy for the tub. We understand from cruiser reports that these curtains may not provide complete protection when it's windy or when in port (just something for the shy to keep in mind). While we haven't yet had the pleasure of experiencing a spa villa ourselves (oh, but we will!), we do want to point out the delightful dry float bed now available (as noted in the Body Purifying treatment above). Jennifer experienced it on a Carnival cruise, which also has Elemis spas—highly recommended! Note that while the Spa Villas are on the Disney Magic only at press time, it is likely that the Wonder will also receive them along with a similar spa expansion when it goes into drydock in October 2006.

Special Treatments—Check your *Personal Navigator* or visit the spa to learn about special treatments offered during your cruise. We've seen Teen Days for hair and nails, Ladies Mornings/Nights, and a Mid-Cruise Booster Package. The Ladies Morning/Night package is a massage, foot massage, and facial in a private room, plus a trip to the Tropical Rainforest where you can enjoy champagne and sweets. Cost is $150 for 120 minutes.

Cabana Massages—Get a private or couples massage in one of the delightful, open-air cabanas on Castaway Cay. Note that the treatments in the cabanas are a bit more expensive than the same ones on the ship. Prices are $139 for a single massage and $278 for a couples massage (choose from Spa Taster or Well Being Massage). Reserve early as they book up quickly. We recommend you avoid the first or second appointment of the day, just in case the ship docks late. Also, keep in mind that the oils they massage into your skin can make your skin more likely to burn later in that Castaway Cay sunshine—bring hats and coverups as well as extra sunscreen. Also see page 250.

Spa Products—The spa personnel may push their spa products during treatments, which is uncomfortable for some guests. The products are Elemis (http://www.elemis.com) and are good, but pricey. If you don't want to buy a product, just say "no thank you" and be firm. You could also indicate on your health form that you don't want to purchase products.

Tipping—It's customary to tip 15%, though really good service may deserve 20%. 10% is fine for treatments like the Exotic Rasul which require minimal staff time, or treatments like the spa villas which have extra private time. Just write in the amount you wish to tip on your bill and it will be charged to your onboard account.

Learning Through Seminars

We keep saying that nobody has to be bored, even on a long cruise, and here's more proof! Disney produces a full schedule of shipboard tours, seminars, and programs on the 7-night and longer cruises for guests 18 and older. You don't even have to register or pay extra in most cases.

Disney's Art of Entertaining—These presentations showcase a senior chef who prepares a dish, of course allowing you to sample it. They also include tips on place setting, decorating, and napkin folding. Some have wine sampling. Programs include Great Expectations: The Appetizer, Dazzling Desserts, and Signature Entrée. Available on the Magic only.

Galley Tour—Enjoy a guided tour of the main galley between Lumière's/Triton's and Parrot Cay. Available on both the Magic and Wonder. See page 106 for more details.

Disney Behind the Scenes—Presentations by a Disney historian, actor, or artist (either a special guest or regular crew member), usually presented in the Buena Vista Theatre. These presentations vary in length and by topic but they are all entertaining and well worth the time. Programs include a Stage Works Tour (meet the stage production crew members—they demonstrate some of the stage effects, answer questions, and allow you to go up on the stage and take a look around at the set and props); Costuming Tour (see and even wear some of the costumes used in the show); and a Q&A session with the Walt Disney Theatre cast (hear stories and get answers to questions). This program is offered on the Magic and on the 4-night cruise on the Wonder.

Disney's Navigator Series—Programs include "The Making of the Disney Magic" (the captain presents a video showing the history of the Disney Magic from concept to construction to maiden voyage and then answers questions) and Captain's Corner (a Q&A session with the senior staff covering just about everything involving the cruise and the ship—it's very impressive, informative, and fun). Available on the Magic only.

Wine Tasting Seminar—This is a good place to mention the "Stem to Stern" Wine Tasting Seminar held on all cruises in either Palo or one of the lounges. For $12/adult (21 and up only), the Cellar Master introduces you to wine types, gives you tips on identifying wines, and shows you how to properly taste a wine. Seminar includes tastings of four to six wines. You may also receive a commemorative pin for attending the seminar. (Pin traders take note!) Reservations are required—stop by Guest Services to make reservations. Available on both the Magic and the Wonder.

Beer Tasting—Check your *Personal Navigator* for a beer tasting session held in Diversions (deck 3 forward).

Towel Animal Folding—Find out how to make those cute animals they leave in your stateroom each night—check your *Personal Navigator* for time and place.

Art of Disney Magic Self-Guided Tour—The Walt Disney Company was founded by an artist, so it's natural that its beautiful ships are full of art—original as well as reproductions. The Art of the Disney Magic tour is a self-guided tour of the art found everywhere on the Disney Magic (sorry, the tour is not available on the Disney Wonder). Pick up a tour booklet at Guest Services—it leads you around the ship, describing and explaining the artwork. Get the booklet early in the cruise so that you can read about the art in the restaurants as you dine in each. If you'd like to see photos of the various stops on the tour, visit http://www.castawayclub.com/dmtour.htm.

Kicking Back and Relaxing

This chapter would not be complete without a few words on how to get the most out of your "down time" on the cruise. You know—relax, bum around, sunbathe, or whatever. This is one of the benefits of cruising, after all!

Relaxing on Deck—Looking for the best place to loll about in a deck chair? Deck 9 is great if you want to be near the pools or people-watch, but it gets very crowded. Try the deck aft of Topsider's/Beach Blanket Buffet after dinner—almost no one goes there. Deck 10 has lots of sun. Deck 7 aft has a secluded and quiet deck. Deck 4 has very comfy, padded deck loungers and lots of shade (see photo below). The lounge chairs on decks 7-10 are made of plastic and metal and recline in several positions, including completely flat. Disney requests that you not reserve the lounge chairs, so don't drape a towel over a chair to use later. If you see loungers being saved with towels, don't be shy about using them. There are also tables and chairs on deck 9 which are mostly in the shade and protected by windows, but decks 4 and 10 can get very windy. Alas, only the larger verandahs at the very aft of the ship are large enough for lounge chairs, but regular deck chairs are on each verandah.

Sunbathing—Sunworshippers typically prefer deck 10. Deck 7 aft works well, too. Decks 4 and 9 are typically too shady. Don't forget sunscreen—the Caribbean sun is harsh.

Reading—With all the things to do onboard, you might not think to bring a book. But if you enjoy reading, you'll absolutely adore reading in a deck chair on your verandah, on deck 4 (our personal favorite), or deck 7 aft.

Strolling—Haven't you always dreamed of perambulating about a deck? Deck 4, also called the Promenade Deck, allows you to walk all around the perimeter of the ship (3 laps = 1 mile). Decks 9 and 10 are also options, though they can get crowded during the day. Deck 10 gets very windy and wet in the evenings, but if you can handle that it makes for fun walks.

Napping—There's nothing like a good nap, especially while cruising. It's something about the lulling effect of the waves. Your stateroom is a great place for a nap, but you may also catch some zzz's in a quiet spot like deck 7 aft.

People-Watching—It's hard to find a spot where you can't people-watch on a ship with this many people! Deck 9 and deck 4 overlooking the atrium are particularly good spots, though.

Spa—The Tropical Rainforest in the Vista Spa (see page 147) is a relaxing spot to spend time.

Shopping—Why not? See page 261.

Relaxing on deck 4

> **Lost & Found**
> Did you leave your half-finished book on your lounge chair before heading to lunch? Report it to Guest Services on deck 3 midship. If you discover you left something behind after disembarking, check with Lost & Found in the terminal or call Disney Cruise Line after returning home. Don't forget to ID all your important items—just in case!

Overlooked Attractions Aboard

Disney is renowned for its attention to detail, and the Disney Cruise Line is no exception. There are any number of smaller, overlooked attractions and activities that may interest you. Here's a list of our favorites:

Hidden Mickey Hunt—How many Mickeys can you find onboard? The internationally-recognized Mickey Mouse head (one big circle and two smaller circles for the ears) has been hidden in murals, railings, foot stools—you name it! We know of more than 25 on the ships, including one in the dinner plate at Palo. Ask at Guest Services for the Hidden Mickey Challenge—it's a fun activity geared towards kids, but still fun for adults. To see the photos of the hidden Mickeys, visit http://www.castawayclub.com/hmick.htm.

Listening Stations—Listen to your favorite tunes in the adults-only lounge (Sessions/Cadillac Lounge) and the Cove Café. Just check the playlist for the music, punch in the code on the pad, and put on the headphones.

Pin Trading—This popular activity that started at the parks has migrated to the cruises! You can buy all sorts of enamel, cloisonné-style pins on the cruise (there are about 500 unique cruise pins) to trade with others. Or bring pins from the parks or from home. Check your *Personal Navigator* for trading sessions. The shopping supplement distributed daily highlights the featured pin for the day (see page 261 for shopping). There's even a PassPorter enamel pin, though you can't trade it for Disney pins—see page 299.

Live Auction at Sea—Unlike the silent auctions on Disney cruises previously, the new live auctions allow cruisers to bid on up to 500 pieces of Disneyana and high-priced artwork. Opening bids can range from $40 to more than $10,000. Here's how it works: Cruisers register in advance (free) to receive a bidding card with a number. Auction items are made available for preview prior to the auction, during which time you can mark which pieces you are interested in to ensure they are brought out for bidding. This is followed by the live auction itself which is open to everyone and quite exciting in its way, even for spectators. The auctions are typically held on sea days in the Promenade Lounge, though we've also seen them in the Lobby Atrium. In addition to the auctions, special artist exhibitions may go on display—check your *Personal Navigator*. If you win an auction, your purchase may be available to take home immediately (especially if it is a low-ticket item), but more likely it will be shipped to you in 6-8 weeks. Payment is made at close of auction. Live auctions are run by a third party, Park West at Sea (http://www.parkwestgallery.com), which does live art auctions on many other cruise lines.

Off-The-Beaten-Path—A thorough exploration reveals several little nooks and crannies. Explore hallways, elevator lobbies, and staircases for art. The secluded deck on deck 7 aft (open from 7:00 am to 11:00 pm) is great for sunbathing. Check out deck 6 behind the midship elevators—you can walk through for a closer look at the mural. Deck 8 aft also has a small deck that is sometimes open. And how about that view from the fitness center?

Religious Services

Seven-night cruisers can attend an interdenominational service in the Buena Vista Theatre on Sunday at 8:30 am. Erev Shabbat (Jewish Sabbath Eve) services are held on Friday at the appropriate time. Or attend services in Cape Canaveral on Sunday—see http://www.marinersguide.com/regions/florida/capecanaveral/churches.html. Western Caribbean cruisers can attend afternoon services on Sunday in Key West—see http://www.marinersguide.com/regions/florida/keywest/churches.html.

Introduction Reservations Staterooms Dining Activities Ports of Call Magic Index

Overlooked Attractions *(continued)*

Lounges—There are many quiet spots onboard to relax with a tropical drink or a glass of wine. Besides the lounges we described on pages 138–139, you'll find Preludes (deck 4 forward), open from 6:00 pm to 9:30 pm for pre-show and afterglow drinks—all ages welcome; Signals (deck 9 forward) is next to the adult pool so it's limited to ages 18 & up—it's typically open until 7:00 pm; Outlook Bar (deck 10 forward) overlooks the adult pool and seems a bit removed from the hustle of the lower decks—all ages welcome; and the Promenade Lounge (deck 3 midship) offers games in the day and live entertainment in the evenings for all ages—it's usually open to midnight.

© MediaMarx, Inc.

The Promenade Lounge

Captain Photo Sessions and Signings—It's always good to meet the Captain! If you're willing to wait in line, you can usually get a handshake and a photo with the Captain. And let's not forget that the Captain's signature is a great souvenir! The Captain typically appears at one of the shops on deck 4. Check your *Personal Navigator* for times and places.

Guest Entertainer Workshops—Seven-night and up cruises have entertainers onboard for the variety shows, and sometimes these entertainers give demonstrations and/or workshops in magic, ventriloquism, juggling, etc. Check your *Personal Navigator*.

Napkin Folding/Towel Animal Folding/Ice Carving Demonstrations—See how each of these amazing creations comes about. Check your *Personal Navigator*.

Coffee or Lunch With the Crew—Have a chat with crew members and learn about life onboard. Various sessions may be offered, some for just singles, some for just adults, and some for everyone.

Treasure Hunts—We just love hunting for "treasure," those little-known bits of trivia and hidden details throughout both the Magic and the Wonder. While there are no organized treasure hunts outside of possible kids' activities, you can certainly make your own and challenge your friends and family. We also host a treasure hunt during our MouseFest cruises each December (see page 265). To top it off, we're publishing a new book on treasure hunts at Walt Disney World and the Disney Cruise Line—it's filled with ready-made hunts for all skill levels (see page 302).

Photo Surfing—While you're onboard, you'll probably have your photo taken by Disney's professional photographers many times. Kids in particular get lots of shots. Regardless of whether you plan to actually buy any of the photos, it's fun to just stop by Shutters and "surf" the photos on display. It's fun to look at photos of other cruisers, too! (And if you find a dreadful photo of yourselves that you'd rather not have anyone seeing, feel free to drop it in one of the containers for unwanted photos.)

Art Browsing—If you enjoy art, take a stroll around the ship to appreciate the various prints, paintings, and sculptures that fill the Disney ships. Stairways contain a good share of the artwork onboard but are often overlooked because many people prefer elevators. And don't forget the Live Auction at Sea items (see page 151), which are placed on display for preview much of the time. Disney Magic guests may also enjoy the "Art of Disney Magic Self-Guided Walking Tour" on page 149.

Hair Braiding—For that authentic "I've been to the islands" look, how about cornrows or braids, ladies? Get the "look" early in the cruise from the braiders up by the pools on deck 9. Hair braiding is also available on Castaway Cay—see page 250.

Dolphin Spotting—Did you know dolphins sometimes frolic in the waters around the ship? The best time to spot dolphins is within the first hour of leaving a port, particularly as you're leaving Port Canaveral. For optimum spotting, you'll want to be looking over either the port or starboard side of the ship, toward the bow. Dolphins like to hitch a ride by using the pressure created in the bow wave of a moving ship. We recommend the big windows on deck 3 or outside on deck 4 for the best views, but deck 10 also offers good views. Taking pleasure in spotting dolphins is an old tradition—Ancient Greek sailors considered dolphin escorts a good omen for a smooth voyage.

Talent Show/Karaoke—If you've got an exhibitionist streak, you may enjoy the opportunity to show your stuff in a talent show or karaoke session. Guest talent shows aren't available on all cruises, but we have recently spotted them on the 7-night and longer cruises—they are typically held in Rockin' Bar D on the last day of the cruise. Look for an announcement in the *Personal Navigator* regarding sign-ups. Crew talent shows are hilarious—if you spot one of these in your *Personal Navigator*, make it a point to attend. Karaoke is much more common and is available for most age groups. Of course, watching other people perform can be almost as much fun as doing it yourself!

Meeting Internet Friends—You may have friends on your voyage and not even know it. If you're a member of an Internet community, just let others know when you're sailing and try to arrange a "meet" or two while you're onboard. Two good places to hook up with fellow cruisers are PassPorter's message boards (http://www.passporterboards.com) and DIS (http://www.disboards.com).

Learning More—Want to know the latest inside scoop on Disney Cruise Line? The single best place to pick up tidbits is at the Navigator's Series Captain's Corner session (see page 149) where the Captain answers cruiser questions. Beyond this, chatting with crew members can yield interesting news, but you'll need to take their unofficial buzz with a grain of salt.

'Til We Meet Again—On the last night of your cruise, the Disney characters and Walt Disney Theatre performers put on a sweet little show along the grand staircase in the lobby atrium. The characters "meet and greet" after the show so you can get that last "kiss" goodnight. It's typically held at 10:15 pm, but check your *Personal Navigator*.

Stuck in Your Stateroom?

Caring for a young one? Feeling queasy? It's not uncommon to be "stuck" in your stateroom for a while and unable to get out to enjoy all these wonderful activities. If you find yourself in this predicament, the stateroom TV is your obvious means of entertainment—note that many onboard talks and even some shows are recorded and later broadcast on the TV during your cruise. If you can't stomach all-TV-all-the-time, reading material is available for purchase in Treasure Ketch. Cove Cafe also has a supply of magazines and books that you can borrow. If you have a verandah, spend as much time outdoors as you can—it'll vastly improve your mood. Here are some other ideas: take a bath at sea • listen to music on the TV (several of the channels play music non-stop) • request a Mickey Bar from room service • try your hand at folding a towel animal • record a personal greeting on your stateroom phone • decorate your stateroom door • use the Disney Cruise stationery in the desk drawer to write letters or keep a journal. Most importantly, keep this in mind: If you had to get stuck in a room somewhere, a pleasant stateroom is a good place to get stuck.

Playing Your Way

If you've read this chapter, you know just how much there is to do aboard a Disney ship. Here are some tips to help you make the most of it all:

- To help you **navigate the ship**, remember this general rule: We had Fun in the Forward (front of ship) and we Ate in the Aft (back).
- Keep in mind that there is **way more to do** on the ship than you can fit in—even on days you visit ports. So don't expect or try to cram in every activity, or you'll be disappointed in the end.
- "I enjoy sitting out on the wonderful deck 4 padded lounge chairs. But in the cooler months the evenings can get chilly. If you like to relax and listen to the sound of the waves even in the cooler temperatures, then **bring a blanket down** and snuggle up like I did. Several people who passed me commented on how cozy I looked and why had they not thought of that. I had brought a favorite travel-sized, down comforter with me—it rolled up quite small and was very light. It proved a much better alternative to the scratchy blankets provided in the staterooms. This was also the way I fought off seasickness on our last evening. My mother headed off to the stateroom and became more ill, while I went down to deck 4 with my blanket and felt much better in the fresh air."

  – contributed by Disney cruiser Penny DeGeer

Magical Memories

- *"It's worth the wait to get to the Walt Disney Theatre early for the shows so you can sit in the first row. During all of the shows we attended on our cruise, special things happened to people on the front row. Guests there often interacted briefly with characters from the show, whether it was to be picked on gently, get a little wink, or whatever. This really made the experience special for kids and adults! In one show, some kids from the front row were called on stage to participate in Hercules, the Muse-ical. And in Disney Dreams, the big blow-up tentacles from Ursula came out from the stage and close to those in the front row. It was great! "*

  ...as told by Disney cruiser Amanda Poole

- *"During our October 2004 cruise on the Disney Wonder, we witnessed a lunar eclipse. As my husband Ron and I sat on deck gazing up at the sky, a woman stopped to ask what we were looking at. We told her to look at the moon! She got so excited. She was from Australia and said she had never seen an eclipse before. A short while later, she returned with her family—the excitement on their faces was magical."*

  ...as told by Disney cruiser Margo Verikas

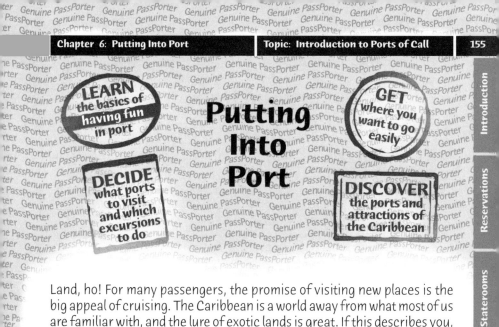

DECIDE what ports to visit and which excursions to do

DISCOVER the ports and attractions of the Caribbean

Land, ho! For many passengers, the promise of visiting new places is the big appeal of cruising. The Caribbean is a world away from what most of us are familiar with, and the lure of exotic lands is great. If this describes you, then this chapter was written with your needs in mind. We hope to help you determine which ports you'd most like to visit (and hence which cruise itinerary to choose) and what you can do while you're in each port.

Each and every port on the various Disney cruise itineraries, including their home port of Port Canaveral and their private island, Castaway Cay, is represented by a "port guide." Each port guide is eight pages long (Port Canaveral is just six pages as it has no Disney shore excursions) and includes general information (time zone, currency, climate, etc.), ambience, history, transportation, safety, walking tour, layout, attractions, sports, beaches, and shopping. In addition to all this, we add one of our own maps of the port and a detailed listing of the shore excursions offered through Disney. These port guides are by no means comprehensive. (That would require an entire book for each port.) Rather, they focus on what's possible and practical during the 8 to 12 hours you'll have in port and should give most day visitors an excellent overview.

For those of you who've "been there and done that" or simply don't want to venture off the ship, feel free to stay onboard while the ship is in port. Disney offers plenty of activities onboard during port days, and you'll enjoy the slower pace and quieter atmosphere of the ship. Do note that the onboard shops will be closed while you're in port, and some places (like Flounder's Reef) will have shorter operating hours.

On all four-night and longer itineraries, you'll have a day (or two, or three—see pages 32–37) when you visit no ports at all. These are called "at-sea" days, and most passengers adore them. The crew offers more stuff to do onboard than usual, and the ship hums with activity. Plus, there's just something special about "being underway" during the day, instead of at night as is more typical on port days.

➢

Island Daze

Feeling adventurous? There's a whole world to explore off-ship. Each of the ports, many of which are islands (even Port Canaveral, which is on a barrier island), offer fun things to do and explore. Here are the details:

If you wish, you can **get off the ship** at each port (guests under 18 will need to be with an adult or have the permission of a responsible adult to go alone) and there is no additional fee to simply visit the ports—Disney folds the port fees into your cruise price, unlike other cruise lines. It does cost extra to book shore excursions (see next page), and if you plan to eat ashore anywhere other than Castaway Cay, that cost is also your responsibility.

It's fun to watch as the **port slides into view**. Check your *Personal Navigator* for the arrival/departure times and observe from deck 4, deck 10, or from your verandah.

Allie watches the ship come into port

While the ship and Castaway Cay have a cashless system, you'll need to **bring cash, major credit cards, and/or traveler's checks** to pay for anything at the other ports. You will also want to have small bills to tip excursion operators, too. Note that there is no ATM (cash machine) on the ship, but there are ATMs at the ports (except Castaway Cay). Keep in mind, however, that ATMs will give you cash in the local currency—this can be good if you're planning to use it immediately, but a drawback if you are taking out any extra or don't understand the local currency-to-dollar rates well enough. So if you're looking for U.S. currency from an ATM, you'll generally only find it at ports that use the U.S. dollar as their main currency—check for this in the small chart at the bottom of the first page of each port description in this chapter.

Some of the ports attract merchants aggressively **hawking their wares or services** near the dock. If this makes you uncomfortable, avoid eye contact and keep walking. Most travelers find that hawkers will respect a polite, but firm, "No thank you."

Some guests like to bring **drinks and snacks** with them during their time onshore (see page 117). Be aware that you can't bring open containers of food back on the ship.

Changing facilities may not always be handy for those **planning to swim** or get wet. We suggest you "underdress" your swimsuit (wear it under your clothing) before going ashore.

Some guests **never get off the ship** at the ports, preferring to stay onboard and enjoy the ship's amenities. We've done this ourselves on non-research cruises. The decision to stay onboard or explore the port is a personal one, however, and no one way is right for everyone. If this is your first visit to a port, we suggest you at least get off and look around for an hour, or book a shore excursion. If you decide you like it, you can explore more!

Disney **does not guarantee** that you'll visit all ports on an itinerary. Bad weather or rough seas can prevent docking, and you may spend the day at sea or at an alternate port instead. Although you will not receive a refund of cruise fare if this happens, you will not be charged for the cancelled Disney shore excursions, either. In addition, you may have port charges for the port you missed refunded to your stateroom account. In any case, Disney will do what they can to make your extra onboard time fun.

Shore Excursions

Disney offers many shore excursions at each port, with the exception of Port Canaveral. These activities incur an additional, per-person fee, anywhere from $6 for Castaway Cay float rentals to $395 (for the Atlantis Deep Explorer in Grand Cayman). In most cases, the excursions are not run by Disney but by outside companies. The good news is that if you book one of these excursions through Disney, virtually all details are taken care of for you. All you need to do is reserve the shore excursion, pay the fees, and show up at the designated meeting point to go ashore. Here are the details:

A **variety of shore excursions** are available, from sightseeing, walking tours, and beach visits to snorkeling, scuba diving, and kayaking. Check the last few pages of each port guide in this chapter for a list of the shore excursions offered at the time of writing. You'll also receive a shore excursion guide with your cruise documentation, and you can check http://www.disneycruise.com (click "Fun Ashore") for a list of the excursions and prices. Note that the excursion details, times, and prices given in this guidebook may change.

Once you've read this chapter carefully, choose and **reserve your excursions in advance**. Some excursions are very popular and get booked quickly. To make advance reservations from 2 to 75 days before your cruise (up to 90 days for Castaway Club members and up to 105 days for guests in stateroom categories 1–3), reserve online at http://www.disneycruise.com or call 877-566-0968 (see page 125 for more details). (Note: You cannot make reservations until you've paid in full.) You can also e-mail excursion requests to dcl.shore.excursion@disneycruise.com, or fill out the form that comes with your cruise documentation and fax to 407-566-7031. You can alter your shore excursion requests any time up to two days prior to sailing. After that time, all excursion reservations are considered final and cannot be changed or refunded. If you do not pre-reserve shore excursions, you can visit the Shore Excursion Desk (deck 3 midship) to check availability and reserve excursions. Use the worksheet on page 255.

When you pre-reserve your excursions, fees are billed to your onboard account and your **excursion tickets** are waiting in your stateroom upon arrival. If you book excursions onboard, you'll receive your tickets in your stateroom the night before the excursion. When you get your tickets, check the time and meeting location printed on it. With each ticket is an excursion waiver form, which you should fill out and sign ahead of time.

On the day of your excursion, bring both the ticket(s) and the signed waiver(s) to the **meeting location** at the assigned time, where they are collected. You'll receive a color-coded sticker to wear, identifying yourself as a member of the excursion group. When ready, a crew member leads the group off the ship and to the excursion.

You can usually book the same excursions offered by Disney for less if you **do it on your own**. The excursion operators are locally known and most have web sites. You'll need to find your own transportation to and from the excursion, but in return you'll have more flexibility and you can take side trips if you wish. Weigh these benefits against the peace of mind you'll have when booking through Disney. We offer tips to do an excursion "On Your Own" at the end of excursion descriptions in this chapter. Then why book with Disney Cruise Line? First, it's simple and easy. One call and everything is arranged. Second, Disney books blocks of excursion tickets, sometimes entire excursions—so you might have trouble getting a ticket on your own. Third, if a Disney excursion is delayed, they'll hold the ship for you—do it yourself, and the ship may sail without you.

➤

Understanding the Shore Excursion Description Charts

We describe each of Disney's shore excursions with our custom-designed, at-a-glance charts. Each chart includes a description, tips, restrictions, typical meeting times, our reviews (when available), cruiser reviews in summary form (when available), information on how to do the excursion on your own, a reader rating, and more! We've organized this array of information into a consistent format so you can find what you need quickly. Below is a key to our charts, along with notes and details.

Key to the Excursion Chart:

Reader Rating[2] Icons[3]

[1] **Excursion Name** [Disney's Code Number] Rating: #	
Description offering an overview of the excursion, what to expect (without giving too much away, of course), historical background, trivia and "secrets," our recommendations and review (if we've experienced it), tips on getting the most out of the excursion, height/age restrictions, typical meeting times, things you should and shouldn't bring with you, a summary of cruiser reviews we've received, and contact information if you want to do the excursion (or something similar to it) "On Your Own"—note that doing it on your own will often be with a different tour operator, however.	**Type**[4] Activity Level[5] Ages[6] Prices[7] Duration[8]

[1] Each chart has an empty **checkbox** in the upper left corner—use it to check off the excursions you want to take (before you go) or those you've taken (after you return).

[2] When available, we note a reader rating from a scale of 0 (bad) to 10 (excellent). These ratings are compiled from the shore excursion reviews we receive (see sidebar below).

[3] Icons indicate what you should (or can) bring along. The sun icon suggests plenty of sunscreen and a hat. The bag icon means you can bring a totebag or backpack along on the excursion. And the camera icon indicates you can bring a camera or camcorder.

[4] The type of activity you can expect on the excursion, such as Sports, Beach, or Tour.

[5] The physical activity level, such as Leisurely (a mild level of activity), Active (a moderate level of activity), and Very Active (a whole lot of activity).

[6] The age requirements for the excursion. Some excursions are for All Ages, while others are for certain ages and up. A few are for teens only.

[7] Prices for adults (and kids, if available). Kids prices are for kids up to 9. Most tours that do not involve a boat transfer will allow kids under 3 to go free. Prices subject to change.

[8] The approximate duration of the excursion. If we offer a range, it's more likely that the excursion will take the maximum time noted, in our experience.

About Our Cruiser Reviews

Excerpts from our cruiser reviews are summarized at the end of each shore excursion description. These reviews are submitted by cruisers via an online form. All reviewers receive a coupon good for PassPorter guidebooks from our online store. Thanks to all who sent in a review! To submit your own review of a shore excursion, visit us at http://www.passporter.com/dcl and click the "Shore Excursion Survey" link.

Introduction | Reservations | Staterooms | Dining | Activities | Ports of Call | Magic | Index

All Ashore! All Aboard!

If you decide to take a shore excursion or simply explore the port on your own, you'll need to get off the ship and on the shore. Here's how:

To find out what time you can **go ashore** at a given port, look for the "All Ashore" time in your *Personal Navigator*—we also give typical times in each of our port guides. This time is typically the earliest you can disembark in the port. (You don't have to go ashore if you prefer to stay onboard.) Ports that put more limitations on disembarking (such as Grand Cayman) may require that guests not on shore excursions meet in the Walt Disney Theatre before going ashore. If this is necessary, the details will be listed in your *Personal Navigator*.

At most ports, the ship **pulls up right alongside the dock** and guests step out right onto the pier. When this isn't possible, guests must be ferried ashore in "tenders." Boarding a tender isn't difficult—you simply step off the ship and onto the tender and enjoy the ride to the shore. If the seas are rough, you are more likely to feel the effects while on the tender. At the time of writing, the only port that always requires tenders is Grand Cayman—other ports may require tenders if Disney cannot secure a berth or if rough seas inhibit docking.

Before you go ashore, pack a day bag with bottled water, sunscreen, hat, raingear, a watch, and any other necessities you may need. You may also want to "underdress" your bathing suit so you don't need to find changing facilities in the port. And make sure everyone has their Key to the World card and, for those over 18, photo ID. (If you lose your Key to the World card, go to Guest Services on deck 3 midship.)

To go ashore, follow the signs in the passageways to locate the specific "**tender lobby**" from which you'll disembark. There are two of these, both located on deck 1 (see page 5). Remember, however, that deck 1 passageways don't extend the length of the ship, so you'll need to take the proper elevator to deck 1 to reach the correct lobby—the signs won't lead you wrong. Note that if you booked a shore excursion through Disney, you'll disembark with the other guests going on the shore excursion. See page 157 for more details.

Once you're in the tender lobby, have your **Key to the World card** (and photo ID) in your hand so the crew may swipe your card and allow you to disembark. Guests under 18 must have an adult accompany them to the gangway to go ashore anywhere other than Castaway Cay. Once you're cleared to go ashore, simply step out onto the dock or into the tender. Watch for a crew member handing out towels for use ashore (towels are bath-size, not beach-size). If they run out of towels at the gangway, the crew members will invite you to take towels from the pool areas on deck 9.

While you're onshore, **keep an eye on the time**—you don't want to miss the boat! The "All Aboard" time is noted in your *Personal Navigator*. If you are late, the ship won't wait for you and it is your responsibility to get to the next port to reboard the ship. The exception to this rule is for guests on one of Disney's own shore excursions—if their excursion makes you late, Disney will hold the ship's departure for you.

Reboarding is simple. Just return to the dock area, present your Key to the World card (and photo ID) to security personnel to enter the dock, show your ID again to the Disney crew to either board the ship or board the tender (which then takes you to the ship). You will need to put your belongings through a security scanner once you're onboard and have your Key to the World card scanned again (so Disney knows you're back on the ship). Don't bring restricted items onboard, such as opened food and black coral.

Shopping Ashore

For some cruisers, shopping is a major reason to visit an exotic port of call. Not only can you find things you can't get at home, but prices on certain luxury items can be remarkably good.

If you plan to shop on shore, pick up the **Shopping in Paradise** port guide at the gangway. It lists recommended stores at which to shop, though keep in mind that these stores are included because they have an advertising relationship with the publishers of the shopping guide. The good news is that if you purchase from one of those listed stores, you'll receive a 30-day guarantee on repair or replacement of an unsatisfactory item (but the guarantee doesn't help if you change your mind about an item). Regardless of this guarantee, you should always ask about return policies before you make a purchase. If you have questions, a knowledgeable crew member is stationed at the gangway or at the Shore Excursion Desk on deck 3 midship. If you need to make a claim after you return from a cruise (and within 30 days of purchasing the item), you must contact the merchant directly and send a copy of your correspondence along with the store name, date of purchase, copy of receipt, and a written description of the claim to Onboard Media, 960 Alton Road, Miami Beach, FL 33139. For more information, visit http://www.onboard.com or call 800-396-2999.

Live presentations on shore excursions and shopping are held during the cruise (freebies may be given out to lucky attendees at the shopping presentation) and later broadcast on your stateroom TV. Check the *Personal Navigator* for times. Stop by the Shore Excursion Desk on deck 3 midship for port and shopping information and excursion brochures (see examples at http://www.dcltribute.com). Desk hours are listed in the *Personal Navigator*, too.

Certain luxury items can be had for less in **particular ports**. Here's where your fellow cruisers have found good deals:

Alcohol: St. Thomas
Cigars: Everywhere but Key West
Cosmetics: St. Thomas, St. Maarten
Jewelry: St. Thomas, St. Maarten (Phillipsburg), Grand Cayman, Cozumel
Perfume: St. Martin (Marigot)
Quirky/Artsy stuff: Key West
Silver jewelry: Cozumel
T-shirts: Key West (though all ports sell t-shirts, of course)
Watches: St. Maarten (Phillipsburg), St. Thomas

Here are some **smart shopping tips** for great deals and quality merchandise:

- Be prepared. Know what you're looking for before you venture out. And be familiar with the typical prices of the items you're interested in so you know whether or not you're getting a good price.
- If you want to deal but aren't successful at initiating it, walk out of the store—this usually gets the clerk's attention.
- If you're shopping for jewlery, ask to go out in the sun to look at it—you may notice flaws in the sunlight that you could not see in the store.
- Check out other stores with similar goods before you buy. And before you leave the store, ask the clerk to write down the item you are interested in along with the price on the back of the shop's card in the event you decide to return.
- Don't settle for something you don't really like.
- Keep your receipts in a safe spot—you'll need them for customs declarations.

Port Canaveral and Cocoa Beach
(All Bahamas/Caribbean Itineraries–Home Port)

Far more than just a place to park a cruise ship, Port Canaveral offers an exciting extension to your Disney cruise vacation. This is Florida's Space Coast, home to the Kennedy Space Center, 72 miles (116 km.) of prime Atlantic beachfront, the Merritt Island National Wildlife Refuge, ecotourism, water sports, sportfishing, etc. Do you have an extra week?

Cocoa Beach at sunrise

AMBIENCE

Thundering rockets, crashing surf, and the total peace of an empty beach come together in the Port Canaveral area. You won't find built-up beach resorts like Daytona or Fort Lauderdale here, though crowds do rise for space shuttle launches. There are just a relative handful of hotels and beachfront condos—so quiet that this is where endangered sea turtles choose to nest! Whether you unwind here prior to your cruise or wind up your vacation with a visit to the astronauts, this can easily be one of the best ports you ever visit.

GETTING AROUND

You'll either want to drive your own car or rent a car to get around (taxis are not abundant). A list of area transportation companies is at http://www.portcanaveral.org/portinfo/groundtrans.htm. The Space Coast region stretches from Titusville in the north to Melbourne in the south (see map on page 165). I-95 runs north/south on the mainland, paralleled by U.S. 1 for local driving. Many attractions are on the barrier islands to the east, across the Banana and Indian Rivers, and the Intercoastal Waterway. SR A1A is the principal route for beach access. Commercial airlines serve Melbourne International Airport and Orlando International. Port Canaveral is just south of Kennedy Space Center, and Cocoa Beach is immediately south of Port Canaveral, roughly halfway between Titusville and Melbourne. See chapter 2 for full details on travel to and from Port Canaveral and the Disney Cruise Terminal.

FACTS

Size: 72 mi. long (116 km.) x 15 mi. wide (24 km.) (Brevard County, Florida)	
Temperatures: Highs: 72°F (22°C) to 91°F (33°C); lows: 50°F (10°C) to 73°F (23°C)	
Population: 476,000 (Brevard)	**Busy Season:** Mid-February to April
Language: English	**Money:** U.S. Dollar
Time Zone: Eastern (DST observed)	**Transportation:** Cars and taxis
Phones: Dial 911 for emergencies, local pay phone calls = 50 cents	

Introduction Reservations Staterooms Dining Activities Ports of Call Magic Index

Exploring Kennedy Space Center and the Astronaut Hall of Fame

KENNEDY SPACE CENTER

It just wouldn't be the Space Coast without the Kennedy Space Center (KSC), located 12 miles from Cocoa Beach. The huge gantries and Vehicle Assembly Building dominate the horizon for miles around. Those aren't high-rise condos along the beach; they're the historic launch towers of Cape Canaveral!

© MediaMarx, Inc.

A view of the KSC gantries from Playalinda Beach

You can easily **spend two days** at the KSC Visitor Complex exploring the history and future of the U.S. space program. Two IMAX theaters, live talks with veteran astronauts, hands-on exhibits, historic spacecraft, and the sobering Astronaut Memorial make the **main visitor complex** an all-day experience. The complex also has a children's play area and shops offering a wide selection of souvenirs. Seven eateries include the Orbit Cafeteria, New Frontier Café, and Mila's, a full-service restaurant. When you're done at the main complex, board a bus to tour the working Space Center (allow three more hours). The bus stops at the huge **Apollo/Saturn V interpretive center**, displaying a Saturn V rocket, an Apollo command module, and Lunar Module, plus several theaters, Apollo Launch Control, a snack bar, and a shop. Visit the **Launch Complex 39** observation gantry, a four-story launch tower affording sweeping views and even more interpretive exhibits.

ASTRONAUT HALL OF FAME

View historic spacecraft and memorabilia, and experience astronaut-training simulators at the **Astronaut Hall of Fame** in nearby Titusville, which is part of the KSC Visitor Complex. Here you can learn about past NASA astronauts and take a ride in various flight simulators to find out just what it is like to be an astronaut. Mission:SPACE fans take note: The G-Force Trainer is a longer, faster cousin of the simulator ride at Epcot—and at four times the force of gravity (4 Gs), it's not for the faint of heart! Almost half of the Hall of Fame is dedicated to hands-on experiences, and all exhibits and motion simulators are included in the price of admission. The Hall of Fame is a nine-mile drive from Kennedy Space Center, but it's worth the trip and good for at least an afternoon's enjoyment.

Exploring Kennedy Space Center and the Astronaut Hall of Fame

ADMISSION

Two-day admission (Maximum Access Badge) to KSC and the Astronaut Hall of Fame: $38/adult and $28/children 3–11. Single-day admission is $31/$21 for KSC; $17/$13 for the Astronaut Hall of Fame. **Two special tours**, NASA Up Close and Cape Canaveral: Then and Now, may be available, too. These tours go even farther, with an expert guide to bring you into restricted areas omitted from the regular tour. The tours last about three hours, each costs an extra $22/$16, and they're well worth it! Also available on most days of the week is a chance to **dine with an astronaut**. These meals add $22.99/adult, $16/child 3–11 to the price of admission.

Another program is the **Astronaut Training Experience (ATX)** available for guests 14 and older at $225/person—it's held from 10:00 am to 4:30 pm at the Astronaut Hall of Fame. This is an in-depth, immersion program which includes motion simulators, exclusive tours, first-hand experiences with veteran NASA astronauts, gear, and lunch. Guests under 18 must be accompanied by an adult. Some simulators have height/weight restrictions. Advance reservations are required—call 321-449-4400.

The Visitor Complex also sells **tickets to Space Shuttle launches**, when KSC is closed to private vehicles. For $34 to $56 you get off-site parking, a ride to the viewing area, and Visitors Complex admission (optional). The official Kennedy Space Center launch schedule is at http://www.kennedyspacecenter.com and click on "Launches."

DIRECTIONS

Directions to Kennedy Space Center: From Cocoa Beach/Port Canaveral take SR 528 west to SR 3 north, and follow the signs for the Visitor Complex. From the mainland, take I-95 or US 1 to Titusville, then take SR 407 east. Visit http://www.kennedyspacecenter.com or call 321-449-4444 for **more information**. Tickets are available on-site and online. Open every day but Christmas. Normal hours: 9:00 am–5:30 pm. The last tour bus departs at 2:15 pm, so be sure to start your day early!

Directions to the Astronaut Hall of Fame: From Kennedy Space Center, take SR 405 west across the Indian River and follow signs to the Astronaut Hall of Fame. From Cocoa Beach/Port Canaveral, take SR 528 to US 1 (Titusville exit), then turn right onto Vectorspace Blvd. From the mainland, take I-95 or US 1 to Titusville, get off at SR 405, and follow signs. Normal hours: 10:00 am–6:30 pm.

Exploring Port Canaveral and Cocoa Beach

PLAYING

Some of Florida's **best beaches** line the Space Coast. Cocoa Beach offers miles of soft, white sand and rolling surf. Beach access is easy, with public access points every few blocks. There's metered parking at the public accesses, or walk from the nearby motels. Cocoa Beach Pier at 401 Meade Ave. offers a variety of on-pier restaurants. For a back-to-nature experience, Canaveral National Seashore's **Playalinda Beach** is located just north of the Kennedy Space Center boundary line. It offers a long, gorgeous beach protected by a tall sand dune and great views of the Kennedy Space Center gantries. It's closed for shuttle launches and landings and closes at 6:00 pm at all times. $5 fee per car per day. Camping on the beach is allowed November–April (permit required). Take I-95 to Titusville exit 220 then SR 406 east to the park. For additional information, call 321-867-4077 or visit http://www.nps.gov/cana.

Endangered species such as bald eagles, manatees, and sea turtles call this area home. **Merritt Island National Wildlife Refuge**, just north of the Space Center, offers hiking trails and incredible wildlife viewing. On your way in, stop by the Wildlife Refuge Visitor Center for information and some museum-style exhibits featuring the wildlife—there's also a delightful boardwalk over a freshwater pond in the back. The seven-mile Black Point Wildlife Drive offers views of many kinds of birds, alligators, river otters, bobcats, and snakes. We visited the wildlife refuge just before sunset in December 2003 and were treated to beautiful panoramas and the sight of many birds roosting for the evening. A special manatee viewing platform is located at the northeast side of Haulover Canal. Located on the road to Playalinda Beach (see above), the refuge closes for shuttle launches and landings. Call 321-861-0667 or visit http://merrittisland.fws.gov.

© MediaMarx, Inc.
Black Point Wildlife Drive

This is the biggest **sea turtle nesting area** in the U.S. Nesting season runs May–August. Turtle encounters are organized at Canaveral National Seashore, Melbourne, and Sebastian Inlet. Call the Sea Turtle Preservation Society at 321-676-1701. More ecotourism opportunities exist, including kayak tours, airboat rides, and guided nature encounters. For listings, visit http://www.nbbd.com/ecotourism, http://www.space-coast.com, or call 800-936-2326.

Dining in Port Canaveral and Cocoa Beach

AREA MAP

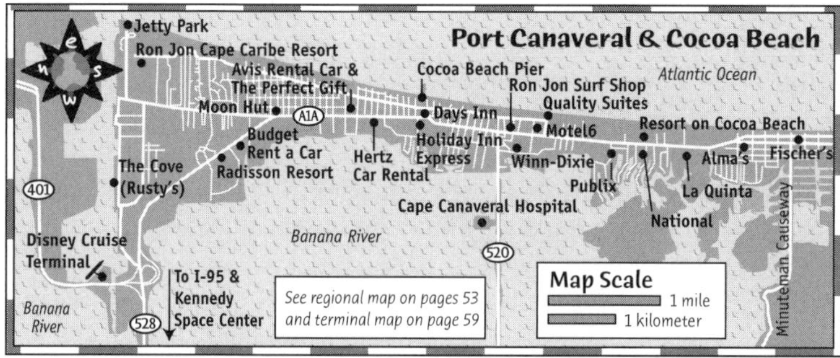

DINING

Looking for a place to eat? There are plenty of **chain restaurants**—in Port Canaveral you'll find a 24-hour McDonald's and a Subway, and down in Cocoa Beach there's a Wendy's, Taco Bell, Denny's, International House of Pancakes (IHOP), Perkins, Blimpie Subs, and a Waffle House. Over on Merritt Island, you'll also find Applebee's, Chili's, Outback Steakhouse, Olive Garden, Red Lobster, and Hooters. If you're looking for something nicer and more "local," here are the restaurants we've tried:

Alma's Seafood & Italian Trattoria—A quirky, moderately priced Italian restaurant with its own hometown charm. The food is decent and the atmosphere is a mix of checkered tablecloths and Space Coast memorabilia. Menu: http://www.dcltribute.com/spacecoast/menus/almas.htm. 306 N. Orlando Ave., Cocoa Beach • 321-783-1981

Cactus Flower Mexican Restaurant—A delightful, atmospheric cafe serving excellent Mexican cuisine. You can dine in or take out. 1891 E. Merritt Island Causeway, Merritt Island • 321-452-6606

Fischer's Seafood Bar & Grill—The moderate restaurant in the trio owned by the Fischer family (see next page). It offers decent seafood for reasonable prices. Info at http://www.geocities.com/bernardsseafood. 2 S. Atlantic Ave., Cocoa Beach • 321-783-2401

Grill's Seafood Deck & Tiki Bar—A fun spot right on the harbor—the menu is equally fun and the food is great. http://www.visitgrills.com. 505 Glen Cheek Dr., Cape Canaveral • 321-868-2226

Zachary's—A basic diner, serving satisfying American and Greek food. http://www.dcltribute.com/spacecoast/menus/zacharys.htm. 8799 Astronaut Blvd., Cape Canaveral • 321-784-9007

Rusty's Seafood & Oyster Bar—Overlooking the port and harbor, this scenic restaurant serves quality seafood. Also owned by the Fischer family. 628 Glen Cheek Dr., Cape Canaveral • 321-783-2033

Playing in Port Canaveral and Cocoa Beach

ACTIVITIES

Fishing (both saltwater and freshwater) is huge in this area. Charters and fishing camps are easy to find, maybe harder to choose from. Check out Coastal Angler Magazine at 888-800-9794 or visit them at http://www.camirl.com.

Lodging rates in this area are reasonable, especially in the off-season (May–December). See pages 64–66 for our lodging suggestions.

Port Canaveral Tips: For seafood, boating, and fishing charters, visit **The Cove**, a waterfront development a stone's throw from the cruise terminals. We had great meals and sunset views at Rusty's and Grill's (see previous page). To get there, exit SR 528 one exit east of the cruise terminals, turn left on George J. King Blvd., turn left on Dave Nisbet Dr., and take it to Glenn Cheek Dr. • **Jetty Park** is a perfect spot to watch space launches, fish, camp, or watch the cruise ships—to get there, exit SR 528 one exit east of the cruise terminals, turn right on George J. King Blvd., take Caribe Dr., then turn left onto Jetty Park Dr.

Cocoa Beach Tips: No trip to the Space Coast is complete without a visit to **Ron Jon Surf Shop** on SR A1A, souvenir T-shirt capital of Central Florida. This large, very pleasant store does sell surfboards and other serious water sports gear, but most visitors exit with items from the huge selection of swimwear, T-shirts, and other outdoor apparel. And it's open 24 hours! • Route A1A in Cocoa Beach varies between pleasant neighborhoods and somewhat seedy sections filled with cheap eats and budget motels. For the most part, though, it's very nice, and the beach is just a few blocks to the east (see photo on page 161). • The Fischer family, who also owns Rusty's in Port Canaveral, runs three fish restaurants under one roof at 2 S. Atlantic Ave. (SR A1A) in Cocoa Beach: Rusty's is cheapest and most informal, Fischer's is the mid-range choice (see previous page), and Bernard's Surf is the most upscale. • Aging sitcom fans might want to follow A1A south and look for "I Dream of Jeannie Lane," in Lori Wilson Park.

Other Space Coast Tips: Farther South, Melbourne is home to a wonderful planetarium and observatory, live theater productions, Montreal Expos Spring Training, and the Brevard County Zoo. The region also hosts a variety of space and nature events during the slow summer months. For information on all these activities and much more, contact the Space Coast Office of Tourism at 800-872-1969 or visit them online at http://www.space-coast.com.

Nassau
(3- and 4-Night Itineraries—First Port of Call)

Two-thirds of all Disney cruisers visit Nassau on New Providence Island in the Bahamas, one of the cruising world's most fabled ports. If you've heard the song Sloop John B ("Around Nassau town we did roam, drinkin' all night, got into a fight"), you might think twice about stepping ashore, but you can have an enjoyable day in this busy capital city if you do your homework.

© MediaMarx, Inc.

A statue of Columbus greets visitors to Government House in Nassau

AMBIENCE

Many cruisers feel uncomfortable walking around Nassau's wharf area, where they're likely to encounter aggressive, enterprising locals intent on their piece of the tourist pie. Hair wrappers, cab drivers, street vendors, and tour hawkers swarm the seedy wharf area—hardly the squeaky-clean welcome Disney crowds prefer. But this large, attractive island boasts a long, British colonial heritage. Historic buildings, large casinos, and attractive beaches await travelers willing to take an excursion or strike out on their own.

HISTORY

Bahamian history starts with the first voyage of Chris Columbus. He called the area "baja mar"—low (shallow) sea—and the name stuck. The Spaniards left in search of gold and the native inhabitants were decimated by disease before the British arrived in the 1600s. Nassau, which was originally called Sayle Island, was a favorite port for fabled pirates like Blackbeard and Anne Bonney, until the islands became a Crown Colony in 1718. Governor Woodes Rogers, a former buccaneer himself, cleaned house and created a town plan which—more or less—remains in effect to this day. The islands became a haven for British loyalists fleeing the American Revolution, and for Southerners during the U.S. Civil War. Trade revived during the Prohibition era, when rum running became a major stock in trade. The islanders voted for and received independence on July 10, 1973, making the Bahamas a member of the British Commonwealth.

FACTS

Size: 21 mi. long (34 km.) x 7 mi. wide (11 km.)	
Climate: Subtropical	**Temperatures**: 70°F (21°C)–90°F (32°C)
Population: 211,000	**Busy Season**: Mid-February to April
Language: English	**Money**: Bahamian Dollar (equal to U.S. $)
Time Zone: Eastern (DST observed)	**Transportation**: Walking, taxis, and ferries
Phones: Dial 1- from U.S., dial 919 for emergencies, dial 916 for information	

Getting Around Nassau

GETTING THERE

Your ship berths at **Prince George Wharf** in the heart of the port. Paradise Island is across the water. A short walk puts you in the heart of town. Disembarkation starts at around 9:45 am (check your *Personal Navigator* for going ashore details), and be sure to bring photo I.D.—wharfside security is tight these days. Enjoy the view from deck 10 to note major landmarks before going ashore, including the Water Tower at the top of the hill, the towering Atlantis resort on Paradise Island, and the arching bridge to Paradise Island. Check your *Personal Navigator* for the "All Aboard" time, usually at 7:00 pm.

GETTING AROUND

Nassau is a **good port for walking**, but several popular attractions, including Paradise Island and Cable Beach, are best reached by taxi, jitney, or water taxi. The taxi stand is to the right as you leave the wharf, beyond the hair braiders stand. • As you leave the pier you'll pass through a new, pier-side welcome center, with a tourist information booth (get free tourist maps here), post office, ATM, telephone/Internet facilities, and a small, pleasant shopping mall. • As you leave the wharf, you'll find Woodes Rogers Walk, which parallels the waterfront. One block inland is the main shopping district, Bay Street. To your left you'll find the grand government buildings near Rawson Square, while a right turn on Bay Street will take you towards the Straw Market. The streets follow a rough grid, and the town is built on a slope. If you get disoriented, just walk downhill to the waterfront. • Small jitneys provide local bus service. The fare is $1 (exact change). Taxi fares are negotiable, but expect to pay $8 for a trip for two to Paradise Island, $12 to Cable Beach, and about $6 for shorter trips. The fare is good for two people, with a $3 surcharge for each extra passenger. Note that the passenger in the front seat may be required to pay the bridge toll • When crossing streets and if you rent a car or scooter, note that Nassau follows the British tradition of driving on the left-hand side of the road.

STAYING SAFE

Safety is often a state of mind, and that's especially true here. Downtown Nassau is **reasonably safe**, but it can be intimidating, with busy streets near the wharf and many locals hustling aggressively. The streets can be empty a few blocks beyond the wharf, so you'll feel better (and be safer) walking with a companion. You can't hide the fact that you're a tourist, so relax, look self-assured, stay alert, keep valuables out of sight, and use your big city street smarts. Panhandlers may offer their "services" as tour guides. Be firm, and don't get sucked in. Carry a few dollars, just in case it's needed to tip a guide.

Touring Nassau

NASSAU MAP

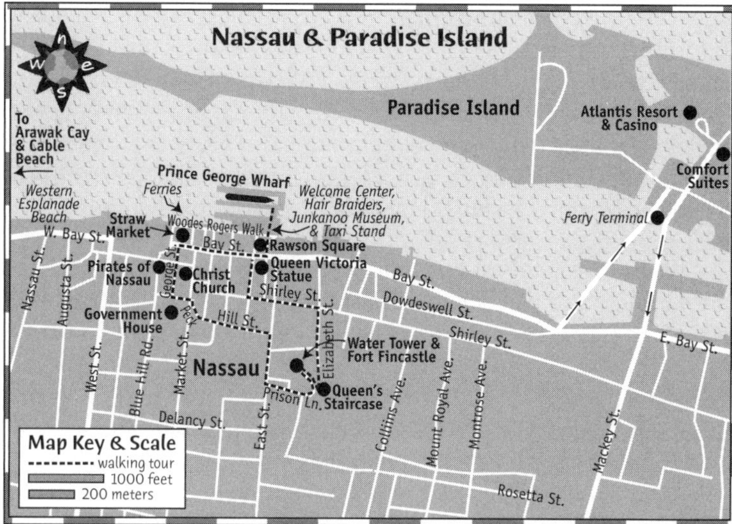

WALKING TOUR

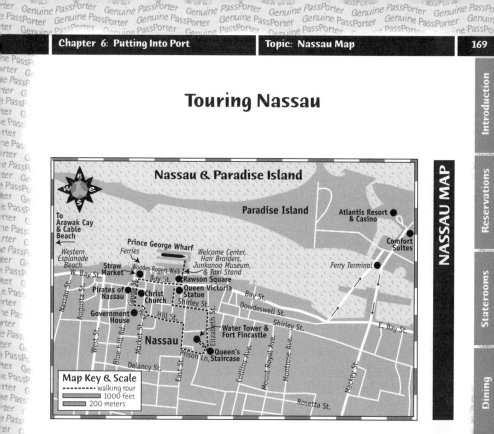

A **self-guided walking tour** around Nassau is a break from the ordinary. Grab one of the free tourist maps distributed on the wharf, play connect-the-dots with your choice of highlighted sights, and trace a route around the perimeter of the downtown district. Allow at least two hours for a non stop walk or more if you want to spend time exploring. Finish before 5:00 pm, when the streets get empty. Here's our suggested walking tour (highlighted on map above): Leaving Prince George Wharf, turn right onto Bay St. Near the corner of Bay and George St. is the famous (or infamous) Straw Market. Turn left up George St. to continue our tour, or follow Bay St. west to the beaches of Western Esplanade and the seafood vendors of Arawak Cay. On George St., you'll soon pass Christ Church and the Pirates of Nassau attraction. Follow George St. to its end, and peer through the gates of Government House (see photo on page 167). Turn left again, cross Market St., and make your way uphill on winding Peck Slope to Hill St. for a commanding view of the port. Follow Hill St. to its end, turn right on East St. to Prison Lane, and follow the lane up to the Water Tower and Fort Fincastle. The tower can be climbed for free, or pay a fare to take the elevator. Exit via the remarkable Queens Staircase and follow Elizabeth St. down the hill. Turn left onto Shirley St., then right onto Parliament St. to view the Library (Old Jail) and the statue of Queen Victoria in Parliament Square. From there, it's a short walk back to the wharf.

Playing in Nassau

ACTIVITIES

Bay St. is lined with **shops** offering the typical selection of upscale luxuries and downscale knickknacks, but Nassau is probably best-known for its Straw Market. There was a time when nobody could leave the port without a straw hat, basket, or handbag, but not every visitor is enchanted by the experience. The stalls and crafters of the market fill a city block between Bay St. and the waterfront—its narrow quarters are shaded by a huge, temporary awning.

The soft, white sands of Nassau are a major attraction. The nearest **public beach** to the wharf is Western Esplanade, along West Bay St. Famed Cable Beach, with its hotels, casino, and water sports, is more attractive and just a few miles farther down the road. Paradise Island has many first-class beaches, best visited as part of a shore excursion. Remote South Ocean Beach is a $33 cab fare from the wharf, or rent a car. Its quiet beauty may be worth the journey.

Casino action centers on Paradise Island's fancy Atlantis Casino and the older Crystal Palace Casino on Cable Beach. A day in either spot offers beach lounging, water sports, and similar distractions for those family members too young or disinclined to gamble. Water taxis serve both destinations from Prince George Wharf.

The **Atlantis Resort** offers aquariums and sea life exhibits to go along with the casino and recreation facilities. All-day admission is $25/adults, $19/kids 3-12, and includes a guided tour, but does not include their 14-acre water park—for that, you need to get a room at Atlantis (http://www.atlantis.com, 888-528-7155) or Comfort Suites (http://www.vacationparadiseisland.com, 800-330-8272).

Nassau offers too many scuba, snorkeling, boating, and sea life encounters to list here, but the Wonder's shore excursions (see next page) offer a good **cross-section** of these activities. Golf, tennis, fishing, and other sporting opportunities abound for those willing to do it on their own. Fortunately, you have a long day in Nassau. For details, visit the Bahamas' official site at http://www.bahamas.com.

"Goombay" and "Junkanoo" have become well known Bahamian catchwords. Goombay is a local musical style that gets its name from the African term for rhythm. The Bahamas famed Junkanoo parades take place when your ship is out of port, but you can view a Junkanoo exhibit right on Prince George Wharf.

Embarking on Shore Excursions in Nassau

Atlantis Beach Day [N07] — Rating: 6

Beach
Active
All ages
$65/adult
$47/child 3-9
2-7 hours

Spend the day lolling about on the beach on Paradise Island. The excursion includes a 20-minute bus ride (to and from Paradise Island)and a meal coupon. Upon arrival, enjoy your reserved spot on the beach, complete with chair and towel. You can explore the resort's casino and shops, but this excursion ***does not include access to the Atlantis water park or aquarium****. Typical meeting time is 9:00 am. Ferries return every 30 min. from 1:30 pm to 5:30 pm. Cruiser reviews are uniform: The bus ride to Paradise Island was "bad" and travelled through a "not so nice area of Nassau." The highlight was the "private beach for cruisers," which is "wonderful" with "beautiful" water "so blue" and with "so many fish." On the beach you are "provided with a towel and chair," and the chair "has an umbrella." The meal coupon left a bit to be desired, as you could only get "certain items" and the food "was not that great." If you want to buy something else, it can be "difficult to pay with cash." And cruisers felt it was unfortunate that they "can't use any of the pools at Atlantis." In sum, the beach is "beautiful" but the rest is just so-so.(On Your Own: Atlantis Resort, http://www.atlantis.com, 888-528-7155)*

Ardastra Gardens and City Tour [N16] — Rating: 7

Tour
Active
All ages
$37/adult
$27/child 3-9
2.5-3 hours

First visit the jungle gardens of the Ardastra Gardens, Zoo, and Conservation Centre, famous for its marching Caribbean Flamingos. After an hour and a half at the gardens, enjoy a city tour in air-conditioned van. A fair amount of walking is required. Typical meeting time is 12:45 pm. Cruiser reviews are mostly positive: The excursion offers "variety" and a way to see a lot in a "short amount of time." Kids enjoy the "zoo" and the animals and birds are "great." The tour's worth "depends on your tour guide." Overall, most "enjoyed it" though a few felt it would have been better to "take a taxi" and do "on your own."(On Your Own: Ardastra Gardens at http://www.ardastra.com, 242-323-5806)

Blackbeard's Cay Beach & Stingray Adventure [N17] — Rating: 9

Sports
Active
Ages 3 & up
$47/adult
$35/child
4.5-5 hours

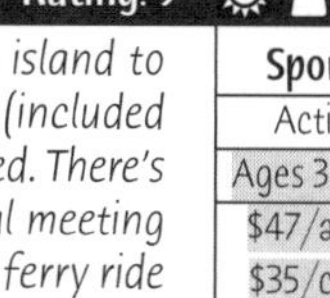

Take a 20-minute boat ride through Nassau Harbor to a private island to snorkel with stingrays, relax on the beach, and enjoy a lunch buffet (included in price). Snorkel equipment and food to feed the stingrays is provided. There's time for swimming and shopping in the little gift shop, too. Typical meeting time is 9:45 am. Cruiser reviews are mixed: The "crowded and hot" ferry ride to the "beautiful little island" with its "pretty beach" is "pleasant." The time with the "stingrays in the penned area" lasted "10 minutes tops" and some kids are "scared," while others "dove right in and started snorkeling" and "loved feeding" the stingrays. Some reported that the "food stunk"–you have your choice of "a burger, a hot dog, or chicken sandwich"–but more recently we've heard that the "food was very good." Cruisers advise you "bring suncreen" and "bottled water because the only drinks available are soft drinks with lunch." If you're in the mood to shop, visit the gift shop early as "the stringray-themed sourvenirs sell out quickly." Most everyone agrees that the beach area is "beautiful" and "great for the kids." Overall, some found the excursion "a waste of time" and "not worth the money," but more felt it was "very relaxing and fun for all" with "friendly stingrays." (On Your Own: ShoreTiprs.com at http://www.shoretrips.com)

See page 158 for a key to the shore excursion description charts and their icons.

Embarking on Shore Excursions in Nassau *(continued)*

Caribbean Queen Snorkel Tour [N04] — Rating: 9

Sports
Very Active
Ages 6 & up
$37/adult
$27/child
2-3 hours

Like the Sunshine Glass Bottom Boat excursion, this trip cruises Nassau Harbour before heading off to Athol Island. Unlike the previously mentioned excursion, you WILL get wet! Snorkel equipment and instruction is provided for your open-water snorkeling adventure. Freshwater showers and cash bar available onboard the 72-foot boat. Typical meeting time is 1:30 pm. Cruiser reviews are consistently good: The "great" excursion crew offers some "sightseeing" along the way to the island. Once there, the snorkeling is "awesome" and there was a "great variety of fish." Younger children and "uptight" people may be "a little frightened at first" but the "crew is wonderful at relieving fears." Chips and beverages ("local beer" plus soda and water) are available for sale on the boat. In sum, "it was great" and cruisers would "do it again." (On Your Own: Stuart Cove's Aqua Adventures at http://www.stuartcove.com, 800-879-9832)

Catamaran Sail & Reef Snorkeling [N14] — Rating: 8

Sports
Very active
Ages 5 & up
$45/adult
$31/child
3.5-4 hours

Set sail on a comfortable, 65-foot catamaran with a large sundeck and shady lounge deck. After a brief tour of Nassau Harbour, you'll sail to a coral reef for snorkeling (equipment provided). Sodas and water are served during the sail, as are snacks and alcoholic beverages after snorkeling. Typical meeting time is 9:00 am. Cruiser comments are mostly positive: The 20-minute sail is "enjoyable" and "relaxing." The snorkeling is "wonderful" though some felt it was in "pretty deep water for beginners" and you cannot "touch bottom." Most report seeing "plenty of fish." Overall, most "loved it!" (On Your Own: Flying Cloud at http://www.bahamasnet.com/flyingcloud, 242-363-4430)

Discover Atlantis [N05] — Rating: 6

Tour
Active
All ages
$39/adult
$26/child
3-5 hours

This excursion begins with a 20-minute bus ride to the Atlantis resort, where you receive a guided tour of the resort and aquarium on Paradise Island. We did this excursion in 2002 and we enjoyed it—be aware that you will do a lot of walking. Typical meeting times are 11:00 am or 1:00 pm. Buses return every half-hour from 1:30 pm to 5:30 pm—don't miss it, or you'll have to pay for a taxi. Cruiser reviews are mixed: This very popular excursion begins with a "capacity-filled" ride to Paradise Island, during which the tour with "very little narrative" could not be "heard or understood over the roar of the engines." Once on the island, you are taken in "smaller groups" to the "stunning" Atlantis Resort, but the walk to it is "boring" because there is "nothing to see." Inside you may "spend a lot of time touring the retail areas," but then are led to the "breathtaking" aquarium, which was by far the highlight for most cruisers. After the aquarium, some felt you were "left somewhere in the hotel to find your own way back" while others enjoyed the "free time to explore." Expect to "spend the entire tour walking." Overall, some cruisers felt the excursion was "awesome" while others felt it "takes way too much time" and "wasn't interesting at all." (On Your Own: Atlantis Resort, http://www.atlantis.com, 888-528-7155)

See page 158 for a key to the shore excursion description charts and their icons.

Embarking on Shore Excursions in Nassau *(continued)*

Nassau Dolphin Encounter [N21]

Rating: 9

Sports
Active
Ages 3 & up
$99/adult $84/child
4-4.5 hours

Despite the hefty price tag, this is the most popular excursion and it typically sells out quickly. Everyone wants the chance to cavort with a friendly dolphin! Guests stand on a platform set at a few feet under the water and play with bottlenose dolphins. (If you want to actually swim in the water with the dolphins, you'll need to book that excursion on your own—see below.) This excursion includes a cruise to the private island of Blue Lagoon (Salt Cay)—a calypso band plays during your ferry trip. Once there, you can swim, sunbathe, and play—water sport equipment rentals are available—in addition to your dolphin encounter. A voucher for lunch is included in the price of the excursion. Professional photos of your dolphin encounter are $8-$35/each and videos are $40-$60/each. Typical meeting time is 9:15 am. Cruiser ratings are mostly positive: The excursion starts with a long, "45-minute" ferry ride some felt was "slow" and "miserable" while others found it "a lot of fun." At the dolphin encounter area, small groups of "10-12" guests stand around a "small pool" and watch a "skit" between the dolphin and "informative handlers." You stand in the "cold" water for about "20 minutes" to "hug, kiss, and dance with" the dolphins, but you only get about "2-3 minutes with a dolphin personally." Cruisers recommend you "wear water shoes" for ease and comfort. All loved the "unbelievably intelligent animal" and the "expertise, friendliness, and humor of the trainers." Some were put off by the "expense" of the photo; others wanted them but "did not know to bring enough money." Overall, most felt it was "exactly as advertised" or "better than expected," though a few felt it was "neat but not worth that much money." (On Your Own: Blue Lagoon Island at http://www.dolphinencounters.com, 242-363-1003)

Nassau Dolphin Observer [N22]

Rating: 8

Tour
Leisurely
All ages
$35/for ages 3+
4-4.5 hours

Just want to go along for the ride with your family or friends to the Nassau Dolphin Encounter (described above)? You can for a reduced price! You get all the same benefits except you don't interact with the animals and you don't get wet. Tip: Bring your camera so you can take photos of your loved ones playing with the dolphins! Typical meeting time is 9:15 am. (On Your Own: Blue Lagoon Island at http://www.dolphinswims.com, 242-363-1003)

Nassau Historic City Tour [N06]

Rating: 6

Tour
Leisurely
All ages
$23/adult $18/child
2 hours

Board an air-conditioned van for a guided tour of historic points of interest in Nassau. The tour visits historic buildings and famous sites, stopping at Fort Charlotte, Fort Fincastle, the Water Tower, and the Queen's Staircase. A good overview without a lot of walking. Typical meeting time is 10:00 am. Cruiser reviews are uniform: Aboard "not very comfortable" but "air-conditioned" vans you see historic sights around Nassau. The driver may not "talk very much" or offer enough "commentary" during the tour, but you will see "much of the city" in a "short time" and stop a few times to "take some photos." Most cruisers enjoyed the climb up to the Water Tower for the "view at the top," but felt it was "more physical activity" than expected. Cruisers were dismayed at the "begging" for tips and "peddlers." Overall, most felt the excursion was a way to see "a lot of things" without a "lot of walking." (On Your Own: Bahamas Experience Tours at http://www.bahamasexperiencetours.com, 242-356-2981, or Henry's Mobile Tours at 242-356-2981)

Embarking on Shore Excursions in Nassau *(continued)*

Scuba Dive Adventure at Stuart Cove [N20] Rating: 3

Sports
Very Active
For certified divers only
Ages 12 & up
$99/adult
4.5–5 hours

If you're a certified diver, this excursion offers an exciting look at the coral reefs and marine life that make their home here. Price includes basic dive equipment (regulator, tank, weight belt, buoyancy control device, mask, snorkel, and fins—wet suits are available for an extra fee). Note that guests ages 12-17 must be accompanied by parent or guardian to participate. Typical meeting time is 11:45 am. Don't forget that underwater camera. Cruiser reviews are uniform: The Disney scuba excursion is "OK" but not "great." The dive takes them "windward" and the waters can be "very rough"—rough enough that most cruisers report that they were able to do only "one of the two dives." The excursion does "provide all equipment," but you may only go "10 to 15" feet deep. The best thing about it is that you don't have to worry about "getting there or back" since it was all arranged through Disney. Overall, the dive was "disappointing" and most felt it would be best to "arrange your own scuba dive" through an outfit like Stuart Cove's. (On Your Own: Stuart Cove's Aqua Adventures at http://www.stuartcove.com, 800-879-9832)

Sunshine Glass Bottom Boat [N02] Rating: 3

Tour
Leisurely
All ages
$25/adult
$17/child
1.5–2.5 hours

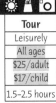

Curious about what's under that aquamarine water? Take this excursion and you won't even have to get wet. The 70-foot boat has one sundeck, a covered deck, restrooms, cash bar, and (what else?) a glass bottom. You'll cruise the Nassau Harbor, then head off to the coral reefs—if the weather permits, you see a shipwreck, too. Typical meeting times are 10:30 am and 2:30 pm. Cruiser reviews are mostly negative. It is a "bit of a walk from the ship to the pier" where the glass bottom boat is moored. Once on the boat, the "scratched up" glass bottom was "way too small" and you may have to stand to see. On the other hand, it "wasn't too expensive" and the "kids really enjoyed it." Overall, the experience was a "complete and total" waste of money for some, while others thought it was a "nice little ride."

Thriller Powerboat [N18] Rating: 5

Tour
Active
Ages 5 & up
$41/31 (5-9)
1.5 hours

This recently-introduced excursion offers an exciting, 45-minute ride through Nassau Harbor and around Paradise Island on a state-of-the-art, custom-built powerboat. You'll need to walk 15 minutes to get to the boat. During the cruise your guide will narrate the sights while you enjoy comfy seats and island music. Pregnant woman, children under 5, and guests with conditions that may be affected by a high speed ride should not go. Typical meeting times is 10:15 am. (On Your Own: Thriller Powerboat Tours at http://www.thrillerboat.com/bahamas, 242-363-4685)

Teen Thriller Powerboat [N19] Rating: n/a

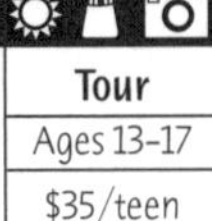

Tour
Ages 13–17
$35/teen

This is basically the same excursion as described above, but it's exclusively for teens! Typical meeting time is 2:30 pm. The powerboat cruise lasts about one and half hours.

See page 158 for a key to the shore excursion description charts and their icons.

St. Maarten/St. Martin

(Eastern Caribbean Itineraries—First Port of Call)

The Dutch say Sint Maarten, the French say St. Martin, but what's in a name? Where else can you visit **two countries** this easily, dine so lavishly, shop so extravagantly, and sun so beautifully? Two nations share this bit of paradise, but if we must take sides, we'll take the French. Alas, the Disney Magic docks on the Dutch side.

Dave and Allie on Pinel Island, St. Martin

AMBIENCE

With the Atlantic to the east, the Caribbean to the west and a lagoon in between, St. Maarten's 37 beaches offer **everything** from roaring surf to gentle ripples, and brisk trade winds keep the island cool. Its 37 square miles (96 sq. km.) include tall, luxuriantly green mountains, two capital cities, hundreds of appetizing restaurants, a dizzying array of shops, and a dozen casinos. Philipsburg, the bustling Dutch capital, hosts up to four cruise ships daily, and offers handy, excellent shopping. Picturesque Marigot, the French capital, offers a lot more charm and sophistication for cruisers willing to go the extra distance.

HISTORY

The **history** of this island begins with the Arawaks, seafaring Indians who discovered salt on the island. Later, Columbus named and claimed this island as he sailed past on the Feast of St. Martin. After harassing the Spanish for some years (here's where New Amsterdam's Peter Stuyvesant lost his leg), the Dutch and French moved in and carved it up in 1647. Relations are friendly now, but the border moved several times during the next 200 years. Sugar cane was the cash crop until slavery was abolished, and sea salt was produced in Philipsburg's Salt Pond, but this was a very quiet place until tourists came to call. And despite this long history, there's still a strong difference in culture and architecture between very French St. Martin and commerce-focused Dutch Sint Maarten.

FACTS

Size: 12 mi. long (19 km.) x 8 mi. wide (13 km.)	
Climate: Subtropical	**Temperatures**: 80°F (27°C) to 85°F (29°C)
Population: 77,000	**Busy Season**: Late December to April
Language: English, French, Dutch	**Money**: Euro or Florin (U.S. dollar accepted)
Time Zone: Atlantic (no DST)	**Transportation**: Taxis and cars
Phones: Dial 011- from U.S., dial 22222 for emergencies	

Making the Most of St. Maarten/St. Martin

GETTING THERE

Your ship docks at the **Captain Hodge Wharf** in Philipsburg in Dutch St. Maarten, at the east end of Great Bay. Taxis and tour buses leave from the wharf, and a water taxi makes two stops along Front Street ($5 buys a pass good for unlimited trips, all day long). A walkway provides direct access to the beach and the shops, casinos, and restaurants of Front Street. It's about a 10–15 minute walk to the near end of Front St., and about a mile (1.6 km) from one end of Front Street to the other. The wharf hosts a tourist information booth. Disembarkation time is typically 8:00 am with an all-aboard time around 7:00 pm.

GETTING AROUND

As with many ports, the real pleasures are found outside of town. Most destinations are within a half-hour drive of Philipsburg, and a **rental car** is the way to get there. Research and book your rental in advance, as rates skyrocket for on-site rentals. All major agencies are represented, but only five have pierside offices. • The island is really two rocky land masses. A pair of sand spits connects the roughly circular main bulk of the island with the small western portion, Terre Basses (the Lowlands). Between the sand spits is Simpson Bay Lagoon. • The French side occupies 21 sq. miles (54 sq. km.) of the northern part of the island, the Dutch 16 sq. miles (41 sq. km.) of the south. A picturesque range of mountains runs north to south, further dividing the island. From Philipsburg, nearly every point of interest, including Marigot, can be reached by driving around the perimeter of the island. • **Taxis** use a government-controlled rate chart. The base fare is for two persons, and each additional person costs about 1/3 the base fare. Sample fares from Philipsburg: Marigot, Orient Beach, Dawn Beach, Maho Resort, all $15; Grand Case, $20. An island tour is $50. • **Public buses** travel between Philipsburg and Marigot. The fare is around $3, U.S. funds are accepted. • Once you're in Philipsburg, Marigot, or any other community, everything will be within walking distance.

STAYING SAFE

There's nothing too unusual about staying safe on "The Friendly Island." No place is crime-free, but St. Maarten does very well. Be wary when carrying parcels, of course. Don't bring valuables to the beach. American and Canadian drivers will be happy, as the island follows U.S. driving practices (right-hand side), but beware of **speed bumps** through towns and resorts. The breeze may fool you into forgetting the sun—be sure to apply plenty of sunblock, especially if you'll be more exposed than usual (if you catch our drift).

Touring St. Maarten/ St. Martin

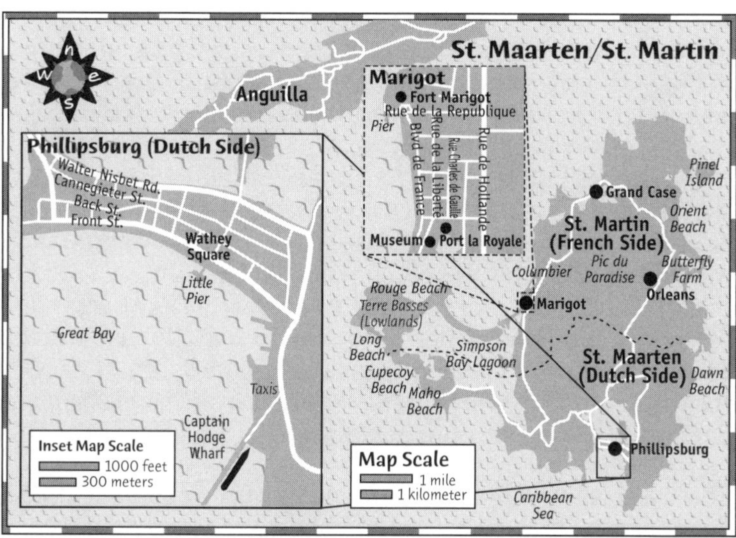

Walking Around in Philipsburg: Philipsburg is a narrow sand spit, just four streets deep and about a mile long (1.6 km.). Front Street runs the length of the town and supplies most of the town's shopping and dining. Back Street is one block over. If you take the water taxi from the wharf you'll arrive at old Little Pier, where the cruise ships' tenders used to dock. Great Bay Beach is right at hand, as are many locals, plying the tourist trade. Leave Little Pier and you'll be in Wathey Square, with its landmark Dutch courthouse. (If you walk from the ship, you'll be at the east end of Front Street, and Wathey Square will be about three blocks west.) You'll find shops, restaurants, and casinos no matter which way you turn. Just walk west until you've had your fill, then retrace your steps.

Walking Around in Marigot: The heart of Marigot is a rough rectangle, bordered on the west by the harbor. On the north, Rue de la Republique offers upscale shopping, with the local pier at its west end. From the pier, head north to climb to the ruins of Fort Marigot, or head south on restaurant-lined Boulevard de France to the Creole graveyard and small museum at the south end of town. Also on the south side, about a block inland, is Port la Royale, a marina surrounded by restaurants and shops—a perfect spot for lunch. Afterwards, head back north on shady Rue de la Liberté or shop-filled Rue Charles de Gaulle.

Playing in St. Maarten/ St. Martin

ACTIVITIES

Great Bay Beach is a short walk from the ship along a new, beachfront promenade. The surf is gentle, and food and shopping are right behind you on Front Street. To the north, **Orient Beach**, with its long crescent of soft white sand and gentle surf, is called the "French Riviera of the Caribbean," but it achieved fame as the island's official nude beach. Beachfront restaurants and resorts have dressed the place up, but bathers at the south end of the beach are still very undressed (not that you have to be). **Maho Beach**, **Mullet Bay**, **Cupecoy Beach**, and **Long Beach** are way out west by the big resorts, past Juliana Airport. All are very pleasant, with Maho offering full resort amenities. Other beaches include remote Rouge Beach (one of Dave's favorites) and Grand Case Beach. Note: With the possible exception of Great Bay beach, you're likely to encounter European-style beach attire (topless women, men in thongs).

The brisk trade winds make the island very popular for **sailing**. For convenience, take one of several "shore" excursions described on the next two pages. Excursions are also available at the marinas near the wharf in Philipsburg. For **snorkeling**, Dawn Beach, several miles to the northeast of Philipsburg, is a top choice.

The island is a **diner's paradise**, with fabulous French, Creole, Indian, Vietnamese, and Indonesian restaurants (and KFC). You'll have no trouble finding a meal along Front Street in Philipsburg, but you'll do better in "France." In Marigot, head toward charming Port la Royale Marina, which is encircled by more than a half-dozen bustling bistros. Note: Many restaurants automatically include a 15% service charge (tip), so watch that bill carefully before you tip.

Twelve **casinos** dot the Dutch side. Four are within walking distance of the wharf, on Front Street in Philipsburg. The largest (and most elegant) casino is the Princess Casino at Port de Plaisance.

The **luxury goods shops** on both sides of the island present a staggering array of French perfumes and cosmetics, crystal, fine porcelain, jewelry, clothing, liquors, and wines. Philipsburg offers many of the French brands you'll find in Marigot at equal or lower prices, but somehow it feels better to shop in Marigot. The huge Little Switzerland luxury goods chain has shops in Philipsburg and Marigot. Cigar fans can find good Cubans, but be sure to smoke 'em before you arrive back home.

Embarking on Shore Excursions in St. Maarten/St. Martin

Pinel Island Snorkel Tour [SM01] — Rating: 6

Sports
Active
Ages 5 & up
$37/$30 (5-9)
3 hours

Pinel Island, which is often called St. Martin's best-kept secret, is an uninhabited island in Orient Bay (French side). You'll take a bus ride, then a water taxi to reach the island. Price includes snorkeling instruction and equipment, with plenty of time to snorkel, swim, sunbathe, or shop. We visited on our own in 2003 and absolutely loved the island. Typical meeting times is 8:00 am. Cruiser reviews are mixed: Some feel the bus ride is "short," while others say it "seems like hours." All agree that the island itself is "very beautiful" with a "sandy beach" and "gradual drop-off." The snorkeling "leaves something to be desired" as it's "often windy" with "poor visibility." Some felt if you visited to "just go swimming" it would be better—others had a "great time."(On Your Own: Scuba Fun at 599-542-2333, ext. 3160)

Shipwreck Cove Snorkel Tour [SM02] — Rating: 5

Sports
Active
Ages 8 & up
$41/$34 (8-9)
3.5 hours

Experienced snorkelers may enjoy this boat trip to Shipwreck Cove to hand-feed the fish that swim among sunken ships and coral reefs. Instruction and snorkel equipment provided, but this excursion is not recommended for non-swimmers. Refreshments, Calypso music, sun decks, and restrooms onboard the boat. Cruiser reviews are mixed: Most felt the snorkeling was "lackluster" in "murky water," while a few others enjoyed "very clear water." The "shipwrecks are real," but were "relocated from somewhere else." In general, most cruisers do "not recommend it," while some "couldn't stop talking about how wonderful it was." Chances are your experience "depends on the weather," which is often windy. Typical meeting time is 1:00 pm. (On Your Own: n/a)

Golden Eagle Catamaran [SM03] — Rating: 9

Sports
Active
Ages 5 & up
$69/$39 (5-9)
4-4.5 hours

Enjoy a half-day jaunt to Tintamar—a real deserted island—aboard the majestic Golden Eagle. The luxurious, 76-foot catamaran sails at up to 30 knots! The excursion price includes pastries, an open bar, and complimentary use of beach floats and snorkel equipment. Typical meeting times are 7:45 am and 1:00 pm. Cruiser reviews are very positive: The ride over is "fun" and "not too fast for kids to enjoy," while the crew "friendly and courteous." The "deserted island" is a "great place to snorkel or just relax on the beach." The "beautiful" beach is "scenic" with "very clear" water. There is "music and singing" during the cruise. All cruisers report that they would "do it again," but some would be sure to "take seasickness medicine" first. (On Your Own: Eagle Tours at http://www.sailingsxm.com or 599-543-0068)

12-Metre Regatta [SM04] — Rating: 10

Sports
Very active
Ages 12 & up
$75
3 hours

Become a crew member aboard one of the famous America's Cup yachts, such as the "Stars and Stripes." You'll compete in an actual race on a shortened version of the America's Cup course. You may get to "grind a winch" or "trim a sail"—no experience is necessary. Wear soft-soled shoes. Typical meeting time is 8:15 am. Cruiser reviews are overwhelmingly positive: This excursion lets you be "as active" as you like—some cruisers were "captain" while others were "in charge of the beverage chest." The "exciting" race is "great fun" with "friendly competition." Cruisers enjoyed the option to purchase a "great photo" of their team. While the seas are "not rough," this is not for anyone "prone to motion sickness." Overall, this excursion is a "highlight of the cruise" and "a blast!" (On Your Own: America's Cup at 599-542-0045)

See page 158 for a key to the shore excursion description charts and their icons.

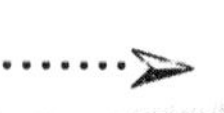

Embarking on Shore Excursions in St. Maarten/St. Martin *(continued)*

Island Drive & Explorer Cruise [SM05] — Rating: n/a

Drive along the Atlantic coast of the island on a guided tour, then board the "Explorer" pleasure boat for a 30-minute cruise to Marigot (the island's French capital). Cash bars onboard. There's time for shopping and sightseeing before you return to Philipsburg. Typical meeting time is 1:15 pm. Cruiser reviews for this excursion were not submitted; it appears it is not very popular. (On Your Own: Eagle Tours at http://www.sailingsxm.com or 599-543-0068)

Tour
Leisurely
All ages
$45/$22 (3-9)
4 hours

Under Two Flags [SM06] — Rating: 7

Board an air-conditioned bus for a scenic, narrated tour of both the French and Dutch sides of the island—you'll see much of the island. The bus makes short 15-minute stops for photos, plus a 45-minute stop in Marigot (the French capital) so you can shop or explore. The tour ends back in Philipsburg. Typical meeting time is 8:45 am. Cruiser reviews are mixed: Most cruisers enjoyed the island drive in a "comfortable, clean bus" with a "friendly driver," though a few did not like to see the "ramshackle houses" along the way. There are several "photo op stops" on "both sides of the island," plus a "French market shopping stop." Most feel this is an "informative," "get acquainted tour" that is "short enough," but some felt the "shopping time is too short" and "kids will be bored out of their skulls." (On Your Own: n/a)

Tour
Leisurely
All ages
$22/$17 (3-9)
3 hours

French Riviera Beach Rendezvous [SM07] — Rating: 8

Enjoy a beach day at Orient Bay, which has been called the "French Riviera of the Caribbean." You'll receive a guided tour on your way to the beach, where you'll be welcomed with a complimentary beverage and a full-service lunch. Then it's off to your reserved beach chair for relaxation. One end of this beach is clothing-optional. Typical meeting time is 9:15 am. Cruiser reviews are mostly positive: The "20-30 minute" bus ride is informative, filled with "facts regarding the island," though some cruisers were uncomfortable with the "visible poverty" on the island. At Orient Beach, you get a "padded lounge chair" to use and a complimentary "fruit punch" with "optional rum." Lunch is "good" with "ribs, chicken, and fish." Cruisers report "topless" bathers and "full nudity," but "forgot about it" after a while. Most felt this excursion is an "adventure" and a "fun experience." (On Your Own: Just take a taxi to Orient Beach!)

Beach
Leisurely
All ages
$57/$40 (3-9)
5 hours

St. Maarten Island & Butterfly Farm Tour [SM09] — Rating: 8

Board a bus for a narrated tour through Philipsburg to the famous Butterfly Farm on the French side of the island. After the farm you'll stop at Marigot for shopping and exploration. Tip: Wear bright colors and perfume if you want the butterflies to land on you. Typical meeting time is 8:00 am. Cruiser reviews are mostly positive: The "great island tour" with "narration" from the "entertaining driver" gave insight into the "rich history" of St. Maarten. The "best part of the trip" was the Butterfly Farm, which "should not be missed" and good for "kids under 12." Most had not seen "so many butterflies so close" and were enchanted when they "landed" on them. Most felt this was a "great overall tour," but some said there are "better butterfly farms at zoos." (On Your Own: The Butterfly Farm at http://www.thebutterflyfarm.com or 599-544-3562)

Tour
Leisurely
All ages
$34/$28 (3-9)
3.5-4 hours

© MediaMarx, Inc.

The Butterfly Farm

See page 158 for a key to the shore excursion description charts and their icons.

Introduction | Reservations | Staterooms | Dining | Activities | Ports of Call | Magic | Index

Embarking on Shore Excursions in St. Maarten/St. Martin *(continued)*

See & Sea Island Tour [SM10] — Rating: 6

Tour
Leisurely
All ages
$51/$36 (3-9)
3.5 hours

Explore the best of both worlds—land and sea—on this guided tour. First you'll take a narrated bus tour to Grand Case. Then you'll board the "Seaworld Explorer"—a semi-submarine—for an underwater glimpse of sea life. Afterwards, there's an hour for shopping and exploring in Marigot. Typical meeting times are 8:15 am and 1:15 pm. Cruiser reviews are mixed: The bus driver is "knowledgeable" and "personable," but the ride was "slow" and "harrowing" at times as the roads are very narrow. The "sea portion" aboard the "semi-sub" was "interesting" and "educational," and the "kids really loved seeing the fish." Some reports suggest that "the sea life is minimal." Overall, some cruisers liked seeing "pretty much all" of the "pretty island," while others felt there were "better ways" to see the island. (On Your Own: Seaworld Explorer at 599-542-4078)

"BUBBA" Fishing Adventure Tour [SM11] — Rating: n/a

Tour
Leisurely
Ages 6 & up
$90/$77
4–4.5 hours

New! Take a five-minute drive to Doc Maarten Marina and hop aboard the custom-built fishing boat for a 45-minute cruise along the St. Maarten coast. At the "secret fishing spot" you'll drop anchor for two hours while you bottom fish for Snapper, Snook, African Pompano, Triggerfish, Barracuda, Grouper, and more. This is a "catch and release" experience with a high-tech rod and reel (provided). Also note that the motion of the boat can be rocky and those who are prone to motion sickness should come prepared. Complimentary beverages are offered during the trip. An opportunity to shop in Philipsburg is available after the cruise. Typical meeting time is 8:15 am. No cruiser reviews are available yet.

St. Maarten Certified Scuba [SM13] — Rating: 8

Sports
Very active
Ages 12 & up
$94
4 hours

Certified scuba divers enjoy visits to some of St. Maarten's famous dive sites. Dive sites are chosen day of the dive according to weather and sea conditions. You must have your scuba certification and have completed at least one dive in the past two years to participate. Typical meeting time is 8:45 am. Cruiser reviews are limited but generally positive: The "two-tank" dive is "great," with "one divemaster per six divers." The tour operators "handled all the equipment" and "took plenty of time" at each location. Even though "St. Maarten isn't the greatest place to dive" due to "choppy waters," once you're underwater it is "beautiful." Those "prone to motion sickness" should take the "appropriate meds" before going. Overall, most felt it "couldn't have been nicer." (On Your Own: Dive Safaris at http://diveguide.com/divesafaris, 599-542-9001 or Aqua Mania at http://www.stmaarten-activities.com, 599-544-2640)

Lotterie Farm Hidden Forest Tour Hike [SM17] — Rating: n/a

Sports
Very active
Ages 8 & up
$80/$48 (8-9)
4.5–5 hours

Ready for a challenging hike up to Pic du Paradise, St. Martin's tallest mountain at 1400 feet (427 m.)? After an air-conditioned bus ride to the Lotterie Farm Hidden Forest, you'll begin your 1 1/2 hour hike through a lush rainforest. After your hike you'll enjoy an open-air lunch and a brief stop in Marigot. Bring good walking shoes and water. Typical meeting time is 8:15 am. No cruiser reviews were received for this excursion. (On Your Own: n/a)

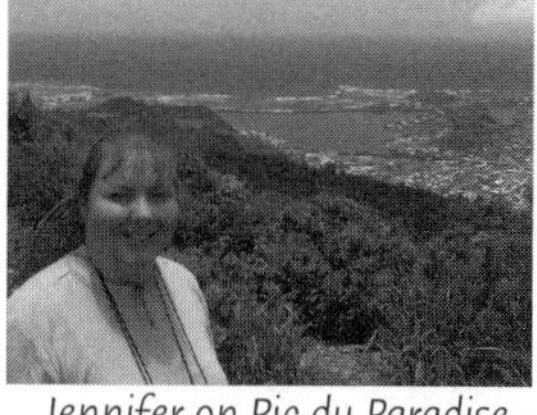

© MediaMarx, Inc.

Jennifer on Pic du Paradise

See page 158 for a key to the shore excursion description charts and their icons.

Embarking on Shore Excursions in St. Maarten/St. Martin *(continued)*

Mountain Bike Adventure [SM19] — Rating: n/a

Sports
Very active
Ages 12 & up
$72
3.5 hours

Need some exercise? This excursion outfits you with a mountain bike and safety gear, then takes you for a bumpy on- and off-road bike tour. You'll ride along the coastline, through the village of Colombier, and encounter at least one steep hill. After your exertions, take 30 minutes to relax and swim at Friar's Bay Beach—includes a complimentary beverage. Typical meeting time is 7:45 am. We received no cruiser reviews for this excursion. (On Your Own: n/a)

Anguilla Dolphin and Stingray Encounter [SM20] — Rating: 8

Sports
Active
Ages 5 & up
$188/$162
7-7.5 hours

Take a 45-minute boat ride to Anguilla, where you'll get to interact and swim with the dolphins and stingrays at Dolphin Fantaseas. Afterwards, relax at Meads Bay, where you'll enjoy a Caribbean barbecue lunch. Note that underwater cameras are not allowed—professional photos are taken for you, but prices can be steep. Typical meeting time is 7:30 am. Cruiser reviews are overwhelmingly positive: Despite the "high price" for this excursion, all cruisers found it "well worth the money." After a "heck of a fun time" on the boat to Anguilla, guests get split into two groups—one group goes to the "stunningly beautiful beach" first while others get their "encounters" first. You get to spend 45 minutes with the dolphins and "swim, dance, play catch, feed, kiss, pet, and race them." When you're "not with the dolphins," you go to "the stingray tank" or "visit with the tropical birds and hermit crabs." The "really neat" stingrays are in a six-foot tank—you can "dive down to pet them and feed them." Most cruisers agreed that biggest drawback is lunch, which is "not the best" (some reported being served goat). Overall, cruisers feel the excursion is "amazing" and the "best ever!" (On Your Own: Dolphin Fantaseas at http://www.dolphinfantaseas.com or 264-497-7946)

Observer at Anguilla Dolphin & Stingray Encounter [SM21] — Rating: n/a

Tour
Leisurely
Ages 3 & up
$129/$101
7-7.5 hours

Just want to go along for the ride with your family or friends to the Anguilla Dolphin Encounter (described above)? You can for a reduced price! You get all the same benefits except you don't interact with the animals and you don't get wet. Tip: Bring your camera so you can take photos of your loved ones playing with the dolphins! Typical meeting time is 7:30 am. (On Your Own: Dolphin Fantaseas at http://www.dolphinfantaseas.com or 800-293-9698)

Rhino Rider and Snorkeling Adventure [SM10] — Rating: 9

Sports
Very active
Ages 10 & up
$84
3-3.5 hours

This newly added excursion offers a chance to zoom about on your own, two-person inflatable boat (the "Rhino Rider") in Simpson Bay. After your cruise, you'll have the opportunity to snorkel (equipment provided). When your adventure is over, you can relax with a complimentary beverage. Note that each boat holds two people maximum, and only those 13 or older can drive. Typical meeting times are 7:45 am and 1:45 pm. Cruiser comments are positive: After a bus ride out to Simpson Bay, guests are given a "brief explanation" on how to use the "two-seater mini boats," which is a bit like a "large jet ski with an inflated rubber bottom." You then take a "30-minute" ride with "great views" to the "good" snorkeling location, where you could also "swim if you prefer." After another 30 minutes, you "take the boat back" to Simpson Bay. If the water is "choppy," you could be a "little sore" afterwards. Most cruisers agree the excursion is "worth it" and offered a "great time." (On Your Own: Atlantis Adventures at http://www.atlantisadventures.com, 599-542-4078)

See page 158 for a key to the shore excursion description charts and their icons.

St. Thomas & St. John
(Eastern Caribbean Itineraries—Second Port of Call)

Welcome to pretty St. Thomas, the **busiest cruise ship port** and duty-free shopping haven in the Caribbean! Pirates once roamed freely here, but your visit will be far tamer, thanks to its status as a U.S. Territory. Shopping not your cup of tea? The neighboring island of St. John is a prime, back-to-nature getaway.

© MediaMarx, Inc.

The Disney Magic in St. Thomas (view from Paradise Point)

AMBIENCE

St. Thomas boasts beautiful beaches like many Caribbean islands, but its **rugged mountain terrain** gives it a distinctive look. St. Thomas is shaped like an elongated hourglass and is about 28 square miles (72 sq. km.) in size, making it the second largest island in the U.S. Virgin Islands (St. Croix is the largest). Shoppers throng the narrow lanes and old, stone buildings of St. Thomas' downtown Charlotte Amalie, a duty-free port since the 1700s. The neighboring island of St. John is just a ferry ride away, home to the hiking trails, wildlife, and remote beaches of 7,200 acre Virgin Islands National Park. Your day in port is brief, so a trip to St. John will take most of your day.

HISTORY

Adventurers from many nations visited St. Thomas, but none put down roots until Denmark colonized in the late 1600s. The Danes made the island's prime harbor a **safe haven** for pirates, cashing in on this early "tourist" trade. They also operated sugar plantations, a thriving seaport, and one of the busiest slave markets in the Americas. Charlotte Amalie's waterfront is still lined with old stone buildings from its commercial heyday. The economy crashed after slavery was abolished in the mid-1800s, so by 1917 the Danes were happy to hand the islands to the U.S. for $25 million (it's now a U.S. Territory). Then in 1956, Laurence Rockefeller donated 5,000 acres on St. John to create the Virgin Islands National Park (and not incidentally, to ensure an attractive setting for his Caneel Bay resort).

FACTS

Size: St. Thomas: 13 mi. (21 km.) x 4 mi. (6 km.) /St. John: 7 mi. (11 km.) x 3 mi. (5 km.)	
Climate: Subtropical	**Temperatures**: 77°F (25°C) to 85°F (29°C)
Population: 51,000 & 4,000	**Busy Season**: Late December to April
Language: English	**Money**: U.S. Dollar
Time Zone: Atlantic (no DST)	**Transportation**: Walking, taxis, cars
Phones: Dial 1- from U.S., dial 911 for emergencies	

Making the Most of St. Thomas and St. John

GETTING THERE

Your ship docks near **Charlotte Amalie**, capital of the U.S. Virgin Islands, normally at the West India Company pier in Havensight, 1.5 miles (2.4 km.) from downtown. Occasionally, guests must be tendered ashore (if this happens, you'll arrive in Charlotte Amalie rather than Havensight). All ashore is typically at 7:30 am, with all aboard around 4:30 pm. All guests must meet with U.S. Immigration officials onboard the ship, regardless of whether you plan to go ashore (see page 272). No guests may disembark until all guests have met with immigration, so there's no sleeping in today (meeting times vary—refer to the letter placed in your stateroom the night before). Visitors traveling to St. John should either book a shore excursion, or take a taxi to the Red Hook ferry on the eastern end of the island—round-trip ferry fare is $6/adults, $2/kids (15-20 minute ride). There's also a ferry from downtown Charlotte Amalie for $14/adults, $6/kids, but again you'll have to take a taxi to the ferry.

GETTING AROUND

There's **plenty of shopping near the pier**, or take a cab into town or to other destinations. Havensight Mall, right next to the cruise pier, offers more than 60 shops, and several other malls are within walking distance. • The Paradise Point aerial tramway ($12/$6) is a short walk from the pier, and offers panoramic views of the island. • There's far more shopping in downtown Charlotte Amalie (1.5 miles/2.4 km). A taxi will cost about $3 (no meters, get the rate in advance). • Car rentals are available at the pier, but taxis and mini-buses are generally a better idea. • Maagens Bay, several miles from Charlotte Amalie on the island's north shore, is a beautiful and well-known beach. Nearby is Mountain Top, famed for its views and banana daiquiris. A half-mile west of Charlotte Amalie is the picturesque fishing village of Frenchtown, known for its restaurants and bars. • If you want to visit **St. John**, Disney offers shore excursions to most of St. John's most famous spots, and with the day's tight schedule, they make sense. If you want to explore on your own, Hertz and Avis both have agencies in Cruz Bay, and taxi fares to the major sights are $3–$9. Ferries arrive in Cruz Bay, and the National Park interpretive center is a short walk away. • The beach at Trunk Bay is most popular. • History buffs may enjoy the ruins of Annaberg Sugar Plantation ($4 day use fee).

SAFETY

Pickpockets and beach theft are the most notable crime problems you'll encounter, so **leave your valuables on board**, and safeguard your purse or wallet while shopping. Drinking water is collected in cisterns from rain water, so you may prefer to drink bottled water.

Touring St. Thomas and St. John

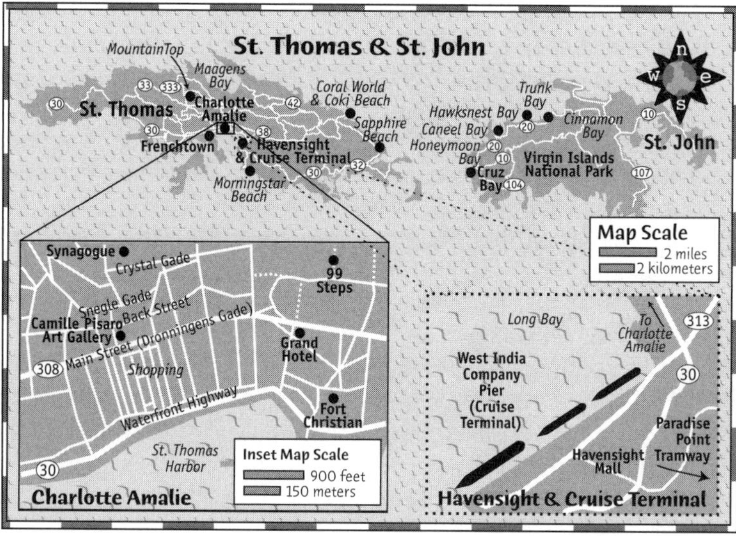

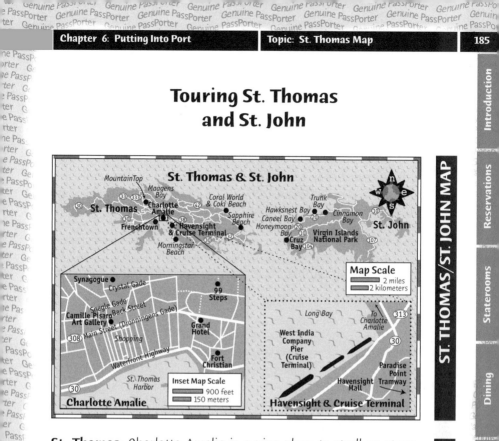

St. Thomas: Charlotte Amalie is a nice place to stroll on steep, narrow streets with Danish names. Most sights are found on the island's many shopping streets, which are within three blocks of the waterfront. Waterfront Highway provides a harborfront promenade. One block inland is Main Street (Dronningens Gade), followed by Back Street, Snegle Gade, and Crystal Gade. More than a dozen Alleys, Gades, Passages, Plazas, and Malls run between Main Street and the waterfront, all lined with shops. Strollers will find historic Fort Christian and the Virgin Islands Museum at the southeast end of downtown. A tourist information center is located nearby, in the former Grand Hotel. One of the New World's oldest Jewish congregations in a charming, 1833 synagogue can be found three blocks inland, near the corner of Crystal Gade and Raadets Gade. Towards the west side of Main Street is the Camille Pissaro Art Gallery, named for the impressionist painter, a St. Thomas native, and featuring works by local artists. Walkers will also enjoy the many brick staircases, including the 99 Steps, that connect the steep streets in the northeast corner of downtown.

St. John's tiny port town of Cruz Bay is good for a short stroll among its cluster of shops and restaurants. The Virgin Islands National Park Visitor Center is a short walk from the dock, and several hiking trails depart from there.

Playing in St. Thomas and St. John

ACTIVITIES

There are no **beaches** within walking distance of the wharf. Morningstar Beach is the closest, and includes all the comforts of the Marriott resort. Maagens Bay ($3/day for adults) is famed for its beauty, but will be thronged with fellow cruise visitors. Sapphire Beach out on the east end offers full, resort-based recreation rentals, and nearby Coki Beach is convenient to Coral World (see below). • On **St. John**, there's a small beach right at the ferry dock in Cruz Bay, but the real attractions are elsewhere. Caneel Beach is a short ride from Cruz Bay, and part of the Caneel Bay resort (stop at the front desk on your way to the beach). Along St. John's north shore, Hawksnest Bay, Trunk Bay, and Cinnamon Bay are easily accessible, offer food, recreation, and other amenities, and are all part of the national park. Trunk Bay ($4/day) is very beautiful, most popular, and features a snorkeling trail. Cinnamon Bay has great windsurfing. • **Snorkeling** equipment can be rented at many beaches. The early departure time makes fishing excursions impractical.

Shopping is St. Thomas' biggest attraction. Shopping is duty-free, sales tax-free, and is conducted in U.S. dollars. As always, while prices can be excellent, know what you'd pay back home for the same goods. Not everything is a "deal." Some shopkeepers will bargain with you. Just ask, "Is that your final price?" With as many as eight cruise ships in port per day, it takes hundreds of shops to absorb the throngs. We suggest you head into Charlotte Amalie and start exploring. If your time is short, the malls and shops in and around the cruise wharf will be most convenient.

Visitors to St. Johns will find the **Virgin Islands National Park** web site very helpful, with a detailed map of the island including its 22 hiking trails. Get more info at http://www.nps.gov/viis.

Coral World Marine Park and Undersea Observatory on St. Thomas' east end (adjacent to Coki Beach) offers underwater observation areas, aquariums, exhibits, stingray encounters, nature trails, and the "Sea Trekkin'" adventure where you get to walk the sea bottom ($50 extra, age 8 and up, reservations suggested). Admission is $18/adults, $9/kids, or $52 for a family of two adults and up to four kids. Visit http://www.coralworldvi.com or call 888-695-2073.

For one of the most informative and well-laid-out **web sites** for the U.S. Virgin Islands, visit http://www.vinow.com.

Embarking on Shore Excursions on St. Thomas and St. John

St. John Trunk Bay Beach & Snorkel Tour [ST01] — Rating: 6

Sports
Active
Ages 5 & up
$42/$34 (5-9)
5–5.5 hours

Travel by sea and land to Trunk Bay, where you'll have 1.5 hours to swim, snorkel (equipment provided), and relax in this beautiful national park. Typical meeting time is 7:40 am. Cruiser comments are mixed: Most report that the "ferry ride" over was "long" and "boring." Once at Trunk Bay, however, cruisers found it to be "one of the most beautiful" and "breathtaking" beaches. There is a "marked snorkel trail" and some cruisers have seen a "lot of fish," "stingrays," and "sea turtles." Most felt this was the "highlight of their cruise," while some "were not impressed." (On Your Own: Take a taxi to Red Hook, a ferry to St. John, and then a taxi to Trunk Bay)

St. John Island Tour [ST02] — Rating: 9

Tour
Leisurely
All ages
$42/$31 (3-9)
5–5.5 hours

Take a boat ride to St. John, then board an open-air safari bus for a guided tour through the unspoiled beauty of this island. Includes a stop at Annaberg Ruins and many stops for photo ops. For all ages. Typical meeting time is 7:40 am. We took this excursion in May 2003 and absolutely loved it. Cruiser reviews are uniformly positive: Most enjoyed the "boat ride" to "beautiful" St. John, though it was "long." The "very good driving tour" "makes a lot of stops for pictures" and the driver is both "entertaining" and "knowledgeable." Some of the roads are "very curvy," which could bother some. Overall, the tour is a "great way" to "see a lot" of the island.

© MediaMarx, Inc.

Dave stops for a panoramic photo on St. John

St. John Eco Hike [ST03] — Rating: 8

Sports
Very active
Ages 6 & up
$59/$49 (6-9)
5.5 hours

Take a ferry to Cruz Bay, where you'll embark on a 90-minute guided hike (1.2 miles). You'll stop at Lind Point Lookout and Honeymoon Beach for swimming. Typical meeting time is 8:10 am. Cruiser reviews are positive: This "wonderful way to see this island" starts with "long ferry ride" then a short walk through the city to meet your "knowledgeable guide." The "very easy" hike is "informative," with a look at "local flora and fauna" ("bring bug spray!"). At the end of the "hot" hike, you get 30 min. to "frolic" in Honeymoon Bay ("wear your swimsuit under your clothes").

5-Star St. John Snorkel & Beach Adventure [ST04] — Rating: 7

Beach
Active
Ages 5 & up
$48/$34 (5-9)
4–4.5 hours

Board the 115-foot "Leylon Sneed" in St. Thomas and cruise to Trunk Bay to snorkel (equipment provided), swim, and sunbathe. Includes a complimentary beverage. Typical meeting time is 7:40 am. Cruiser reviews are mixed: Most cruisers appreciated the cruise on the "1939 Chesapeake Bay Oyster Buy Boat replica," but found the trip "long" (45 minutes) and "a little crowded." Those cruisers that made it to Trunk Bay thought it "simply beautiful" with "great snorkeling," but a significant number of reviews noted that they were "detoured to St. James" island because of "rough seas," and this was "disappointing."

See page 158 for a key to the shore excursion description charts and their icons.

Embarking on Shore Excursions on St. Thomas and St. John *(continued)*

Maagens Bay Beach Break [ST27] — Rating: 9

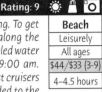

Relax on the beautiful white sands of Maagens Bay and go swimming. To get there, you'll take a 25-min. scenic drive, stopping at Drake's Seat along the way so you can take photos of the great views. A beach chair and bottled water are included in the price of the excursion. Typical meeting time is 9:00 am. Cruiser reviews for Disney's excursion were not available because most cruisers do this excursion on their own for less money (this excursion was added to the Disney roster in 2004). Those that visited Maagens Bay found the beach "wonderful" and "absolutely beautiful." They also "enjoyed the ride from the pier" as "some of the views going over the mountain were absolutely gorgeous." "Restrooms and a snack bar" are available. Most cruisers recommend you "do the excursion on your own" because "it's so easy to do and much cheaper than paying what Disney charges per person for the same thing." (On Your Own: Just take a taxi from the pier to Maagens Bay for about $6/person each way, and then pay $3/person admission to the beach.)

Beach
Leisurely
All ages
$44/$33 (3-9)
4-4.5 hours

Atlantis Submarine Adventure [ST06] — Rating: 5

Climb aboard the "Atlantis XV" and dive down to 90 feet (26 m.). Typical meeting times are 9:15 am, 10:15 am, and noon. Guests must be 36" tall. Cruiser reviews are mixed: This "expensive" excursion takes place in a "fairly spacious" sub which you "board in water (no dock)" "after a choppy 25-minute ride." It has portholes "running along the sides." Two people need to "share a porthole" to gaze out at the "cloudy water" with "some sea life" but "nothing spectacular." A "knowledgeable guide" points out specifics along the way. Most cruisers "enjoyed it" but probably wouldn't "do it again." (On Your Own: http://www.atlantisadventures.net or 340-776-5650)

Tour
Leisurely
Ages 4 & up
$89/$57 (4-9)
2.5 hours

Doubloon Sail & Snorkel [ST08] — Rating: 9

Help hoist the sails of the 65-foot "Doubloon" schooner and cruise to Turtle Cove on Buck Island. Snorkel (equipment provided) and swim. Includes snacks and drinks. For ages 5 & up. Typical meeting time is 8:15 am. Cruiser reviews are positive: This "fun" excursion with a "heavy pirate theme" is fun for "kids and adults alike." While it's not a "major sailing experience," it is "enjoyable" and the "crew is attentive." Snorkeling at Buck Island is "good," though you may not be able to walk on the beach due to "nesting birds." "Rum punch," "beer," and "soda" is served. Overall, most cruisers "recommend it."

Sports
Active
Ages 5 & up
$49/$32 (5-9)
3.5 hours

St. Thomas Island Tour [ST11] — Rating: n/a

Take an open-air safari bus tour to St. Peter's Great House and Mountain Top, the highest point on the island. The bus does make some stops for photo opportunities. Typical meeting times are 8:00 am and 12:15 pm. We received no cruiser reviews for this excursion, however cruisers who visited Mountain Top on their own claim it is "amazing" how you can "see so much!"

Tour
Leisurely
All ages
$35/$24 (3-9)
2.5 hours

See page 158 for a key to the shore excursion description charts and their icons.

Embarking on Shore Excursions on St. Thomas and St. John *(continued)*

☐ Coral World Ocean & Island Drive [ST12] Rating: 7

Tour
Leisurely
All ages
$41/$30 (3-9)
3.5 hours

Take a guided tour to Mountain Top (highest peak) and Coral World in St. Thomas. Typical meeting times are 8:00 am and noon. Cruiser reviews are mostly positive: Coral World is a "wonderful adventure," a bit like "Sea World" but "more science-oriented." "Kids love it," and "see all kinds of sea life" and "pet a shark." The disappointments were the drive which was "not well narrated," and the length of time at Coral World ("only an hour and a half"). Cruisers did enjoy Coral World, but many suggested they'd "do it on their own" next time. (On Your Own: See page 186 to save money and see Coki Beach, too!)

☐ Water Island Bike & Beach Adventure [ST13] Rating: 10

Sports
Very active
Ages 10 & up
$69
3.5 hours

Enjoy a short boat ride to Water Island where you'll explore the terrain by mountain bike. Includes all necessary equipment. Includes a beach stop. Typical meeting time is 12:15 pm. Cruiser reviews are overwhelmingly positive: Get a ride to Water Island on a "large pontoon boat" and listen to the "history" of the island. Once on the island, you get a "quick how-to" on the bikes, "fit you for your helmet," and you're off. Most of the ride is "downhill," but it does cover ground with "gravel and loose rocks." After reaching Honeymoon Bay, you can "beach it" or "keep biking" a mostly "uphill trail." Cruisers of "all shapes and sizes" enjoyed this excursion.

☐ Kayak Marine Sanctuary Tour [ST14] Rating: 9

Sports
Very active
Ages 10 & up
$60
3.5-4 hours

Paddle two-person kayaks through the mangroves in a St. Thomas marine sanctuary. Along the way, snorkel or swim at Bovini Point. Bring water shoes. Typical meeting time is 8:20 am. Cruiser reviews are very positive: While "no kayak experience is necessary," this "fascinating" excursion is a "bit of a workout." The "helpful guides" explain the "mangrove habitat" you pass on your kayak "adventure." Snorkeling is "interesting" with "plenty of sea creatures," but the water is a "bit murky." "Cold water" and "bite-size candy bars" are provided after snorkeling. All cruisers agree this excursion is "great!"

☐ Golf at Mahogany Run [ST15] Rating: 10

Sports
Active
Ages 10 & up
$164
5-6 hours

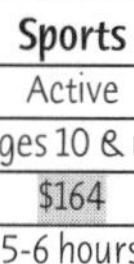

Play a round of golf at this 6,022-yard course designed by George and Tom Fazio. Price includes greens fees, golf cart, and transportation. Rental clubs are additional (about $20). Typical meeting time is 8:15 am. Cruiser reviews are very positive: The excursion "includes transportation" to and from the "beautiful course" with "awesome views." Players are "matched by handicap" and play in "foursomes." Some cruisers report that the course is "challenging," but "lots of fun." Other cruisers suggest you "carry your own golf shoes" to ensure a "comfortable fit." (On Your Own: Mahogany Run Golf Course at http://www.st-thomas.com/mahogany)

☐ Certified Scuba in St. Thomas [ST16] Rating: n/a

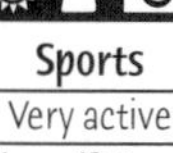

Sports
Very active
Ages 12 & up
$94
4 hours

Certified scuba divers can take a two-tank dive to a maximum depth of 60 feet. Equipment and transportation are provided; wet suit not included. Typical meeting time is 8:00 am. Cruiser reviews are limited: Most cruisers enjoyed this "well-organized" tour and had a "great dive." In general, most agree that St. Thomas is a "far better location for diving" than St. Maarten. (On Your Own: Coki Beach Dive Club at http://www.cokidive.com, 800-474-2654)

See page 158 for a key to the shore excursion description charts and their icons.

Embarking on Shore Excursions on St. Thomas and St. John *(continued)*

St. John Barefoot Catamaran Sail & Snorkel [ST21] — Rating: 7

Sports
Active
Ages 5 & up
$75/$55 (5-9)
4-4.5 hours

After a scenic drive from the port you'll board a catamaran and sail to St. John where you'll swim, snorkel, and sunbathe. Snacks, snorkel gear, and open bar included. Typical meeting time is 7:45 am. Cruiser reviews are mostly positive: This "great sailing trip" "over and back to St. John" is "excellent." The crew is "terrific" and served "drinks and snacks" both coming and going. Snorkeling at Honeymoon Bay is "very good" with "clear water, lots of fish, and even stingrays," but be aware that if you just want to lounge on the beach you'll need to "swim a short way from the catamaran to the beach." Overall, this excursion is "highly recommended" but a few would "do something else next time."

Charlotte Amalie Historical Walking Tour [ST22] — Rating: 5

Tour
Leisurely
All ages
$31/$20 (3-9)
3.5 hours

Explore the quaint town of Charlotte Amalie—along the way you'll admire a stunning vista of the town and visit Notman's Manor. Wear comfortable walking shoes. Typical meeting time is 8:15 am. Cruiser reviews are mixed: Guests board a "van" and "drive up to the highest point" on the tour. From there, you "walk downhill" and listen to your "knowledgeable tour guide" point out sites and divulge the "history of the island." This is an "interesting tour" if you are a "history buff," otherwise it is a "bit dry." There are a "lot of stairs" and the tour is boring for "toddlers and young kids."

Paradise Point Tramway [ST23] — Rating: 7

Tour
Leisurely
All ages
$15/$8 (0-5 free)
1 hour

Enjoy a great view (see photo on 183) in this suspended tram. Bird shows are held twice daily. You can do this excursion anytime after 9:00 am. Jennifer tried this and found it a fun diversion with great views, but not a don't-miss. Cruiser reviews are mostly positive: The tramway is an "easy 10-15 minute walk" from the pier (but if you tender in, it's a "$3/person taxi from town" instead). The view from the tram is "just amazing" and you get a "great view of the Disney Magic." The "birds are cute" (shows are at "10:30 am and 1:30 pm") and there are some "nice shops" to browse. There is also a quarter-mile "nature walk" and a "little cafe." Most cruisers didn't bother with the excursion through Disney, but simply walked over (you can see the tramway from the pier) and purchased tickets on their own (same price). (On Your Own: http://paradisepointtramway.com)

© MediaMarx, Inc.

Boarding the tram

Captain Nautica's St. John Snorkeling Expedition [ST25] — Rating: 9

Tour
Active
Ages 8 & up
$69/$57 (8-9)
4 hours

Enjoy a speedboat ride to two different snorkeling sites. Price includes snorkeling equipment, snacks, and beverages. Typical meeting times are 7:50 am and noon. Cruiser comments are very positive: The "adventurous" speedboat ride is "pretty fast" and "lots of fun." The crew is "friendly" and "helpful." The reported snorkeling sites are either "Turtle Cove off Buck Island" or "Christmas Cove," plus "Honeymoon Bay." Snorkeling is "wonderful" with "many colorful fish." The only complaint reported was with the snacks, which "weren't all that great." Overall, cruisers "loved it" and "would do it again." (On Your Own: http://www.captainnautica.com)

See page 158 for a key to the shore excursion description charts and their icons.

Antigua
(Special 10- & 11-Night Caribbean Itineraries in 2006)

INTRO

Encircled by protective reefs and blessed with sheltered anchorage, Antigua (say "an-TEE-ga") boasts **365 beaches** for sunning, and fair harbors for sailing. Alas that you'll have but eight hours in port—you'll have to take in a new beach every minute to see them all (or come back and spend a year visiting a new beach every day!)

AMBIENCE

Ruined fortresses, old sugar plantations, and modern, beach-front resorts reflect a **rich history and a prosperous present**. With the tourist economy responsible for 75% of the island's income, you'll find pleasant shopping opportunities right at the pier, but a jaunt across the island will take you back to the glory days of Britain's Royal Navy. Whether you stay close to port in St. John's, or head for historic English Harbour (Nelson's Dockyard), you'll find first-rate beaches less than 10 minutes away by taxi. If history isn't your thing, the island offers a rich selection of water sport-based activities, from sailing and snorkeling to stingray swims.

HISTORY

Although named by Columbus, European settlers didn't arrive in Antigua until the mid-1600s. The first settlements were those of the Siboney (an Arawak word meaning "stone-people"), who date from about 2400 B.C. After the Siboney came the Arawaks, who were agricultural by nature. The Arawaks were displaced by the Caribs, an aggressive people. The earliest European contact came with Columbus' second Caribbean voyage in 1493, but European settlements didn't take root for another century due to the lack of fresh water and the Carib resistance. While the island was home to very prosperous sugar cane plantations, the British Navy prized the island for its **easily protected, safe harbors**. English Harbour was the British Navy's base of operations in this part of the Caribbean. Captain Horatio Nelson spent several unhappy years here, and many a man-o'-war was overhauled in what's now called "Nelson's Dockyard," naturally hidden from any enemy warship cruising by. With the exception of a brief occupation by the French, the island remained firmly under British rule until 1981, when it achieved full independence.

FACTS

Size: 14 miles (23 km.) long by 11 miles (18 km.) wide	
Climate: Subtropical	**Temperatures**: 81°F (26°C) to 87°F (30°C)
Population: 68,000	**Busy Season**: Late December to April
Language: English	**Money**: E. Carib. Dollar (1 = 37 U.S. cents)
Time Zone: Atlantic (no DST)	**Transportation**: Walking, taxis, cars
Phones: Dial 1- from U.S., dial 911 for emergencies	

Making the Most of Antigua

GETTING THERE

Your ship docks at **Heritage Quay** (pronounced "key"), in the heart of Antigua's capital city, St. John's. This pier, and nearby Redcliffe Quay, are the town's principal tourist shopping destinations, mixtures of renovated old buildings and fresh construction. If shopping and casino gaming are your only interests, you can do it all right on Heritage Quay. You'll also find a tourist information booth on the pier, and plenty of taxis awaiting your fare. On the 10-night holiday itinerary, the Magic lists an "all ashore" time at 7:30 am and an all-aboard time at 6:00 pm. The 10-night S. Caribbean itinerary lists an earlier "all aboard" time of 4:30 pm, while the 11-night itinerary shows a later "all aboard" time of 7:30 pm. Your actual "all ashore" and "all aboard" time may differ, particularly if you stop at this port because of bad weather elsewhere.

GETTING AROUND

The shops and restaurants at the pier, and Redcliffe Quay, are all within **walking distance** of the pier. Redcliffe Quay is about a 10 minute walk from the ship. • Taxi fares to English Harbor (Nelson's Dockyard) and many of the most worthwhile beaches will cost more than $20 for up to four passengers. Rates are set by the government, and drivers are required to carry an official rate card. Be sure to agree on the fare before you hop in. • Antigua is another island where car rentals are not advisable. Antigua's 60 miles of paved roads are in poor repair, you'll be driving British-style (on the left), and you must pay $20 for a local driving permit. If you do decide to drive, please drive with care and note that there are very few road signs—be sure to have a good map handy. • As nearly all points of interest are likely to be visited by shore excursions, excursions remain, as always, your safest bet.

SAFETY

There's **safety in numbers** on Antigua. With so many remote, unguarded beaches, beach crime is a serious concern. Bring the bare minimum with you if you set off in search of secluded sands. Leave valuables back on the ship and keep your Key to the World card, I.D., cash, and credit cards in a secure location on your person, such as a waterproof case. As always, do not carry large amounts of cash or jewelry. With most decent shopping so close to the pier, you should have no problems getting your packages safely onboard. Vendors near the pier can be pushy about selling their goods or services—a firm "no thank you" will do the trick. As mentioned above, Antiguans drive on the left-hand side of the road—don't forget this when crossing the street.

Touring Antigua

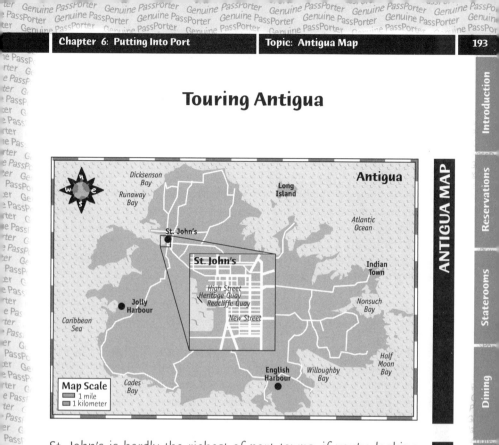

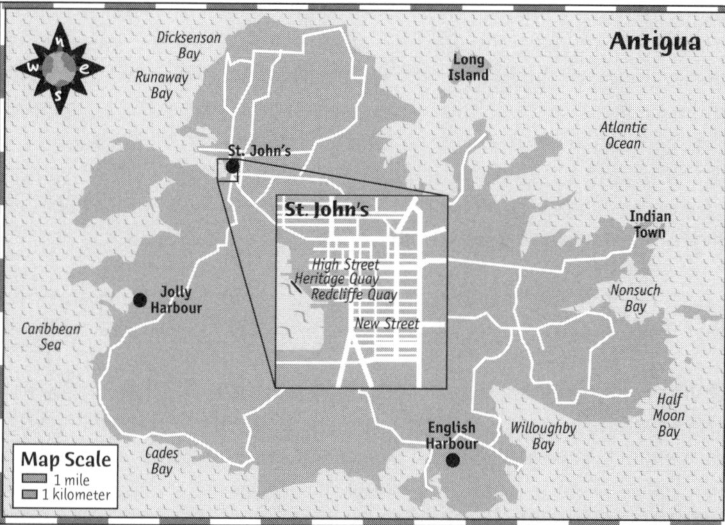

St. John's is hardly the richest of port towns, if you're looking for a walking tour. There are a handful of **historic sites** to visit, including the Museum of Antigua and Barbuda on Long Street, just two blocks north and a few inland from Heritage Quay. In addition to worthwhile historical exhibits, the museum may offer a self-guided walking tour of the town for a nominal price. Other sights include the ornate Anglican Cathedral and the restored buildings on Redcliffe Quay. English Harbour National Park offers greater opportunities for history hounds. About 8 miles southeast of St. John's, this historical park is one of the Caribbean's foremost historical attractions. Restored buildings and anchorages abound, including Nelson's Dockyard, and no fewer than four fortresses set up to guard the mouth of the harbor and command nearby Shirley Heights. The most photographed portion of Nelson's Dockyard is a group of 12 massive columns that used to support a huge boathouse where ships could get their sails and rigging repaired. Nelson's Dockyard is also famous for its English pubs and restaurants. If you'd rather, the park also offers several nature trails. Some visitors liken English Harbour to Colonial Williamsburg in Virginia. Detailed information can be found at the Visitor's Center in the Royal Artillery Barracks on Shirley Heights.

Playing in Antigua

ACTIVITIES

The **closest decent beach** to Heritage Quay is Fort Bay, near the northern mouth of the harbor. Runaway Bay and Dickenson Bay are just a little farther north up the coast (about 5 to 10 minutes by taxi), and offer calm, sheltered waters and the civilized niceties that go along with the adjoining beachfront resorts. Half Moon Bay is reputed to be among the island's finest beaches, but it's all the way cross-island from St. John's. If you're visiting English Harbour, Pigeon Beach is nearby (short drive or 20 minute walk).

The only **casino**—Kings Casino—is located moments from the ship, on Heritage Quay. Visit http://www.kingscasino.com.

Golfers can play a round at the **Jolly Harbour Golf Club**, an 18-hole championship course. Visitors can play for a daily fee and club rental is available. Visit http://www.jollyharbourantigua.com/golf.html.

Scuba, snorkel, and windsurfing are all popular activities, thanks to miles of encircling reefs, and the brisk winds on the Atlantic (eastern) side of the island. Snorkeling is possible at many of Antigua's beaches. Cades Reef is part of a designated off-shore underwater park, and very popular for snorkeling and scuba-diving. The wreck of the Andes, a three-masted merchant ship that sank in 1905, is another popular spot. Sailing is also very popular here—the island hosts an annual major regatta.

Looking for a **stingray and/or dolphin experience**? Antigua has those, too. For more information on stingray and dolphin encounters, visit http://www.dolphindiscovery.com/antigua.

Devil's Bridge at the northeastern point of the island is an amazing natural arch, created when the soft limestone was eroded away by the seawater. Devil's Bridge is located in Indian Town, one of Antigua's National Parks. Numerous blowholes spouting water surround Indian Town, making for quite a sight.

Cricket is a big sport on Antigua! If this sport interests you, matches can be found on the island at almost any time. For more information, visit http://www.antigua-barbuda.org/agcri01.htm.

For more details on Antigua, visit http://www.antigua-barbuda.org.

Embarking on Shore Excursions in Antigua

Disney's next visit to Antigua is in 2006 and it has yet to announce its round-up of shore excursions. We provide these listings to acquaint you with the possibilities, based on typical offerings by other cruise lines.

Antigua Historical Tour

Explore the capital city of St. John's in a bus, with stops along the way for photos and closer looks. Along the way you may visit Heritage Quay, Nelson's Dockyard, Dow's Hill Interpretation Center, Falmouth, English Harbour, Blockhouse Ruins, and Shirley Heights' Lookout (a strategic British lookout point from which enemy vessels could be clearly seen in the early days). Bring comfortable shoes as some walking will be necessary.

Tour | Leisurely | $36-42 | 2.5-3 hours

Island Safari Jeep Tour

Drive a four-person, 4x4 off-road vehicle and get off the beaten track! You can expect to travel dirt roads up to Buckley's Village with its gorgeous views and even drive through a rainforest. Afterwards, stop at a beach along the South Coast and cool off with a swim. This is likely to be a very bumpy ride, so pregnant women and those with bad backs are not advised to take it.

Tour | Active | $60–70 | 3–3.5 hours

Catamaran Snorkel Cruise

Board a large catamaran for a swift cruise along the Antigua coastline. When you reach your snorkel site, you'll be provided with instruction and equipment. Swimming may also be available on a nearby beach. Afterwards, cruise home with complimentary beverages.

Sports | Active | $50–55 | 3 hours

Circumnavigate Antigua (Around the Island EcoTour)

Go around the island of Antigua in a purpose-built, rigid inflatable boat. Your circumnavigation begins along the North Coast with its mangroves and sea life. Then head down the East Coast via the "Devil's Bridge," stopping along the way to snorkel and swim for about 45 minutes. Then it's back on the boat to cruise along the South Coast with its large volcanic structures and old forts. You may even have the chance to visit Nelson's Dockyard. Finally, you'll travel up along the West Coast to see the largest barrier reef in Antigua. The ride may be a bit bumpy along the way, so it's not recommended for pregnant women or those with back problems. Those prone to motion sickness may also want to skip this excursion or start taking their preventative medicine well in advance of the excursions departure.

Tour | Active | Ages 12 & up | $80 | 4 hours

Jolly Roger Pirate Cruise

Board an authentic wooden, two-masted schooner with billowing scarlet sails, skull-and-crossbones, and pirate wannabes. Enjoy island music and a fun-loving party as you ply the West Coast. Beverages may be included, perhaps even an open bar (we hear they make a wicked rum punch). And the crew may encourage guests to participate in a limbo competition or even an impromptu wedding or two. You may also anchor in one of Antigua's coves for swimming or beachcombing. The large schooner holds over 200 and has a sundeck, a shaded seating area, changing facilities, and "heads" (restrooms). (On Your Own: Jolly Roger Antigua Limited at http://www.geographia.com/antigua-barbuda/jolly-roger or 268-462-2064)

Tour | Active | $20-39 | 3 hours

Embarking on Shore Excursions in Antigua *(continued)*

Miniboat Adventure	
Take a taxi or bus ride to a marina where you'll board two-person miniboats. Cruise along the open water to a hidden lagoon where you'll have the time to swim or simply explore the area. Beverages (water and soda) are provided at the beach. Minimum age to drive a miniboat is 18; guests ages 12 to 17 must be accompanied by an adult or guardian.	**Sports** Active Ages 12 & up $75-80 3.5 hours

Stingray Village Swim and Snorkel	
Venture out to Antigua's Stingray Village by boat for the opportunity to swim and snorkel among these gentle sea creatures. You'll visit a natural sand bar and stand in about four feet of water to meet the various stingrays. Snorkel equipment and instruction is provided. After snorkeling, complimentary beverages are provided.	**Sports** Active Ages 8 & up $65-70 3 hours

Dolphin and Stingray Experience	
Board a boat from the pier and journey to a natural, 5.5 million gallon saltwater lagoon at Marina Bay. After a briefing, you'll have the chance to get in the water and play with the dolphins for about 25 minutes—learn how to feed them, pet them, and listen to them. Snorkel equipment will be provided during this time. After your dolphin encounter, head on over to the stingrays to touch, pet, and feed them as they swim and glide around you. (On Your Own: Dolphin Fantaseas at http://www.dolphinfantaseas.com/locations/antigua.htm, 268-562-7946)	**Sports** Active Ages 5 & up $145 3 hours

Antigua Beach Break (Millers by the Sea)	
Take a 15-minute bus from the pier to one of Antigua's best West Coast beaches. The secluded spot at Dickenson Bay offers you your own beach chair, changing facilities, a complimentary beverage, and a BBQ lunch. The beach is home to the open-air hotspot, Millers by the Sea, which features calypso and reggae music. Bring a towel and plenty of sunscreen.	**Beach** Leisurely All ages $40-50 5 hours

See page 158 for a key to the shore excursion description charts and their icons.

Antigua On Your Own

For those that want to get a headstart on their excursion plans, or just want to do it on their own, here is some information on tour operators in Antigua. Please note that we have not used these operators, nor is any mention here an endorsement of their services. A variety of excursions are offered through **Antigua Adventures**, and it's a popular operator with cruisers. Choose from sailing, powerboating, 4x4 adventures, helicopter rides, ecotours, hikes, and fishing excursions. For information, visit http://www.antiguaadventures.com or call 268-727-3261. If you'd like to go diving, **Big John's Dive Antigua** offers several dive excursions. For more information, visit http://www.diveantigua.com. For unique ecotours, **Antigua Paddles** offers it all—kayaking, swimming, snorkeling, hiking, and boat rides, all in one four-hour tour! You visit Bird Island to snorkel and hike, and Antigua's North Sound Marine Park to cruise in a boat. Minimum tour age is 7 and all guests must be able to swim. Complimentary bottled water and a snack is served while kayaking, and nutmeg rum punch is served on the return trip. For more information, visit http://www.antiguapaddles.com.

St. Lucia
(Special 10- & 11-Night Caribbean Itineraries in 2006)

INTRO

Towering mountains covered in lush vegetation, bubbling sulfurous hot springs, and black-sand beaches combine to make St. Lucia (pronounced "LOO-sha") a memorable stop for Caribbean vacationers. Watersport and eco-tourism opportunities abound—if only we had more time in port to hike those mountains and explore the forests!

AMBIENCE

St. Lucia is about as French as any British island can be. Most place names are French, including Les Pitons, those **twin mountains** rising a half-mile from the sea. Les Pitons are possibly the most-photographed mountains in the Caribbean. Your entry port of Castries, alas, has little of its old architecture remaining, due to several disastrous fires. Unless your goal is to shop, head out of town to enjoy the island's many sights and activities.

HISTORY

St. Lucia is called "the Helen of the Caribbean." Like Homer's Greek heroine, the **island's beauty** is notable. Like many Caribbean islands, the Arawak Indians were settled here two thousand years ago, only to be later ousted by the aggressive Caribs in 800 A.D. The first European to set foot on the island is widely believed to be Juan de la Cosa, a prolific explorer. The first European settler was Francois Le Clerc, a.k.a. "Pegleg," who set up house on Pigeon Island and attacked passing Spanish ships. The French and British battled over "Helen" for more than 150 years—the island changed hands fourteen times during that period. The British had the final triumph in 1814 (thanks to victory in Europe over Napoleon), so cars drive on the left-hand side, but the French influence is still huge—most place names are French, and the French-based Creole patois is still widely spoken. The volcanic hot springs were developed as a military health spa under the direction of King Louis XVI, only to be destroyed several years later during the French Revolution. As with most islands in the region, St. Lucia achieved independence in the late 1970s, and is now part of the British Commonwealth. St. Lucia's tourism has grown steadily over the last 20 years.

FACTS

Size: 26 miles (42 km.) long by 13 miles (21 km.) wide	
Climate: Tropical	**Temperatures**: 76°F (25°C) to 86°F (29°C)
Population: 158,000	**Busy Season**: Late December to April
Language: English, French	**Money**: E. Carib. Dollar (1 = 37 U.S. cents)
Time Zone: Atlantic (no DST)	**Transportation**: Taxis, cars
Phones: Dial 1- from U.S., dial 911 for emergencies, dial 999 for police	

Making the Most of St. Lucia

GETTING THERE

Your ship will likely dock at **Pointe Seraphine Pier** across the harbor from Castries, the capital city of St. Lucia. If that pier is busy, however, you may dock at the Elizabeth II pier. Both are located in Port Castries on the west coast of the island and are indicated on the map on the next page. On the 10-night holiday itinerary in 2006, the Magic lists an "all-ashore" at 9:30 am and an "all abourd" at 6:15 pm. Both S. Caribbean itineraries show "all ashore" time at 12:00 pm and an "all aboard" at 9:15 pm. Taxis are available at the dock to take you into town or to another destination, or you may simply walk to the nearby shopping.

GETTING AROUND

There's **good shopping near the pier** at Pointe Seraphine, a red-roofed, harbor front shopping complex with over 20 shops, many of which offer duty-free goods. You can walk there easily. • Due to the rugged terrain of this island, shore excursions and taxis are the best way to get around. You can get a taxi right at the pier—taxis do not have meters, but rates for common routes are set by the government. A typical fare from Castries to Rodney Bay is $40 for up to four people. Confirm the fare before getting in. • If you're thinking about a rental car, we think it may be more trouble than it's worth. You are only in port for seven hours, and a temporary driver's permit is necessary (you can get these from car rental agencies for $20). Also be aware that St. Lucians drive on the left side of the road, like the British. If you have your heart set on renting a car, there are half a dozen rental agencies at the pier—prices start around $50/day. • Beaches at Pigeon Island or Choc Beach are about 20 minutes away by taxi.

SAFETY

Petty street crimes and beach theft are the most notable crime problems you'll encounter, so **leave your valuables on board**, and safeguard your purse or wallet while shopping. It's best to stay on the main roads and not wander into alleys or away from downtown Castries on your own. Lockers aren't easy to come by on the island. As always, know your prices before you shop, and agree to taxi fares in advance. Sunblock is a must. Apply it before you leave your stateroom, and dress according to your planned activities—changing rooms aren't always easy to find. Wear cover-ups while shopping or walking in town, as local customs are conservative. You should also note that it is a local offense for anyone outside of the police force to dress in **camouflage clothes**, and topless bathing is illegal.

Touring St. Lucia

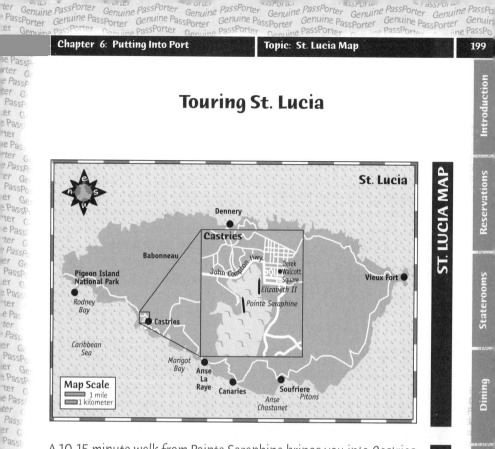

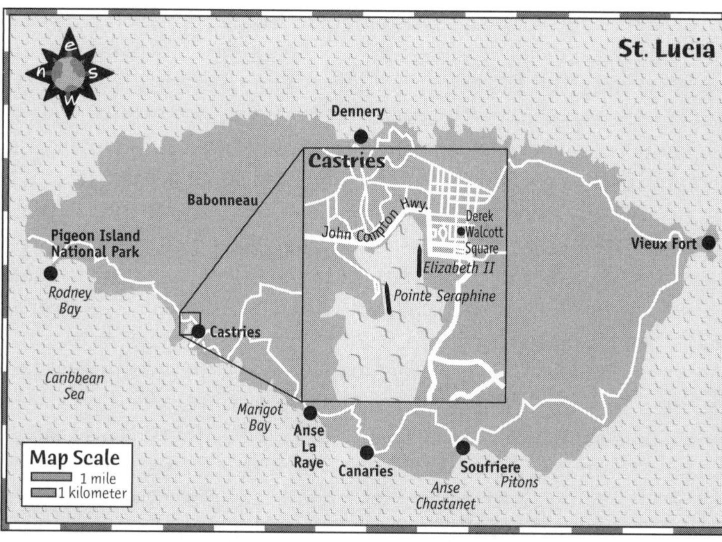

A 10-15 minute walk from Pointe Seraphine brings you into Castries proper, where you can view historical monuments, the busy harbor, and the city's farmer's market. We suggest you start your walking tour at the north end of Peynier Street where you'll find the newly-built **Central Market**, a bustling farmer's market in the mornings. In addition to the produce and spices you'd expect to find here (neither of which you can bring back into the U.S.), you'll find baskets, T-shirts, carvings, straw hats, and plenty of silly souvenirs. Across the street is Vendor's Arcade, which houses more craft stalls. Your next visit may be to **Derek Walcott Square**, located between Micoud and Brazil Streets. The square is named for the island's poet laureate, who won the Nobel Prize in 1992. In the recently refurbished square you'll see a statue in honor of the Nobel Laureate, a 400-year old Massav tree, and monuments to St. Lucian soldiers lost in the Second World War. Lining the square are historic buildings displaying both the French and English architecture of the island. The large Cathedral of the Immaculate Conception is located on one corner of the square—you can take a look inside the ornate interior unless a Mass is underway. There are plenty of other sites to see along the way, as well as the local flavor of the city. We suggest you pick up a good tourist map on your walk into town. If you feel intimidated about touring on your own, Solar Tours offers the Castries Heritage Walk—get more information at http://www.solartoursandtravel.com or call 758-452-5898.

Playing in St. Lucia

ACTIVITIES

St. Lucia is known for its **beautiful beaches**, all of which are public (though some can only be reached by boat or by passing through private property). Closest to the pier is Vigie Beach, just a mile and a half from Castries and parallel to the nearby airport. It's a clean, pretty beach. The best beaches are a short taxi ride away. Choc Beach (sometimes known as Palm Beach) is about 20 minutes away by taxi and offers a gorgeous stretch of white sand with swaying coconut palms. This is a great family beach with calm, crystal-clear waters and plenty of amenities. The secluded beaches at Pigeon Island National Park are also a favorite among visitors, offering water sports, a restaurant, and even a small historical museum. It isn't actually an island anymore—it was connected to the mainland in the '70s by a causeway. Those interested in snorkeling should visit Anse Chastanet on the southwest side of the island, about 12 miles from the pier. This is the site of a Marine Park and the Anse Chastanet Reef, which has been buoyed off specifically for snorkeling. The beautiful beach here has a volcanic black sand blanket and views of the twin Piton peaks. Be aware that a taxi trip to Anse Chastanet could take at least an hour, however, due to the steep, hilly roads and blind turns.

Shopping on St. Lucia is pretty easy. The Pointe Seraphine shopping complex (see previous page) is just steps from the pier, and the Central Market with its crafts and souvenir stalls is in downtown Castries. Note that bargaining is not customary on St. Lucia. Shopping is duty-free, sales tax-free, and is conducted in U.S. dollars. As always, while prices can be excellent, know what you'd pay back home for the same goods.

Golfers may enjoy a visit to the St. Lucia Golf & Country Club, an 18-hole golf course offering great views of both the Atlantic Ocean and Caribbean Sea. Rental clubs are available. For more information, visit http://www.stluciagolf.com or call 758-450-8522.

St. Lucia is a treasure trove of **beautiful natural resources**, including Pigeon Island National Park, the "drive-in volcano" near Soufriére (which means "smells of sulphur," by the way), and the famous Piton peaks which rise almost a half mile into the sky. These are all worth visiting if you're able!

For more information on St. Lucia, visit http://www.stlucia.org.

Embarking on Shore Excursions in St. Lucia

Disney's next visit to St. Lucia is in 2006 and it has yet to announce its round-up of shore excursions. We provide these listings to acquaint you with the possibilities, based on typical offerings by other cruise lines.

North Coast Tour and Beach Break

Tour
Leisurely
$22–36
3–4 hours

Board an air-conditioned bus for a tour of the Castries area with its beautiful views. Then it's on to Morne Fortune and it's impressive mountain range. After this, you'll visit Bagshaws at La Toc and see a demonstration of the 2000-year-old batik fabric making craft. Back on the bus you'll tour the countryside, visit Pigeon Island, and pass the Rodney Bay Marina. Your last stop is Reduit Beach for an hour or so of swimming and relaxing. A complimentary beverage and a reserved beach chair are waiting for you.

Waterfall Island Bike Tour

Sports
Very active
Ages 12 & up
$65
4–4.5 hours

Travel down the East Coast of the island into the rainforest, where you'll meet your tour guide, get your mountain bike and safety equipment, and listen to a short orientation. Then it's off the trail to explore banana plantations, stopping along the way to sample the local fruit. You'll end up at beautiful Errard Falls, where you'll receive a complimentary beverage and have a chance to cool off with a swim at the base of the falls. This bike tour is along routes with gentle inclines, and is recommended for experienced mountain bikers and/or those in excellent physical condition.

Soufriére Cruise and Swim

Tour
Leisurely
$40-50
5.5 hours

Board a large boat for a relaxing cruise down to Soufriére. You'll pass the Anse La Raye fishing village and the Canaries village, catching a glimpse of St. Lucia's famous Pitons, twin peaks towering 2,500 ft. above the sea. Once you reach Soufriére, you'll board mini-buses and journey to Sulphur Springs, the "world's only drive-in volcano." You may also have the chance to visit Fond Doux estate, a 250-year-old working plantation. Back on the boat you'll be treated to snacks while you take a 45-minute cruise to Cochon Beach. At the beach there will be time to take a swim and enjoy a complimentary beverage.

Pirates of the Caribbean Adventure

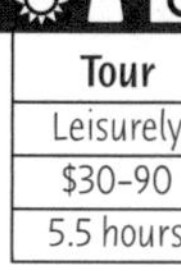

Tour
Leisurely
$30–90
5.5 hours

Imagine an opportunity to board an actual ship used in Disney's film, "Pirates of the Caribbean: The Curse of the Black Pearl." The Brig Unicorn is a replica of a 138 ft., 19th century tall ship, and appears in both "Pirates of the Caribbean" (where it was named "Black Pearl") as well as "Roots." Your adventure begins in Vigie Cove, near Castries, where 16th-century pirates once docked their warships. After boarding you'll sail the same waters once dominated by genuine Caribbean pirates—you may even have the chance to swing from the ropes or walk the plank. You can expect to visit historic Pigeon Island and Fort Rodney, which was the scene of several important naval battles between the British and French. The crew even treats you to a mock pirate attack, during which you'll hear the ship's working cannons. You'll then go ashore to explore and play, with time for swimming and hiking. You may also have the chance to go on a pirate treasure hunt while ashore! Back onboard there are snacks, rum punch, and soda. (On Your Own: Sun Link Tours at http://www.sunlinktours.com, 800-786-5465)

See page 158 for a key to the shore excursion description charts and their icons.

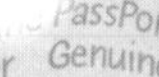

Embarking on Shore Excursions in St. Lucia *(continued)*

Deep Sea Fishing

Hunt for blue marlin, wahoo, barracuda, and other big game fish off the waters of St. Lucia, home to some of the best deep sea fishing in the world. You'll fish aboard a fully-equipped fishing boat; fishing tackle, bait, and "fighting chair" are all included. Catch-and-release only. This excursion is not recommended for those who are prone to motion sickness.

Sports
Active
$130
4 hours

St. Lucia Beach Snorkel

Take a 60-minute ferry boat ride along the St. Lucia coast to a marine preserve. After receiving your snorkel equipment and instruction, enter the waters from a special beach at the preserve. You'll have the opportunity to snorkel the Anse Chastanet Reef, voted one of the ten best snorkeling sites in the Caribbean. A complimentary beverage is served after snorkeling. (On Your Own: Scuba St. Lucia at http://www.scubastlucia.com, 758-459-7755)

Sports
Active
Ages 5 & up
$65
3.5 hours

Off-Road Adventure and Hike

Would you like to see areas of St. Lucia that are normally inaccessible to regular vehicles? Board an off-road, open-air, safari vehicle and drive through Castries, up Mourne Rouge, into the Cul-De-Sac Valley, over a volcanic hill, and deep into the rainforest. From here, you'll continue on foot to the upper part of the Anse La Raye valley and along a river to a waterfall. Then it's back in the vehicles to visit the La Sikwi Sugar mill for rest, a brief tour, and a complimentary beverage. You should be in excellent physical condition for this excursion, as there is moderate to heavy walking. You may have the chance to cool off with a swim, so we recommend you underdress your swimsuit.

Sports
Very active
Ages 6 & up
$58
3.5 hours

Pigeon Island Sea Kayaking

Transfer to Rodney Bay for a 30-minute paddle in a two-person kayak. Safety instructions and kayaking lessons will be provided. As you paddle the calm waters, your tour guide points out local flora and fauna, as well as historical trivia. Once you reach Pigeon Island National Park, you'll have time to swim and explore the ruins of a British fortification. A complimentary beverage and light snack will be served after kayaking.

Sports
Active
Ages 6 & up
$65
3 hours

See page 158 for a key to the shore excursion description charts and their icons.

St. Lucia On Your Own

For those that want to get a head start on their excursion plans, or just want to do it on their own, here is some information on tour operators in St. Lucia. Please note that we have not used these operators, nor is any mention here an endorsement of their services. For land and sea adventures, try **SunLink Tours**—they have cruises on the Brig Unicorn "pirate" ship (see previous page), dolphin and whale-watching, deep sea fishing, island tours to Soufriére, 4x4 safari tours, rainforest hikes, and biking tours. For more information, visit http://www.sunlinktours.com or call 758-456-9100. Those interested in scuba diving and snorkeling should check out **Scuba St. Lucia**, which is located on the southwestern shore near the Anse Chastanet Reef. A variety of diving and snorkeling excursions are offered. For more information, visit http://www.scubastlucia.com or call 758-459-7755.

Barbados
(Special Southern Caribbean Itineraries in 2006)

INTRO

Goodness gracious! This easternmost of all Caribbean isles is heir to a long British Colonial heritage and is popular with English tourists. Barbados boasts **soft, sandy beaches** to the west, rugged Atlantic surf to the east, a chance to explore bygone plantation life, and enough natural wonders to fill several days.

© Corel

North Point

AMBIENCE

Sugar plantations, rum distilleries, and modern, beachfront resorts all reflect a rich history and a prosperous present. With the tourist economy responsible for 75% of the island's income, you'll find pleasant shopping opportunities right at the pier, but the island really begins to shine when you head out of town to visit the rolling hills of "Scotland," the tropical ravines, and the beautiful coastline.

HISTORY

Named **Barbados ("bearded ones")** by the Portuguese, presumably for the abundant "bearded" fig trees, the only Spanish cultural contribution was the disease that annihilated the native Carib Indians. This coral island, lifted from the seabed by plate tectonics, is underlain by subterranean freshwater lakes and caverns, and its soil has been enriched by volcanic ash fall from islands to the northwest. The English arrived in 1627 to raise cotton and tobacco, but soon switched to sugar cane. Slavery was key to the island economy, and a brief slave revolt in 1816 preceded emancipation in 1834. If someone tells you, "George Washington slept here," believe it. He brought his brother here for the tuberculosis "cure" (which didn't succeed), and the president-to-be caught his famous case of smallpox here. Washington swore off all foreign travel after that ill-fated visit, ensuring that he was home when his country called. Sugar (and rum) remained the principal business well into the late 20th century. Home to the world's third-oldest parliamentary government, Barbados was ruled by the British until independence in 1966.

FACTS

Size: 21 miles (34 km.) long by 14 miles (22.5 km.) wide	
Climate: Tropical	**Temperatures**: 82°F (28°C) to 86°F (30°C)
Population: 279,000	**Busy Season**: Late December to April
Language: English	**Money**: Barbadian dollar ($2 =$1 U.S.)
Time Zone: Atlantic (no DST)	**Transportation**: Walking, taxis, cars
Phones: Dial 1- from U.S., dial 211 for emergencies	

Making the Most of Barbados

GETTING THERE

The Disney Wonder docks at the **Bridgetown Cruise Terminal**, a large pier and retail facility that, on the days the Wonder is scheduled to visit, you'll have all to your own. Inside the air conditioned terminal are 25 shops offering typical duty-free wares, "pushcart" vendors offering native goods, a post office, telephone center/Internet cafe, and tourist information office. Just outside is "Chattel House Village," a collection of shops offering handmade garments, plus several bars and eateries. You'll also find plenty of taxis and shuttles awaiting your fare. Nearby is Pelican Village, an attractive marketplace area featuring craft shops and craft demonstrations. "All ashore" time is about 7:30 am, and "all aboard" time is at 5:00 pm.

GETTING AROUND

The **heart of Bridgetown** is about a mile from the pier. You can certainly walk, but a cab is convenient, especially if you're returning to your ship with purchases. The architecture downtown on Broad Street is an interesting mix of British and Island style, but the shopping isn't much different or better than what you'll find in the cruise terminal. Taxi fares are set by the government, but there are no meters. Be sure to agree on the fare before you hop in. For longer jaunts, expect to pay about $30 per hour. There are several car rental agencies at the Bridgetown Cruise Terminal. We recommend you reserve ahead of time to get the best deal. You must pay $10 for a local driving permit (supplied by the rental agency), and you'll be driving British-style (on the left). While the map makes island navigation seem simple, with major routes all radiating from Bridgetown, an intricate web of secondary roads will make navigation more challenging—obtain a more detailed map if you plan to strike out on your own. Ask yourself: Are you *sure* you want to drive? As nearly all points of interest are likely to be visited by shore excursions, they remain, as always, your safest bet.

STAYING SAFE

Traffic flows English-style (left-hand side), so **look both ways** before crossing streets. This may seem like a minor thing, but you'd be surprised how many Americans forget this little detail and step out right into oncoming traffic. The cruise terminal provides a secure shopping environment, and the native "Bajans" like to be known for their friendliness, but conventional safety and security warnings are still in effect. Leave valuables on the ship, and be mindful at all times.

Touring Barbados

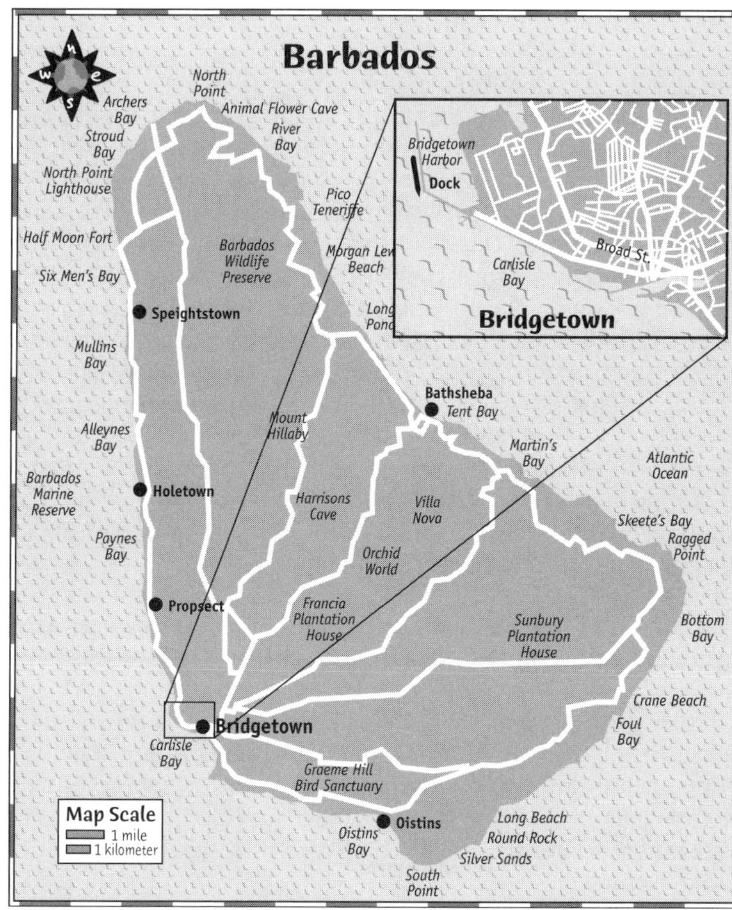

Harrisons Cave and Welchman Hall Gully, near the center of the island, are a **top excursion stop**. Electric trams take visitors down into beautiful limestone caverns traversed by underground rivers and waterfalls. The "gully" is a lush, tropical ravine with wildlife that survived the island's development. Orchid World, the Flower Forest, and Andromeda Botanic Garden are other destinations displaying tropical wonders. Mount Gay Rum and Mailbu Rum both operate visitor centers in Bridgetown—the local sugar becomes rum rather than children's candy! These and many more attractions are detailed at http://www.barbados.org, one of the most extensive and useful tourism sites you'll find for the Caribbean.

Playing in Barbados

ACTIVITIES

All beaches on the island are **open to the public**, and there are more worthy beaches here than we have space to catalog. We'll start with the calm seas of the western beaches. The closest practical beach to the cruise terminal is Brandon's Beach, a bit to the north by the Malibu Rum visitor's center. The beach is within walking distance of the pier, or a cab will do. Weiser's on the Bay and the Malibu Visitor's Center and Beach Club add a wide range of comforts, water sport rentals, dining, and plenty of rum-based beverages. A bit beyond Brandon's Beach are Batt's Rock and Paradise Beach, which are a good bit quieter. North from there is Paynes Bay Beach, and Sandy Lane Beach, known for its beauty and its proximity to one of the Caribbean's more exclusive upscale resorts. Heading south from Bridgetown, we reach the southern beaches, which become a bit more turbulent and are famous for windsurfing and snorkeling. The beaches of Needham's Point (Pebbles, Needham's Point, and Drill Hall) are just south of Bridgetown and offer a wide variety of recreational opportunities, sightseeing, and comforts.

Needham's Point was home to the British Navy's dockyards before they were moved to Antigua in 1816. The Garrison Area is home to a fortress, a huge collection of rare, vintage cannons, "George Washington House," and historic barracks, offering enough historic interest to sate most appetites. Some of the cannon are one-of-a-kind finds, dating back into the 17th century. Beach resort comforts can be found at the Hilton Hotel on Needham's Point beach.

Scuba, snorkel, and wind surfing are all popular activities, especially at the beaches on the south side of the island. Surfing and surfing lessons can also be found. Have you ever wanted to tag along with "Crush," the surfer-dude sea turtle from Finding Nemo? Several shore excursions offer swim-with-the-sea-turtles opportunities, an interesting twist on the more common stingray and dolphin excursions you'll find on other islands.

Attention, shoppers—Barbados is known for its clothing industry (look for cashmere sweaters), china, crystal, liquor, and local crafts (batiks, mahogany carvings, basketry, and jewlery).

Embarking on Shore Excursions in Barbados

Disney's first visit to Barbados is in 2006, and it has yet to announce its round-up of shore excursions. We provide these listings to acquaint you with the possibilities, based on typical offerings by other cruise lines.

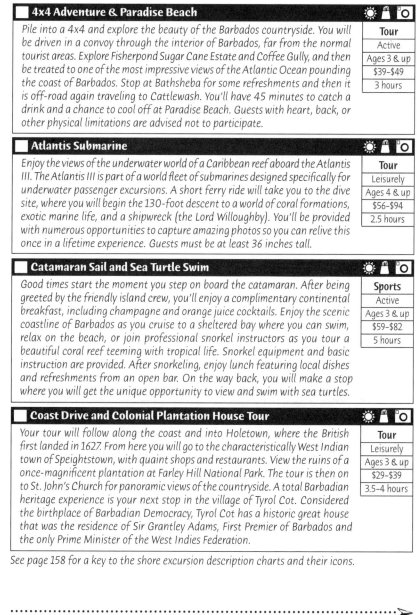

4x4 Adventure & Paradise Beach

Pile into a 4x4 and explore the beauty of the Barbados countryside. You will be driven in a convoy through the interior of Barbados, far from the normal tourist areas. Explore Fisherpond Sugar Cane Estate and Coffee Gully, and then be treated to one of the most impressive views of the Atlantic Ocean pounding the coast of Barbados. Stop at Bathsheba for some refreshments and then it is off-road again traveling to Cattlewash. You'll have 45 minutes to catch a drink and a chance to cool off at Paradise Beach. Guests with heart, back, or other physical limitations are advised not to participate.

Tour
Active
Ages 3 & up
$39-$49
3 hours

Atlantis Submarine

Enjoy the views of the underwater world of a Caribbean reef aboard the Atlantis III. The Atlantis III is part of a world fleet of submarines designed specifically for underwater passenger excursions. A short ferry ride will take you to the dive site, where you will begin the 130-foot descent to a world of coral formations, exotic marine life, and a shipwreck (the Lord Willoughby). You'll be provided with numerous opportunities to capture amazing photos so you can relive this once in a lifetime experience. Guests must be at least 36 inches tall.

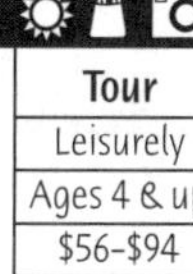

Tour
Leisurely
Ages 4 & up
$56-$94
2.5 hours

Catamaran Sail and Sea Turtle Swim

Good times start the moment you step on board the catamaran. After being greeted by the friendly island crew, you'll enjoy a complimentary continental breakfast, including champagne and orange juice cocktails. Enjoy the scenic coastline of Barbados as you cruise to a sheltered bay where you can swim, relax on the beach, or join professional snorkel instructors as you tour a beautiful coral reef teeming with tropical life. Snorkel equipment and basic instruction are provided. After snorkeling, enjoy lunch featuring local dishes and refreshments from an open bar. On the way back, you will make a stop where you will get the unique opportunity to view and swim with sea turtles.

Sports
Active
Ages 3 & up
$59-$82
5 hours

Coast Drive and Colonial Plantation House Tour

Your tour will follow along the coast and into Holetown, where the British first landed in 1627. From here you will go to the characteristically West Indian town of Speightstown, with quaint shops and restaurants. View the ruins of a once-magnificent plantation at Farley Hill National Park. The tour is then on to St. John's Church for panoramic views of the countryside. A total Barbadian heritage experience is your next stop in the village of Tyrol Cot. Considered the birthplace of Barbadian Democracy, Tyrol Cot has a historic great house that was the residence of Sir Grantley Adams, First Premier of Barbados and the only Prime Minister of the West Indies Federation.

Tour
Leisurely
Ages 3 & up
$29-$39
3.5-4 hours

See page 158 for a key to the shore excursion description charts and their icons.

Embarking on Shore Excursions in Barbados *(continued)*

Jolly Roger Pirate Cruise

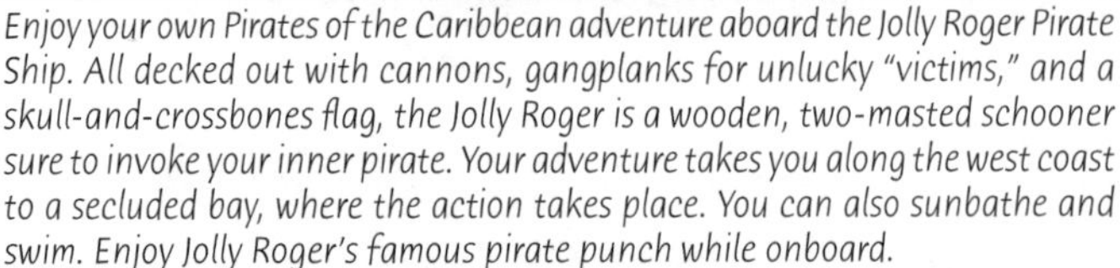

Enjoy your own Pirates of the Caribbean adventure aboard the Jolly Roger Pirate Ship. All decked out with cannons, gangplanks for unlucky "victims," and a skull-and-crossbones flag, the Jolly Roger is a wooden, two-masted schooner sure to invoke your inner pirate. Your adventure takes you along the west coast to a secluded bay, where the action takes place. You can also sunbathe and swim. Enjoy Jolly Roger's famous pirate punch while onboard.

Tour
Leisurely
Ages 3 & up
$54
3 hours

Kayak and Sea Turtle Encounter

Set out for an exciting kayak tour adventure. You'll start with a scenic boat ride to a secluded beach, where you will set out on your kayak tour. Kayaks, paddles, and safety gear are provided, as is basic kayak instruction. Paddle along the scenic Barbados coast to the snorkel location, where you will don your mask, snorkel, and safety vest. Then join your guides as they feed the sea turtles. On your return boat trip, enjoy some complimentary beverages.

Sports
Active
Ages 5 & up
$52–$75
3–3.5 hours

Rainforest Hike and Cave Adventure

This two-part tour starts with a hike through a rainforest and includes a descent into a cave for an underground adventure. Walk a lush forest trail where you're surrounded by rock formations, towering trees with hanging vines, and rare palms. From here, you'll enter a cave with fascinating natural rock formations. After a short hike back to the surface, you'll enjoy some refreshments before your return to the ship. Guests should be in good physical health as this is a strenuous tour. Light clothing and suitable footwear should be worn.

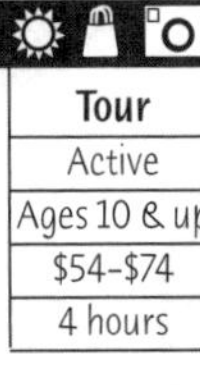

Tour
Active
Ages 10 & up
$54–$74
4 hours

Ocean Park Aquarium and Island Drive

View scenic, panoramic views of Barbados on your way to the Ocean Park Aquarium. Featuring large displays of marine life in their natural environment, this aquarium park is uniquely Caribbean. Thirty-three displays feature both freshwater and Caribbean sea life, including freshwater waterfalls, ray pool, Ocean encounter, and a shoreline discovery pod. Don't miss the Caribbean ocean exhibit with its viewing window and the walk-through coral reef exhibit.

Tour
Leisurely
All ages
$34–$44
3 hours

Sail, Fish-Feeding, and Snorkel Adventure

Soak up all that is Barbados as you sail and snorkel the gentle waters of the Caribbean. After a short drive, enjoy a 50-minute cruise to the snorkel site with a shipwreck that is home to fish you can feed by hand. Snorkel equipment is provided. There may even be a coral reef nearby that you can explore. Back onboard, you'll enjoy cool refreshments and relax in the sun as the catamaran sails back to Bridgetown. Plenty of shade and freshwater showers are onboard.

Sports
Active
Ages 8 & up
$34–$59
3.5 hours

Barbados On Your Own

For those who want to get a head start on their excursion plans or just want to do it on their own, consider spending the day at one of the local beaches such as the Boatyard or Accra Beach. You may also consider going on a private shore excursion with companies like Glory Tours (http://www.glorytours.org, 246-231-2932) or Ocean Adventures (http://www.oceanadventures.bb, 246-438-2088).

St. Kitts (St. Christopher)
(Special Southern Caribbean Itineraries in 2006)

This **peaceful little paradise** in the Caribbean's chain of Leeward Islands is a respite from some of the more frenetic islands. The island is dominated by the 3,792-foot-tall Mount Liamuiga (say "Lee-a-mweega"), a dormant volcano carpeted by dense tropical forests.

© Corel

North and South Friars Bays, St. Kitts

AMBIENCE

St. Kitts' volcanic origins give the island its **distinctive geography** and abundant vegetation. The jungle-covered central peaks of the island are mostly uninhabited, with most people living in the flatter areas near the coasts. Fascinating features include lava formations, tropical forests, and numerous lagoons. Its sister island, Nevis, is a single peak slightly more than two miles away. Nevis comes from the Spanish word for snow and it is named so because of the crown of white clouds that often covers its peak. The old sugar plantation homes are now more often grand hotels, and quaint Colonial architecture is evident throughout the towns.

HISTORY

Christopher Columbus first spotted St. Kitts in 1493 on his second voyage. There's been speculation that he even named the island after himself (**St. Kitts is a shortened form of St. Christopher**, Columbus' patron saint). The British arrived in 1623 to establish its first colony in the West Indies among its lush forests and fertile soil. The island's strategic location and vigorous sugar trade played a large role in the formation of the new world, and St. Kitts became known as the "Mother Colony" of the Caribbean. At one time, 68 sugar planations operated on St. Kitts alone. In 1983, St. Kitts and Nevis gained independence from the United Kingdom, and they are now collectively an independent country. Hurricane Georges tore through the islands in 1998, but they've rebounded well and damages have been repaired.

FACTS

Size: 18 miles (29 km.) long by 5 miles (8 km.) wide	
Climate: Subtropical	**Temperatures**: 79°F (26°C) to 87°F (30°C)
Population: 39,000	**Busy Season**: November to May
Language: English	**Money**: E. Carib. dollar ($1 = $0.37 U.S.)
Time Zone: Atlantic (no DST)	**Transportation**: Walking, taxis, cars
Phones: Dial 1- from U.S., dial 911 for emergencies	

Making the Most of St. Kitts

GETTING THERE

The Disney Wonder docks in Basseterre, capital of St. Kitts. The new **Port Zante** dock is a deep-water, 27-acre cruise ship facility that allows large cruise ships to pull right up for debarkation—no tendering is necessary in most cases. The facility offers a welcome center as well as some shopping and dining. The city is within walking distance, as is more shopping at the Pelican Mall (see map on next page). Taxis are available right at the port if you want to venture outside Basseterre. You should be able to disembark by 7:30 am (check your *Personal Navigator* for going ashore details). "All Aboard" time is expected to be 4:30 pm.

GETTING AROUND

If you're not on a shore excursion, you'll probably just want to **hoof it around Basseterre**—we suggest a stroll to Independence Square (once the site of the largest slave market in the Caribbean) and the "Circus" (a roundabout modeled after London's famous Piccadilly Circus). If you want to go further afield, take a taxi—rates are fixed and posted. Expect to pay about $30–40 U.S. to reach most destinations. A four-hour taxi tour is about $60 U.S. Plenty of rental car agencies (including Avis and Thrifty) are located in Basseterre within walking distance of the ship, but you'll need a local driving permit (about $10 from the rental car agency) and driving is on the left side of the road. If you do rent a car, drive slowly—many animals (cows, goats, donkeys) use the roads, and they have the right of way. The road that circumnavigates St. Kitts is well maintained and marked. A ferry ($6–$8 U.S.) is available to Nevis (and the ferry dock is near Port Zante), but the passage takes 45 minutes each way. With the 4:30 pm port departure, we don't recommend you risk the ferry. If you must visit Nevis, look for a shore excursion offered by Disney instead.

STAYING SAFE

Your health and safety when exploring a foreign land should be your number one priority. Tourists everywhere are targets for robbery—St. Kitts is no exception, but don't let that discourage you from exploring. Just exercise caution and leave extra cash and valuable items behind on the ship in your in-room safe. Remember that traffic in St. Kitts drives on the left-hand side, so be sure to look in both directions before crossing the road. Water is generally safe to drink here—it comes from volcanic springs.

Touring St. Kitts

ST. KITTS MAP

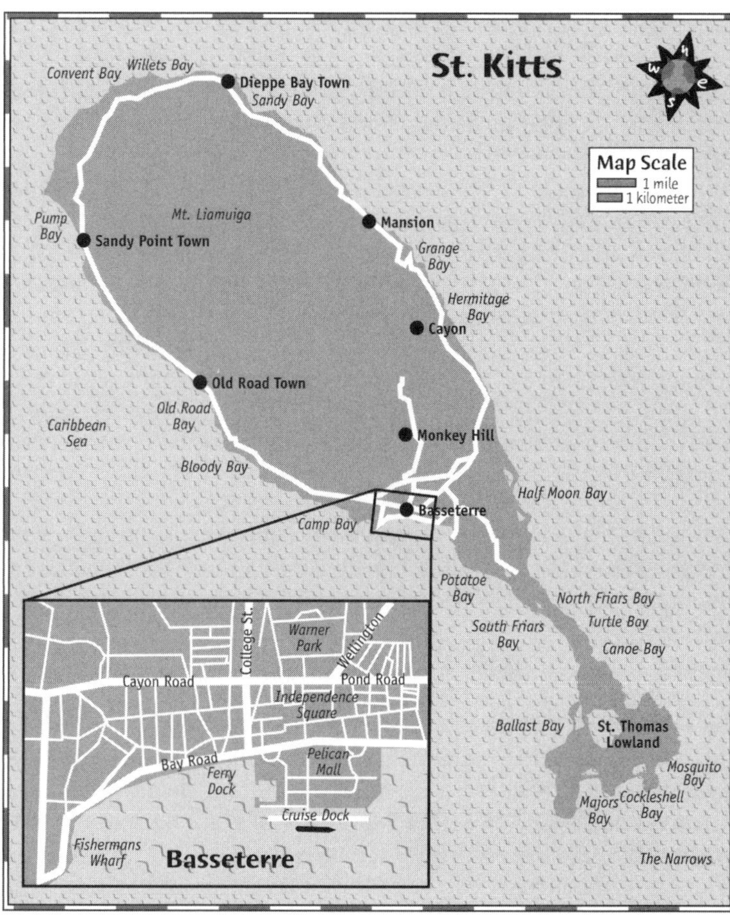

HIKING

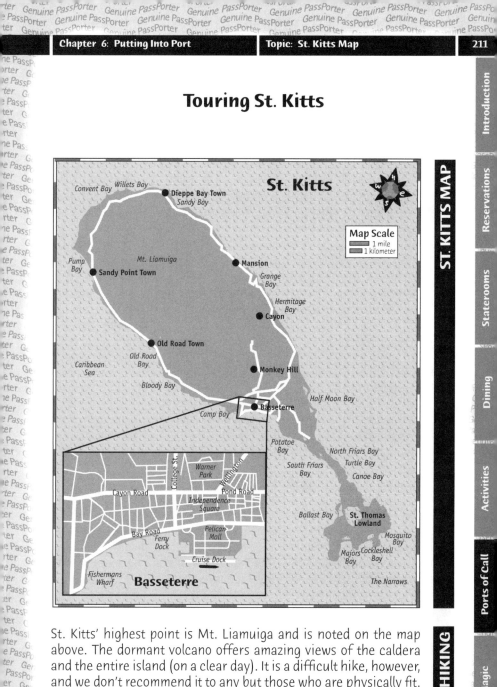

St. Kitts' highest point is Mt. Liamuiga and is noted on the map above. The dormant volcano offers amazing views of the caldera and the entire island (on a clear day). It is a difficult hike, however, and we don't recommend it to any but those who are physically fit. This is a full day's activity as it takes about 2.5 hours to hike each way. If you want to try it, check to see if any of the shore excursions Disney offers goes up. If not, check with Greg's Safaris at 869-465-4121 or http://www.gregssafaris.com (this tour operator also offers rainforest hikes and sugar plantation tours).

Playing in St. Kitts

ACTIVITIES

From walking on sugar-fine sand to playing in gray volcanic sand, St. Kitts offers some of the most **beautiful beaches** in the Caribbean. The beautiful white sand beaches of the Southeast Peninsula are accentuated by the panoramic views of sister island Nevis. With the emphasis on preserving the environment, the minimally developed beaches of Turtle Beach and Sand Bank Bay are exceptionally clean and relaxing. Years of erosion have made the black volcanic rock that is abundant throughout the island into an intriguing, gray sand. Found at numerous beaches at the northern end of the island, the gray sand is certainly worth a look, especially if you are looking for an alternative to the white sandy beaches usually found on St. Kitts. Travel to Frigate Bay for two beaches: on the western side, the Caribbean Sea offers calm waters to play and relax in; on the eastern, the Atlantic Ocean offers large waves that are ideal for body surfing.

While St. Kitts is not a major **dive destination**, some interesting sites do exist. Both shallow inshore and offshore shoals provide good diving, as does the coral reef between St. Kitts and Nevis. If you are certified and want to try a dive, contact Kenneth's Dive Center (see page 214 for contact information).

Brimstone Hill Fortress, a stop on several shore excursions, is a UNESCO World Heritage Site and a fascinating place for those who enjoy history and architecture. It's quite large and has both a visitor center and a museum. It also provides stunning views—on a clear day, you can see several neighboring islands. If you want to visit on your own, you can get a taxi at the port for about $30 U.S. Admission is $8 U.S. (Kids are $4 U.S.) Hours are 9:30 am–5:30 pm. For more information, visit http://www.brimstonehillfortress.org.

Another must-see attraction in St. Kitts is **Romney Manor**, which was once owned by Thomas Jefferson's great-great-great-grandfather. The manor has 10 acres of majestic grounds—look for the 350-year-old saman tree that covers half an acre! This is also the site of Caribelle Batik—you can watch artists create batik items as well as purchase them (there's also a store in downtown Basseterre if you can't make it there). For more information, phone 869-465-6253 or visit http://www.caribellebatikstkitts.com. Admission is free.

Embarking on Shore Excursions in St. Kitts

Disney's first visit to St. Kitts is in 2006, and it has yet to announce its round-up of shore excursions. We provide these listings to acquaint you with the possibilities, based on typical offerings by other cruise lines.

Basseterre Walking Tour	
Stroll the charming capital of St. Kitts with a knowledgeable tour guide. Your leisurely walk will likely take you by the Treasure Building, the Circus, Pretoria Gardens, Berkeley Memorial, Independence Square, and St. George's Anglican Church. A light refreshment will probably be served on your tour. Afterward, you may opt to go shopping or get transportation back to the dock.	**Tour** Active All ages $49-$42 2 hours

Catamaran Sail	
Board a catamaran and sail to the island of Nevis. You'll stop at a protected cove for snorkeling (equipment and orientation provided). Back onboard, you'll sail to the 3-mile-long Pinneys Beach, where a barbecue awaits you. Complimentary beverages are served throughout the cruise (alcoholic beverages served after snorkeling). You must remain barefoot while on the catamaran.	**Sports** Active Ages 6 & up $95-$119 6 hours

Highlights Tour	
Board an air-conditioned bus and take a scenic 30-minute coastal drive to the 300-year-old Brimstone Hill Fortress National Park, Romney Gardens, and Caribelle Batik Studio. Time to tour each of these sites is provided. You'll even get a view of Mt. Liamuiga as you return to the cruise dock. Some stair climbing is involved, as is walking at each of the tour stop locations.	**Tour** Leisurely All ages $40-$52 3-4 hours

Mountain Biking Tour & Beach Time	
Set off from Basseterre to Timothy Hill and the Frigate Bay resort area on a mountain bike. Time for a rewarding swim at Frigate Bay Beach is provided, along with refreshments. This excursion is for experienced mountain bikers in very good physical shape. Closed-toe shoes are required. Safety equipment is provided (and required). Minimum height is 60"/153 cm.	**Sports** Very active Ages 12 & up $78-$89 4 hours

Nature Kayak and Snorkel Adventure	
Your adventure begins with a scenic drive to White House Cove in the southern peninsula, where you receive a safety briefing and kayak orientation. Then you board your two-person ocean kayak and paddle along the beautiful coastline to Friars Bay (about a 90-minute trip, or one-and-a-half miles). An opportunity to snorkel and snorkel equipment are provided, as are soft drinks and snacks after your paddle. You return to the ship by minivan. This excursion is for guests in good physical condition. Wear your swimsuit under your clothing.	**Sports** Very active Ages 10 & up $65-$79 3 hours

Nevis Highlights and Botanical Gardens	
Take a 45-minute ferry to the island of Nevis, enjoying the scenic coast along the way. Once on Nevis, drive through Charlestown, stopping at Alexander Hamilton's Museum and finally arriving at the eight-acre botanical gardens with a glass conservatory, re-created temple, and a variety of gardens. Fruit punch is provided at Martha's West Indian Tea House before your return.	**Tour** Leisurely All ages $109-$129 3.5 hours

See page 158 for a key to the shore excursion description charts and their icons.

Embarking on Shore Excursions in St. Kitts *(continued)*

Panoramic Island Drive

Journey from Basseterre in an air-conditioned bus for an informative overview of St. Kitts' history and heritage. The narrated tour takes you through the city, into the "sugar country," and down the island's southern peninsula for views of Frigate Bay. You may even spot the island of Nevis in the distance. Some roads are unpaved, and you may experience bumps.

Tour
Leisurely
All ages
$28–$44
2 hours

Peninsular 4x4 Safari

Travel to St. Kitts' southern peninsula in 4x4 troop trucks. Your adventure will likely take you past Frigate Bay, Timothy Hill, and an old Overseer's House, where you can get out and explore the ruins. You'll continue to the extreme southern point of St. Kitts (Cockleshell Bay) to relax on the beach, enjoy fruit and juice, and catch a glimpse of Nevis. You return via the same route.

Tour
Leisurely
Ages 6 & up
$54–$62
3.5 hours

Rainforest Tour

After a 30-minute scenic drive, you arrive at Romney Gardens, where you'll have an opportunity to tour the manicured gardens and batik studio. Then you're off on a two-hour nature walk through the cool rainforest with a tour guide who provides commentary on the local flora and fauna. Enjoy fruit and juice at the end of your walk. Wear closed-toe shoes and bring raingear.

Tour
Active
Ages 4 & up
$38–$69
4 hours

Sail and Snorkel

Board a catamaran for a 45-minute cruise along St. Kitts' pristine coast as you head to the southern peninsula. After dropping anchor at the special site, you can explore the underwater world with the provided snorkel equipment or just swim. You may see parrotfish, trumpetfish, angelfish, and sand sharks. Soft drinks will be provided onboard.

Sports
Active
Ages 4 & up
$59
3 hours

Scenic Rail Tour

Enjoy a circuit of the entire island of St. Kitts on a one-of-a-kind narrow gauge railroad built nearly a century ago. The double-deck railcars feature an upper level with an open-air observation deck as well as a lower level with air conditioning (and you will have a seat available on both levels). Complimentary drinks, island music, and island narrative are provided during your journey. You'll cross steel bridges, spot neighboring islands, and pass small villages, towns, and popular tourist attractions. Seating is first-come, first-serve.

Tour
Leisurely
All ages
$80–$100
3.5 hours

See page 158 for a key to the shore excursion description charts and their icons.

St. Kitts On Your Own

For those who want to get a head start on their excursion plans or just want to do it on their own, here is some information on tour operators in St. Kitts. Please note that we have not used these operators, nor is any mention here an endorsement of their services. Many visitors love the "**private taxi tours**" which you can get right near the dock—expect to pay $40 for a peninsular tour and $60 for an island tour. Catamaran and snorkeling cruises are offered by **Blue Water Safaris** (869-466-4833, http://www.bluewatersafaris.com). Dives are available through **Kenneth's Dive Center** (869-465-2670, http://www.kennethsdivecenter.com) and **Dive St. Kitts** (800-621-1270, http://www.divestkitts.com).

Key West
(Western Caribbean Itinerary–First Port of Call)

Casually hanging out at the tip of the fabled Florida Keys, Key West is the southernmost point in the Continental U.S. Famous for Ernest Hemingway and Jimmy Buffett (and their bars); charming homes, sunsets, sport fishing; historic spots, and a way-laid-back lifestyle. You won't be in town long enough to waste away, but you sure can try.

© MediaMarx, Inc.

Key West's Mallory Square at sunset

AMBIENCE

As Florida's southernmost landfall, Americans will feel more secure wandering Key West than any other port of call. The charm of its century-old buildings and the small-town air will put you right at ease. Most attractions are a short stroll from the cruise ship piers, and streets head off in (mostly) straight lines. To visit the sights, just head there under your own power.

HISTORY & CULTURE

Spaniards called this flat, sun-drenched outpost "Cayo Hueso" (Island of Bones). The English (some buccaneers among 'em) were soon mispronouncing it "Key West." The U.S. Navy banished the pirates and has been stationed here ever since. Nearby, treacherous reefs sank countless vessels in the New Orleans trade, making salvage crews fabulously rich. A lighthouse turned that boom into a bust, and the town has been reborn again and again as a capital for spongers, cigar rollers, a President, treasure seekers, wealthy vacationers, artists and writers (James Audubon, Tennessee Williams, Robert Frost, Ernest Hemingway, and Thornton Wilder) and generations of dropouts from the rat race. Islanders declared the Conch Republic in 1982 to protest a Federal roadblock that choked access to the Florida Keys. They soon had enough media attention to restore free passage, but the Republic's flag still flies high.

FACTS

Size: 4 mi. (6.5 km.) wide x 2 mi. (3 km.) long	
Climate: Subtropical	**Temperatures**: 72°F (22°C) to 82°F (28°C)
Population: 24,832	**Busy Season**: Mid-February to April
Language: English	**Money**: U.S. Dollar
Time Zone: Eastern (DST observed)	**Transportation**: Walking, scooters
Phones: Dial 1- from U.S., dial 911 for emergencies	

Introduction Reservations Staterooms Dining Activities Ports of Call Magic Index

Getting Around Key West

GETTING THERE

Your ship docks around noon right at the **Hilton Marina** (Pier B), which is an easy five-minute walk to Mallory Square and Front Street. Tendering is not necessary, unless the ship is unable to dock (rare). You should be able to disembark by 12:00 pm or 1:00 pm (check your *Personal Navigator* for going ashore details). The marina is on the northwest corner of the island, looking out to the Gulf of Mexico. For those exploring on foot, most of the major destinations are within easy reach of the marina. Check your *Personal Navigator* for the "All Aboard" time, usually 1:00 am.

GETTING AROUND

This is one of the **easiest ports to navigate**, thanks to its small size and pedestrian-friendly streets. Most visitors here just **walk**, and even many of the residents don't bother with cars. Almost all of Key West's streets near the docks run on a grid, making it easy to get around with a map. If you'd rather not walk, try one of Key West's famous **tram tours**. The Conch Tour Train (described on page 221) is $20/adults, $10/kids 4 to 12 (3 & under free)—board the tram near Mallory Square. If you'd prefer to get off and look around, the Old Town Trolley makes nine stops (see page 221) for $20/adults, $10/kids 4–12 (3 & under free)—board near the dock. • The Key West **bus system** is less expensive than the trams at just 75 cents/adults and 35 cents/kids and seniors (kids 5 & under are free). There are always two buses running—one goes clockwise around the island, the other goes counter-clockwise. Call 305-293-6435 for bus info. • **Taxis** are also available—the meter starts at $1.40 and adds 35 cents per quarter mile. You can get taxis near the dock—if you need to call for one, try Florida Keys Taxi (305-284-2227). • Need your own transportation? Try a **scooter** rental. Adventure Scooter (601 Front Street, 305-293-9933, http://keywest.com/scooter.html) rents scooters for about $24/day—see the coupon at their Web site.

STAYING SAFE

The "key" to **staying safe** in Key West is simple common sense. The biggest potential dangers here are overexposure to sun (bring that sunscreen and hat) and overindulgence at a local bar. Key West is very laid-back—we didn't encounter any street hawkers on our visit and we felt secure walking around on our own. If you rent a scooter, be sure to wear your helmet. If you swim, note the color-coded flags which indicate swimming conditions at the beach: blue = safe, yellow = marginal, and red = dangerous and prohibited. If you walk, wear comfortable, well broken-in walking shoes. And bring a watch so you don't lose track of time and miss the boat!

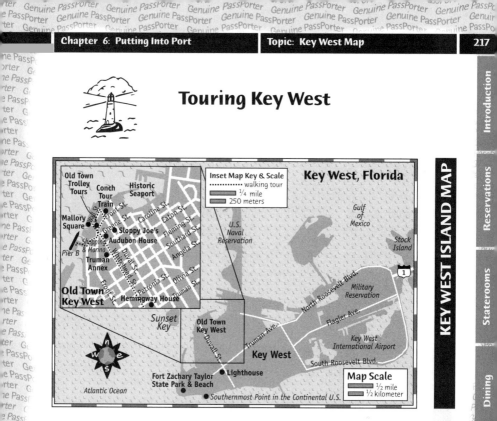

Touring Key West

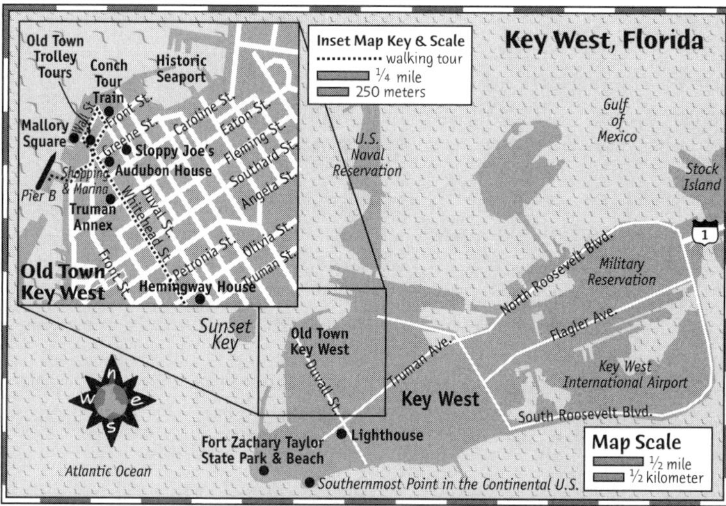

KEY WEST ISLAND MAP

WALKING TOUR

Key West is one of the best ports for a **casual walking tour**. Take along our map or pick one up at the Chamber of Commerce at 402 Wall Street. We've marked a walking tour on the map above. From the pier, you first reach the Truman Annex waterfront shopping area. Near the junction of Front and Greene Streets, is the brick 1891 Custom House and its Museum of Art and History. Turn left onto Front Street, passing the U.S. Customs House (and Post Office) and the Naval Coal Depot building. At the corner of Front and Whitehead is the Key West Art Center, showcasing local artists. Nearby is the Key West Shipwreck Historeum ($9/adult, $4/kids 4 to 12) with its 60-foot lookout tower, and the Key West Aquarium ($9/adult, $4.50/kids 4 to 12), Key West's oldest tourist attraction. Turning onto Wall St. you'll find the Chamber of Commerce (free maps and info), and famous Mallory Square (see next page for sunset viewing tips). Continue along Wall St., rejoining Front St., where you can board the Conch Tour Train (see previous page), or stroll another block along Front to the Historic Seaport boardwalk. Follow Front St. back towards the ship, crossing Duval St. then turn onto Whitehead for its charm and many museums. Stop where you will, but if you're in a walking mood, follow Whitehead nine blocks to the Lighthouse and Hemingway House. Whenever you've had enough, retrace your steps towards the waterfront to explore Duval and nearby side streets, or re-board the ship. For a more directed tour, try the "Key West Walking Tour" shore excursion (see page 222).

Playing in Key West

ACTIVITIES

Sloppy Joe's isn't the original Hemingway hangout; that's Captain Tony's, which used to be Sloppy Joe's. Captain Tony's gave Jimmy Buffett his first place to waste away, but now Jimmy can afford his own Margaritaville. Got all that? Regardless of your choice, these and many other atmospheric bars are a short crawl from the ship.

One of the joys of Key West is its **architecture**. Walk along Whitehead Street and turn down a few of the side streets. The old, clapboard homes, trimmed with Victorian gingerbread and surrounded by flowering foliage and white picket fences, are a delight. Household eaves are painted sky blue to ward off bugs, demons, or some such.

This isn't really a **beach zone**. The rocky bottom isn't swim-friendly. Fort Zachary Taylor State Park offers an attractive, nearby place to sun (enter via the Truman Annex gate on Thomas St.).

Your day in port is too short for an all-day **fishing or diving trip**, but a half-day may work. Plan in advance. Visit the Florida Keys & Key West Visitors Bureau at http://www.fla-keys.com or call 800-FLA-KEYS for information and lists of charter operators.

Want some authentic **Caribbean junk food**? Try hot, greasy, conch fritters for a fair price at the stand by the Aquarium entrance. For seafood and Key Lime Pie, just follow your nose.

The daily **Mallory Square sunset ritual** gathers thousands of revelers to watch the legendary sunset, and the harbor overflows with party boats. We surveyed the superb scene from deck 10. Go to http://www.mallorysquare.com and click WebCam for a preview. Sunset time is printed on the front of your *Personal Navigator*, or visit http://www.usno.navy.mil and click on "Sun Rise/Set."

Key West has too many **museums** for a brief cruise ship visit. Choose just one or two. Whitehead St. is the equivalent of Museum Mile, with nearly every attraction listed here either on the street or a block away. For glimpses inside beautiful historic homes, visit Audubon House, Harry S. Truman Little White House, Hemingway House, and/or Oldest House. All charge admission.

Key West and **T-shirts** seem to go together. Nearly every bar sells its own, Hog's Breath Saloon, Sloppy Joe's, and Margaritaville among 'em. Try the Conch Republic Store for local color. Brand luxuries can be had at U.S. prices, but you'll also find items by local designers.

Embarking on Shore Excursions in Key West

As of March 2005, Disney offers ten shore excursions in Key West, all of which are described below and on the following pages. Note that the Key West Beach Break excursion previously offered is no longer available. We don't think you need to go on one of these shore excursions to enjoy your time in Key West, but in general they are excellent. If you want to try one of these activities on your own, we also offer information on arranging your own tours and excursions at the bottom of each description.

Sail, Kayak, & Snorkel [K01] — Rating: n/a

Sports
Very Active
For more experienced snorkelers
Ages 10 & up
$79/person
5-5.5 hours

This is the "smorgasboard" of shore excursions, offering three different adventures in one. You'll start with a sail in a two-masted schooner to mangrove islands. At the islands, you'll hop into kayaks and paddle about the backcountry mangrove creeks for an hour. When you're done, its time to don snorkeling equipment (provided) and explore underwater for 45-60 minutes. Top it all off with a refreshing snack of fruit, chips, salsa, and beverages back at the pier. Meeting time is typically 12:10 pm. Bring an extra pair of dry shorts for the return trip. Unfortunately, we received no reviews for this excursion, nor could we find anyone who'd experienced it. Most cruisers preferred the Back to Nature Kayak Tour or the Key West Catamaran Sail & Snorkel Tour, described later. (On Your Own: JavaCat Charters at http://www.keywestkayak.com, 305-292-3188)

Catamaran Racing [K02] — Rating: 9

Sports
Very Active
For beginners and all levels
Ages 6 & up
$69/adult
$56/child
2.5-3.5 hours

You'll board your catamaran right at the pier, where your skipper assigns tasks (from navigator to timekeeper) and explains how the boat and the race works. Then you and your teammates sail out to the race course and do three timed runs. Back at the pier all sailors are treated to a victory party with a complimentary beverage, and the winning teammates get to pose for pictures with a trophy (our team won—see photo below). Don't bother with cameras or camcorders—they might get damaged. Bring sunglasses to shield your eyes from the sun and wind. Meeting time is typically 12:30 pm. We did this in May 2002 and had a blast! Even though neither of us are sailors, we never felt "out of our depth" and enjoyed the friendly competition. Cruiser reviews are positive: This "wonderful" catamaran sail is great for "adults and kids"—a "great time" is "had by all." Your "captain" teaches you "how to sail" or do whatever needs to be done, and tells you what "route" to follow. There is a "great sense of adventure" and "freedom" on this race. Be sure to "wear plenty of sunscreen" and a "hat" or you will get "burned." Overall, all cruisers who submitted reviews "loved this excursion" and would "recommend it to other cruisers." (On Your Own: Key West Cup Regatta at 305-293-8812)

Jennifer and Dave hold the winning trophy aboard the catamaran that won the race!

See page 158 for a key to the shore excursion description charts and their icons.

Introduction | Reservations | Staterooms | Dining | Activities | Ports of Call | Magic | Index

Embarking on Shore Excursions in Key West *(continued)*

Back to Nature Kayak Tour [K03] — Rating: 8

Sports
Very Active
For beginners and all levels
Ages 10 & up
$59/adult
3-3.5 hours

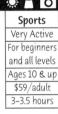

Looking for wildlife beyond Duval Street? Take a boat to the Key West Wildlife Preserve and paddle around in two-person, stable kayaks. Your tour guide leads you through the protected salt ponds and points out the many species of birds and marine life in their natural habitat. Typical meeting times are 12:15 pm and 1:50 pm. Bring an extra pair of dry shorts for the return trip—cameras and binoculars are a good idea, too. Water and soft drinks are provided. Cruiser comments are positive: You start with a 20-minute boat ride ("board at the pier") to a mangrove wash called "Archer Key." From here you board yet another boat to "receive a short lesson on using the two-person kayaks." You then kayak "beside the mangroves" and down "some passages." The "interesting guide" points out the "local birds and sea life," plus "natural history." The kayaking "is not difficult," except for those cruisers who experienced "stiff winds."

Sunset Sail: Western Union Schooner [K04] — Rating: 5

Tour
Leisurely
For beginners and all levels
All ages
$59/adult
$24/child
3-4 hours

The sunset sail is a quintessential Key West activity, but you must be willing to forego the early seating dinner or early show. First you explore Key West via the Conch Train Tour or Old Town Trolley (see pages 199). After your tour board the historic, 130-foot tall ship for a two-hour sunset sail. Includes live music, snacks, soda, beer, and wine. Meeting time is typically 4:15 pm. Cruiser reviews are lackluster: Some cruisers report that you "travel to the schooner" in an "air conditioned bus," "not the Conch Train or Trolley." Once aboard the "crowded" schooner, you "motor out" of the harbor then "the sails go up." There are a "lot of people" on board—"be prepared to stand." There's not "a whole lot to interest kids," and "very little sightseeing." A few cruisers "fell in love with it" and rave about the "fabulous Key West Ice Cream." The highlight is the "pretty Key West sunset." (On Your Own: http://www.schoonerwesternunion.com or 305-292-1766.) Note: You'll probably miss dinner, so order room service.

© MediaMarx, Inc.

The Western Union during a Key West sunset

Key West Catamaran Sail & Snorkel Tour [K05] — Rating: 6

Sports
Active
For all levels
Ages 5 & up
$47/adult
$27/child
3-3.5 hours

Set sail on a 65-foot comfortable catamaran with large sundecks, shady lounge deck, restrooms, and a fresh-water shower. The catamaran takes you about 6.5 miles (10 km.) south of the harbor to the only living coral reef in the continental U.S. Snorkeling equipment is provided for you to explore the reefs. Bring an underwater camera. Sodas and water are served, as is complimentary beer and white wine after snorkeling. Typical meeting time is 12:30 pm. Cruiser reviews are mixed: The "great crew" motors the "super clean" sailboat out of the harbor, though a few cruisers report "no sailing, just motoring." The snorkeling location "feels like the middle of the ocean" with depths of "20 feet or so." Some cruisers report that "snorkeling is great" with "plenty of coral and fish," while others note that "surge can be strong" and "kids may be afraid to snorkel" in the "bobbing water." Overall, most "enjoyed it" but "probably wouldn't do it again." (On Your Own: Fury Catamarans at http://www.furycat.com, 305-294-8899 or 800-994-8898)

See page 158 for a key to the shore excursion description charts and their icons.

Embarking on Shore Excursions in Key West *(continued)*

Conch Republic Tour & Museum Package [K08] — Rating: 4

Tour
Leisurely
All ages
$45/adult
$24/child
2–2.5 hours

Yes, you can do this all on your own, but if you'd prefer a more directed tour at a slightly steeper price, this is for you. First take an hour-long tour aboard the Conch Tour Train or the Old Town Trolley (see below). After the tour, you'll disembark at Mallory Square to visit the Aquarium and Shipwreck Museum on your own. Wear comfortable walking shoes and bring a camera. Typical meeting time is 12:00 pm. Cruiser reviews were uniform: The "city tour" is "great," conveying a "lot of info" in a "short amount of time" (good enough that some say it "made them want to visit Key West in the future"). The downfall seemed to be the Shipwreck Historeum, for which you "have to wait outside for the group before entering" and "then listen to a guide" before you are "free to explore on your own." The Aquarium is "ok" but many have "seen better at home." In general, this excursion has "too much waiting around." (On Your Own: See pages 217–218.)

Western Union Schooner [K07] — Rating: 5

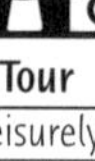

Tour
Leisurely
For all levels
All ages
$46/adult
$23/child
3–4 hours

If the schooner appeals to you but you don't want to miss dinner or a show, take this midday sail on the Western Union Schooner instead. You'll start your excursion with a tour on the Conch Tour Train or Old Town Trolley (see below) and then set sail on this beautiful ship, which is registered as a National Historic Landmark. You'll hear history, lore, and stories on your two-hour sail. The crew may also invite you to lend a hand. Includes snack and drink. Typical meeting time is 12:40 pm. Cruiser reviews are similar to those for the sunset sail, described on the previous page. The best part about this excursion compared to the other is that you don't miss dinner and "it's quite delightful on a sunny day." (On Your Own: http://www.schoonerwesternunion.com, 305-292-1766)

Old Town Trolley or Conch Train Tour [K09] — Rating: 6

Tour
All ages
$24/adult
$12/child
1–1.5 hours

A great way to get an overview of Key West and learn something on the way. The one-hour tour (either the trolley or the train) passes 100 points of interest and your tour guide offers historical and cultural commentary. We've done the Conch Tour Train and recommend it to first-time visitors as a friendly overview to Key West. Bring a camera. Young kids may get bored. Typical meeting time is 12:35 pm. Cruiser reviews are mostly positive: The "informative" tour is a "lot of fun." A complete circuit of the tour route "takes about an hour," which is "good for kids who can sit still long enough." The "friendly tour guide" "driver" provides "plenty of information about the history and architecture" of "Key West." The downfall to booking this excursion through Disney is that "you cannot get on and off it" like you can when you book it yourself and want to use it as transportation as well as a tour. (On Your Own: There's not much reason to book this one with Disney—see page 216 for more information.)

© MediaMarx, Inc.

The Conch Tour Train

See page 158 for a key to the shore excursion description charts and their icons.

Embarking on Shore Excursions in Key West *(continued)*

Glass Bottom Boat Tour on the Pride of Key West [K10] Rating: 1

Tour
Leisurely
All ages
$39/adult
$18/child
2-3 hours

If you'd like to see the underwater world of Key West but don't want to get wet, this catamaran is your ticket. The catamaran boasts an air-conditioned viewing area and an upper-level sun deck. Your guide delivers a narrated eco-tour as you visit the continental U.S.'s only living coral reef about 6.5 miles (10 km.) south of Key West. Typical meeting time is 1:20 pm. Cruiser reviews were mostly negative: The boat's "bottom viewing window" is "way too small for everyone to use." And while the viewing area is air-conditioned, the sun deck is "miserably hot" with "no shade." The only refreshments were "sodas for a buck a pop." Some cruisers also report that they did not visit the reef because "the tide was too strong." Overall, most cruisers "were not impressed." (On Your Own: Key West Famous Glassbottom boats at http://www.seethereef.com, 305-289-9933)

Key West Walking Tour [K11] Rating: n/a

Tour
Active
Ages 3 & up
$20/adult
$13/child
1.5-2 hours

Here's another excursion you can do on your own at little to no cost, so you're really paying for your tour guide. This 1.5-hour walking tour visits the oldest house in South Florida (built in 1829), the Key Lime Pie Company (where you get a sample), a cigar factory (where you can watch cigars being made), and tropical gardens. Wear comfy walking shoes and bring your camera. Typical meeting time is 1:15 pm. We received no cruiser reviews for this excursion. (On Your Own: See page 217)

Pirate Soul and Shipwreck Historeum [K13] Rating: n/a

Tour
Active
All ages
$31/adult
$16/child
2.5 hours

New! Ahoy, mateys! Discover your inner pirate on this adventure to the new Pirate Soul museum with Audio-Animatronics, interactive displays, and real pirate treasures (including one of only two Jolly Roger flags known to exist and the only authentic pirate chest in the U.S.). Afterward you'll visit the Shipwreck Historeum to explore Key West's maritime heritage. Typical meeting time is 12:30 pm. We have yet to get cruiser reviews for this excursion. (On Your Own: http://www.piratesoul.com and http://www.shipwreckhistoreum.com)

See page 158 for a key to the shore excursion description charts and their icons.

Key West On Your Own

Many cruisers prefer to embark on non-Disney excursions in Key West. While we don't have experience with these tour operators ourselves, here are some popular options: The **Sunset Watersports** allow you to drive your own speedboat through the back country mangrove channels, with time for snorkeling and swimming. For more information, visit http://www.sunsetwatersports.com or call 305-296-2554. • For less expensive transportation, try the **Bone Island Shuttle** bus at $7/person for the entire day. It makes about 12 stops throughout both ends of the island including Mallory Square, Duval Street, and the historic waterfront. For more details, visit http://www.boneislandshuttle.com or call 305-293-8710. • Another fun option is to rent a funky-yet-fun electric car from a place like **Tropical Rent a Car** for about $60 for two hours (2-seater) or $80 (4-seater). They also rent scooters and bicycles. They are located at 1300 Duval St. For more information, visit http://www.tropicalrentacar.com or call 305-294-8136.

Grand Cayman

(Western Caribbean Itinerary–Second Port of Call)

In these days of corporate scandals, the Cayman Islands have come to symbolize shady dealings hidden by offshore banks. Cruise visitors find a different pleasure waiting offshore; some of the most spectacular coral reefs in the Caribbean. Whether you snorkel, scuba, tour by submarine, or swim with the fishes at Stingray City, Grand Cayman is the perfect island for **watery recreation**.

Dave plays with stingrays in Grand Cayman

AMBIENCE

Of all Disney's ports of call, Grand Cayman seems the **quaintest**. Visitors arrive at a small pier, adjoining a relatively modest shopping street. We find scattered, free-standing buildings and several outdoor malls. The real action is taking place off shore, where fleets of excursion boats help visitors enjoy the island's sea life and fabled coral reefs. Alas, Grand Cayman was hit hard by Hurricane Ivan in September 2004 and the island will need time to regrow its vegetation. The beaches and Stingray City are in good shape, however.

HISTORY & CULTURE

A wayward breeze pushed the Cayman Islands onto the map in 1503, when Columbus stumbled upon these essentially flat outposts. He named them "**Tortugas**," for the plentiful local sea turtles, but soon the islands were renamed the Caimanas, after some other local reptilians (either crocodiles or Blue Iguanas, depending on who you ask). For centuries nobody bothered to settle here, but many ships visited to gather fresh turtle meat for their crews. Famed pirates visited frequently, but eventually the islands were ruled from British Jamaica. Still, with the exception of some mahogany-logging operations, there was little development here until well into the 20th century, and its famous banking industry didn't arrive until the 1950s. When Jamaica voted for independence from Great Britain in 1962, the Cayman Islanders chose to remain a British Crown Colony.

FACTS

Size: 22 mi. long (35 km.) x 8 mi. (13 km.) wide	
Climate: Subtropical	**Temperatures**: 78°F (25°C) to 84°F (29°C)
Population: 37,000	**Busy Season**: Mid-February to April
Language: English	**Money**: Cayman Islands Dollar (= $1.25 US)
Time Zone: Eastern (no DST)	**Transportation**: Walking, taxis, cars
Phones: Dial 1- from U.S., dial 911 for police, or dial 555 for an ambulance	

Introduction Reservations Staterooms Dining Activities Ports of Call Magic Index

Making the Most of Grand Cayman

GETTING THERE

Currently, this is the only Disney Cruise Line destination that regularly **requires tendering**. The ship anchors a short distance offshore of George Town, Grand Cayman—capital of the Cayman Islands. Tenders ferry guests to the pier in a matter of minutes, and run continuously throughout the day. Tenders returning to the ship depart from the South Terminal pier. You'll receive a notice in your stateroom describing current tendering procedures. A taxi stand is just a few steps from the dock, and the island's duty-free shopping district is tightly clustered within several blocks of the pier. The nearest beach is Seven Mile Beach, a short drive north of George Town. Typical all ashore is 7:30 am, with all aboard around 4:30 pm.

GETTING AROUND

Grand Cayman is **shaped like a sperm whale**, with its capital of George Town where a whale's "fluke" would be (see map on next page). It's easy to get around on foot in town. • Grand Cayman hardly overflows with sights to see, so while car rentals are available, we don't suggest them. Shore excursions can take you to nearly every sight, and taxis are fine for those who want to tour on their own. Taxis use a rate chart that is posted at the taxi stand by the cruise pier. Most car rental agencies are at the airport. Reserve in advance and arrange to have the car waiting at the pier for you. • Due north of George Town are Seven Mile Beach and the settlement of West Bay, home to the Cayman Turtle Farm and a tourist trap named Hell. Just to the east, kettle-shaped North Sound takes a big bite out of the north shore. A long coral reef guards the entrance to this bay, and just south of the reef, miles from shore, is "Stingray City," where excursion boats gather and guests cavort with the gentle stingrays in warm, waist-deep water (see photo on previous page). • The resort-and-beach destination of Rum Point is at the easternmost extreme of North Sound. • A single road follows the perimeter of the island (except for a huge gap between West Bay and Rum Point) connecting the island's many scuba dive destinations. • One of the most famous dive sites is Wreck of the Ten Sails, just beyond the village of East End and as far from George Town as you can be.

SAFETY

For water-based excursions, **leave your valuables** (and change into your swimwear) on the ship. Lockers aren't easy to come by on the island. Wear cover-ups, as local customs are sedately British, and carry lots of sunscreen. As always, know your prices before you shop, and agree to taxi fares in advance (fares are posted at the pier's taxi stand).

Touring Grand Cayman

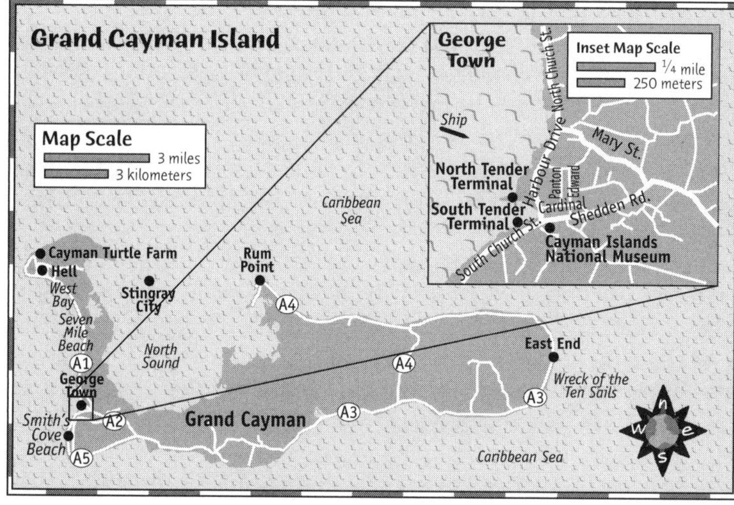

GRAND CAYMAN ISLAND MAP

WALKING TOUR

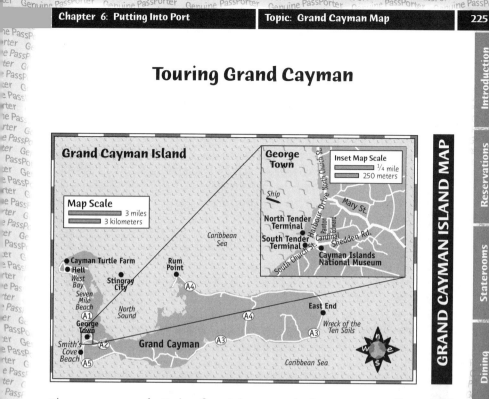

There are **many shops** but few sights to see in George Town. After several hours of walking and shopping you'll be ready to head back to the ship. Your tender arrives at South Terminal pier, a few steps from a tourist information center, the taxi stand and tour bus loading area. North Terminal pier is just across the tiny harbor. A single road, known alternately as North Church St., Harbour Drive, and South Church St. lines the waterfront. As you face inland, North Church will be to your left, and South Church to your right. Cardinal Ave., opposite North Terminal, heads directly inland from the waterfront into the heart of the shopping district. Shops and malls line Cardinal and wrap around onto Panton St. and Edward St. You'll find the Post Office at the corner of Cardinal and Edward. The shops of Anchorage Centre can be reached from Cardinal or Harbour Drive, directly across from the docks. The worthy Cayman Islands National Museum ($5 U.S./adults, $3/children) is across from the terminal, at the corner of South Church and Shedden Rd. Follow Harbour Drive a block northward to reach Blackbeard's Rum Cake shop, and two blocks beyond, Cayman Auto Rentals and the Nautilus undersea tours. Follow South Church southward to reach Atlantis Submarines and a cluster of shops and restaurants including the local Hard Rock Cafe, Blue Mountain Cyber Cafe, and the Tortuga Rum Cake Bakery. A long walk or short cab ride along South Church brings you to small Smith's Cove Public Beach, the closest sunning spot to the pier.

Playing in Grand Cayman

ACTIVITIES

The **shopping** is passable in this duty-free port, offering the usual selection of jewelry, luxury goods, and island wares. Serious shoppers report less-than-wonderful experiences, but if you know your prices and can cut a bargain, you may do fine. The principal "native" item is rum cake (yo ho, yo ho). Many visitors stock up on small sampler packages, perfect for gift giving. Turtle and coral-based items cannot be brought into the U.S., so don't buy them!

Certified scuba divers may be tempted to bring their own gear on the cruise and make their own dive arrangements. The Cayman Islands Department of Tourism at http://www.divecayman.ky has a useful online guide. Several shore excursions also exist for divers who don't want hassles. Snorkeling excursions are a good choice for those lacking scuba credentials.

While several **beaches** can be found around the perimeter of the island, we suggest you take an excursion to either Seven Mile Beach or Rum Point. Seven Mile Beach starts a short cab drive north of the port, with most of its length dominated by resorts and condos. A public beach with restrooms is found towards the beach's north end. Small Smith's Cove Beach at the south end of George Town also has restrooms, and is a long walk or short cab ride from the pier.

Unless the island's legendary coral reefs draw you elsewhere, you may want to consider an excursion that includes **Stingray City**, a submerged sand bar out in the middle of a huge bay. Guests climb from the boat right into the waist-high water for an encounter with friendly stingrays. We were instructed to "Stingray Shuffle" (shuffle your feet in the sand—the rays only sting if you step on them), and members of the crew introduced us to their aquatic protégé. While the rays are wild creatures, they've become willing partners in this enterprise—anything for a free handout (think pigeons in the park). On the ride to the sandbar one of our crew members spent his time cutting bait (frozen squid). The rays will swim right up to (or even into) a wader's arms for a snack, and the boat's crew shows us how to snuggle-up with the rays (see photo on page 223). Silky-soft rays swim among the guests, brushing past legs, sucking bait out of loosely-closed hands, and tolerating all sorts of petting zoo behavior. While the squeamish need some time to get used to the activity, eventually everyone becomes captivated by this up-close and personal encounter with these very gentle, odd creatures.

➢

Embarking on Shore Excursions on Grand Cayman

Grand Cayman's shore excursions offer jaunts to less-than-sterling tourist sights and several attractive water-based activities.

Atlantis Deep Explorer [G01]

Rating: 10

Tour
Leisurely
Ages 8 & up
$345
1–1.5 hours

This is a very pricey trip in a real research-class submarine that dives to impressive depths of 800 feet/244 m. Your undersea voyage takes you down to explore the Cayman Wall. The sub holds only two passengers, plus the pilot, so availability is extremely limited. Note that due to the very small size of the sub, height and weight restrictions are as follows: 6'2" max. height and 230 max. pounds per person; passengers traveling as a pair must weight less than 425 lbs. combined. Typical meeting times are 7:35 am & 12:50 pm. Cruiser reviews are overwhelmingly positive: Passengers start by taking a tender "out to sea," where the sub surfaces and you board. This "once in a lifetime opportunity" goes down to depths where the "external light" may give you views of a "wreck,"a lot of marine life," "weird-looking sponges," and "huge limestone haystacks." Cruisers suggest you "wear something red" as there is a "cool light spectrum effect" at certain depths. All cruisers felt this excursion was "well worth the money" and "recommend doing this if you can," though it is "not good for the claustrophobic." (On Your Own: http://www.atlantisadventures.com/cayman or 345-949-7700 or 800-887-8571)

Two-Tank Dive Tour [G03]

Rating: n/a

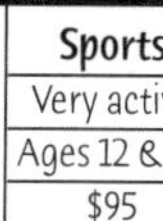

Sports
Very active
Ages 12 & up
$95
4 hours

Certified scuba divers can take this two-tank dive. The first dive will be along the Cayman Wall, followed by a shallow dive of 50 feet (15 km.) or less. All equipment is provided. Typical meeting time is 7:45 am. We received no cruiser reviews for this excursion, but we do know it is very popular (Grand Cayman is an excellent diving spot) and has been known to fill up more than 30 days in advance. If you find this excursion is full, here are some other scuba operators used by Disney cruisers: Bob Soto's Reef Divers at http://www.bobsotosreefdivers.com, 800-262-7686 (from the U.S.) or 345-949-2022 • Abanks Scuba Diving Diving Center, http://caymanislandsdiscounts.com/AbanksDiveCenter.htm, 345-946-6444 • Don Foster's Dive Cayman at http://www.donfosters.com, 800-833-4837 (from the U.S.) or 345-949-5679. Note that Red Sail Sports (http://www.redsailcayman.com) is the exclusive dive operator for Disney Cruise Line, but you cannot book directly with them.

SafeHaven Golf [G05]

Rating: n/a

Sports
Active
Ages 10 & up
$130
5 hours

Play a round at Grand Cayman's only championship 18-hole course. Includes greens fees and golf cart. Club rental not included. Guests must wear a collared shirt. Typical meeting time is 7:35 am. We received no cruiser reviews for this excursion, nor could we find cruisers who had experienced it. (On Your Own: The Links at SafeHaven, http://www.safehaven.ky/links.htm, 345-945 4155)

Nautilus Undersea Tour and Reef Snorkel [G07]

Rating: 8

Beach
Leisurely
Ages 5 & up
$45/$40 (5-9)
2 hours

Board a semi-submarine for a peek at shipwrecks and the Cheeseburger Reef, then spend some time snorkeling (equipment included). Typical meeting time is 7:30 am. Cruiser reviews are positive: This excursion is "great if you have both snorkelers and non-snorkelers in your group." The "tour is short" and "you stay close to the shore." Snorkeling is "great" and "views are phenomenal," with "fish," "plants," and a "wreck." (On Your Own: http://www.nautilus.ky or 345-945-1355)

See page 158 for a key to the shore excursion description charts and their icons.

Embarking on Shore Excursions on Grand Cayman *(continued)*

Stingray City Snorkel Tour [G08] Rating: 9

Sports
Active
Ages 6 & up
$45/$35 (6-9)
3 hours

Enjoy a ride in a double-decker catamaran to snorkel with the stingrays in 3-6 feet of water along a natural sandbar (see photo on page 207). All snorkeling equipment is provided. Complimentary water and lemonade served after snorkeling. If you want to see stingrays, this is the excursion we recommend. Cruiser reviews are very positive: You start with "hot," "20-minute van ride" to a harbor, where you board the "great" catamaran. The cruise to Stingray City is "fun," with "great scenery." The stingrays are "amazing," but be aware that "some kids may be afraid at first" and the "water may be over their heads" if it's "high tide." Overall, this "unique" excursion is one "the whole family can participate in." Typical meeting times are 7:30 am and 1:00 pm. (On Your Own: Captain Marvin's–see page 214 or Native Way Water Sports at http://www.nativewaywatersports.com, 345-916-5027)

Seaworld Explorer Semi-Submarine [G10] Rating: 9

Tour
Leisurely
All ages
$39/$29 (0-9)
1-1.5 hour

Take a ride on this semi-submarine to discover shipwrecks and sea life. A marine expert is on board to provide narration and answer your questions. Note that this excursion is very similar to the Nautilus Undersea Tour (see below). Cruiser reviews are very positive: This "short" excursion takes you down "five feet below the water" to view "Cheese Burger Reef" and two "shipwrecks," with "coral reefs" and "many fish." The "viewing windows" are "generous" and "clear." Cruisers note that it is a bit cheaper to "book this one on your own ($32/adult)." Overall, a "fun time for the whole family!" Typical meeting times are 8:10 am and 11:15 am. (On Your Own: Atlantis Adventures at http://www.atlantisadventures.com/cayman or 345-949-7700)

Atlantis Submarine Expedition [G11] Rating: 6

Tour
Leisurely
Ages 4 & up
$75/$50 (4-9)
1.5 hours

This submarine dives down to 90 feet (27 m.). Guests must be at least 36"/91 cm. tall). Typical meeting times are 9:20 am and 1:15 pm. Cruiser reviews are very similar to those on same excursion in St. Thomas (see page 178), but it gets a slightly higher rating thanks to the better views and visible sea life. (On Your Own: http://www.atlantisadventures.com/cayman or 345-949-7700)

Nautilus Undersea Tour [G12] Rating: 9

Tour
Leisurely
All ages
$39/$29 (3-9)
1-1.5 hours

Cruise on a semi-submarine with a marine expert. The Nautilus glides like a boat and never entirely submerges. This excursion is very similar to the Seaworld Explorer described earlier, except that kids under 3 are free on the Nautilus. Typical meeting time is 9:00 am. Cruiser comments are positive: The "view is phenomenal" and cruisers loved seeing "actual wrecks," "sea creatures," and "water plants." The "friendly" crew identified the wrecks and sealife. The "comfortable" boat was "a lot of fun."(On Your Own: http://www.nautilus.ky or 345-945-1355)

Rum Point Beach Adventure [G13] Rating: 6

Beach
Leisurely
All ages
$43/$35 (3-9)
5-5.5 hours

Enjoy a relaxing half-day at a secluded beach. Includes lunch and a soft drink. Watersport rentals available for extra fee. Cruiser reviews are mixed: Take a "long journey ("first a bus then a 45-min. ferry") to reach the "nice" but "small" beach. Cruisers suggest you "try to secure beach chairs as soon as you arrive." Lunch is "good" with a "variety of food." Overall, some cruisers enjoyed "being able to relax" while others felt "herded like cattle." Typical meeting time is 8:20 am.

➤

Embarking on Shore Excursions on Grand Cayman *(continued)*

Rum Point Beach Adventure & Stingray City Tour [G14] Rating: 7

Add a visit with the stingrays to the previous excursion for $22–25 more. After playing at the beach, you'll board a glass bottom boat and cruise out to Stingray City to snorkel. Cruiser reviews were mixed but very similiar to those for Rum Point Beach Adventure and Stingray City tours on the previous page—basically the big winner is the stingrays. Typical meeting time is 8:20 am.

Sports | Active | Ages 6 & up | $65/$60 (6-9) | 5.5 hours

Shipwreck and Reef Snorkeling [G15] Rating: 9

Explore one of the Cayman's most famous shipwrecks, the "Cali," where you'll learn a history of the ship and snorkel. You'll also visit a coral reef for more snorkeling. Includes snorkel gear and soft drinks (water and lemonade). Cruiser reviews are very positive: This "great" excursion is "good for beginners." Some cruisers report snorkeling "within sight of the Disney Magic," where they explored the "way cool" "shipwreck" which rests in about "15 to 20 feet of water." Then move about a "quarter mile" down to snorkel among "protected reefs" and see "awesome" sea "critters." Overall, cruisers "loved" this "fun excursion." Typical meeting times are 7:45 am and 1:40 pm.

Sports | Active | Ages 6 & up | $35/ $30 (5-9) | 2-2.5 hours

Stingray City Observatory and Island Tour [G18] Rating: n/a

Take in the island's sights on an air-conditioned bus—you'll see the Governor's House, Seven Mile Beach, Cayman Turtle Farm, and Hell. Then head out to sea to board a moored, semi-submarine for an underwater peek (so you won't get wet) at the stingrays. Ends with a trip to George Town with time to shop. A variety excursion! We received no cruiser reviews for this excursion, as it appears most would prefer to actually swim with the stingrays, an option not offered by this excursion (and you can always just observe on the other stingray excursions). Cruiser reviews on the island tour portion of this excursion are given below. Typical meeting time is 7:30 am.

Tour | Leisurely | Ages 6 & up | $55/ $45 (3-9) | 3-3.5 hours

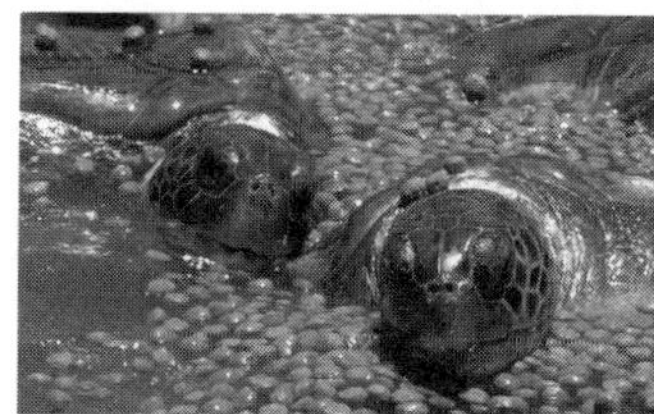
© MediaMarx, Inc.

Turtles at the Cayman Turtle Farm

Grand Cayman Island Tour [G17] Rating: 7

Take an air-conditioned bus tour through the streets of George Town, past the Gingerbread House, on through Hell, and to the Cayman Turtle Farm. This is very touristy—we personally didn't enjoy it much and felt like it was mostly a tour of souvenir shops, but other cruisers liked it. Cruiser reviews are mostly positive: A "nice overview" of the island in "cool" air-conditioned "buses." The tour guide is "informative" and "friendly." The turtle farm is "the best part" and "fun for the kids" (ask if you can "hold a turtle"), though some may be "appalled by the crowding of the turtles in the tanks.". Hell was "not a favorite" and "didn't impress" most cruisers, however. Highlights are the "low price" and "learning the history in a short time;" downfalls are the "short stops" and "no interaction with locals." Overall, most cruisers felt it "worth their time" even though is "isn't a sophisticated" excursion. Typical meeting times are 10:00 am and 1:25 pm.

Tour | Leisurely | All ages | $27/ $21 (3-9) | 2 hours

See page 158 for a key to the shore excursion description charts and their icons.

Embarking on Shore Excursions on Grand Cayman *(continued)*

Island Tour and Snorkeling with Stingrays [G19] — Rating: 8

Sports
Active
Ages 6 & up
$60/ $50 (6-9)
3.5 hours

Take an air-conditioned bus for a tour of several tourist highlights on Grand Cayman (see previous excursion for a more detailed description and cruiser reviews). Then board a ferry and cruise out to the Stingray City sandbar to snorkel with the rays. (See previous stingray excursion descriptions for more details on this.) This is just another set of options that may fit your schedule and interests. We did this excursion in May 2002—we loved the stingrays but didn't care for the island tour. Cruiser reviews gave this a slightly higher rating than the Island tour alone thanks to the interaction with the stingrays. Typical meeting times at 7:20, 10:00, and 11:00 am. About 3.5 hours. (On Your Own: Captain Marvin's—see below.)

Stingray City Reef Sail and Snorkel — Rating: n/a

Sports
Active
Ages 5 & up
$40/$30 (5-9)
3 hours

Yet another stingray excursion, this one featuring a nice, seven-mile sail in a 65-foot catamaran. For details on the stingray experience, see pages 226, 228 and 229. Includes snorkel equipment and beverages (water and lemonade). This excursion is relatively new, so we have no cruiser reviews to offer. Typical meeting time at 12:40 pm.

Aquaboat & Snorkel Adventure — Rating: n/a

Sports
Active
Ages 10 & up
$79
3 hours

Another new excursion with an exciting twist—piloting (or riding) in your own, two-person inflatable motorboat. You'll cruise along Grand Cayman's shores, then explore an uninhabited island (Sandy Cove). Then it's off to Smith's Cove to swim and snorkel (equipment provided). On your way back, you'll stop at the Cali shipwreck. When it's all done, enjoy a complimentary beverage (fruit or rum punch) at Rackams Bar on the dock. Note that guests must be 13 or older to pilot a boat, and must be accompanied by a parent or guardian. We have no cruiser reviews for this excursion yet as it is still new. Typical meeting time at 12:45 pm.

Island Tour & Butterfly Farm — Rating: n/a

Tour
Leisurely
All ages
$49/39 (3-8)
3.5-4 hours

Introduced in 2004, this excursion is very similar to the Grand Cayman Island Tour described on the previous page , but it also adds in a visit to the Grand Cayman Butterfly Farm. The butterfly farm is operated by the same folks who run the St. Maarten butterfly farm (see page 180). For more information on the butterfly farm, visit http://www.thebutterflyfarm.com. Typical meeting times are at 8:00 am and noon.

See page 158 for a key to the shore excursion description charts and their icons.

Grand Cayman On Your Own

Grand Cayman is another port where you find cruisers going on non-Disney excursions. Here are some popular options, though please note that we have no experience with these tour operators: **Captain Marvin's Watersports** is a very popular and well-liked outfit that offers snorkeling, island tours, and fishing charters at great prices, fewer crowds, and excellent service—visit http://www.captainmarvins.com or 866-978-0022. Another option is **Captain Bryan's Stingray City Sailing Charters**, which offers nicer boats with large sundecks and restrooms—better than the typical excursion boats. For details, visit http://www.cayman.org/captainbryan or 345-949-0038. A third option, also popular, is **Native Way Water Sports**—they have excursions to Seven Mile Beach and Coral Gardens in addition to Stingray City. Visit http://www.nativewaywatersports.com or 345-916-5027.

Note: Cozumel was heavily damaged by Hurricane Wilma in 2005. The island is still in recovery, so attractions and excursions may not fully match the descriptions.

Cozumel

(Western Caribbean Itinerary—Third Port of Call)

Welcome to **Mexico**! The island of Cozumel, just off the northeastern tip of Mexico's Yucatan peninsula and a bit south of Cancun, offers the Disney Cruise Line's primary taste of the Caribbean's Hispanic heritage. You can stay on the island, or visit the Mayan ruins on the mainland. Cozumel offers a wide range of enticing activities and Mexican handcrafted goods.

© MediaMarx, Inc.

Relaxing on the beach on Cozumel

AMBIENCE

Cozumel is a **destination of contrasts**. For some, it's a crowded shopping port, intimidatingly foreign to some, exciting for others. It can be a jumping-off point for a visit to ancient ruins, or a gateway to some of the world's greatest reef diving. A unique nature park offers underwater and jungle adventure, and white, powdery beaches offer sheltered, resort/upscale experiences on the western shore, or remote, raucous rolling surf on the eastern shore.

HISTORY & CULTURE

With a history as a **religious destination** dating back into Mayan pre-history (the name Cozumel derives from the Mayan for *island of swallows*), this is one port where you can visit ruins that actually pre-date Christopher what's-his-name. The island's substantial population was destroyed after the Conquistadores brutal arrival, and its many coves and inlets served as hideouts for pirates such as Jean Lafitte and Henry Morgan. Settlers returned in the mid-1800s and cultivation of rubber here and on the mainland made this once again a trading center. The island's beautiful beaches made it part of the State of Quintana Roo's "Mexican Riviera." Undersea explorer Jacques Cousteau really put the island on the tourism map in the 1960s, thanks to the island's prime coral reefs, part of the second-largest coral reef formation in the world (after Australia's Great Barrier Reef).

FACTS

Size: 30 mi. (48 km.) long x 9 mi. (16 km.) wide	
Climate: Subtropical	**Temperatures**: 75°F (24°C) to 90°F (32°C)
Population: 65,000	**Busy Season**: Mid-February to April
Language: Spanish, English	**Money**: Nuevo Peso ($10 Pesos = $1 U.S.)
Time Zone: Central (DST observed)	**Transportation**: Walking, taxis, scooters
Phones: Dial 011- from U.S., dial 060 for emergencies, dial 20092 for police	

Making the Most of Cozumel

GETTING THERE

Your ship docks at the new **Punta Langosta** pier in the city of San Miguel de Cozumel, on the island's western shore. Tendering is not required. You can see Playa del Carmen on the mainland—the channel is just two miles (3 km.) wide. The typical all ashore time is 10:30 am, with all aboard at 10:00 pm. A tourist information office is at the end of the pier, as is the glitzy Punta Langosta shopping plaza. The plaza is reached via a pedestrian bridge over Avenida (Avenue) Rafael Melgar, and provides a convenient, secure shopping and dining destination. There is no beach within walking distance.

GETTING AROUND

You disembark the ship near the **center of town**, about five blocks south of Muelle Fiscal, the city's central plaza and ferryboat dock (ferries to the mainland). Several miles to the south are the International and Puerta Maya piers, in the resort hotel district. The waterfront road, Avenida Rafael Melgar, goes right past the pier, and leads to most of the sights in town and on the island's west shore. Just five blocks north you'll find Avenida Benito Juarez, which heads directly to the San Gervasio ruins and the beaches of the eastern shore. Drive south on Ave. Rafael Melgar to reach Chankanaab Nature Park, San Francisco Beach, Playa Del Sol, and Palancar Reef. • Car and scooter rentals are advisable for those who wish to set off on their own, but taxis ($4 for up to four passengers) are more convenient for in-town travel. Four wheel drive vehicles are especially useful if you head for the eastern beaches. Executive Car Rental (529-872-1308) is located in the Punta Langosta Mall, and several other agencies are nearby. Note that cars are driven on the same side of the road as in the U.S.

STAYING SAFE

Safety is always, in part, a **state of mind**. Certainly the crowds of sprawling San Miguel will put most travelers on the defensive, as may the dominant, Spanish language (though most shop owners speak some English). Take typical big-city precautions, then try to relax and enjoy. A polite, friendly attitude towards the locals will ease your way—it always helps to treat your host with respect. "Do you speak English?" is a good way to start your conversations. Drinking water and food safety are a classic concern for visits to Mexico. Be sensible. Drink bottled water and commercially-prepared beverages, and think twice about dining from street vendors. However, most restaurants will be well up to stateside health standards. As always, sunblock is a must. Dress according to your planned activities—changing rooms are hard to find at the beach.

Touring Cozumel

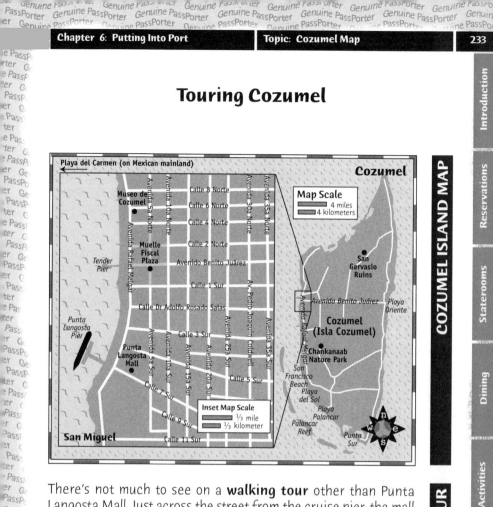

COZUMEL ISLAND MAP

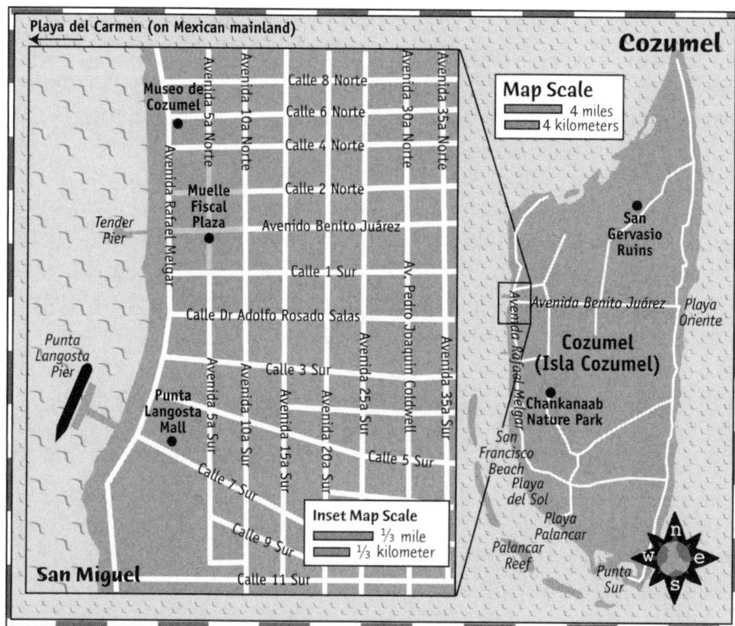

WALKING TOUR

There's not much to see on a **walking tour** other than Punta Langosta Mall. Just across the street from the cruise pier, the mall is brand-new, with stylish architecture reminiscent of fashionable stateside malls (it reminds us a bit of Downtown Disney in Orlando). You'll find upscale souvenir and luxury shops, the popular bars Carlos 'n' Charlie's and Señor Frog, a Tony Roma's Steakhouse, and a Burger King. While the Punta Langosta Mall offers a secure experience, you'll get a better taste of the town by taking a short stroll or cab ride five blocks north to Muelle Fiscal, the town's central plaza. A six-block area has been converted to a pedestrian mall, featuring many restaurants, shops, and a large souvenir and crafts market. Three blocks farther north on Ave. Rafael Melgar is the island's museum ($3 admission), which features two floors filled with archaeological and ecological exhibits and a very popular rooftop restaurant (Del Museo), which is open until 1:30 pm. Most tourist-oriented restaurants and shops are clustered along a 10-block stretch of Avenido Rafael Melgar between Punta Langosta on the south and the museum on the north. However, if you're bargain-hunting, the shops on the side streets and a block inland may offer better deals.

Playing in Cozumel

ACTIVITIES

The best of the island's and mainland's **play spots** and attractions are featured in shore excursions on the next four pages, which we recommend for most visitors. Many are day-long experiences. Serious divers may prefer to make their own arrangements.

The island does not produce much in the way of local crafts, but you can find a wide range of silver, carved wood and stone, and other Mexican specialties, imported from the mainland. **Shops** near the cruise pier will tend to be the most expensive. Know your prices, and be prepared to bargain. Silver items are typically sold by weight, and black coral cannot be brought back into the U.S.

White, powder-soft sands and clear, turquoise waters make the island's **beaches** very attractive. The strong undertow found on the east coast beaches, such as Playa Oriente, can be perilous for swimmers, but the big surf, dunes, stretches of rocky coastline, and small crowds are very tempting. Playa Oriente is at the far eastern end of the central, cross-island road, and others can be found by turning right and following the paved road southward. Several of these beaches offer restaurants and watersport rentals. The safe, gentle beaches on the sheltered west side of the island are generally built-up, offering a wide variety of recreational and dining opportunities. Top picks (all south of San Miguel) include San Francisco Beach, Playa del Sol, Playa Francesa, and Playa Palancar.

Palancar Reef, at the island's southwest corner, is probably at the top of most serious divers' list, but dozens more **dive sites** dot the map. Visit http://www.travelnotes.cc/cozumel/links/scuba.html for a good introduction to Cozumel diving, listings, and reviews.

Chankanaab Park offers first-rate snorkel, nature, and wildlife encounter opportunities. • On the mainland, the **Xcaret** Eco-Archeological Park offers many unusual opportunities (book an excursion for either of these). The island's archeological sites are quite minor, with the most developed at San Gervasio, near the island's center. Archeology buffs should book an excursion to Tulum Ruins, about 80 miles (128 km.) away on the mainland. Alas, famed Chitchen Itza is a bit too far for a day trip.

Your schedule allows for both **lunch and dinner** ashore. Carlos 'n Charlies is a town fixture, relocated to Punta Langosta Mall. In the center of town, Casa Denis and La Choza offer regional specialties.

Embarking on Shore Excursions on Cozumel

Cozumel's Golf Excursion [CZ01] — Rating: n/a

Play a round at the Cozumel Country Club on a course designed by the Nicklaus Group. Includes greens fees, golf cart, and golf balls. Lunch and club/shoe rentals are additional. Golf attire required. Typical meeting time is 10:20 am. We received no cruiser reviews for this excursion. (On Your Own: Cozumel Country Club, http://www.cozumelcountryclub.com.mx, 987-872-9570)

Sports
Active
Ages 10 & up
$145
5-6 hours

Certified Scuba Tour [CZ02] — Rating: 9

Certified divers enjoy two dives—first to Palancar Reef (70'-80' or 21–24 m.) and then to a shallower dive (50'-60' or 15–18 m.). Includes equipment, fruit, and drinks. Typical meeting time is 11:35 am. Cruiser reviews are positive: Two "drift dives" offer the opportunity to see more "unique underwater life" than in many other ports. Palancar Reef is "phenomenal" and the reef wall is "very deep" with "lots to see." Visibility is "incredible." (On Your Own: Eagle Ray Divers, http://www.eagleraydivers.com, 987-872-5735)

Sports
Very active
Ages 12 & up
$94
4-4.5 hours

Dolphin Discovery Cozumel [CZ04] — Rating: 7

This popular excursion takes you to Chankanaab National Park where you'll encounter dolphins in waist-deep water. Afterwards, stay and enjoy the park. If you want to swim with the dolphins, you will need to book that on your own—see below. Typical meeting times are 10:20 am, noon, 1:00 pm, and 2:00 pm. Cruiser comments were mixed: Listen to a "brief training session," don "bulky life jackets," then enter one of five "water areas" where you stand in the water. Several cruisers report that the "waist-high" water was in fact "chest-high" or even "chin-high" instead, and that it could be over the heads of guests under 7. Most cruisers loved being able to "touch and interact" with the "amazing" dolphins. Cruisers note that you cannot wear "water shoes." Some feel this excursion isn't really great for cruisers "under 12" due to the depth of the water. (On Your Own: Dolphin Discovery Cozumel at http://www.dolphindiscovery.com/cozumel/, 800-417-1736)

Encounter
Leisurely
Ages 3 & up
$110/$96
3-3.5 hours

Mayan Frontier Horseback Riding Tour [CZ05] — Rating: 6

Giddyup! Mosey on down a Mayan trail on horseback, passing ruins on your way. Afterwards, visit a ranch. Includes complimentary soft drinks and beer after riding. Typical meeting time is 11:15 am. Cruiser reviews were mediocre: The "very friendly staff" is "helpful," but the "saddles are old and unpadded." The horses are also "over the hill" (which could be a good thing as they are more sedate than younger horses). Cruisers also note that some of the "ruins and artifacts" are "not real." Younger guests "enjoyed it," but most cruisers were "not impressed."

Sports
Very active
Ages 12 & up
$85
4 hours

Tulum Ruins and Beach Tour [CZ06] — Rating: 9

An all-day adventure to the mainland for a visit to the sacred ruins. Includes a beach visit, drinks, and sandwiches. Note that there is an extra fee if you bring a camcorder. Typical meeting time is 9:40 am. Cruiser reviews are positive: The "boat to Mexico" is "large and comfortable," though a "little bouncy." The "fantastic" tour guides are "knowledgeable," making the ruins "way more interesting than you'd expect." The "beautiful" beach is "perfect," but be aware there are "no changing rooms." Overall, a "worthy" and "fun" excursion.

Sports
Active
Ages 5 & up
$97/adult
$72 (5-9)
7-7.5 hours

See page 158 for a key to the shore excursion description charts and their icons.

Embarking on Shore Excursions on Cozumel *(continued)*

Sea Lion Discovery and Snorkel Tour [CZ07] — Rating: 7

Sports
Active
Ages 7 & up
$55/$45(7-9)
3.5-4 hours

Journey to Chankanaab National Park to enjoy the sea creatures at the Sea Lion Show. Afterwards, snorkel for 45 minutes. Stay longer at the park if you wish. Typical meeting time is 12:30 pm. Cruiser reviews are mostly positive: This "cute" and "entertaining" show is "a lot of fun for kids," particularly "young ones" (under 10). Also includes a "bird show," though a common complaint is that there are "too many people" and "not everyone gets the chance to hold a bird." Afterwards, go snorkeling at the "pretty beach" but beware of "crowded conditions" where you may "constantly bump into one another in the water." All agreed this is a "beautiful park." (On Your Own: Just take a taxi to Chankanaab National Park.)

Chankanaab Sea Lion Discovery [CZ08] — Rating: 8

Tour
Leisurely
All ages
$40/$30 (3-9)
3-3.5 hours

Just the Chankanaab's Sea Lion Show and the Wacky World of Birds Show mentioned above (no snorkeling), but it still includes transportation. Stay at the park longer if you wish and explore the botanical gardens. Typical meeting time is 12:30 pm. Cruiser reviews are very similar to the those mentioned in the previous description, but considered slightly better without the snorkeling.

Tropical Jeep Safari Tour [CZ09] — Rating: 7

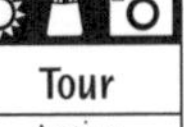

Tour
Active
Ages 10 & up
$85
4.5 hours

Drive a four-person, standard-shift, 4x4 vehicle through the "tropical" scrub. After bump-bump-bumping along the dirt roads, enjoy a yummy lunch on the beach and explore some low-key ruins. If you're a party of two, you'll share a vehicle with another couple and take turns driving. Cruiser reviews are mostly positive: After a "long walk," you get into your "open air" vehicle ("no air conditioning") and "take a fun drive" through town. Once on the dirt roads, it's "very bumpy and dusty" but "adventuresome." Lunch at a "beautiful beach" is "very good," though the ruins are "unimpressive." Overall, most cruisers enjoyed the "entertaining tour guides" and "had a good time." Typical meeting time is 12:20 pm.

© MediaMarx, Inc.

Our Jeep Safari

Xcaret Eco Archeological Park [CZ10] — Rating: 9

Tour
Active
All ages
$99/$77 (3-9)
7-7.5 hours

This mainland park is a favorite—it's like a natural water park. Swim, visit an aquarium, and see ruins. Includes transportation, lunch, and entrance fee. Bring cash. Regular sunscreen is not allowed; you will be provided with environmentally-friendly sunscreen upon arrival. Cruiser reviews are very positive: While the "travel time is long" (about "1.5 hours"), the "beautiful nature park" is "well worth the journey." A favorite feature is the "unique underground fresh water river" that you "float through" (but beware that it is "cold water"). There are also "good spots for snorkeling" with "lots of fish." Many cruisers feel this excursion is the "highlight of their trip." Typical meeting time is 9:45 am.

Snorkeling at Chankanaab National Park [CZ11] — Rating: 5

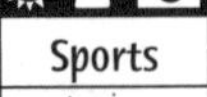

Sports
Active
$47/36 (5-9)

Snorkel in a lovely nature park. Afterwards, relax or explore gardens. For ages 6 & up. Typical meeting times are 9:45 am and noon. About 3 hours. Cruiser reviews indicate the snorkeling is hampered by crowds and is not highly recommended.

Embarking on Shore Excursions on Cozumel *(continued)*

Fury Catamaran Sail, Snorkel, & Beach Party [CZ12] Rating: 10

Sports
Active
Ages 5 & up
$49/$28 (5-9)
4.5-5 hours

Board a 65-foot catamaran and cruise out to snorkel in 3'-20' (1-6 m.) of water. Afterwards, party on the beach with free soft drinks, margaritas, and beer. Typical meeting time is 12:30 pm. Cruiser reviews are overwhelmingly positive: Enjoy a 35 minute sail on a "large," "unexpectedly smooth" catamaran with an "exceptional" crew. Then snorkel for 45 minutes in a "beautiful" area with "many fish and coral." Hop aboard for "short," "20 minute" sail to a "gorgeous beach" with "plenty of shady areas." The food served at the beach is "very good" (about "$8/person"). Then it's back onboard for a "30-45 minute" sail back, with "music" and "dancing." "Plenty of free drinks." "Bring cash" for food and tips. Note that you "do need to be mobile to exit and reenter the catamaran at sea." Overall, cruisers had a "great time" and would "do it again." (On Your Own: Fury Catamaran at http://furycat.com/cozumel.htm, 987-872-5145)

Fury Catamaran Teen Cruise [CZ13] Rating: 7

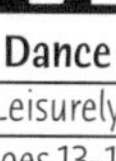

Dance
Leisurely
Ages 13-17
$37
2.5 hours

Teens can take an evening cruise aboard a 65-foot catamaran—includes music, snacks, and beverages. Chaperoned by counselors from the teen-only club. The cruise is similar to the one described above, but without the snorkeling, beach, or alcoholic beverages. Teen cruiser reviews are mixed: Some thought it was "way fun" others just "so-so." Like all teen events, its success probably depends on who attends. Typical meeting time is 6:00 pm. (On Your Own: Don't bother)

Clear Kayak & Beach Snorkel Combo [CZ24] Rating: n/a

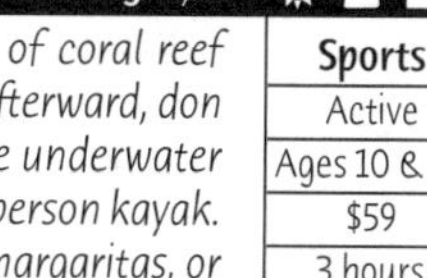

Sports
Active
Ages 10 & up
$59
3 hours

New! Paddle in transparent kayaks over the unspoiled beauty of coral reef formations, watching tropical fish swim right under your kayak. Afterward, don the provided snorkel equipment to get an even closer look at the underwater world. Then relax on Uvas Beach. Weight limit of 350 lbs per two-person kayak. Includes fruit and two complimentary drinks (soda, water, beer, margaritas, or daiquiris). Bring biodegradable sunblock. Typical meeting time is 9:45 am.

Cozumel Beach Break [CZ15] Rating: 8

Beach
Leisurely
All ages
$59/$46 (3-9)
5-5.5 hours

Bum around the Playa del Sol Beach. Price includes taxi fare to and from the beach, admission, use of pool and beach, open bar (mixed drinks, beer, soda, and juice), water toys, recreation, entertainment, and lunch buffet. Typical meeting time is 10:30 am. Cruiser comments were mostly positive: The beach has a "family party atmosphere" with "lots to do," including "water trampolines" and "a climbing iceberg" (though these are "pretty far out in the water"). Keep in mind that while the drinks may be free, they are also "watered down." Lunch is "good" by most accounts, though you have to "contend with vendors" to get to the food area. (On Your Own: Playa Sol at http://www.playasol.com.mx, or Mr. Sanchos—see next page)

Caverns Exploration and Beach Tour [CZ18] Rating: n/a

Tour
Active
Ages 6 & up
$88/$63 (6-9)
7.5 hours

Take an all-day journey via a ferry and air-conditioned bus to the Mexican mainland to explore natural caverns in Playa del Carmen. Afterwards, relax on the beach with your own beach chair. Includes a Mexican lunch and beverages. Note that there are rocky areas and rough terrain; strollers are not allowed. Typical meeting time is 9:25 am. We received no cruiser reviews for this excursion.

See page 158 for a key to the shore excursion description charts and their icons.

Introduction | Reservations | Staterooms | Dining | Activities | Ports of Call | Magic | Index

Embarking on Shore Excursions on Cozumel *(continued)*

Cozumel Ruins & Beach Tour [CZ19] Rating: 3	
Tour the San Gervasio Ruins, then it's off to Playa Del Sol Beach for an hour and a half of relaxation. Includes soft drinks (food is extra). Watersports available for extra fee. Typical meeting time is noon. Cruiser reviews were mostly negative: While the "water is beautiful," there "wasn't enough time" to spend at the beach. The food at the beach "didn't seem fresh." Most of your time is spent at the "ancient sites" which are "interesting," but not "spectacular." "Bring bug spray!" Overall, cruisers were not impressed and "do not recommend it."	**Tour/Beach** Leisurely Ages 5 & up $49/$33 (5-9) 4-4.5 hours

Atlantis Submarine Expedition [CZ20] Rating: 6	
Board the "Atlantis" submarine and dive up to 110' (33 m.), viewing tropical fish and 30' (9 m.) coral heads. Includes beverages. Height restriction of 36"/91 cm. minimum. Typical meeting times are 12:35 and 2:35 pm. Cruiser reviews are very similar to those on same excursion in St. Thomas (see page 188), but it gets a slightly higher rating thanks to the better views and visible sea life. (On Your Own: http://www.atlantisadventures.com/cozumel or 987-872-5671 or 866-546-7820)	**Tour** Leisurely Ages 4 & up $89/$57 (4-9) 2.5 hours

Reef Snorkel [CZ21] Rating: n/a	
Take a taxi to Playa Corona, where you get to snorkel the beautiful reefs of Cozumel. Snorkel gear, instruction, and transportation provided. This is a good excursion for beginners as you enter the water from the beach. Typical meeting time is 9:55 am. We received no cruiser reviews for this excursion. (On Your Own: Bring your snorkel gear and take a taxi to Playa Corona.)	**Sports** Active Ages 5 & up $32/$23 (5-9) 2.5-3 hours

Ocean View Explorer Tour [CZ22] Rating: 5	
Explore the coral of Paradise Reef in this semi-submersible. Typical meeting times are 11:00 am and 12:45 pm. Cruiser reviews on this excursion are limited, but those we received were mixed: Some felt it was a good "compromise" between the Atlantis sub and a snorkeling excursion, while others felt it was "boring" and would not do it again. Compared to the Atlantis, it is less expensive and allows kids 0-3. (On Your Own: AquaWorld at http://www.aquaworld.com.mx)	**Tour** Leisurely All ages $42/31 (0-9) 1.5-2 hours

See page 158 for a key to the shore excursion description charts and their icons.

Cozumel On Your Own

Want to set out on your own? There are several popular tour operators and destinations preferred by Disney cruisers. While we haven't tried these outfits ourselves, we offer the information here for your reference: **Mr. Sancho's Cozumel Beach Club** is a nice alternative to the Cozumel Beach Break excursion—just take a taxi to Mr. Sancho's and enjoy a less expensive day at the beach with plenty of amenities should you wish to use them. For more information, visit http://www.mrsanchos.com. **Wild Tours ATV** is an adventurous excursion during which you can tool around the "jungle" in an ATV, go kayaking, then do a bit of snorkeling. For more information, visit http://gocozumel.com/wild-tours-atv or call 987-872-2244. And for those that want something more familiar, try **Cozumel Mini-Golf** with a fun, tropical course just a short distance from the pier. For more information, visit http://cozumelminigolf.com or call 987-872-2244.

Costa Maya
(Special 7-Night Western Caribbean Itinerary)

Ruins and coral and beach, oh my! The port of Costa Maya isn't even on most maps. Development in this **quiet corner** of Mexico's Yucatan coast began in 2000, headed by the same group that made Cancun what it is. The nearby village of Majahual is dwarfed by this, the first Mexican port created for the cruise industry.

© Corel

Costa Maya's port complex

AMBIENCE

The port of Costa Maya and its "**Mayan Pavilion Park**" are more like Disney's Castaway Cay and Downtown Disney than a traditional port. That can be reassuring—virtually no signs of poverty, no uncomfortable encounters with the locals—just shopping mall-style commerce; clean, safe swimming; free entertainment; and excursions to exciting Mayan ruins. It has everything a Western Caribbean vacationer can expect of a 10-hour port visit, with the exception of a dolphin encounter (it's probably on its way). If "adventure" calls, a short walk brings you to the beachfront village of Majahual.

HISTORY & CULTURE

Native American empires have risen and fallen in the southeast corner of Mexico's Yucatan, but all has been quiet for many centuries. The 80-mile-long "**Costa Maya**" **(Mayan Coast)** is dotted by some 800 Mayan historical sites (mostly unexcavated) and small villages peopled by Mayan descendants. Such was the village of Majahual (population 200) until the year 2000, when developers seized on the area as the next big thing. To the north is the huge Sian Kaán Biosphere Park, which buffers this region from Cozumel and Cancun. Scant miles to the south is the ecotourism-friendly nation of Belize. Promised to be eco- as well as tourist-friendly, Costa Maya has become a popular stop for most major cruise lines, providing "private island" conveniences on the Mexican mainland. Virtually untouched by the hurricanes that ravaged Grand Cayman, Cozumel, and Cancun, Costa Maya has provided alternate accommodations to displaced cruise ships.

FACTS

Size: 1 mile long by ½ mile wide	
Climate: Subtropical	**Temperatures**: 80°F (26°C) to 87°F (30.5°C)
Population: 2,000	**Busy Season**: Mid-December to April
Language: Spanish	**Money**: Mexican Peso (10.50 Pesos = $1 U.S.)
Time Zone: Central (DST observed)	**Transportation**: Walking, taxis
Phones: Dial 011- from U.S., dial 060 for emergencies, dial 20092 for police	

Introduction Reservations Staterooms Dining Activities Ports of Call Magic Index

Making the Most of Costa Maya

GETTING THERE

Costa Maya's pier can berth three large cruise ships (even the huge Queen Mary II docks here). Visitors are shuttled down the long quay in Disney-style trams, directly to the **modern port complex** (see photo on previous page). From there, it's a short walk to your tour bus, or you can "hang" in a complex that includes 70,000 sq. ft./6,500 sq. m. of shopping, a crafts market, a salt water pool, live entertainment, cultural presentations, and several restaurants. The swimming, lounge chairs, and entertainment are all free, included in the port fees paid by Disney Cruise Line. Water sports rentals are available, too. Independent tour operators can be found just outside the complex's gates. The "New" Majahual, a planned town with a target population of 20,000, is growing just beyond the pier facilities, and the village of Majahual is about a half mile to the south (left as you leave the port). The Disney Magic typically docks at 7:30 am and departs at 5:30 pm.

GETTING AROUND

Until recently, only a rutted, dirt road served Majahual and nearby villages. With planned development comes a few paved roads, but we strongly recommend that you **stick to the shore excursions** if you want to venture far afield. An anti-smuggling government roadblock guards the road out of town. We haven't located a local car rental agency. The nearby airport has been under development, but service is slim, so if you're stranded when the boat leaves, you may have an adventure on your hands. The Uvero Beach excursion includes unlimited use of shuttle buses that depart every 35 minutes. If you have the urge to abandon tourist heaven and find the "real" Majahual fishing village, it's about a half mile south of the pier area. Taxis and shuttles are available for $2–$3 per person each way, or you can walk.

STAYING SAFE

Costa Maya is about as **safe as any port can be**. Access to the port area facilities are well guarded, and let's face it, anyone who doesn't belong is going to be pretty conspicuous. Much the same can be said for all the shore excursion destinations. Still, leave valuables on board and take advantage of the port facilities to shuttle purchases back to your room. As always, sunscreen is a must, and insect repellent is a very good idea, especially on excursions that venture near the jungle or visit ruins.

Touring Costa Maya

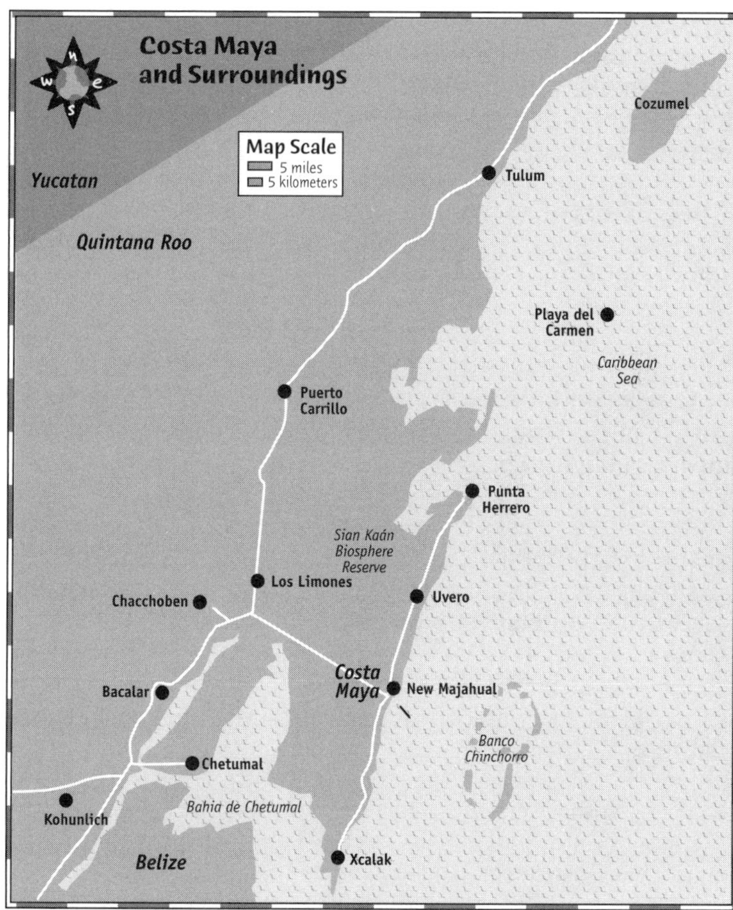

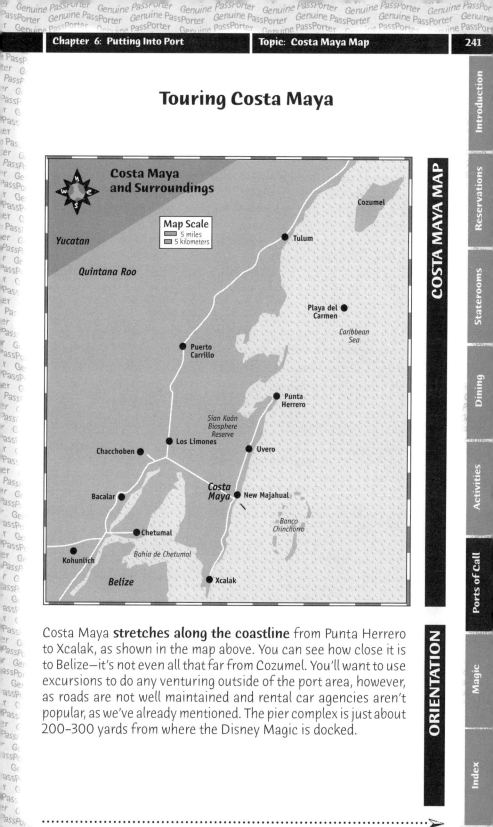

Costa Maya **stretches along the coastline** from Punta Herrero to Xcalak, as shown in the map above. You can see how close it is to Belize—it's not even all that far from Cozumel. You'll want to use excursions to do any venturing outside of the port area, however, as roads are not well maintained and rental car agencies aren't popular, as we've already mentioned. The pier complex is just about 200–300 yards from where the Disney Magic is docked.

Playing in Costa Maya

ACTIVITIES

With the growth of cruise ship tourism, the **village of Majahual** has begun to compete with the port's offerings. Parasailing, jetskiing, scuba, snorkel, and fishing excursions are all available without reservations once you leave the confines of the Costa Maya port facilities (see page 240 for tips on how to do this).

A **beachfront of sorts** has developed near the village, with water sports operators, restaurants, bars, and shops popping up, but it still has small-town charm and is far less "touristy" than the main port area.

So far, there's not a Carlos 'n Charlie's or Señor Frog's (the Mexican equivalents of TGIFridays and Bennigan's) in sight, at either the port or in the village. Cruisers report happy experiences at the **locally run eateries**, which focus on fresh seafood.

There are also no sites of significant historical or cultural interest near the port. The shore excursions take you to historic sites that are under development to serve Costa Maya. The excursion that takes you to the **state capital of Chetumal** will give you the best glimpse of "urban" culture. The city of 120,000 retains old-time charm, has a decent history museum, and like the rest of this corner of Mexico, has so far been relatively untouched by the tourist trade.

You can **swim** within the secure arms of the Costa Maya complex in a free-form salt water pool, but the nearby beach is for sunning only. "Downtown" Majahual has a better beach, with part roped off to protect swimmers from power boats. Uvero Beach is 15 miles up the coast and is a very popular "beach break" excursion with cruisers. The beach is beautiful, the facilities are modern, and water sports rentals are plentiful. Food is optional on the excursion.

Scuba and snorkel are popular activities, thanks to the same huge barrier reef that makes Cozumel so famous. Banco Chinchorro, 18 miles off shore, is the Northern Hemisphere's largest coral atoll. No organized excursions go here (it's an hour each way by boat), but you can make arrangements on your own, either on the spot or from several dive operators that are listed on the web.

Embarking on Shore Excursions in Costa Maya

4 x 4 Jeep Safari [CM12] — Rating: n/a	
Drive (or ride in) a 4x4 vehicle through the fishing village of Majahual, into the tropical Mexican jungle, and past ocean vistas. Drivers must be 21 years of age and have a valid driver's license. The ride is bumpy and we do not recommend it for guests who have back or neck problems or those who are pregnant. The excursion includes a barbeque lunch. This appears to be very similar to the Tropical Jeep Safari Tour on page 236. Typical meeting time is 11:00 am.	**Tour** Active Ages 10 & up $85/person 3.5–4 hours

All-Terrain Truck Expedition [CM09] — Rating: n/a	
Board a special all-terrain, military-style truck and go off road into the coastal jungles of Costa Maya. A bilingual tour guide does the driving along the bumpy terrain. Your destination is a beach where you can swim, play volleyball, or even kayak for an hour and a half. A light snack and soft drinks/bottled water are provided at the beach. This excursion is not recommended for pregnant women or guests with back problems. Typical meeting time is 12:00 pm.	**Tour** Active All ages $75/adult $55/child 3.5–4 hours

Beach Snorkel Adventure [CM07] — Rating: n/a	
Beginner and intermediate snorkelers can experience an ecosystem with parrotfish, butterfly fish, and angelfish visible at depths from 3 to 15 feet. Your adventure starts from the beach, so you can snorkel at the depth that is most comfortable for you. The excursion includes equipment and basic snorkel instruction. It's not clear if snacks or soft drinks are provided, so bring them if needed. Typical meeting time is 10:30 am.	**Sports** Active Ages 5 & up $45/adult $35/child 4–4.5 hours

Bike and Kayak Adventure [CM08] — Rating: n/a	
Explore the Costa Mayan coastline in two ways—by bike and kayak. After donning safety gear and adjusting your bike, you're off on a 30-minute ride along a dirt road to the village of Majahual. Next, board two-person kayaks and paddle along the reef. After kayaking, you bike back to Costa Maya along a different route. This excursion is not recommended for guests over 6 feet tall due to the size of the bikes. Typical meeting time is 11:00 am.	**Sports** Very active Ages 10 & up $45/person 2.5–3 hours

Catamaran Sail and Snorkel [CM01] — Rating: n/a	
Hop aboard a catamaran at Fisherman's Pier for a delightful cruise along the virgin coast of Costa Maya. Mid-point through the cruise, the catamaran will drop anchor so you can snorkel for about 45 minutes. Equipment (mask, fins, and float jacket) and instruction are provided. Transportation to the pier and a soft drink is provided with the excursion. Time to shop is provided back at the pier. Typical meeting time is 1:30 pm.	**Sports** Active Ages 5 & up $48/adult $38/child 3–3.5 hours

Chaccohoben Mayan Ruins [CM03] — Rating: n/a	
Board a motorcoach to explore the Mayan ruins of Chacchoben deep in the jungle near Belize. Chacchoben, which means "the place of red corn," is believed to have been settled around 200 B.C. The 10-acre site is mostly unexcavated, but there is a grand pyramid and several temples. A lot of walking over uneven ground is required during this tour, as well as stair climbing. Time to shop is provided back at the pier. Typical meeting time is 12:00 pm.	**Tour** Active Ages 5 & up $69/adult $59/child 4.5–5 hours

See page 158 for a key to description charts and their icons.

Embarking on Shore Excursions in Costa Maya

Chetumal Mayan Museum & Spanish Fort [CM04] — Rating: n/a

Immerse yourself in Mexican history as you learn about the great Mayan empire and the fateful arrival of the Spanish conquistadors. The excursion begins with a ride in an air-conditioned bus to the Museum of Mayan Culture, which is filled with artifacts and stone carvings. Then it's off to a restored Spanish fort in the city of Bacalar overlooking the Lagoon of Seven Colors. A cold soft drink is served enroute. Typical meeting time is 10:15 am.

Tour | Active | All ages | $85/adult, $75/child | 6.5 hours

Clear Kayak and Beach Break [CM10] — Rating: n/a

Want to peek underwater without getting wet? This excursion allows you to experience the beautiful underwater world in a two-person, transparent acrylic ocean kayak. You'll glide over colorful reef and coral formations. After your adventure, relax with fresh fruit and a soft drink on the beach. All necessary equipment and basic kayaking instruction is included in this excursion. Typical meeting time is 11:30 am.

Sports | Very active | Ages 10 & up | $59/person | 3–3.5 hours

Dune Buggy Exploration [CM11] — Rating: n/a

If the Jeep and all-terrain truck don't push your buttons, how about a four-person, customized dune buggy convertible? Bump along dirt roads as a driver or a rider. Enjoy the beach halfway through your drive. Drivers must be 21 years of age and have a valid driver's license. The ride is bumpy, and we do not recommend it for guests who have back or neck problems or who are pregnant. Typical meeting time is 11:00 am.

Tour | Active | Ages 10 & up | $85/person | 3.5–4 hours

Horse Back Adventure [CM05] — Rating: n/a

Saddle up for a trek through the Costa Mayan prairie and through lush jungles. After a safety briefing and basic riding instruction, your guide leads you and your horse to a neighboring horse ranch. A cold drink awaits you at the end of the trail. Guests should wear long pants and closed footwear. Maximum weight limit is 250 lbs.; guests who have back/neck injuries or who are pregnant may not participate. Typical meeting time is 11:00 am.

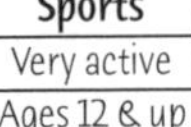

Sports | Very active | Ages 12 & up | $82/person | 3.5 hours

Jungle Beach Break [CM02] — Rating: n/a

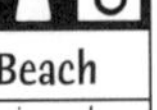

Board a bus for a 30-minute trip to Uvero Beach, a popular beach with white, powdery sand, palm trees, and plenty of beach activities. The beach can get crowded, but if you venture farther down the beach, you can find quiet spots. Food and shopping is nearby. You decide when you're ready to leave and board the appropriate shuttle in the parking lot. Typical meeting time is 10:30 am.

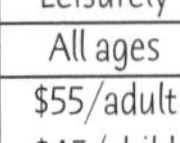

Beach | Leisurely | All ages | $55/adult, $45/child | 4–4.5 hours

Kohunlich Mayan Ruins [CM06] — Rating: n/a

Travel by air-conditioned bus to a secluded jungle near the border of Belize to reach these famous ruins. A broad range of architectural styles in a naturally beautiful setting await you, including the Temple of the Large Masks. A soft drink is served onboard the bus. The tour includes a lot of walking on uneven terrain and stair climbing. If you bring your video camera, expect to pay a $5–$8 fee to use it (no tripods allowed). Typical meeting time is 10:00 am.

Tour | Active | All ages | $85/adult, $75/child | 6.5 hours

Castaway Cay
(All Caribbean Itineraries)

We saved our **favorite port** for last (and so has Disney). Castaway Cay is Disney's private island, exclusively for the use of Disney Cruise Line guests and crew. It's clean, safe, and well-themed, and lunch is complimentary on the island. We recommend you get up early on your Castaway Cay day—you don't want to miss a minute of the fun!

© MediaMarx, Inc.

Megan and Natalie on Castaway Cay

AMBIENCE

Castaway Cay (pronounced "Castaway Key") is a **tropical retreat** with white sandy beaches, swaying palm trees, and aquamarine water. What makes it so magical is its theming—it's not unlike visiting one of Disney's excellent water parks, such as Typhoon Lagoon. The island even has its own legend—they say three explorers set sail with their families to the scattered islands of the Bahamas in search of fame and fortune. Their adventures brought them to this island, where they found sunken treasures, the secret of youth, and the skeletal remains of a giant whale. The explorers and their families remained on the beautiful island for years as castaways—you can still see the original structures and artifacts left behind.

HISTORY

Disney may call this out-island Castaway Cay, but in its previous incarnation it was **Gorda Cay**. The island is a part of the Abaco Bahamas island archipelago. Its history is murky. It may have first been inhabited by Lucayan Indians, "discovered" by the Spanish, later used as a harbor for pirates, and was long used by the Abaconians for farming pumpkins and sweet potatoes. In the '70s and '80s, the island was a base for drug operations. Disney leased the island and, over the next 18 months, spent $25 million to fix up 55 acres (only about 5% of the island). 50,000 truckloads of sand were dredged to make the beautiful beaches. Its extensive facilities are the best in the cruise industry. For more history, visit: http://web.outsideonline.com/magazine/0199/9901blackbeard.html

FACTS

Size: 2 mi. (3.2 km.) x 1.25 mi. (2 km.)	**Distance**: 260 nautical miles from home port
Climate: Subtropical	**Temperatures**: 66°F (19°C) to 88°F (31°C)
Language: English	**Money**: U.S. Dollar/stateroom charge
Time Zone: Eastern (DST observed)	**Transportation**: Walking, bicycles

Making the Most of Castaway Cay

GETTING THERE

Thanks to a deep channel Disney dredged when it acquired the island, **your ship pulls right up to the dock** on Castaway Cay. Typical all ashore time is 8:30 am, and you have until about 4:30 pm (or just eight hours) to play on this delightful island. When you alight from the ship, proceed down the dock (picking up towels on your way) to the island—it's about a 3-minute walk to the tram. Be aware that when the seas are rough, the ship may be unable to dock at Castaway Cay, and therefore you'll be unable to visit. This is most likely to happen in January and February, but it can occur at anytime.

GETTING AROUND

Castaway Cay is the **easiest port to get around**, thanks to the well-marked paths and convenient trams. As you walk down the dock to the island, you'll pass the Castaway Cay post office on your right and Marge's Barges sea charters dock on your left, after which you'll reach a tram stop—hop aboard the next tram, or simply take the 10-minute walk to the family beach. Once you're at the family beach, you can continue down the path past buildings that house the restrooms, shops, and services. At the far end of the main path is the teen beach. The adults-only beach is accessible by another tram (or a long, hot, 25-minute walk down the airstrip) near the end of the main path. All locations are marked on the map on the next page, as well as on the color map Disney provides with your *Personal Navigator*.

DINING

Unlike the other ports, the Disney Cruise Line provides lunch on Castaway Cay. For complete details on Castaway Cay dining, see page 114 (we've repeated some of the same information here for your reference). Everyone can eat at **Cookie's BBQ** across from the family beach. Cookie's typically serves from 11:30 am to 2:00 pm, and offers the best selection with burgers, BBQ ribs, chicken sandwiches, corn on the cob, fruit, frozen yogurt, and cookies. Food is served buffet-style. Plenty of covered seating is nearby. Basic beverages (including sodas) are also provided, or you can buy an alcoholic beverage across the way at the Conched Out Bar. Adults can eat at the **Castaway Cay Air Bar-B-Q** located at Serenity Bay, the adults-only beach, from about 11:00 am to 1:30 pm. Offerings include burgers, salmon, potato salad, fresh fruit, and fat-free frozen yogurt. Alcoholic beverages can be purchased at the bar nearby. If you choose not to visit Castaway Cay, a buffet is served in Parrot Cay, usually from 8:00 am to 1:30 pm.

Exploring Castaway Cay

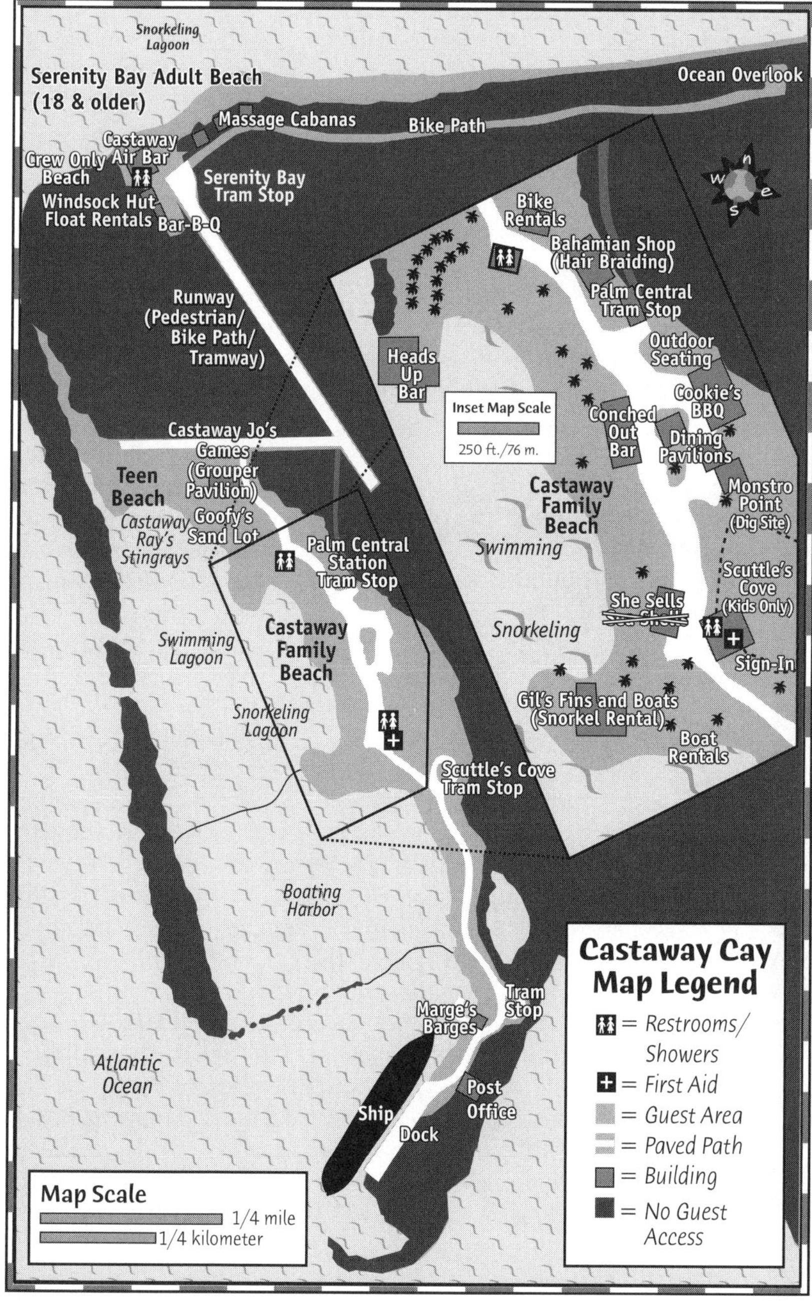
Snorkeling Lagoon
Serenity Bay Adult Beach (18 & older)
Ocean Overlook
Massage Cabanas
Bike Path
Castaway Air Bar
Crew Only Beach
Serenity Bay Tram Stop
Windsock Hut Float Rentals
Bar-B-Q
Runway (Pedestrian/ Bike Path/ Tramway)
Bike Rentals
Bahamian Shop (Hair Braiding)
Palm Central Tram Stop
Outdoor Seating
Heads Up Bar
Inset Map Scale
250 ft./76 m.
Cookie's BBQ
Conched Out Bar
Dining Pavilions
Castaway Jo's Games (Grouper Pavilion)
Teen Beach
Castaway Ray's Stingrays
Goofy's Sand Lot
Castaway Family Beach
Monstro Point (Dig Site)
Swimming
Palm Central Station Tram Stop
Scuttle's Cove (Kids Only)
She Sells
Snorkeling
Castaway Family Beach
Swimming Lagoon
Sign-In
Gil's Fins and Boats (Snorkel Rental)
Snorkeling Lagoon
Boat Rentals
Scuttle's Cove Tram Stop
Boating Harbor
Castaway Cay Map Legend
= Restrooms/ Showers
= First Aid
= Guest Area
= Paved Path
= Building
= No Guest Access
Tram Stop
Marge's Barges
Atlantic Ocean
Post Office
Ship
Dock
Map Scale
1/4 mile
1/4 kilometer

Playing in Castaway Cay

ACTIVITIES

Some **activities** on Castaway Cay require advance booking (see details on page 252). You can reserve floats, bikes, and snorkel equipment rentals in advance, though these are usually available on a walk-up basis. Strollers and beach wheelchairs are free for use on a first-come, first-served basis—while beach wheelchairs are designed to roll on the sand, they are still very hard to push.

The **beautiful beaches** are a big draw at Castaway Cay. The family beach is the largest and busiest—arrive early to get a good beach chair. Float rentals are available near Gil's Fins snorkel rentals and at the bike rental shack. The adults-only beach—Serenity Bay—is a wonderful place to spend a little grown-up time. The beach there is a little more barren than the family beach. Bring some water shoes as the bottom is coarser and sometimes uncomfortable. Walk farther down the beach for the most privacy. The teen beach—which is exclusively for teens—offers teen activities like volleyball and dancing.

© MediaMarx, Inc.

The kids water play area

Stingray encounters, a popular shore excursion on many islands, have finally arrived at Castaway Cay. See page 253 for details.

Would you like to see a bit more of the island? You can **rent bicycles** near the family beach—prices are $6/hour for all ages. It takes about one hour to cycle down the airstrip and along the unpaved trail that borders the Serenity Bay beach and back again. Child seats can be requested. Water is provided along the bike trail, too.

Kids have their own supervised playground at **Scuttle's Cove**. If you've registered your kids for Oceaneer Club or Lab, you can check them in here while you go play at Serenity Bay. Counselors guide kids in structured activities, but they do not take them swimming. Beside Scuttle's Cove is Monstro Point, which has a huge whale "skeleton" to dig up! Programming ends at 3:30 pm. Note that kids can check out sand toys at Scuttle's Cove—first come, first served.

Playing in Castaway Cay

Snorkeling is a very popular activity on Castaway Cay and an excellent spot for beginners to try out the sport. You can rent equipment at Gil's Fins near the family beach—prices are $25/adult and $10/kid (includes masks, fins, and vest). You can reserve your snorkel rental in advance (see page 252), though this is not necessary. The snorkeling lagoon is extensive—there's plenty of fish and sunken treasure to discover, as well as a submarine from Walt Disney World's "20,000 Leagues Under the Sea." Look for the map that shows the snorkeling course before you get in. Put sunscreen on your back—the water intensifies the sun's rays and you can get badly sunburned. Consider clipping a water bottle to your vest to rinse out your mouth—the saltwater can be bothersome. Note that there is an unofficial snorkeling lagoon at Serenity Bay (it's straight out from the first massage cabana)—rent your equipment at Gil's and tote it over. You can use your own snorkel gear in the lagoons, too. (Disney requires that all snorkelers wear a flotation device—you may need to pay a small fee of $6 for its use.) Some families like to bring their own (better) equipment, or simply purchase cheap snorkel sets for kids and then leave them behind.

Boat rentals are primarily available at the boat beach (Relay Bay). Rent paddle boats ($8 for two-seater, $10 for four-seater), Aqua Trikes ($15), sea kayaks ($8 for one-seater, $10 for two-seater), small Aqua Fins sailboats ($15), and Hobie Cat sailboats ($18)—all prices are for a half-hour. (Underlined boats may also be at Serenity Bay, along with Banana Boats.) No advance reservations for rentals other than Banana Boats.

© MediaMarx, Inc.

Watercraft on Castaway Cay

Family games are available at Castaway Jo's (also known as the Grouper Pavilion), a shaded patio with shuffleboard, billiards, foosball, Ping-Pong, basketball/football toss, horseshoes, a giant checkerboard, and a sandbox with toys. This area is often overlooked, yet can really be a lot of fun, especially when you or a family member need some time out of the sun.

Playing in Castaway Cay

Goofy's Sandlot is the **sport beach** on Castaway Cay—it's right next to Castaway Jo's. You can play volleyball and tetherball here. Watch for an organized volleyball game in the late morning. The sport beach is often very quiet and uncrowded, making it an ideal spot for families to hang together. And its proximity to the teen beach (right next door), Castaway Jo's, and the Heads Up Bar make it very convenient, too. This is also a good spot to find a hammock if they are all occupied on other beaches.

Adults can reserve a popular **cabana massage** near Serenity Bay. If you do just one spa treatment, this is the one we recommend. Cabana massages are $139/person—reserve it on your first day to avoid disappointment. If you are sensitive to the sun, book a massage for later in the day—the oils make your skin more likely to sunburn. You can bring your sunscreen and ask to have it applied at the end of the massage.

A massage cabana on Castaway Cay

Shopping is limited to three small shops. She Sells ~~Sea Shells~~ is a Disney themed shop with unique Castaway Cay logo items. Visit this shop early, as the crowds are huge later in the day and some items and sizes get gobbled up quickly. Two Bahamian-run retail shops near the end of the family beach sell crafts, shirts, and trinkets—this is also where you can get hair braiding for $1/braid or $2/cornrow—expect to pay about $30 for the whole head (which takes about 3 hours). There is sometimes a merchandise cart at Serenity Bay, too. The shops on the ship are closed while the ship is docked at Castaway Cay.

Your can meet your favorite **Disney characters** on Castaway Cay. Check the back of the Disney-provided Castaway Cay map for times. Photo opportunities are available all over the island. Look for ship's photographers near the ship and at the family beach.

Playing in Castaway Cay

While it's not possible to **hike** around the island, you can take a leisurely stroll down the bike path near the adult beach. Water is provided along the trail, and there's a scenic ocean overlook at the end of the hike. If you're looking to see parts of the island that are normally off-limits, we recommend the Walking and Kayak Adventure excursion described on page 254. It's quite delightful, and it was fascinating to see the undeveloped parts of the island that are usually considered "backstage."

A new **"Pirates in the Caribbean" Scavenger Hunt** was added to the roster of available activities on Castaway Cay in 2005. Watch your *Personal Navigator* for a "Hunt Orientation" session the day before your scheduled day in Castaway Cay. At this session, you'll receive a short briefing on the scavenger hunt and the all-important packet of items that you need for the hunt! (Tip: If you can't make it to this session, ask a friend or tablemate who can attend to pick up a hunt packet for you.) Once you dock at Castaway Cay, you're free to begin your scavenger hunt–it will take you over a wide range and call on your keen observation skills. This is really an adult or family activity, as some of the clues require good reading or logic skills. Record your results in your hunt packet as you go along. If you're following a clue and you're not sure if you've found the right answer, look for a small round plaque–these mark the general location of the answers and are handy for confirming your guesses. Once you've completed your hunt, the answer tells you where to go to claim your treasure. This last step seems to stump a lot of people because not everyone knows the names of the various spots around the island. (Tip: Use our Castaway Cay map!) There's no reward for being the fastest to solve the scavenger hunt, and the reward isn't anything valuable, but it is a lot of fun and we really enjoyed it!

Let's not overlook one of our favorite activities on Castaway Cay–**relaxing**! You can do it practically anywhere, but we really like lounging about in hammocks on the family beach or adults-only beach. We've had the best luck finding empty hammocks behind Gil's Fins (the snorkel rental shack). If you find a hammock, please enjoy it, but don't try to save it by leaving your things on it.

Advance Rentals on Castaway Cay

These rentals are nonrefundable unless your cruise skips Castaway Cay.

Snorkel Equipment [C01]

Explore Disney's 12-acre snorkeling lagoon—price includes all-day rental of mask, fins, and vest (light flotation). Beginners can take the Discover Trail; experienced snorkelers may like the longer Explorer Trail. Both trails have lots to see. Pick up your snorkel equipment at Gil's Fins. Note that children under 13 must be with an adult. (On Your Own: Bring your own equipment and use the lagoon!)

Sports | Active | Ages 5 & up | $25/adult, $10/kids 5-9

Float Rentals [C03]

Enjoy the water with a lounge float or tube. (On Your Own: Purchase inflatable floats from a dollar store at home and bring along on your cruise.) Ages 5 & up.

Beach | $6/each

Bicycle Rental [C04] Rating: 8

Dozens of bikes are available for rent. Training wheels, child seats, and helmets are available. The biking paths are on flat terrain, and there's plenty of drinking water along the way. Look for the ocean outlook at the end of the bike path! Cruiser reviews are positive: The bikes are "comfortable" and the "trail is beautiful." At the end of the trail is a "very peaceful," "secluded beach."

Sports | Active | All ages | $6/hour

Castaway Cay Getaway Package [C05] Rating: 7

This package includes a float rental, snorkel equipment rental, and a bike rental for one hour, for a savings of $5-6. Very popular—book early. But don't bother if you are planning other activities—there's not enough time for it all! Cruiser reviews are positive: Cruisers enjoyed having the rentals "secured" and felt it is "good deal," though many noted they weren't able to use all three rentals.

Sports | Active | Ages 5 & up | $32/adult, $16/child

Banana Boat Rides [C06] Rating: 8

Ride a big, yellow, inflatable water "sled" around Relay Bay and out around the ship. The banana boat holds 10 people and is pulled by a Jet Ski. You must be able to swim, as you could fall off. Departure times are every 30 minutes beginning at 8:50 am (Wonder) or 10:30 am (Magic). When we rode it, half the passengers fell off when we hit a big wave. Cruiser reviews are positive: This "very bouncy," "fun" ride is "exhilarating" and "very fast." Many cruisers did get "bounced off" in the water, but "enjoyed it." Most cruisers agree that this is "great fun." We are in the minority as we didn't like this—it was much too rough and we couldn't enjoy the scenery with all the saltwater spray in our eyes. Tip: Wear swim goggles.

Sports | Very active | Ages 8 & up | $15/person | 20 minutes

Parasailing [C08] Rating: 9

If you've never tried parasailing, this is a great experience for beginners. You can go solo or tandem, and you'll take off from the boat and land in it when you're done. Expect to be airborne for 5-8 minutes, with 600 feet of rope between you and the boat. Guests must be 90-350 lbs. (40-158 kg.) to parasail. Tandem parasailing is possible if you're both under the maximum weight combined. Be sure to take a disposable camera for some amazing photos while in the air! Cruiser reviews are very positive: "No experience is necessary" to enjoy this "amazing flight" over the water. The "views" are "stunning." It's a "real adrenaline rush" and a "genuine highlight" of the cruise. "Book early" as "spots fill up quickly." Cruisers say "go for it!"

Sports | Active | Ages 8 & up | $75/person | 45 minutes

See page 158 for a key to description charts and their icons.

Embarking on Shore Excursions on Castaway Cay

Castaway Cay Bottom Fishing [C02] — Rating: 9

Fishing
Active
Ages 6 & up
$117/person
3 hours

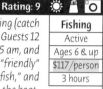

Up to six guests can enjoy a ride around the Abaco Islands for bottom fishing (catch and release). Tackle, bait, and beverages (soda and water) are provided. Guests 12 and under must wear life jackets. Typical meeting times are 9:00 am, 9:15 am, and 1:00 pm. Very popular—book early! Cruiser reviews are very positive: The "friendly" captain takes you out to a "beautiful setting" to fish. There are "lots of fish," and "plenty to catch." Cruisers do note that there is no "head" (restroom) on the boat. All cruisers had a "great time" and considered it a "highlight" of their cruise. This excursion may be suspended without notice depending on the season and other conditions.

Castaway Ray's Stingray Adventure [C13] — Rating: 9

Sports
Active
Ages 5 & up
$35/adult
$29/ages 5–9
1 hour

We were fortunate enough to be one of the first to experience this new excursion in September 2005. The adventure begins when you check in at the Castaway Ray's Stingray Hut near the Teen Beach (see Castway Cay map on page 247). After receiving your snorkel equipment (mask, snorkel, and flotation vest), guests gather under a shelter for a fascinating and educational orientation on the stingrays. This program was developed in partnership with The Living Seas at Epcot, and cast members from Epcot are often the ones to give you your orientation. After your briefing, you wade into the shallow water with the stingrays. A guide accompanies you and encourages the stingrays to come closer so you can view them up close and touch them. You may even have the chance to feed them! Special U-shaped ramps (see photo below) were created and the stingrays were trained to swim up them, giving you an unparalleled look. After this, there's free time to don your snorkel equipment and swim among the stingrays for an underwater look. Note that children under 16 must be accompanied by an adult. A portion of the proceeds from this excursion go to Disney's Wildlife Conservation Fund. Typical meeting times are every hour from 9:00 am to 3:00 pm. Cruiser reviews are very positive: The experience was "enjoyable" as well as "educational." The "innovative" stingray ramps gave cruisers "a better look at the rays" than on other stingray excursions. The stingrays "don't bite" and their "barbs have been removed." Cruisers "did not feel threatened" but the "snorkeling was poor" due to the stirred-up sand. Overall, most cruisers say they want to "do it again" on their next cruise.

© MediaMarx, Inc.

Dave meets a stingray at Ray's

Glass-Bottom Boat Scenic Voyage [C11] — Rating: 2

Tour
Leisurely
All ages
$35/$25 (3–9)
1.5 hours

Board a 46-foot trawler with a glass bottom for an hour-long ecotour of the barrier reefs surrounding Castaway Cay. Typical meeting times are 9:45 am, 11:15 am, 12:45 pm, and 2:15 pm. Cruiser reviews are uniform: The "rocky," "overcrowded boat" is filled with people "pushing and shoving" to see out the "cloudy" glass bottom. "Very limited fish" are visible. There are "very few seats," meaning most have to stand the entire time. Overall, cruisers say "don't bother."

Embarking on Shore Excursions on Castaway Cay

Personal Watercraft Eco Tour [C12] Rating: 9

Sports
Active
Ages 8 & up
$95 single
$160 double
1 hour

Explore Castaway Cay on a personal watercraft (also known as a "waverunner" or "jet-ski") with a knowledgeable tour guide accompanying you. Note that you must be 18 years or older to drive the personal watercraft (guests ages 16 and 17 may drive with written authorization from parents.) Typical meeting times are 9:45 am, 10:30 am, 11:15 am, 12:00 pm, 1:00 pm, 1:45 pm, and 2:45 pm. Cruiser reviews are very positive: Guests love "riding the waverunners" at a "brisk pace" while getting "gorgeous views" of Castway Cay and the Abacos. Cruisers recommend you "bring watershoes" and a "waterproof camera" as there are "good photo-ops on the tour." Those who've done this excursion remind us that "just hanging on to the waverunner for a long time as you navigate through the waves can leave you a bit tired and even a little sore." Parents also point out that kids who ride double with you "just hang on to your waist—there are no buckles or restraints" to keep them from falling into the water. Most cruisers found this an "excellent excursion" and "highly recommend it" to others.

Seahorse Catamaran Snorkel Adventure [C09] Rating: 4

Sports
Active
Ages 5 & up
$52/$30 (5-9)
2-2.5 hours

If the snorkeling lagoon doesn't satisfy your itch to snorkel, this excursion puts you aboard a 63-foot catamaran to sail to a prime snorkeling area. Snorkel gear and instruction provided. Complimentary beverages and snacks are served after snorkeling. Typical meeting times are 9:15 am and 1:15 pm. Cruiser reviews are mixed: The "excellent" catamaran trip was "delightful" for most. The snorkeling proves trickier, however—some enjoyed an "abundance of sea life," while others battled with "wind and currents." All agreed the "snack" is "unimpressive" ("a couple of bowls of potato chips"). Cruisers felt the "open water can be choppy" and this is "not good for those prone to motion sickness or snorkeling beginners."

Walking and Kayak Nature Adventure [C10] Rating: 7

Sports
Very active
Ages 10 & up
$64
2.5-3 hours

Explore areas of Castaway Cay normally off-limits to guests! Start with a 40-min. nature hike to reach your kayak launch site, then enjoy an hour-long kayak trip through mangroves. Afterward, swim at a deserted beach, then take a 20-min. walk back. Typical meeting times are 9:00 am, 9:15 am, and 12:45 pm. We did this ourselves and really enjoyed it—we recommend it to anyone who wants to be active and explore the ecosystem. Wear appropriate footwear. We think it's best for those who've visited the island before. Cruiser reviews are mixed—most think the kayaking is "awesome" but other felt the overall "pace was too slow." Kids were "bored" with the nature aspects and "didn't do much paddling." Cruisers report seeing "lots of wildlife."

The Wild Side (for Teens Only) [C07] Rating: 9

Sports
Very active
Ages 13-17
$35/teen
4 hours

Retrace the adventures of the first teens on the island—Molly and Seth. There's plenty of action, and you'll get to do some snorkeling, biking, and sea kayaking. Typical meeting time is very early for teens—8:20 am at Aloft or 9:00 am at The Stack. Teen cruiser reviews are overwhelmingly positive: First, "wait until you see who else is going" before you book—this tour "is best when you go with people you know" (but don't wait too long—it can book up). On Castaway Cay, you "do the bike ride first," "kayak for about 20 minutes," then bike back to go "snorkeling." After lunch at Cookies, you "hook up with other teens at the teen beach." Many think this was the "highlight" of their cruise; those that disagree had issues with "other teens," not the excursion.

Port Activity Worksheet

Use this worksheet to keep track of the activities and shore excursions you want to do most on your cruise. List your activities in order of preference—when booking shore excursions with Disney, you'll be more likely to get an excursion if you list a second and third choice along with the first. When you're ready to book your shore excursions through Disney, reserve online or call 877-566-0968 no later than 2 days in advance of your sail date (see page 157). Note that you cannot make excursion reservations until Disney has received your final payment for your cruise. Check off any excursions you've booked with a notation in the "Reserved?" column. Once you know what excursions you're confirmed for, circle them and cross off the others.

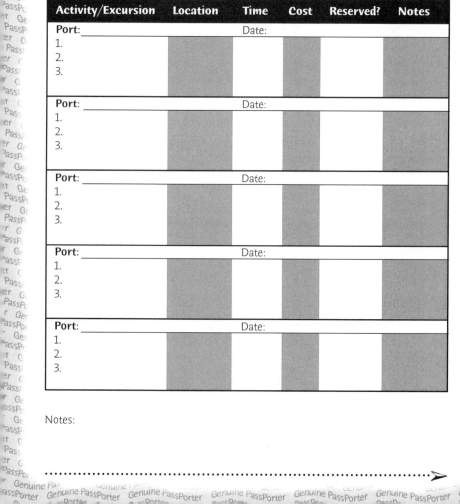

Activity/Excursion	Location	Time	Cost	Reserved?	Notes
Port:		Date:			
1.					
2.					
3.					
Port:		Date:			
1.					
2.					
3.					
Port:		Date:			
1.					
2.					
3.					
Port:		Date:			
1.					
2.					
3.					
Port:		Date:			
1.					
2.					
3.					

Notes:

Cavorting in Port

We predict that some of your favorite cruise memories will be made at your ports of call! Below are tips to help you get the most out of your jaunts, as well as port memories to get you in the mood.

- You can mail a **postcard home from the Castaway Cay post office** and get your stamp cancelled with a cool Castaway Cay postmark (see page 16). Be sure to bring some cash to purchase your stamps as you can't use your shipboard charge here. Small bills and change are best, as it can be difficult for the staff to break large bills.

- Pack a disposable **underwater camera**! You'll love it when you swim and snorkel, and you won't worry about it getting wet or stolen.

- The **Caribbean sun** is brutal. Be sure to wear sunscreen on your visits to the shore—you are likely to be in the sun more often than the shade. Sunglasses also come in handy against the glare of the bright sun off sidewalks and water. And don't forget hats with wide brims to protect your face and neck and shield your eyes. You'll find a soft fabric, crushable hat with a chin strap to keep it on your head is invaluable on shore, especially on active excursions.

- "Bring a **handheld GPS** with you. We brought one along on our Mexcian Riviera cruise and it was great when our kids asked, 'Exactly where are we?' Because the ship keeps the land just over the horizon, we had trouble knowing whether we were close to Mexico, still near San Diego, etc. With the GPS, we could see the ship's progress as it traveled up and down the coast. We also were able to see the exact speed of the ship. As this was our first cruise, we found it interesting to see that the ship slows down for dinner!"

  – contributed by Kris Romero

Magical Memory

- *"Our visit to Key West on the Disney Magic was magical. We live in Barrow, Alaska, which is the northernmost town in the United States. Barrow is at the very top of Alaska and sits next to the Arctic Ocean. While we were in Key West, we made a point of going to the southernmost location. At the spot, there is a buoy painted black and red, and it states 'Southernmost point in the continental U.S.' We had our pictures taken next to the buoy and often chuckle when we think about having been at both the northermost and southernmost points in our lives. We had a great time on our cruise and have fond memories of our visit to Key West."*

  ...as told by Disney cruiser Jennifer Litera

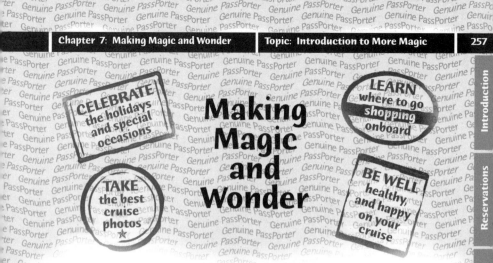

Making Magic and Wonder

Is your mind still filled with nagging little questions? This chapter may just banish the last of those concerns. Among other topics, we'll discuss toddler care, special occasions, seasickness, meeting Disney characters, clearing U.S. Customs, how much to tip, and what happens when you arrive back in Port Canaveral. These are some of the little (and not so little) things that can make the difference between an ordinary vacation and a trip filled with magic and wonder.

Is your tot too small for the regular children's programs? We tour Flounder's Reef, the ship's childcare center. Children of all ages can get the lowdown on meeting Disney characters. Learn how to preserve fond memories with your own photographs and glossies from the ship's photographers. Do you have money left after shopping in port? We describe all the stores and shopping opportunities on board, too.

While modern cruises aren't the fancy dress extravaganzas they used to be, every cruise includes opportunities to dress up. In fact, the seven-night sailings include officially-designated formal and semi-formal nights (one of each). Here's where we button-down all the details on appropriate attire, tuxedo rentals, and other dress-up options. Do you want a real excuse to dress up? We describe special and celebrity cruises, and deliver tips for creating your own special celebrations on board, whether you're tying the knot or want to give a loved one an extra-special send-off.

Next, there's the business of staying healthy and avoiding that curse of the deep, *mal de mer* (seasickness). Plus, a few tips on keeping up-to-date with your business back home.

It's also time to set your feet back on shore in Port Canaveral. Nobody likes this part, but now is the perfect time to explore the mysteries of "customary gratuities" (tipping), the rules and regulations of U.S. Customs, and the rituals of debarkation. We've had a great time cruising with you! Alas, that it had to end so soon. Bon voyage!

Introduction
Reservations
Staterooms
Dining
Activities
Ports of Call
Magic
Index

Cruising With Kids

Disney cruises and kids go together like peanut butter and jelly! We've had the pleasure of cruising with kids many times, with our son Alexander (at 4 months, 11 months, 13 months, and 16 months), our daughter Allie (at 9 and 12), our nieces Megan (3 and 5) and Natalie (2 and 4), our nieces Kayleigh (13 and 16), Melanie (11 and 14), and Nina (10 and 13), and Dave's second cousins Bradley (2) and Andrea (1). So we've been "around the deck," so to speak. Here are our tips for happy cruising with kids, along with tips from Jennifer's sister Kim Larner, mother of Megan and Natalie.

Introduce kids to Disney cruising before you go. Order the free video/DVD, have a family showing, and encourage your child(ren) to watch it on their own. It builds excitement, and also breeds familiarity, which is important to kids.

Your stateroom choice depends on your budget, but spring for an **outside stateroom** if possible. Kim says, "The split-bathroom units were very convenient and the large porthole made the room feel very open." These are big pluses when cruising with kids.

Kids absolutely love **swimming**, and the pools onboard are lots of fun. They also tend to be very crowded, however, and "you'll need to keep an eagle eye on your kids in the pools," according to Kim. She also suggests you make time to go swimming in the ocean at Castaway Cay—"the kids loved the warm water, and found crabs and starfish."

The **Oceaneer Club and Lab** tend to be big hits with most kids, though there can be downfalls. Allie tells us she was disappointed when she was put in the age 8 to 9 group and her cousin Nina was in the 10 to 12 group. And while Megan fell in love with the Oceaneer Club, she had a "potty accident" due to the exciting and unfamiliar environment, and wasn't allowed back in to the Club for a while. Certainly let the kids know about the Oceaneer Club and Lab before you go, but don't build it up too much in the event there are disappointments. Kim also suggests you "put your kid(s) in the Club/Lab for at least one of your meals to allow you the chance to really enjoy the dinner."

Speaking of meals, **early seating** tends to work much better than late seating for kids, especially young kids. Kim says, "the kids enjoyed the start and end of the meal, but were impatient during the middle." Older kids like Allie also get impatient—consider letting older kids go to the Oceaneer Club or Lab if it's appropriate.

The **stage shows** are popular with kids, though very young kids may find it hard to sit through one of these hour-long shows. On-stage characters can present difficulties, too. Kim says that "both Megan and Natalie wanted to go up to the stage and give the characters a hug, and Natalie cried for some time about not being able to do it."

Of all the **cruise activities**, it's most common for kids to love swimming and Castaway Cay the best. You may want to take at least two swimsuits so you always have a dry one.

Overall, we've observed that a Disney cruise is **better than a Walt Disney World vacation** when you're with young kids. There's less walking, less overstimulation, less exhaustion, and just as much magic. On every Disney vacation we've gone on with young kids (under 5), the kids (and their parents) were much happier on the ship than at the parks. Kim says, "The cruise was the best part of our vacation."

Childcare

Yes, parents, this is your vacation, too! While family time spent together is golden, Disney makes sure there's plenty of time and space for adults-only relaxation and fun. So what do the kids do while the grownups play? They're having a party of their own, in some of the **best childcare** programs you'll find on land or sea.

Kids at least three years of age and potty-trained can enjoy supervised play at the Oceaneer Club or Lab—see pages 132–134 for all the details. If your child is between twelve weeks old and three years old, or not yet toilet-trained, you can use the **Flounder's Reef Nursery**. Flounder's is the ships' full-service childcare center located on deck 5 aft, beside the Buena Vista Theatre. The nursery is equipped with a playroom filled with age-appropriate toys, Disney movies, baby bouncers, and rocking chairs, as well as a separate sleeping room with cribs for infants and mats for toddlers. A smaller third room holds changing tables.

Reservations are required for Flounder's, and you can now make them in advance online (see page 125). If you don't reserve in advance, do it very soon after boarding, because it's a popular place. Only a limited number of spaces (about 20) are available, as Disney strives to maintain a child/counselor ratio of 4:1 (infants) and 6:1 (toddlers). You can make reservations in Flounder's on embarkation day, typically from 1:30 pm to 3:30 pm and again from 4:00 pm to 5:00 pm. Disney may limit the number of spaces you can reserve in order to accommodate more guests. After the initial reservation period, services are offered on a space-available basis. If you are planning to dine at Palo, coordinating the two reservations can be tricky. Get your Palo reservation first, then do your Flounder's Reef Nursery reservation.

Unlike the Oceaneer Club and Lab, which are included in your fare, Flounder's Reef Nursery charges **$6/hour** for the first child and $5/hour for additional children. There is a two-hour minimum. Flounder's is open daily, typically from 1:00 pm to 4:00 pm and again from 6:00 pm to midnight, though times may vary for at-sea days and some port days may offer extended hours to accommodate guests going on shore excursions.

When you **check in** your young cruisers to the nursery, bring diapers, wipes, and anything else that may be needed, such as pre-made bottles, pacifiers, security items (such as a blanket), or sippy cups. If you are nursing your infant, you can return to Flounder's Reef in mid-session to nurse—when Jennifer visited with baby Alexander, the staff moved a rocking chair into the back room for privacy. See page 115 for more feeding tips. If your child has any special needs at all, be sure to mention them so they can accommodate your child. You will be given a pager when you drop off your child, in the event you need to be contacted for any reason during your child's stay. Please note that no medication can be dispensed to a child by a crew member, and children with obvious symptoms of illness will not be accepted.

Tip: Parents **traveling with infants** can request a highchair in the dining room and a pack & play crib for their stateroom.

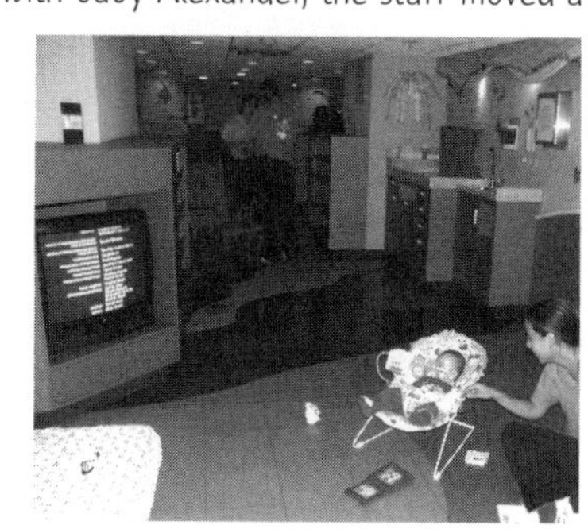

© MediaMarx, Inc.

Baby Alexander got excellent treatment at Flounder's Reef Nursery

Photographs

Say cheese! Whether you're taking your own photos or letting a ship's photographer snap the shot, a Disney cruise is the perfect photo op!

Bring your own camera and plenty of film and batteries. Should you forget this essential bit of cruising equipment, you can buy Pentax and Olympus cameras ($200+), Kodak single-use cameras, film, and batteries onboard. We use a digital camera, which allows us to take as many photos as we like and not bother with film—we recommend it! Camcorders are also very popular—if you bring yours, be aware that the high humidity in the Caribbean can be a problem for your camcorder. To keep moisture out of your camcorder, keep it in the shade whenever possible and allow at least 30 minutes to adjust to different environments (such as when you go from your air-conditioned stateroom to a steamy port).

Onboard photo processing is offered in **Shutters Photo Gallery** (deck 4 aft). Drop off your film before 11:00 am and it'll be ready the same day by 5:00 pm—otherwise your photos are ready the next day. For every roll of film you develop at Shutters, you get a free photo of the ship and a trading pin (as of press time). Developing costs are about $5 for 12 4x6 prints or $10 for 24 (double prints are 35 cents). Shutters processes regular 35mm film and Advantix film, as well as prints from underwater, single-use, and digital cameras. Tip: You can have your digital photos downloaded to a CD for $14.95.

Ship's photographers are everywhere. In fact, the moment you board the ship, you'll be asked to pose for a portrait. Your embarkation photo will be available in Shutters between 5:00 pm and 11:00 pm that same evening. Candid and posed photos may be snapped throughout the cruise—just swing by Shutters to see the photos. Photos taken during the day are typically available in the evening, while photos taken after 5:00 pm or so are displayed the following day. Note that older photos are no longer removed from the displays to make room for new ones. If you aren't sure which photos you want to buy, collect all your photos and stack them behind one another on the display to keep them together. Also, be sure to save your receipts, as you may get quantity discounts. And consider waiting until the end of the cruise to purchase photo packages. If you need photo reprints after your cruise, negatives may be archived for up to ten weeks after your cruise—call 800-772-3470 ext. 11.

Dave poses for a portrait in the atrium

© MediaMarx, Inc.

The **professional photos** at Shutters come in two sizes: 6 x 8 prints are $10 each (10 for $85, 15 for $120, or 20 for $150); 8 x 10 prints are $20 each. Formal portraits and some other shots only come in 8 x 10. Purchased photos are placed in flexible cardboard folders, or you can buy padded folders or frames. Photos are copyrighted and you can be fined up to $500 for unauthorized duplication at a photo lab—download a copyright release waiver at http://www.image.com/guest-postcruise.htm. Tip: If you cruise during the holiday season, Shutters can turn your family portrait into greeting cards with lots of "character!"

Shutters is **open** all day on at-sea days, and from about 5:00 pm to 11:00 pm on port days. Note that Shutters is also open debarkation morning from 6:45 am to 8:30 am. We recommend you avoid the last night and morning, as they are incredibly busy.

Shopping Onboard

Both ships sport a 5,500-square-foot shopping area—combine that with extra shopping opportunities aboard and great shopping in port (see chapter 6), and you'll find it easy to shop 'til you drop anchor. As you might imagine, prices are a bit on the high side, but the quality is excellent.

Due to U.S. Customs regulations, the onboard shops **cannot be open while in port**. Check your *Personal Navigator* for shop operating hours, and keep in mind that the last night of your cruise is your last opportunity to shop. And before you splurge on that big-ticket item, see page 272 for details on customs allowances.

Mickey's Mates (deck 4 midship) is the Disney character and logo shop, filled with stuffed animals, souvenirs, logowear, trading pins, postcards, etc.

© MediaMarx, Inc.
The shopping area onboard the ship

Treasure Ketch (deck 4 midship) is right across the hall from Mickey's Mates, and offers more upscale and practical merchandise, such as resortwear, jewelry (including loose gemstones and "gold by the inch"), collectibles, toiletries, film, batteries, books, and magazines. Tax-free gifts are also available here, such as watches and sunglasses. Collectors, check your *Personal Navigator* for Captain's signings—he'll sign posters, hats, T-shirts, pins, and ship models for free.

Preludes Snacks (deck 4 forward) is a small bar that sells packaged snacks such as candy bars, chips, and popcorn. Typically open from 6:00 pm to 10:00 pm.

Up Beat/Radar Trap (deck 3 forward) offers duty-free liquor (over 45 brands), fragrances (over 60 brands), cigars (over 25 brands), and cigarettes, as well as snacks, candy bars, cameras, film, and batteries. Note that duty-free orders are delivered to your stateroom on the last night of your cruise—yes, that means you cannot consume that liquor you bought here while you're onboard. The shop is typically open evenings until midnight.

Shutters (deck 4 aft) sells compact cameras, frames, and photos. See previous page.

Live Auction at Sea (deck 4 forward) features fine art and collectible Disney Cruise Line items auctioned to the highest bidder. See page 151 for all the details.

Pin Trading Station (deck 3 or 4 midship) opens nightly on the port side of the Atrium Lobby, typically from 7:30 pm to 8:30 pm. This is a great place for limited edition pins.

A pool-side merchandise cart may be parked near the **Mickey Pool** on certain days.

Let's not forget the **onboard gift brochure** you receive with your cruise documentation before you embark—any items ordered from this brochure will be waiting for you in your stateroom when you board.

Check the "**On-Board Shopping**" **supplement** distributed with your *Personal Navigator* for daily specials, featured items, operating hours, and a list of where to find what onboard.

Shops are **busiest** from 7:00 pm to 10:00 pm, so you may want to go earlier or later.

Formal and Semi-Formal Occasions

What is it about a cruise that brings out our Fred Astaire and Ginger Rogers? It may be passé ashore, but a formal night at sea is still magical!

On the **3- and 4-night** Wonder cruises, there are no official formal nights. Instead, your semi-formal nights are determined by your dining rotation. On your Triton's night, you can wear semi-formal attire, such as a jacket for men and a dress or pantsuit for women, but it isn't required. Wear semi-formal attire for Palo. The other nights are casual or tropical.

On the **7-night** Disney Magic cruises, you have one formal night–day 2 on Eastern Caribbean itineraries and day 3 on Western Caribbean itineraries–and one semi-formal night on day 6 of both itineraries. (Longer cruises have 1–2 more formal and semi-formal occasions.) Formal night is "black tie optional." Many men wear tuxedos or suits and women typically wear evening gowns, but semi-formalwear is fine, too. During the formal and semi-formal nights, the crew sets up backdrops and takes formal portraits (see page 260). In addition, you are asked to wear semi-formal attire when you eat dinner in Lumière's.

Men's Formalwear: Fortunately, you don't have to rent a tuxedo and haul it across the country and back. Cruise Line Formalwear supplies men's formalwear on the Disney Cruise Line, and cruise-long rentals range from $85 to $120 (this price includes everything but the shoes), plus accessories ($5 to $20). Order at least two weeks before you cruise with the order form in your cruise documents, online at http://www.cruiselineformal.com or on the phone at 800-551-5091. You can also view the tuxedos and accessories on their web site. When you order a tuxedo from them, it'll arrive in your stateroom on your first day aboard (try it on right away to see if it needs any alterations). When the cruise ends, just leave it in your room. Note that Cruise Line Formal does keep extra inventory onboard for exchanges and last-minute rentals. Another option is to buy a tuxedo (try a local tux rental shop or http://www.ebay.com). Perhaps you'd like a Disney-themed vest and tie set to go with your own tux? If so, check on the Internet at http://www.tuxedosdirect.com.

Jennifer and Dave decked out at Palo

Women's Formalwear: If you don't happen to have an evening gown or old bridesmaid's gown hanging in your closet, you can make do with a nice dress on both semi-formal and formal evenings. A "little black dress" is a popular choice. Feel free to wear your dress more than once on your cruise–accessorize to change the look. Consider adding a wrap for chilly dining rooms. Formal evenings see most women in long evening gowns–try shopping the department stores (such as J.C.Penney's) for good deals. You could also try Chadwick's (http://www.chadwicks.com) and Victoria's Secret (http://www.victoriassecret.com).

Kids' Formalwear: Obviously, many parents don't want to buy their kids nice suits or dresses for a cruise because they grow out of them so quickly. Dressing the boys in slacks and a button-down shirt is just fine. If your boy really wants to dress up like Dad in a tux, special order rentals are available through Cruise Line Formalwear. You can also look for a good deal at http://www.ebay.com or at http://www.tux4boys.com. The girls look great in sun dresses, and this is the perfect opportunity to wear Disney princess dresses (available beforehand at the Disney Store and onboard in Mickey's Mates). Of course, that's if they even dine with you. Some kids prefer the company of their peers and have dinner with the Club/Lab.

Special/Celebrity Cruises

Looking for something a bit special on your next cruise? Disney plans many special cruises each year—some are once-in-a-lifetime events, while others just feature celebrity guests. Here are some past and upcoming events to give you an idea of what to expect:

Inaugural Cruises—The first sailing of a new ship, or the first sailing of a ship on a new itinerary is a big deal. On the up side, you get the thrill of being "the first" to sail, and you may get a few extra treats—on the Western Caribbean Inaugural Cruise in May 2002, we were treated to a Mexican mariachi band before embarking, given special "fans" to wave as we set sail, and presented with complimentary champagne glasses. On the down side, an inaugural cruise often doesn't have all the glitches worked out yet (though we didn't notice anything wrong on our inaugural cruise). There are no dates set for the next inaugural cruise (new ship? new itinerary? who knows!), so watch our web site for details.

Celebrity Cruises—Many cruises have at least a minor celebrity or notable speaker, while others feature bigger names. For example, Roger Ebert and Richard Roeper usually do an annual Film Festival at Sea in the autumn on the Disney Wonder. A special packag typically includes a sail-away cocktail reception with the famous film critics, screenings of four of their favorite films, open discussion sessions, and a book signing. Most celebrity guests have some connection with Disney, and include actors, artisans, and authors–recent guests have included Ernie Sabella (voice of "Pumbaa" in Disney's The Lion King—see photo below), Leslie Iwerks (granddaughter of Ub Iwerks), Raven, and former presidents George H.W. Bush and Jimmy Carter. Disney rarely announces their celebrities or speakers ahead of time, but you can call 888-DCL-2500 to inquire.

Holiday Cruises—If your cruise coincides with a major holiday, you can bet Disney has something special planned. Halloween cruises have costume contests, Thanksgiving cruises offer traditional dinners, December cruises feature magical holiday decorations and special holiday events, and so on. New Years Eve cruises are very, very popular—book early if you're interested in one. Note also that religious holidays (Ash Wednesday, Easter, Passover, Hanukkah, Christmas, etc.) have clergy onboard for observances.

Fan Cruises—Disney fans love to cruise together, and usually one group or another is organizing a group cruise. We're doing a 4-night PassPorter reader cruise as part of MouseFest 2006 on December 3-7, 2006—check http://www.mousefest.org for all the details (see page 265, too). And when your authors are cruising, we like to host a casual meet onboard—you can get details on these meets at the above address also.

Other Cruises—Keep an ear out for more special cruises, such as pin trading cruises, Disney Vacation Club and/or Annual Passholder cruises, and movie premieres. There are also cruises that feature two stops at Castaway Cay in 2006—check with Disney Cruise Line for sail dates.

Ernie Sabella and Dave at Castaway Cay

Celebrating Special Occasions

We firmly believe there's always something to celebrate... even if it's just the fact that you're going on a cruise! And, of course, there are always birthdays, anniversaries, and holidays to remember. If you are celebrating a special occasion while you're onboard, be sure to let your travel agent or Disney reservation agent know when you book your cruise, or at least three weeks before you sail.

Bon Voyage Celebrations—Why not throw a party before you depart for your cruise? Invite your friends and family and make 'em jealous! Or if you happen to know someone going on a cruise, surprise them with a send-off party or a gift in their stateroom (see sidebar below). And don't forget about a celebratory drink when you board! Note: Only passengers are allowed on board or in the terminal, so parties with non-cruisers must take place before your arrival at the cruise terminal.

Birthdays—Let Disney know about your celebration in advance, and you'll be serenaded by your serving team and receive a small cake. You may also get a birthday pin!

Honeymoons—The Disney Cruise Line is popular with honeymooning couples, and Disney offers some "romance" packages for the celebration (see page 43). Be sure to let Disney know about your honeymoon even if you aren't on a package.

Anniversaries—We celebrated Dave's parents' 50th wedding anniversary aboard the Wonder in 2001—it was magical! Again, tell Disney about your celebration ahead of time and you may get a surprise.

Holidays—Disney does the holidays in grand style, particularly on Christmas and New Years Eve—look for Santa Goofy, a three-deck-tall tree, holiday feasts, a New Years Eve party, and a New Years Day tailgate party.

Tip: **Decorate your stateroom** and/or stateroom door in honor of your celebration! You can order basic stateroom decorations from Disney (see sidebar below) and they'll put them up before you arrive. Or bring your own decorations from home. Another fun idea is to buy (or make) magnets or banners with which to decorate your metal stateroom door (see photo).

Door decorations for Dave's "Who Wants To Be A Millionaire —Play It!" winning cruise

Stateroom Gifts

Disney Cruise Line offers a variety of gifts that you can order ahead of time and have waiting for you in your stateroom (or that of a friend or family member). Check the brochure that comes with your cruise documents, visit http://www.disneycruise.com and search on "gifts," or call 800-601-8455. If you're looking for something extra special, the Cape Canaveral-based company, The Perfect Gift, delivers delightful cruise baskets at good prices to your stateroom—you can even custom design your gift baskets. Call 800-950-4559 or visit http://www.theperfectgift.cc for more information.

Reunions and Group Cruises

A Disney cruise is ideal for a reunion or group event. Unlike a gathering on land, say at Walt Disney World, the Disney cruise allows groups to stay within close proximity of one another, offers a number of built-in activities and meals, and offers fun reunion packages. We've planned a number of reunions and group cruises over the years—here are our tips for a successful gathering:

Pick the best dates. Consult with the members of your group to find the dates that work best for their schedules and wallets. While spring and summer breaks may be best for groups with kids, those are also the priciest and may prevent some from joining you. Whenever possible, go for the less-expensive seasons, such as January, February, May, or early December.

If you're cruising as a family or small group, it may be possible to select staterooms in **close proximity** to one another, which facilitates communications and meetings. But if you cannot, don't fret—the ship isn't that big of a place. You may also be able to get rooms in closer proximity around final payment time (75 days before), when other cruisers cancel.

Keep in **close communication** with your group both before and during your cruise. Simple notes or newsletters, via e-mail or on paper, can be very helpful for educating and notifying them of events. Once onboard, you can leave voice mail and notes on stateroom doors.

When you book your cruise, let Disney know that you're traveling as a group and ask them to **link the reservations together** so you can dine in close proximity to one another. The dining room tables usually hold up to eight guests—on one of our family reunion cruises we had a family of 16, and we were seated at two tables of eight, end to end. We've found that having this time together at dinner is very important to the success of a group cruise. Keep in mind, however, that everyone in your party needs to be on the same dinner seating—discuss early vs. late seating with your group before making a unilateral decision.

If your group wants to **dine at Palo**, make your reservations online as early as possible! Large groups are hard to accommodate and space goes quickly. Several small tables may be a better idea. Note: If your group's reservations are linked in Disney's system and you book a Palo table large enough to accommodate your group, be aware other members of your group may not be able to make their own, separate Palo reservations.

Don't expect or try to do everything together. The beauty of a Disney cruise is that you don't have to hang together all the time to enjoy your group. You'll inevitably do some activities together during the day, bump into one another during free moments, and then enjoy quality time together at dinner.

PassPorter Gathering and MouseFest Cruise

Interested in joining other PassPorter readers and Disney Internet fans on a fun cruise? Each year in early December we host a 4-night cruise—this year it is December 3–7, 2006. We plan all sorts of special activities and enjoy the company of like-minded individuals. And there are fabulous deals available through various travel agents. If you're interested in joining us, visit http://www.mousefest.org for information and an RSVP form. Everyone is invited!

Weddings and Vow Renewals

Ah, what is more romantic (or simple) than getting married or renewing your vows aboard a cruise ship? Disney Cruise Line makes it very easy to do both, and when compared to a land-based wedding, the prices are a good value, too!

First, if you're interested in either a wedding or vow renewal ceremony onboard a Disney ship, be aware that this isn't something you can arrange on your own. You'll need Disney's assistance, and you'll need to purchase their wedding or vow renewal package. To get started, visit http://www.disneycruise.com, click "Reservations," then choose either the "Weddings at Sea" package or the "Vow Renewal" package. This is where you'll find prices and package details. You can also call 321-939-4610 for information.

When you're **ready to book**, call a professional Disney wedding consultant at 321-939-4610 or contact your travel agent. You can book a wedding or vow renewal up to 12 months in advance, though it is not necessary to book it so early—you can plan a cruise wedding or vow renewal in as little as a month or two (based on availability).

Ceremony locations vary. Most wedding ceremonies are held outdoors at the Head's Up Bar at the far end of the family beach on Castaway Cay—the lagoon and ship provide a beautiful backdrop. You can also get married in either Sessions (Magic) or Cadillac Lounge (Wonder) on deck 3 forward. The lounges and Palo are also the typical spots for Vow Renewal ceremonies. Other locations may be possible under certain circumstances—inquire with your Disney wedding consultant.

Wedding ceremonies are **officiated** by an administrator of the Bahamas. Vow renewal ceremonies are usually performed by the Captain or a high-ranking officer.

Those getting married should note that you'll have a **private, legal ceremony** in the cruise terminal before your ship leaves Port Canaveral. This means you're technically married for your entire voyage, even though your public ceremony happens later in the cruise.

The **"Disney Weddings" e-book** by Andrea Rotondo Hospidor may be helpful, even though it concentrates on Walt Disney World weddings. Many of the tips on working with Disney's Fairy Tale Weddings department apply, as does much of the information on intimate weddings and vow renewals. For more details on this e-book, visit http://www.yourfairytale.com. The book is $19.95 and available for immediate download.

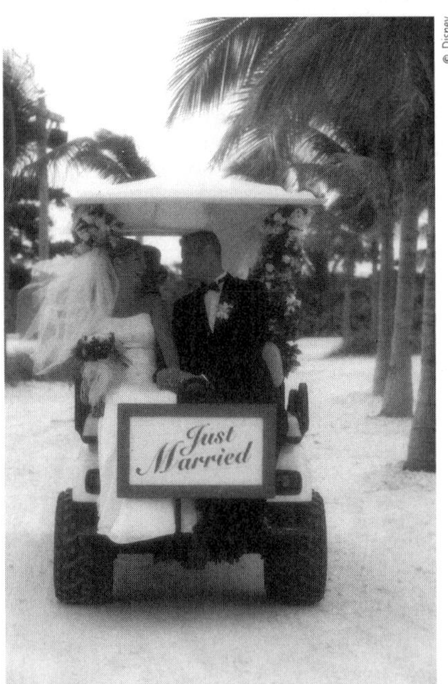

A Castaway Cay wedding

Preventing Seasickness

Seasickness—just the thought of it can make some of us a little queasy. And if you actually have it... no, let's not think about it. Let's think about how fortunate we are to be sailing on a large, modern cruise ship on some of the calmest waters in the world. Two huge stabilizer fins take the bite out of the worst wave action, and modern medicine has provided more than one helpful remedy. If you're looking for that ounce of prevention, read on!

✔ **Purely natural**—Go topside, take deep breaths, get some fresh air, and look at the horizon. The worst thing you can do is stay in your stateroom. Sea sickness is caused by the confusion between what your inner ear senses and what your eyes see. If you can look at something steady, it helps your brain synchronize these. Eventually your brain will get used to the motion and you get your "sea legs," but that can take a day or two. Drink lots of water and have some mild food, such as saltine crackers—avoid fatty and salty foods, and eat lightly.

✔ **Herbs**—Ginger is reported to help reduce sea sickness. It comes in pill and cookie form—even ginger ale can help. It's best to begin taking this in advance of feeling sick.

✔ **Bonine, or "Dramamine Less Drowsy Formula"**—These are brand names of Meclizine, which has far fewer side effects than its older cousin Dramamine (which we don't recommend). Try it at home before your cruise to check for side effects, then take it a few hours before departure for maximum effectiveness. Note that Bonine is only for those 12 years or older; use Dramamine (original formula) for kids ages 2 to 12. Tip: The onboard medical facility (discussed on the next page) provides free chewable Meclizine tablets (25 mg.) from a dispenser next to its door on deck 1 forward. Guest Services (on deck 3 midship) may also have some Meclizine if you can't make it down to deck 1.

✔ **Sea bands**—These are elastic wrist bands that operate by applying pressure to the Nei Kuan acupressure point on each wrist by means of a plastic stud, thereby preventing sea sickness. Some people swear by them, some say that they don't work. Either way, they are inexpensive (unless you buy them on the ship) and have no medical side effects. They don't yet come in designer colors to match your formal evening gown, however.

✔ **Scopolamine Transdermal Patch**—Available by prescription only. It is the most effective preventative with the least drowsiness, but it also comes with the most side effects, such as dry mouth and dizziness. For more information about scopolamine, speak to your doctor and visit http://www.transdermscop.com.

✔ **Ship Location**—A low deck, midship stateroom is generally considered to be the location on a ship where you'll feel the least movement. If you know you're prone to seasickness, consider requesting a stateroom on decks 1-2, midship. But once you're onboard and you find yourself feeling seasick, the best thing to do is get out of your stateroom, go to deck 4 midship, and lie down in one of the padded deck chairs—then use the tips noted in "Purely Natural" above.

✔ **Choose Excursions Wisely**—Those prone to motion sickness may want to avoid shore excursions that rely heavily on smaller boats such as ferries and sailboats. Read the excursion descriptions in chapter 6 carefully for mentions of motion sickness or rough seas. If you don't want to miss out on anything, begin taking your preferred seasickness remedy well in advance of the excursion.

➤

Staying Healthy

Staying healthy is easy with some preparation and knowledge. Folks who are already healthy may only have to worry about getting seasick (see the previous page) or picking up a virus. Here's what you can do to prevent illness:

Getting a virus is less likely than seasickness, but still possible—any time you get people together for more than two or three days at a time you're going to have some percentage become ill. Cruise ships are significantly less vulnerable than schools, hotels, nursing homes, and restaurants, contrary to the media attention the Norwalk-like virus received in November/December 2002—cruise ships account for 10% of the outbreaks, while restaurants, nursing homes, and schools account for over 70%. The Centers for Disease Control (CDC) report that normally 1-2% of a cruise population gets sick on a regular basis; during the Norwalk-like virus epidemics, this number may only rise to 2-4%. Nonetheless, Disney takes many precautions to avoid illness on its ships, including thoroughly disinfecting surfaces that are touched, encouraging hand washing, providing hand wipes in particular situations, and refusing passage to visibly ill passengers to reduce the risk of transmitting a virus to others.

To avoid catching a bug, get a full night's sleep before you embark, eat well, drink lots of water, and wash your hands thoroughly and frequently. Hand-washing cannot be emphasized enough. Wash your hands for at least 15 seconds after using the bathroom, after changing a diaper, and before handling, preparing, or consuming food. Regular soap and water does the trick—there's no need for antibacterial soaps (in fact, the Centers for Disease Control suggest that antibacterial soaps may contribute to the problem, and suggest you do not use them). Alcohol-based hand sanitizer can be used as a supplement in between times hands are washed, but it should not replace soap and water. There's no need to bring your own Lysol either—all surfaces are disinfected before you board as well as while you're underway (besides, Lysol does nothing to stop the Norwalk-like virus). Tip: To make sure both you and your kids wash your hands for long enough, try singing or humming the "Happy Birthday" song slowly while washing your hands—when the song ends, your hands are clean.

If you get sick, be aware that reporting illness to the cruise staff is taken seriously—the cruise line is required to report any onboard cases of gastrointestinal illness to the CDC. You may be required to visit the medical facility onboard (see below), and if you're found to have a gastrointestinal illness, you may be restricted to your stateroom to avoid passing the illness to others. And if you're sick when you check-in at the terminal, you may need to visit a medical professional before boarding—you may even be refused passage.

Viruses aside, there's one medical problem that far too many cruisers contract during their cruise—**sunburn**. Bring that sunscreen (SPF of 30 or higher) and use it. And wear hats and cover-ups whenever possible. Don't take your chances with a sunburn.

As much as we don't like to think about it, accidents happen and guests get sick. Knowing that this is unavoidable, Disney has put a well-equipped **medical facility** aboard—it's equipped with modern medical equipment such as cardiac life support equipment, ventilators, and an X-ray machine. Two doctors and three registered nurses are on staff. The care, we hear, is excellent and the fees are reasonable. Any medical care you receive is billed to your stateroom account and you bill your insurance company separately.

Doing Business Onboard

We know, we know... "work" is a four-letter word on a cruise. If you can avoid your work entirely on the cruise, we heartily recommend it! Alas, we know better than anyone that sometimes your business doesn't take a vacation just because you do. If you need to keep up with work while you're cruising, here are our tried-and-true tips:

Phone Calls—You have four options when making phone calls: use Disney's ship-to-shore phone system (the phone in your stateroom) for $6.95/minute, use your cellular phone when in port or sailing past islands with cell roaming service, use a pay phone in port, or use a service such as Skype (see page 144) to make calls on your laptop with wireless access. Your stateroom phone system is detailed on page 93. If you opt to bring a cell phone, call your wireless provider to inquire about international roaming.

Laptop Computers—We always bring along our laptop, and now that we can connect to the Internet with it via wireless access onboard, doing business is much easier. Typically, we use the laptop to download photos from the digital camera, but on one cruise we had to do some printing (we used our portable printer hooked up to our laptop) and faxing (we had Guest Services fax for us). Be sure to bring all necessary cables!

Internet Access—We've devoted two full pages to the Internet Access, on pages 144–145. If you're relying on Internet access to keep up with work, keep in mind that the Internet Cafe is the least busy earlier in the day and late at night. Note also that the Internet Cafe may not open on debarkation morning, though recently it has stayed open. We noticed no pattern to the occasional and short downtime experienced with wireless access onboard.

Faxes—You can send and receive faxes from the Guest Services desk (deck 3 midship). Cost is the same as ship-to-shore phone calls—$6.95/minute. We faxed several sheets during a 4-night cruise and found that each page takes about one minute to fax, though fax transmission time does depend on the density of the page.

Copies—The Guest Services desk is also the place to have copies made.

Meeting Space—Both Disney ships have public spaces that may be rented at certain times. You can also get audio-visual equipment. Call Disney for details.

Tip: If your work is portable, take it outside to one of the patio tables behind Topsider's/Beach Blanket Buffet (deck 9 aft) or enjoy the solitude of the small area on deck 7 aft.

Joining the Ship's Crew

Ever thought of working on a Disney ship? If you are at least 21 years old, there are job opportunities. From what we understand it takes a huge time commitment (you typically sign a six-month contract and work about 70–80 hours a week) and it's difficult to be away from home for the long stretches required. On the flip side, Disney does offer several perks, such as crew-only areas (including a beach on Castaway Cay and an onboard pool), free theme park admission, and so on. If you'd like to learn more, call the job line at 407-566-SHIP or visit http://www.dcljobs.com.

Disney Characters

One of the benefits of a Disney cruise is the opportunity to meet your favorite Disney characters—you won't find them on any other cruise in the world. Typically, the Disney celebrities joining you on your cruise include Mickey, Minnie, Goofy, Pluto, Donald, Chip, Dale, and Stitch (often in tropical attire) as well as appearances from special "face" characters like Cinderella, Snow White, and Alice. Here's where to meet your Disney friends onboard:

Character Appearances—The Lobby Atrium (both decks 3 and 4) is a popular gathering place for Disney friends, typically in the evenings for photo opportunities. If you forget your camera, there are often ship's photographers to snap a shot. You'll also find characters in the terminal before you board, at deck parties, the kids' clubs, and near the Mickey Pool. For schedules, check your *Personal Navigator*, the character appearance display in the Lobby Atrium (or outside Shutters), or call 7-PALS on your stateroom phone.

Character Autographs: Bring a notebook or autograph book to the character meets—you can buy them in Mickey's Mates or just make one at home before you board (see photo on right). Take a photo of the Disney character autographing the book and you can later attach a copy of the picture to each autographed page—this makes a great keepsake!

© MediaMarx, Inc.

A home-made autograph book

Character Breakfasts—Guests on the seven-night and longer cruises get the opportunity to mingle with Mickey, Minnie, Goofy, Pluto, Chip and Dale at a character breakfast in Parrot Cay. For more details, see page 108.

Tea With Wendy—This is a special character event on the seven-night (and longer) cruises. Check your *Personal Navigator* for the day and time to pickup tickets (at no extra charge) and arrive early—this is a popular event and tickets go quickly. The half-hour "tea" is held in Studio Sea (deck 4 midship) on certain afternoons. As you might have guessed, the tea is hosted by Wendy Darling (from Disney's Peter Pan), who demonstrates the proper way to serve tea, and tells a story. Chocolate chip cookies and iced tea are served. The event is attended predominantly by young girls, but everyone is welcome—young or old, male or female. After tea, guests may greet Wendy personally and get a photograph with her. Tip: Crew members select two boys from the audience to play John and Michael, Wendy's brothers.

Character Parties—In addition to the Disney character appearances at the deck parties, there is another special character party for which to check your Personal Navigator. 'Til We Meet Again is a farewell party in the Lobby Atrium held on your last evening (usually at 10:00 or 10:15 pm)—most of the characters come out to bid everyone a special goodbye.

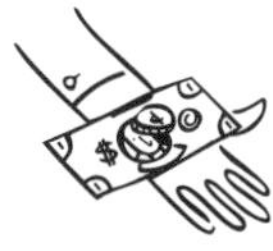

Tipping and Feedback

Tipping is your way of thanking the crew members for their fine service. Here are the recommended gratuity guidelines for each guest:

Crew Member/Service	Per Night	3-Night	4-Night	7-Night
Dining Room Server	~$3.75	$11.00	$14.75	$25.75
Dining Room Asst. Server	~$2.75	$8.00	$10.75	$18.75
Dining Room Head Server	~$1.00	$2.75	$3.75	$6.50
Stateroom Host/Hostess	~$3.60	$10.75	$14.50	$25.25
Palo Server	Your discretion (on top of the $10/person service charge)			
Bartender/Lounge Server	If no tip was automatically added, 10% to 15%			
Room Service	Your discretion (usually $1 to $2/person)			
Kids' Counselors	Not necessary, but do reward good service			
Shore Excursion Tour Guide	$1 to $2/person			
Baggage Porters (at terminal)	$1 to $2/bag			

Disney's tipping guidelines are **not etched in stone**. Exceptional service deserves an exceptional tip, and substandard service should earn a lesser reward. But don't save all your compliments for the tip envelope—people thrive on appreciation.

On your last day, **tip envelopes** will be left in your stateroom so you may give gratuities to the first four crew members noted in the chart above. Fill them with cash, or charge the tips to your stateroom account at Guest Services and they will give you receipts to put in the envelopes (avoid Guest Services on the last evening—it's very busy). Give the filled envelopes to each crew member—servers typically receive theirs at the last dinner.

Tipping is a form of feedback for services received, but you can give **additional feedback** on your experience. Neither we nor Disney Cruise Line would be where we are today without your feedback. For instance, did you know that those obstructed-view category 7 staterooms we mentioned on page 85 were reclassified (and lowered in price) based on cruiser feedback? And even with PassPorter, our depth of detail is a direct reader request.

The night before you disembark a **questionnaire** is placed in your stateroom. Take the time to fill it out and deposit it in the collection boxes at breakfast the next morning or on the gangway. If you had problems, there is a very small section to describe what happened—if you need to communicate more, read on.

To send **detailed comments** (complaints or compliments) to Disney once you return home, write a letter and mail it to: DCL Guest Communications, P.O. Box 10238, Lake Buena Vista, FL 32830. You can also send e-mail to dcl.guest.communications@disneycruise.com or visit http://disney.go.com/mail/disneycruiseline. Disney is typically very responsive to guest feedback, and you should hear back from them within six weeks.

Contacting us at **PassPorter Travel Press** is even easier. E-mail feedback@passporter.com or send a letter to P.O. Box 3880, Ann Arbor, MI 48106. You can fill out a survey about this guidebook at http://www.passporter.com/dcl/surveyintro.htm. We also recommend you visit http://www.passporter.com/register.htm to register your copy, which is another perfect opportunity to tell us what you think. When you register, we'll send back coupons good for discounts on future PassPorters and accessories!

Customs Allowances

Ah, U.S. Customs. While we dreaded customs on our first cruise, we quickly found that the rules aren't hard to understand, and the process is smooth if you pay attention. If you feel unsure about customs and debarkation in general, attend the debarkation talk on the afternoon of your Castaway Cay day (or catch it on TV in your stateroom later that evening).

You are required to declare everything that you purchased or were given as a gift on the ship, in your ports of call, and on Castaway Cay. Fill out the **U.S. Customs Declaration Form** left in your stateroom on your last night (extra forms are available at Guest Services) Fill it in and sign and date the form—you will hand it to customs during debarkation.

Each guest is allowed a **total duty-free allowance** of $800 (3- and 4-night cruises and 7-night Western Caribbean cruises) or $1200 (7-night Eastern Caribbean cruises)—these allowances were last increased on 11/4/2002. Liquor and tobacco have special limits. One liter of liquor per person over 21 years of age is exempt from duties (Eastern Caribbean cruisers are allowed four more liters from the Virgin Islands). One carton of cigarettes and 100 cigars (other than Cuban cigars, which are not allowed at all) are exempt (Eastern Caribbean cruisers can add four more cartons of cigarettes if purchased in St. Thomas). If you exceed the customs allowances, you must report to the Customs Inspector before you debark the ship—check the debarkation sheet left in your stateroom. If you exceed your customs allowances, you will need to have cash on hand to pay your duties—no checks or credit cards are accepted.

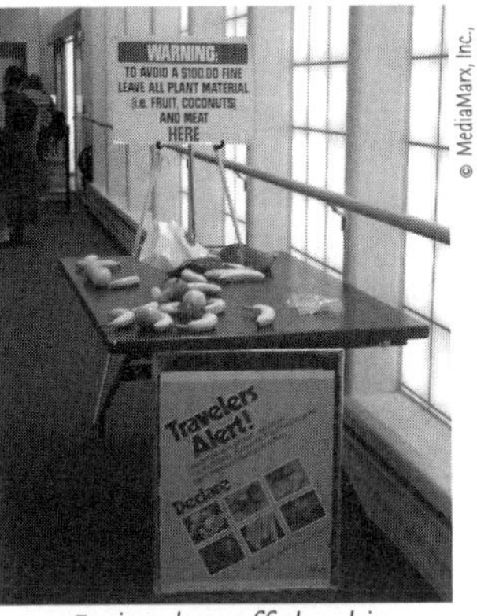

© MediaMarx, Inc.,

Fruit taken off the ship

Read more about the **U.S. Customs Laws** online at http://www.cbp.gov/xp/cgov/travel (click "Know Before You Go!"). Keep in mind that anything that you don't declare is considered smuggled—don't forget any items you won onboard. The duties on declared items are low, but the penalties for smuggled items are high. And don't try to carry off items that aren't allowed, such as fresh fruit or flowers—you can face a stiff fine. You'd be surprised how many try to "smuggle" a banana unwittingly (see photo).

Immigration and International Guests

As we mentioned earlier in the guidebook, international guests yield their passports before boarding the ship. U.S. Immigration requires that all non-U.S. guests (and anyone who joined the ship enroute) present themselves at every U.S. port of entry. International guests on all itineraries must go through immigration in Port Canaveral. On the 7-night Eastern Caribbean cruise, immigration inspection is also held at St. Thomas for all passengers (U.S. and non-U.S.). In both cases, you will be directed to reclaim your passport—the details will be on a note placed in your stateroom the evening before. Alas, immigration happens pretty early in the morning—typically at 5:30 am to 6:00 am. Be sure to bring all members of your party and your passport receipt. All guests must clear immigration before any guests can debark in St. Thomas or Port Canaveral.

Debarkation

Yes, your cruise is really over. Wouldn't it be nice if you could just stay onboard and sail forever? Even when it's time to go, nobody gets you to the exit more smoothly than Disney. This is the company that made crowd control a science. There's no waiting in line to depart, nobody calls out your name, and things seem to just flow. Here's the drill:

First, you need to **settle your onboard account**. If you put a credit card on your account at check-in, you're all set. Otherwise, visit Guest Services (deck 3 midship) to pay the total with credit card, traveler's checks, or cash. Do this the day before you debark.

On your **last night aboard**, pack your bags, remove old cruise tags, and attach the new tags provided (more tags are at Guest Services if you need them). Don't forget to fill out the tags and make a note of the tag color. When you're ready, place your tagged luggage in the passageway by 11:00 pm–you will not see it again until you're off the ship. Thus, it's crucial that you pack a small day bag to hold your toiletries, nightclothes, and valuables. And don't forget to keep out an outfit (and shoes) to wear the next morning! If you're hoping to get off the ship quickly the next morning, consider keeping your luggage with you and carrying it off the ship yourself–not as convenient, but a bit quicker. This is a good time to fill out the customs forms placed in your stateroom (see previous page). Also, if you have a pager for the kids clubs, return it to deck 5 midship this evening.

On **debarkation morning**, take your day bags and go to breakfast in the same restaurant in which you dined the previous evening (unless you ate at Palo, in which case you go to the restaurant you would have been in). Guests with early seating eat at 6:45 am, while late seating guests eat at 8:00 am. If you prefer, you can get "early bird" coffee and Danish pastries at 6:00 am to 6:30 am at the Beverage Station (deck 9 aft) or a continental breakfast from 6:30 am to 8:00 am at Topsider's/Beach Blanket Buffet (deck 9 aft). Be aware that guests must vacate their staterooms by 8:00 am. Shutters is open from 7:00 am to 8:30 am, but all other shops are closed. Drop off your questionnaire (see page 271) at breakfast or as you debark. Typically the first guest debarks at 7:45 am and the last guest debarks at 9:45 am.

Now it's time to **say goodbye** to all your "family." After breakfast, go to the gangway (deck 3 midship), stroll off the ship with your day bags, and head off to Customs. Keep your photo I.D., birth certificate, and/or passport handy. At the Customs area, claim your checked baggage in the color-coded area. Photography is not allowed in the Customs area–keep your camera down to avoid complications. Pass through Customs (usually you just present your customs forms and walk right through) and you're soon in your Disney motorcoach, car, or limousine. Porters are available to help you–don't forget to tip them. If you're flying out of Orlando Airport, several airlines (American Airlines, Delta, Northwest, US Air, and Continental) give you the option of checking your bags at the port, just outside of Customs.

Castaway Club

Once you've got a Disney cruise under your belt, you're an automatic member of Disney's Castaway Club. As a Castaway Club member, you get perks for future cruises, such as a special toll-free number, special check-in area, onboard reception with ship officers, and free gift in your stateroom. If you don't receive any information on the Castaway Club after your cruise, call Disney at 888-DCL-2500 to request it.

Magical and Wonderful Tips

Creating a "magical" and "wonderful" cruise takes a dash of planning, a pinch of knowledge, and a bit of pixie dust! Here are some more tips:

- Check your *Personal Navigator* for information on getting the complimentary **Bridge Tour** tickets—tour spaces fill up quickly. The tour is informative and interesting. If you're sailing on the Disney Wonder before it goes into drydock in October 2006, you can get a peek at the bridge without the tour. Head up to the Vista Spa's fitness/exercise room, and there in front of the treadmills are windows looking down into the forward part of the bridge as well as a wonderful view out the two-story bridge windows. The bridge is most interesting to watch when the ship is entering or departing a port and there is more bridge activity.

- Write to us and **share your experiences, memories, and tips**. If we use them in a future edition, we'll credit you by name and send you a free copy when it's published! Write to us at P.O. Box 3880, Ann Arbor, MI 48106 or e-mail us at feedback@passporter.com.

Magical Memories

- *"Before I left for my cruise, I made my own autograph book. I cut transparencies (the kind used for overhead projectors) to 5x6 inches. I put a plain piece of white paper behind each transparency to make each page easier to see. I punched two holes in the top of each page and used rings to fasten it into a book. I attached a permanent "Sharpie" marker with a piece of ribbon. On the cruise, I collected a bunch of character autographs, particularly of the ones I photographed. After the cruise, I printed out my digital photos, took my autograph book apart, cut off the 1-inch edge that had the two hole punches in it and I now had a 4x6 transparency with autograph on it. I laid the transparency directly on top of my photo and now it looks like each photo is autographed!"*

  ...as told by Disney cruiser Melissa Hatcher

- *"On our way to dinner one night, we were pushing our twin three-year-olds in their double stroller. As we turned toward the dining room, we spotted Chip heading our way to a character greeting. Our boys' eyes lit up! Chip started to goof around with them and our boys held up their best Buzz Lightyear phaser arms and took aim at Chip. Once Chip realized he was being 'phasered' by two Buzz Lightyears, he fell 'dead' to the floor. It was a Disney magical moment I will never forget!"*

  ...as told by Disney cruiser Brenda S.

- *"My sister and I live about 1,500 miles apart and only see each other every couple of years. This year, we are cruising and we've planned the entire trip via e-mail. The trip is still months away, but we are zipping e-mails back and forth every day in anticipation."*

  ...as told by Disney cruiser Mary Jane Ross

Glossary of Terms

While this guide isn't exactly overflowing with salty terms, we thought a brief glossary could be useful, and a bit of fun.

Aft—Towards the rear. The *after* section of the ship. Also *abaft.*
All Ashore—The earliest time a passenger may disembark in a port.
All Aboard— The latest time a passenger may board in a port.
Amidships—The center of the ship, between fore and aft. Also *midship.*
Assistant Server—The crew member who assists your server, typically by looking after drinks, clearing the table, and carrying trays to and from the kitchen. On the Disney Cruise Line, a single assistant server attends your needs throughout your voyage.
Beam—The widest portion of a watercraft.
Berth—Any bed on a ship, but more commonly, the fold-down or fold-out beds in a stateroom.
Boat—A small watercraft, sometimes carried onboard a ship.
Bow—The forward-most section of the ship, pronounced *bough.*
Bridge—The location from which a ship is steered and speed is controlled.
Bulkhead—A vertical wall or partition.
Captain—Ship's officer responsible for the operation and safety of the vessel. See *Master.*
Cast Member—An employee at Disney's land-based theme parks and resorts.
Castaway Club—Disney's free club for past Disney cruisers.
Catamaran—A very stable, fast watercraft with two parallel, widely-spaced hulls joined by a broad deck.
Crew Member—A shipboard employee.
Cruise Director—Officer in charge of all passenger entertainment and recreational activities, including shore excursions. "Is everybody having a good time?"
DCL—Abbreviation for the Disney Cruise Line.
Deck—The covering over a vessel's hull, or any floor on a ship.
Diesel Electric—Propulsion system used by ships of the Disney Cruise Line. Diesel generators provide electricity to operate the ship's propulsion motors and other systems.
Displacement—Weight of the water displaced by a vessel, equivalent to the vessel's weight.
Dock—To come alongside a pier. See also *pier.*
Draft—The depth of the submerged portion of a watercraft.
Fathom—A measure of depth. One fathom is equivalent to 6 feet/1.8288 m.
Fender—A device for padding the side of a watercraft or pier to prevent damage.
Fore—Forward. Towards the front. Also, a golfer's warning call.
Gangway—A location on the side of a vessel where passengers and crew can board and disembark. Also, *a retractable walkway broader than a gangplank, connecting ship to shore.*
Guest Relations—Disney's term for a hotel's front desk operations. On the Disney Cruise Line, equivalent to the Purser's Office. Located on deck 3, adjacent to the Atrium Lobby.
Hawser—Long, thick mooring lines for fastening a ship to a pier.
Head Server—The crew member who supervises dining room servers and assistant servers. A single head server attends your needs throughout your voyage.
Hotel Manager—Ship's officer in charge of all passenger-related operations, including accommodations, housekeeping, food & beverages, and entertainment.
Hull—The main body of a watercraft. From Middle English for *husk.*
Keel—One of the main structural members of a vessel to which frames are fastened.
Key to the World card—Your personal room key, admission, identification, and charge account. Each member of your party has his/her own Key to the World card.

Glossary *(continued)*

Knot–A measure of speed equal to Nautical Miles Per Hour (6076 feet/1852 meters). Also, an undesired tangling of hair.
Latitude–Position north or south of the equator, expressed in degrees.
League–20,000 Leagues = 60,000 miles = 96,560 kilometers
Leeward–Away from, or sheltered from, the wind.
Line–Rope and cord used on a watercraft, or a tall tale told at a bar.
Longitude–Position east or west of Greenwich, England, expressed in degrees.
Mal de Mer–(French) Seasickness. Popular English language euphemism, akin to "green around the gills."
Master–The captain of a ship. *Master Mariner* is a government-issued license for merchant ship captains.
PFD–Personal Floatation Device. Life jacket. Sometimes known as a Mae West, for the pulchritude (physical appeal) added to those who wear it.
Pier–A platform extending from shore for mooring and loading watercraft.
Pitch–The rising and falling of the bow and stern. See *Roll*. Also, black, tar-like substance used for waterproofing wooden vessels.
Port–The left side of the watercraft when facing Forward. Also, harbor. Also, a fortified wine named for the Portuguese port town of Oporto.
Porthole–An opening in the hull of a vessel. A round window.
Porthos–One of Alexandre Dumas' Three Musketeers.
Propeller–A rotary fan-like device connected to the ship's engines. When it turns, the ship moves. When stationary, the ship is at rest.
Purser–The ships officer responsible for banking, payroll, and passenger records. See Guest Relations.
Roll–Side-to-side, rocking motion of a vessel. In extremes, this can lead to capsizing.
Rudder–A flat, submerged surface at the stern, used to steer a vessel while underway.
Server–The crew member who attends your table in the dining room, takes food and beverage orders, and supervises the assistant server. Similar to a restaurant waiter. On the Disney Cruise Line, the same server attends your needs throughout your voyage. Also, a networked computer providing services to network users.
Ship–A large watercraft, typically oceangoing, too dignified to be called a boat and big enough to carry boats of its own.
Shorex–Cruise industry abbreviation for Shore Excursion.
Stabilizer–Horizontal, mechanized, submerged flaps that can be extended from a vessel to reduce rolling motion.
Staff Captain–A ship's second-in-command, responsible for crew discipline and ship's maintenance. Also known as "Number One."
Starboard–The right-hand side of the vessel when facing Forward.
Stateroom Host/Hostess–The crew member responsible for your stateroom's housekeeping, baggage pickup/delivery, and your housekeeping-related requests. Sometimes known as a Stateroom Attendant or Steward.
Stem–The part of the bow that is farthest forward.
Stern–The rear-most section of the ship. Also, humorless.
Tender–A watercraft used to convey passengers and cargo from a ship to the shore. Also, easily chewed, as in Filet Mignon.
Thruster–A propeller positioned to move the ship laterally while docking and at other times when the ship has little or no forward motion.
Waterline–A line painted on the hull of a watercraft to indicate its typical draft when properly loaded.
Whorf–A character on "Star Trek the Next Generation." See *Pier*.
Windward–Travel into the wind.

Index

We feel that a comprehensive index is very important to a successful travel guide. Too many times we've tried to look something up in other books only to find there was no entry at all, forcing us to flip through pages and waste valuable time. When you're on the phone with a reservation agent and looking for that little detail, time is of the essence.

You'll find the PassPorter index is complete and detailed. Whenever we reference more than one page for a given topic, the major topic is in **bold** to help you home in on exactly what you need. For those times you want to find everything there is to be had, we include all the minor references. We have plenty of cross-references, too, just in case you don't look it up under the name we use.

P.S. This isn't the end of the book. The Web Site Index begins on page 283.

A

B

C

D

E

Introduction | Reservations | Staterooms | Dining | Activities | Ports of Call | Magic | Index

Web Site Index

(continued on next page)

Site Name	Page	Address (URL)
Abanks Scuba Diving Center	227	http://caymanislandsdiscounts.com/AbanksDiveCenter.htm
About.com	28	http://cruises.about.com
Acuario Tours (Acapulco)	254	http://www.acapulco.com/en/tours/acuario
All Ears Net	11, 28	http://www.allearsnet.com
Amazon.com	139	http://www.amazon.com
American Automobile Association	46	http://www.aaa.com
Amtrak	52	http://www.amtrak.com
Antigua Adventures	196	http://www.antiguaadventures.com
Antigua Official Travel Guide	194	http://www.antigua-barbuda.org
Antigua Paddles	196	http://www.antiguapaddles.com
AOL E-Mail	144	http://aolmail.aol.com
AOL Instant Messenger	144	http://www.aim.com
Aqua Mania (St. Maarten)	181	http://www.stmaarten-activities.com
AquaWorld	222	http://www.aquaworld.com.mx
Ardastra Gardens	171	http://www.ardastra.com
Art's Shuttle	66	http://www.artsshuttle.com
Atlantis Adventures	212, 222	http://www.atlantisadventures.net
Atlantis Adventures (St. Thomas)	188	http://www.atlantisadventures.net/stthomas
Atlantis Resort (Nassau)	170	http://www.atlantis.com
AutoPilot	52	http://www.freetrip.com
AvidCruiser	28	http://www.avidcruiser.com
Bahamas Experience Tours	173	http://www.bahamasexperiencetours.com
Bahamas Official Site	170	http://www.bahamas.com
Barbados Tourism	205	http://www.barbados.org
Bidding For Travel	59	http://www.biddingfortravel.com
Blue Water Safaris (St. Kitts)	214	http://www.bluewatersafaris.com
Bob Soto's Reef Divers	227	http://www.bobsotosreefdives.com
Bone Island Shuttle	222	http://www.boneislandshuttle.com
Brevard Medical Equipment	94	http://www.brevardmedicalequip.com
Brimstone Hill Fortress (St. Kitts)	212	http://www.brimstonehillfortress.org
Butterfly Farm (St. Maarten)	180	http://www.thebutterflyfarm.com
Canada's Passport Office	69	http://www.ppt.gc.ca
Canaveral National Seashore	164	http://www.nps.gov/cana
Captain Bryan's Stingray Tours	230	http://www.cayman.org/captainbryan
Captain Marvin's Stingray Tours	230	http://www.captainmarvins.com
Captain Nautica's Snorkeling	190	http://home.att.net/~captainnautica
Caribelle Batik Studio (St. Kitts)	212	http://www.caribellebatikstkitts.com
Cayman Islands Dept of Tourism	226	http://www.divecayman.ky
Centers for Disease Control	22	http://www.cdc.gov/nceh/vsp
Chadwick's (women's formalwear)	262	http://www.chadwicks.com
Coastal Angler Magazine	166	http://www.camirl.com
Coki Beach Dive Club	189	http://www.cokidive.com
Comfort Suites (Paradise Island)	170	http://www.vacationparadiseisland.com

Web Site Index *(continued from previous page)*

Site Name	Page	Address (URL)
Intercot.com	11	http://www.intercot.com
Interstate 75 Online	52	http://www.i75online.com
I-95 Exit Information Guide	52	http://www.usastar.com/i95/homepage.htm
JavaCat Charters (Key West)	219	http://www.keywestkayak.com
Joanne's Disney Site	28	http://www.wdisneyw.co.uk/cruise.html
John Wayne/Orange County Airport	66	http://www.ocair.com
Jolly Harbour Antigua Golf	194	http://www.jollyharbourantigua.com/golf.html
Jolly Roger Pirate Cruise	195	http://www.geographia.com/antigua-barbuda/jolly-roger
Kennedy Space Center	162-163	http://www.kennedyspacecenter.com
Kenneth's Dive Center (St. Kitts)	214	http://www.kennethsdivecenter.com
Key West Adventure Scooter	216	http://keywest.com/scooter.html
Key West Glassbottom Boats	222	http://www.seethereef.com
Key West Jungle Tour Mini-Boats	222	http://www.jungletour.com
Key West Sunrise/Sunset Times	218	http://www.usno.navy.mil
Key West Visitors Bureau	218	http://www.fla-keys.com
Kingdom Magic Travel	46	http://www.kingdommagictravel.com
Kings Casino	194	http://www.kingscasino.com
Kolb Family Disney Cruise Site	28	http://www.kolbfamily.com/2000cruise/disney_cruise
LaughingPlace.com	11	http://www.laughingplace.com
Magical Disney Cruise Guide	10, 11, 28	http://www.allearsnet.com/cruise/cruise.shtml
Magical Journeys	46	http://www.yourmagicaljourneys.com
Magical Mouse, The	28	http://www.themagicalmouse.com/dcl
MagicTrips.com	11, 28	http://www.magictrips.com
Mahogany Run Golf Course	189	http://www.st-thomas.com/mahogany
Mallory Square (Key West)	218	http://www.mallorysquare.com
Mariners Guide	187	http://www.marinersguide.com
Maritime Telecom Network	93	http://www.mtnsat.com
MEI-Travel	11, 46	http://www.mei-travel.com
Merritt Island National Refuge	164	http://merrittisland.fws.gov
Motel 6	65	http://www.motel6.com
MouseEarVacations.com	11, 46	http://www.mouseearvacations.com
MouseForLess, The	11, 26	http://www.themouseforless.com
MousePlanet	11, 30	http://www.mouseplanet.com
MouseSavers.com	1, 11, 27	http://www.mousesavers.com
Mr. Sancho's Cozumel Beach Club	238	http://www.mrsanchos.com
Native Way Water Sports	230	http://www.nativewaywatersports.com
Nautilus Undersea Tour	227, 228	http://www.nautilus.ky
Ocean Adventures (Barbados)	208	http://www.oceanadventures.bb
Onboard Media	160	http://www.onboardmedia.com
Orbitz.com	46, 51	http://www.orbitz.com
Orlando International Airport	54	http://www.orlandoairports.net
Orlando Sanford Airport	55	http://www.orlandosanfordairport.com
Paradise Island (Bahamas)	170	http://www.nassauparadiseisland.com
Paradise Point Tramway	190	http://paradisepointtramway.com
Perfect Gift, The	264	http://www.theperfectgift.cc
Pettit's Disney Cruise Site	28	http://www.richpettit.com/vacations/ourvacations.htm
Photo Copyright Release Waiver	260	http://www.image.com/guest-postcruise.htm

Web Site Index *(continued from previous page)*

PassPorter Sites	Page	Address (URL)
PassPorter Main Page	15, 42	http://www.passporter.com
PassPorter Disney Cruise Line	2, 15, 28	http://www.passporter.com/dcl
PassPorter Deck Plans	5	http://www.passporter.com/dcl/deckplans.htm
PassPorter Registration	300	http://www.passporter.com/register.htm
PassPorter Surveys	271	http://www.passporter.com/dcl/survey.htm
PassPorter Gathering	263, 265	http://www.passporter.com/gathering.htm
PassPorter Internet Portal	145	http://www.passporter.com/dcl/porthole.htm
PassPorter Luggage Log	70	http://www.passporter.com/wdw/luggagelog.htm
PassPorter Message Boards	11	http://www.passporterboards.com
PassPorter Store	299, 301	http://www.passporterstore.com
PassPorter Page Updates	300	http://www.passporter.com/dcl/updates.htm

Your Favorite Sites	Address (URL)

Introduction
Reservations
Staterooms
Dining
Activities
Ports of Call
Magic
Index

Notes

Watching the ship leave the harbor

Notes

An evening at Palo

Notes

© MediaMarx, Inc.

Chilling out on the verandah

Notes

A view of the Disney Wonder from Castaway Cay

Notes

Introduction
Reservations
Staterooms
Dining
Activities
Ports of Call
Magic
Index

Notes

Notes

Notes

Notes

Notes

Notes

PassPorter Gear

PassPorter was born out of the necessity for more planning, organization, and a way to preserve the memories of a great vacation! Along the way we've found other things that either help us use the PassPorter better, appreciate our vacation more, or just make our journey a little more comfortable. Others have asked us about them, so we thought we'd share them with you. Order online at http://www.passporter.com/store, call us toll-free 877-929-3273, or use the order form below.

PassPorter® PassHolder is a small, lightweight nylon pouch that holds your Key to the World card, ID cards, passports, money, and pens. Wear it wherever you go (see photo on page 263) for quick access to your essentials. The front features a clear compartment, a zippered pocket, and a velcro pocket; the back has a small pocket and two pen slots. Adjustable cord. Royal blue. 4 7/8" x 6 1/2"	**Quantity**: ____ x $7.95 
PassPorter® Name Badge personalized with your name! Go around the "World" in style with our oval name badge. Price includes personalization with your name shipping, and handling. Please indicate name(s) with your order.	**Quantity**: ___ x $4.00 Name(s): ________
PassPorter® Pin is our new collectible, cloissone pin. The current version depicts our PassPorter logo amidst an open book which reads, "The World is an Open Book." Watch for new pins each year!	**Quantity**: ___ x $6.00 

Please ship my PassPorter Gear to: Name .... Address .... City, State, Zip .... Daytime Phone .... Payment: ❑ check (make payable to "MediaMarx") ❑ MasterCard ❑ Visa ❑ American Express ❑ Discover Card number .... Exp. Date. .... Signature	Subtotal: Tax*: Shipping**: **Total**: ** Include 6% sales tax if you live in MI.* ***Shipping costs are:* *$5 for totals up to $9* *$6 for totals up to $19* *$7 for totals up to $29* *$8 for totals up to $39* *Delivery takes 1-2 weeks.*

Send your order form to P.O. Box 3880, Ann Arbor, MI 48106, call us toll-free at 877-WAYFARER (877-929-3273), or order online http://www.passporterstore.com/store.

PassPorter Online

A wonderful way to get the most from your PassPorter is to visit our active web site at http://www.passporter.com/dcl. We serve up valuable PassPorter updates, plus useful Disney Cruise information and advice we couldn't jam into our book. You can swap tales (that's t-a-l-e-s, Mickey!) with fellow Disney fans, enter contests, find links to other sites, get plenty of details, and ask us questions. You can also order PassPorters and shop for PassPorter accessories and travel gear! The latest information on new PassPorters to other destinations is available on our web site as well. To go directly to our latest list of page-by-page of PassPorter updates, visit http://www.passporter.com/dcl/updates.htm.

Register this guidebook and get more discounts

We are **very** interested to learn how your vacation went and what you think of the PassPorter, how it worked (or didn't work) for you, and your opinion on how we could improve it! We encourage you to register your copy of PassPorter with us—in return for your feedback, we'll send you coupons good for discounts on PassPorters and gear when purchased directly from us. You can register your copy of PassPorter on the Internet at http://www.passporter.com/dcl/register.htm. Or you can write us a letter to tell share your thoughts and suggestions for the guidebook—mail it to P.O. Box 3880, Ann Arbor, Michigan 48106. Thanks!

Cruise with Jennifer & Dave in December 2006

We invite you to join us at MouseFest 2006 aboard the Disney Wonder and at Walt Disney World. This is our annual gathering of PassPorter readers, fellow Disney fans, friends, and family... and the fourth year we take to the sea! This is a casual, family-friendly affair for the PassPorter and Disney fan community, during which we and our community members host informal events—everyone is welcome! Most of our events are free (though you may need to be on the Disney Wonder or have park admission to participate), while a few events have a small registration fee (to cover supplies or prizes) or have prerequisites. To learn more about MouseFest, visit http://www.mousefest.org. (Of course, if you check this site after December 2006, you'll learn about our next gathering!) You can make travel arrangements on your own, through your favorite travel agent, or through other travel agents who are offering excellent deals for this event. Hope to see you there!

More PassPorters

You've asked for more PassPorters—we've listened! At our readers' request, we developed the Deluxe Edition of same book you hold in your hands—it's proven phenomenally popular! And we also have a best-selling, award-winning guidebook to the Walt Disney World Resort. To learn about these and other PassPorters, visit http://www.passporter.com.

Deluxe Cruise Edition

Design first-class cruises with this loose-leaf ring-bound edition. Our popular Deluxe Edition features the same great content as this field guide, plus fourteen of our famous organizer "PassPockets" to plan and record your trip. Special features of the Deluxe Edition include ten interior storage slots in the binder to hold maps, ID cards, and a pen (included). The Deluxe binder makes it easy to add, remove, and rearrange pages... you can even download, print, and add updates and supplemental pages from our web site. Refill pages and pockets are available for purchase. Learn more about the Deluxe Edition and order a copy at http://www.passporter.com/wdw/deluxe.htm. The Deluxe Edition is also available through bookstores by special order—just give your favorite bookstore the ISBN code for the 2006 Deluxe Edition (1587710315).

PassPorter Walt Disney World Resort

It all started with Walt Disney World (and a mouse)! Our Walt Disney World guidebook covers everything you need to plan a practically perfect vacation, including fold-out park maps, resort room layout diagrams, KidTips, descriptions, reviews, and ratings for the resorts, parks, attractions, and restaurants, and much more! This edition also includes 14 organizer pockets you can use to plan your trip before you go, hold papers while you're there, and record your memories for when you return. Learn more and order at http://www.passporter.com/wdw or get a copy at your favorite bookstore. Our Walt Disney World guide is available in a spiral-bound edition (ISBN: 1587710277) and a Deluxe Edition (ISBN: 1587710285)—both have 14 PassPockets. You can order either on our web site or through a bookstore.

To order any of our guidebooks, visit http://www.passporterstore.com or call toll-free 877-929-3273. PassPorter guidebooks are also available in your local bookstore. If you don't see it on the shelf, just ask!

Note: The ISBN codes above apply to our 2006 editions. For the latest edition, ask your bookstore to search their database for "PassPorter."

Even More PassPorters

PassPorter's Walt Disney World For Your Special Needs

Includes coverage of Disney Cruise Line! It's hardly a one-size-fits-all world at Disney's Orlando resort, yet everyone seems to fit. Consider the typical multi-generational family planning a vacation: pregnant and nursing moms, parents with infants, cousins "keeping Kosher," grandparents with declining mobility, a child with food allergies, an uncle

struggling with obesity, a teenaged daughter recently "converted" to vegetarianism ... everyday people coping with everyday needs. Authors Deb Wills and Debra Martin Koma have prepared more than 400 pages of in-depth information for Walt Disney World and Disney Cruise Line vacationers of all abilities, delivering in-depth coverage of every ride, attraction and resort on Walt Disney World property from a distinctive "special needs" perspective. This is a perfect supplement to your favorite guidebook. Learn more and order your copy at http://www.passporter.com/wdw/specialneeds or get a copy at your favorite bookstore (ISBN: 1587710188).

PassPorter Disneyland Resort and Southern California Attractions–First Edition

New for 2006! PassPorter tours the park that started it all! California's Disneyland Park, Disney's California Adventure, and Downtown Disney get PassPorter's expert treatment, and we throw in Universal Studios Hollywood, Knott's Berry Farm, Hollywood and Downtown Los Angeles, San Diego, SeaWorld, the San Diego Zoo and Wild Animal Park, LEGOLAND, and Six Flags Magic Mountain. All this, and PassPorter's famous PassPockets and planning features.Whether you're making the pilgrimage to Disneyland for the big celebration or planning a classic Southern California family vacation, you can't miss. Learn more and order a copy at http://www.passporter.com/dl, or pick it up at your favorite bookstore (ISBN: 1587710048). Also available as a Deluxe Edition in a padded, six-ring binder (ISBN: 1587710056).

PassPorter's Treasure Hunts at Walt Disney World

New for 2006! Have even more fun at Walt Disney World! Jennifer and Dave's treasure hunts have long been a favorite part of PassPorter reader gatherings at Walt Disney World, and now you can join in the fun. Gain a whole new appreciation of Disney's fabulous attention to detail as you search through the parks and resorts for the little (and big) things that you may never have noticed before. Great for individuals, families and groups, with hunts for people of all ages and levels of Disney knowledge. Special, "secure" answer pages make sure nobody can cheat. Prepared with plenty of help from Jen Carter, famous for her all-day, all-parks scavenger hunts. Learn more about this fun new book and order at http://www.passporter.com/wdw/hunts or get a copy at your favorite bookstore (ISBN: 1587710269).